Apparitions, Daemons, and Emanations

SUNY series, Intersections: Philosophy and Critical Theory
―――――――――
Rodolphe Gasché, editor

Apparitions, Daemons, and Emanations

Poetry and Painting in the
Work of Georges Bataille, Pierre Klossowski,
and Henri Michaux

CHARLES FREELAND

Published by State University of New York Press, Albany

© 2024 State University of New York

All rights reserved

Printed in the United States of America

No part of this book may be used or reproduced in any manner whatsoever without written permission. No part of this book may be stored in a retrieval system or transmitted in any form or by any means including electronic, electrostatic, magnetic tape, mechanical, photocopying, recording, or otherwise without the prior permission in writing of the publisher.

For information, contact State University of New York Press, Albany, NY
www.sunypress.edu

Library of Congress Cataloging-in-Publication Data

Name: Freeland, Charles, 1947– author.
Title: Apparitions, daemons, and emanations : poetry and painting in the work of Georges Bataille, Pierre Klossowski, and Henri Michaux / Charles Freeland.
Description: Albany : State University of New York Press, [2024]. | Series: SUNY series, intersections: philosophy and critical theory | Includes bibliographical references and index.
Identifiers: LCCN 2023023661 | ISBN 9781438496658 (hardcover : alk. paper) | ISBN 9781438496665 (ebook) | ISBN 9781438496641 (pbk. : alk. paper)
Subjects: LCSH: Bataille, Georges, 1897–1962—Criticism and interpretation. | Klossowski, Pierre—Criticism and interpretation. | Michaux, Henri, 1899–1984—Criticism and interpretation. | French literature—20th Century—History and criticism. | Art, French—20th century.
Classification: LCC PQ2603.A695 Z667325 2024 | DDC 841.9109—dc23/eng/20230920
LC record available at https://lccn.loc.gov/2023023661

10 9 8 7 6 5 4 3 2 1

Contents

Acknowledgments	vii
Abbreviations	ix
Introduction	1
Chapter 1 Apparitions: Georges Bataille, Lascaux, and the "Birth of Art"	15
Chapter 2 Diabolo scilicet: Pierre Klossowski: The Work of Art as Demonology	79
Chapter 3 Emanations: The Painting and Poetry of Henri Michaux	169
Postface: Poésie par le gouffre	229
Bibliography	271
Index	281

Acknowledgments

A very special thanks goes to Prof. Rodolphe Gasché and everyone at the SUNY Buffalo Department of Comparative Literature who, many years ago, invited me to present my essays on Klossowski and Bataille. Their very encouraging reception prompted me to rework these essays into their new, present form. I would also like to thank the editors at SUNY Press, Rebecca Colesworthy, Diane Ganeles, and Carly Miller, for their help in preparing my manuscript for publication. Finally, my thanks to my anonymous reviewers whose comments have been helpful in improving this book for publication.

Abbreviations

The following abbreviations have been used for references in the text. In instances where the English translation of a book and its French language original are both referenced, page numbers are given in pairs separated by a slash. The first number is for the pagination for the English translation, the second is for the French original. Thus *DB* 16/20 references page 16 of the English translation, *Diana at Her Bath*, and 20, references the page from the French original, *Le bain de Diane*.

Chapter 1

OC Georges Bataille, *Oeuvres complètes*, vols. I–XII (Paris: Gallimard, 1970–1988).

Chapter 2

B Pierre Klossowski, *The Baphomet*, trans. Sophie Hawkes and Stephen Sartarelli (Hygiene, CO: Eridanos Press, 1988). Originally published as *Le Baphomet* (Paris: Mercure de France, 1965), referred to in chapter 2 as *B*.

DB *Diana at Her Bath*, trans. Sophie Hawkes and Stephen Sartarelli (Boston: Erianos Press, 1990). Originally published as *Le bain de Diane* (Paris: Gallimard, 1972), referred to in chapter 2 as *BD*.

LH *Les lois de l'hospitalité* (Paris: Gallimard, 1965). English translation, *Roberte Ce Soir & The Revocation of the Edict of Nantes*, trans. Austryn Wainhouse (New York: Grove Press, 1969).

NVC	*Nietzsche and the Vicious Circle*, trans. Daniel W. Smith (Chicago: University of Chicago Press, 1997). Originally published as *Nietzsche et le cercle vicieux* (Paris: Mercure de France, 1969).
R	*Ressemblance* (Alpes, Côte d'Azur: Office Régional de la Culture, Éditions Ryoan-ji, 1984).
SDD	*Such a Deathly Desire*, trans. Russell Ford (Albany: State University of New York Press, 2007). Originally published as *Un si funeste désir* (Paris: Gallimard, 1963).
TV	*Tableaux vivants: Essais critiques 1936–1983*, ed. Patrick Mauriès (Paris: Gallimard, 2001).

Chapter 3

OC	Georges Bataille, *Oeuvres complètes*, vols. I–XII (Paris: Gallimard, 1970–1988).
OC	Henri Michaux, *Oeuvres complètes*, vols. I–III, ed. Raymond Bellour with Ysé Tran (Paris: Gallimard, Bibliotheque de la Pléiade, 2004).

Introduction

> How can we live without the unknown in front of (*devant*) us?
>
> Men of today want the poem to be in the image of their lives, composed of such little consideration, of such little space, and burned with intolerance.
>
> Because it is no longer given to them to act supremely, in this fatal preoccupation of self-destruction at the hands of their fellowmen, because of their inert wealth holds them back and enslaves them, men of today, their instinct weakened, lose—still keeping alive—even the dust of their names.
>
> Born from the summons of becoming and from the anguish of retention, the poem, rising from its well of mud and of stars, will bear witness, almost silently, that it contained nothing which did not truly exist elsewhere, in this rebellious and solitary world of contradictions.
>
> —René Char, "Le poème pulvérisé"

René Char asked, "How can we live without the unknown before us?"[1] But how to speak of the "unknown"? Not as an intellectual category opposed to the "known," opposed to and replacing the unknown with what we might call the book of knowledge, but the unknown as the summons of a night, of a void, of an infinite "becoming" and an "anguish," something that can only be named in a neutral voice, as Blanchot suggests in his essay on

---

1. René Char, "Le poème pulvérisé," in *Furor and Mystery & Other Writings*, trans. and eds. Mary Ann Caws and Nancy Kline (Boston: Black Widow Press, 2010), 244–45. Quoted in Maurice Blanchot, *l'Entretien infini* (Paris: Gallimard, 1969), 439. Trans. by Susan Hanson as *The Infinite Conversation* (Minneapolis: University of Minnesota Press, 1993), 298.

Char.² This is what is exceptional in the voices we shall hear in the pages that follow: that "the unknown" is not something "before" or "in front of" them, as though it were a future, looming possibility, something always and already ahead of us, like death, a vanishing point of intentionality. They speak not *of* the unknown but *from* the unknown. The "unknown" in this context has its best equivalents in words having no gender, no specific assignation, words that were once the currency of ancient myth and have returned to form the song of our modern myths: Night—"la jouissance de la nuit," as Bataille wrote³—Void, Excess, Laughter, the Impossible, what can only be "non-savoir," as Bataille phrased it. How can we live without the "Impossible" before us, the poet asks? Not the impossible as a yet to be realized possibility, but only as something ever not possible, yet included in the poem in all its unrealizable impossibility as what might be called the limit-figure of its existence. An irreducible, impossible unknown that marks the limit-experiences, the "tests," the *épreuves* undergone by these authors, Bataille, Michaux, and Klossowski. This is an irreplaceable, irremovable unknown that draws the reader into these works, a centrifugal pull experienced as we seek answers to what are not questions, really, but paradoxes, enigmas, voices telling us of strange voyages they have endured and turned back from, telling us from the limits of the possible for language what they have seen, what they have heard, what they have suffered, and where they have found joy.

Hence our title. The songs, the poems, the writings and works of art these three, Bataille, Klossowski, and Michaux, have left us do not come from the unspeakable depths directly, clearly, and unequivocally. Rather they come indirectly, obliquely, as "apparitions," as "emanations," as "pulverized" poems, as a "virulence of phantasms," not the writings and paintings of an "author" but of a "daemon," a being, a force unknown, an impossible being.⁴

---

2. Blanchot, *Infinite Conversation*, 298.

3. Georges Bataille, "Le non-savoir," in *OC* XII, 286. See also, "L'évidence de la nuit," in *Henri Michaux: Oeuvres récents* (Paris: Le Point Cardinal, 1985), unpaginated: "l'épanchement lyrique de la nuit qui recouvre le silence du ciel."

4. As Bataille wrote, "When a man or woman (*l'homme*) seeks to represent him/herself, no longer as a moment of a homogenous process . . . but as a new tear (*déchirement*) at the interior of an already torn nature (*nature déchirée*), the levelling phraseologies that stem from the understanding will be of little avail: he/she can no longer recognize him/herself in the degrading chains of logic . . . to the contrary, recognizes him/herself only in the virulence of his/her phantasms." "Dossier de l'oeil pineal (1)," in *OC* II, 22; trans. mine.

Little need, let us hope, to introduce the lives and works behind the names Bataille, Klossowski, and Michaux. They are all well-known French writers and artists. Georges Bataille was first and foremost a writer. He died in 1962, but since then there has been a renaissance of interest in his writings when Éditions Gallimard published his *Oeuvres complètes*, beginning in 1970 with volume I and finishing with volume XII in 1988. An amazing production from the hands of a man mostly famous in the popular imagination for his self-recorded dissipations in Parisian bordellos and bars.[5] In fact, he was anguished and yet joyfully driven to writing,[6] writing as a means of escaping the dark fingers of madness, perhaps, or of facing his madness in the madness of writing. Of the incendiary novels, three titles have especially attained notoriety: *Histoire de l'œil*, published in 1928 under the humorous pseudonym Lord Auch; the 1937 *Madame Edwarda*, first published in 1941 (Éditions du Solitaire), also anonymously, this time under the pseudonym Pierre Angélique; and *Le Bleu du ciel*, written in 1935, first published in 1936 in Bataille's journal *Minotaure*, then in 1943 in *L'Expérience intérieure*. Roger Laporte considers these Bataille's supreme achievements, not just for their raw, scandalous subject matter but for their savage beauty and economy of writing. Yukio Mishima strikes a similar tone in his introductory essay to the English translation of three of Bataille's novels: *My Mother, Madame Edwarda*, and *The Dead Man*.[7] Bataille's more philosophical works—and this is a characterization that can only be applied with considerable reservations and discussions as to what would constitute a "philosophy" in this case—*L'Expérience intérieure*, for just one example, collected under the title *La Somme athéologique*, underscore his readings of Hegel in connection with the Kojève seminars (1933–1939) and his readings of Nietzsche, especially his *Sur Nietzsche*, published by Gallimard in 1945. Likewise, his essays on eroticism seem more academic in tone. As Laporte phrases it, they only

---

5. See, for example, one of Bataille's many self-descriptions: "I differ from my friends in not caring a damn for any convention, taking my pleasures in the basest of things. . . . Ending up, drunk and red-faced, in a dive full of naked women." *L'Impossible*, in *OC* III, 107. Trans. by Robert Hurley as *The Impossible* (San Francisco: City Lights, 1991), 17.

6. Bataille: "Comment nous attarder à des livres auxquels, sensiblement, l'auteur s'a plus été contraint?" ("How can we linger over books to which their authors have manifestly not been *driven*?"). *Le Bleu du ciel*, in *OC* III, 381. Trans. by Harry Mathews as *The Blue of Noon* (New York: Urizen Books, 1978), 153.

7. Yukio Mishima, "Georges Bataille and *Divinus Deus*," in *My Mother, Madame Edwarda, The Dead Man*, by Bataille, trans. Austryn Wainhouse (London: Marion Boyars, 1989), 9–21.

4 | Apparitions, Daemons, and Emanations

talk about eroticism from the exterior vantage point of a book, unlike the early novels that seem afire in the sexual hells they narrate. Laporte also points to the "anthropological works" from the postwar period, especially the 1955 Skira edition on Lascaux. But as chapter 1, "Apparitions," shows, the roots of Bataille's "anthropological" interests actually date from the late 1920s, during the very years he was also writing his erotic novels, when he published several essays and photographs of "anthropological interest." "L'art primitif," for example, now published in the first volume of the *Oeuvres completes*, first appeared in Bataille's journal *Documents* in 1929, or the entry *Abattoir*, part of the *Dictionnaire critique*, was also published in 1929 in *Documents*. Chapter 1 also shows the importance of Bataille's *Le Bas materialism et la gnose* (*Documents*, 1930), for his essays on Lascaux's art.

Michel Leiris, who was a contributor to *Documents*, described *Documents* as "a war machine against received ideas."[8] "Primitivism" had become the fashion in art and was seeping into popular culture. The Josephine Baker Revue in 1927 was a sensation and became iconic for the jazz age that followed. Bataille's ethnographic studies in *Documents*, for example, were aimed against all of that, trying to free ethnography, trying to free "the primitive" from the grips of both exploitative capitalism and idealism.

Critical reception of Bataille's anthropological writings has not been kind. Michel Surya's biography of Bataille, for example, is curtly dismissive of Bataille's writings on prehistoric art from the 1950s.[9] Laporte likewise considers Bataille's anthropological essays to be the weak side of his *Oeuvre* because, as he puts it, Bataille is too much the prisoner of "une grille de concepts," such as the oppositions between play and seriousness, work and art, transgression and interdiction. The erotic works, by comparison, have a more "savage freedom."[10]

Perhaps the time has come to reread Bataille's texts on prehistoric art and religion. We shall see that Bataille's interpretation of the art at

---

8. [8] Michel Leiris, "De Bataille l'impossible à l'impossible Documents," in *Critique* 195–96 (Aug.–Sept. 1963): 689. Also quoted by Dawn Ades and Fiona Bradley, introduction to *Undercover Surrealism: Georges Bataille and DOCUMENTS* (Cambridge, MA: MIT Press, 2006), 11. Leiris's essay is a valuable source for firsthand insights into *Documents*.

9. Michel Surya, *Georges Bataille: La mort à l'oeuvre* (Paris: Garamont, Librairie Séguier, 1987), 406. Here he mentions *Lascaux and Les larmes d'Eros* as "livres d'un intérêt moindre." Surya, *Georges Bataille: An Intellectual Biography*, trans. Krzysztof Fijalkowski and Michael Richardson (London: Verso, 2002), 417.

10. Roger Laporte, *A l'extrême pointe: Proust, Bataille, Blanchot* (Paris: P.O.L., 1998), 52.

Lascaux—if art is what it "is"—does not merely apply preexisting oppositions and categories. Even in the essays from the late 1940s and early 1950s that preceded the Lascaux book, essays that were somewhat of a continuation of the perspectives opened by the founding of the Collège de Sociologie (1937–1939), dedicated as it was to research "the sacred" in all its manifestations, the opposition between work (utility) and play (sovereignty) was used not to buttress received metaphysical oppositions but to contest them.[11] With the exception, perhaps, of Caillois's 1950 *L'Homme et le sacré*, the usual interpretations of the "sacred" and prehistoric art had been entirely based on considerations of utility. By drawing upon such a "grid of concepts" that had been scattered throughout the nonscientific literature, Bataille proved himself to be not so much a "prisoner" of concepts as he was able to use these notions to transform the study of prehistoric art, ejecting it from the category of anthropological writings and making it something bordering on poetry. Bataille's papers on prehistoric art seek to name, to provide an account of the creative force that left its marks on the grotto walls at Lascaux, not the utilitarian interests that overshadow most scientific accounts but the creative force that emerges from within the materiality of Lascaux so as to transform that materiality into a visual poetry we still struggle today to comprehend. In chapter 1 we shall ask to what extent Bataille is indeed a prisoner of anything, let alone preestablished concepts and ways of thinking. We shall see how Bataille not only offers a way to transform the established ways prehistoric art has been viewed, questioning whether all its unknowns can be reduced to knowns, but also shows how, by looking back at the ancient past of humanity and its earliest works of large-scale art, we can also look forward, to the future of our humanity and art, to the unknown that always lies "before us." The freedom of Bataille's collected papers on Lascaux lies in its freedom of thought, its freedom from the tyranny of stereotypes or inherited ideas, and the way it was also a questioning challenge posed to the increasingly technological and hostile world of "modern men" that was the 1950s context for Bataille's writings on Lascaux. This makes us wonder if there is something of a Hölderlin-like moment in Bataille: a feeling that the times were in a bad way, "in dürftiger Zeit" as Hölderlin called it, a nullity

---

11. See for example, "L'amitié de l'homme et de la bête" (1947)," in *OC* XI, 167–71; "Le passage de l'animal à l'homme et la naissance de l'art"; "La guerre et la philosophie du sacré"; a review of Roger Caillois's 1950 *L'Homme et le sacré*; and "Au rendez-vous de Lascaux, l'homme civilisé se retrouve homme de désir" (1953)," in *OC* XII, 259–77, 289–92.

hollowed out by the absence of gods, and, in the Europe of the 1950s, by the domination of a secular world of practical affairs, material values, and a far-reaching technology that was taking their place. Bataille's 1960 address "Unlivable Earth?" suggests the necessity of a renewed *"rende-vous"* with a world lost to modern human beings. Yet that past still communicates with us in the grandeur of the images it left behind like a gift destined for a future it could never know. Against a backdrop of an international arms race and the very real and ever-present threat of nuclear annihilation, Bataille contrasted the evident joy and creative richness of Lascaux with the spiritual impoverishment of the modern world. How could the joy that infuses the animal images of Lascaux become the will to destruction that haunts the modern world? With little or nothing to be expected from the Surrealist Revolution, too riddled, as it was in Bataille's view, with failed idealists, the keys to an alternative world yet-to-come might lie in the past, in a world before time and writing.

Bataille's friend Pierre Klossowski was a manifold figure from the very outset. As Georges Perros says of him in his article in *L'Arc*, "This man seems to have come from distant places."[12] His family background is Eastern European, but his culture is French and German, Roman Latin, and Catholic. He was tutored by Rilke and then worked as a youthful secretary to Gide. He prospered in the intellectual and artistic circles of prewar Paris. Like Bataille, he also struggled with the power of stereotypes and other "grids" that suppress the "unknown before us" into something more manageable, more measurable, something "speakable." In a phrase recalling Bataille, he described himself as "neither a 'writer,' nor a 'thinker,' nor a 'philosopher,' or whatever else might be in any mode of expression—nothing at all before having been, before being and remaining a monomaniac."[13] This monomania shall be the "unknown" that lies before us in our reading of Klossowski.

Klossowski met Bataille in 1933 or 1934 while he collaborated with him on the journal *Acéphale* (1933–1939). Klossowski's 1969 book on Nietzsche, *Nietzsche et le cercle vicieux*, is the culmination of work he had begun during this collaboration three decades prior: the task of safeguarding German culture against its distorted appropriation by the Nazi propaganda machine. Sarah Wilson's important essay "Épiphanies et secrets" notes how

---

12. Georges Perros, "Le Moans qu'on puisse dire," in *L'Arc* 43 (Paris: Librairie Duponchelle, 1970), 45.

13. Pierre Klossowski, "L'indiscernable," in *Ressemblance* (Alpes, Côte d'Azur: Office Régional de la Culture, Éditions Ryoan-ji, 1984), 91.

Nietzsche's work in particular was important to them. In a footnote to that essay, she notes that the second number of *Acéphale*, January 1937, bore the subtitle "Réparation à Nietzsche." Georges Bataille's 1945 *Sur Nietzsche* is an extension of this task.[14] Meanwhile, Klossowski also did translations of Friedrich Sieburg on the theme of German nationalism and another on Robespierre. But, as noted with *Documents*, *Acéphale* was also "a war machine against received ideas," but this time it is the Fascistic transmogrification of Nietzsche and Fascism's more general threat to Europe that are the dangers and the signatures of the destitution of the times.

Klossowski also worked with the Collège de Sociologie, which was directed by Bataille, Caillois, and Maurice Heine. Not despite all these rich ethnographic and political connections during the 1930s, Klossowski was first of all a translator of Latin and Germanic authors: Ovid, Wittgenstein, Nietzsche, Heidegger, Hölderlin, but never Freud. In fact, it was while translating Hölderlin that he discovered Sade. Writing and spirituality, that was his quest in those days. Beginning in 1939, Klossowski was a novice Dominican monk at La Lesse, near Chambréy. But that adventure lasted only a few months until he was told his way of thinking was not very Christian.[15] In the context of the Spanish Civil War, rising Fascism, and the formation of a united front against Fascism in France, which had Walter Benjamin and Bertolt Brecht amongst its growing numbers of *emigré* members, Klossowski was in the "orbit" of the Convent Saint-Maximin, where he studied theology, and on the occasion of the 150th anniversary of the French Revolution, gave a conference on Sade, which was published in the first edition of *Sade mon prochain*.

After these years of spiritual wandering, during which time he continued his studies of Sade, he returned to Paris in 1943, and soon, at the "soirée de Moré," he again met up with both Bataille and Jacques Lacan. Klossowski was already quite familiar with psychoanalytic thinking. During the 1930–1933 period he had been a secretary to the psychoanalyst René Laforgue and had published an article, "l'Éléments d'une étude psychanalytique sur le marquis de Sade," in the *Revue de psychanalyse*. Laforgue was scandalized by the essay, prompting him to fire Klossowski.[16] So Klossowski's

---

14. Sara Wilson, "Épiphanies et secrets," in *Pierre Klossowski: Tableaux vivants*, catalog to an exposition organized by Sara Wilson with the Whitechapel Gallery, London, and the Ludwig Museum, Cologne (Paris: Gallimard, 2007), 31, 41–42, n. 20–21.
15. Alain Arnaud, *Pierre Klossowski* (Paris: Seuil, 1990), 187.
16. Arnaud, 186–87. Most of the above-cited biographical material is from Arnaud's book.

links with Bataille, Lacan, and psychoanalysis do go back to the 1930s, although, as we shall see in chapter 2, "Diabolo scilicet," this alone does not allow us to apply, like a grid of concepts, psychoanalytic concepts as the key to an interpretation of Klossowski's writing and drawings. Nonetheless, between Lacan, Blanchot, Bataille, and Klossowski we have a very thought-provoking milieu situated between the Surrealists, the Communists, and the psychoanalysts that shall be important for our reading. But all three alternatives were rejected: the Surrealists, too much the idealists, too much the aesthetes; the Communists, too much the censors, the gatekeepers of prisons, and the murderers of artists and poets; and the psychoanalysts, although influential, also rejected or marginalized by all except Lacan insofar as the Freudian truth of the unconscious was rejected.

During the 1940s, Klossowski converted to Lutheranism (hence his interest in the eighteenth-century philosopher Hamann), published his book on Sade, *Sade mon prochain*, and, most importantly, married Denise Marie Roberte Morin-Sinclair, who was to become his model for his most of his drawings, photographs, and films. By the mid-1950s, his *Roberte, ce soir* and his first "graphic expressions" had been published, and in 1956, *Le bain de Diane*. These works are contemporaries of Bataille's papers on Lascaux. In both, there is a search for a sacred language, or for a mythic, almost bestial interaction between gods and humans far too extraordinary and indeed violent to be seen or heard.

But it is his *Nietzsche et le cercle vicieux*, published to general acclaim amongst his peers G. Deleuze, M. Foucault, and many others, that was to be his last major work on a philosopher. He did publish *La Monnaie vivante* in 1970 and participate in 1972 in the famous Cerisy-la-Salle collogium on the theme "Nietzsche, aujourd'hui," with Deleuze, Derrida, Lyotard, M. de Gandillac, and B. Pautrat, but it was also during this period in the early 1970s that Klossowski turned away from writing and toward drawing. It is his book on Nietzsche, coming as it does during these pivotal years, that shall be of primary importance for chapter 2. Klossowski's art is given special attention in the later sections of that chapter. How to communicate a vision of the Eternal Recurrence, Nietzsche's vision, Nietzsche's shattering experience—how to communicate this? Hence the role, so important to Klossowski, of the simulacre, of a *ressemblance* that does not do the work of resemblance or representation so much as it is a mode of exorcism of the monomania at the center of his work and life. Hence, the daemon, creator of simulacra.

Yes, Klossowski does come to us from distant places, yet he remains always before us, the unknown Klossowski.

Henri Michaux, the third author-artist in this volume, is a figure who started out in life a bit of a loner, mystic, and recluse who had dreamed of becoming a Benedictine monk but ended up a becoming a famous literary-artistic figure in Paris, with many books and art works to his credit. From 1914 to 1918, when Belgium was under German occupation, Michaux was a student interested in music and Latin and the writings of Ernest Hello, the fourteenth-century mystic John van Ruysbroeck, Angèle de Foligno, Tolstoy and Dostoyevsky, and especially Lautrémont. Through these authors he discovered the power of words. From 1922, he was a correspondent with the renowned Belgian author Franz Hellens, director of the literary journal *Le Disque vert*. Then, in 1924, after having moved to Paris, he probably met Jean Paulhan, editor of the *Nouvelle Revue Française* (NRF), and the poet Jules Superville. He collaborated with Paulhan over the years, as in 1935 when they teamed up to launch the new luxury literary journal *Mesures*, directed by Henry Church. Michaux first attracted critical attention in 1927 with his poetry collection *Qui je fus* (*Who I Was*), published by Éditions de la NRF.

Michaux was first a voyager: voyages through both his interior life, "l'espace du dedans," as he called it in his 1966 title,[17] and across seas and through distant exotic cultures, voyages of "expatriation," he called them, voyages to "drive his country out of him, to shed his attachments to all kinds and whatever elements of Greek and Roman culture or Belgian habits that he had become attached to, despite himself. Whether from within (dedans) or across oceans, "He travels *against:*" Turkey, Italy, North Africa, England, Ecuador, the Orient.[18] And with these voyages he brought back travel books: *Ecuador* (1929, NRF) and *Un Barbare en Asie*, the journal of his travels in 1931–1932 to India, China, and Japan.[19]

---

17. Henri Michaux, *L'Espace du dedans* (Paris: Gallimard, 1966).

18. "Il voyage *contre*." Henri Michaux, "Quelques renseignements sur cinquante neuf annés d'existence," in *Henri Michaux: Oeuvres completes*, vol. I, ed. Raymond Bellour (Paris: Gallimard, Bibliothèque de la Pléiade, 1998), cxxxiii. Trans. by David Ball as "Some Information About Fifty-Nine Years of Existence," in *Darkness Moves: Henri-Michaux Anthology 1927–1984*, trans. and ed. David Ball (Berkeley: University of California Press, 1994,) xxxiii; emphasis in original.

19. *Un Barbare en Asie* (Paris: Librairie Gallimard, 1933; repr. 1945).

In January 1933, *Un barbare en Asia* appeared to general critical acclaim. By the early 1940s, as Europe descended into another catastrophic war, his metamorphosis was complete: the man born in Belgium as Henry Michaux, the solitary seeker and wanderer through far Eastern ports and exotic locales, had become Henri Michaux, Parisian poet, painter, and assimilated personality, a subject of literary discussions and critical inspection.[20] André Gide tried to launch a conference on Michaux in 1941, which was supposed to have convened in Nice in May of that year, but had to be canceled due to the war. Gide's essay for the conference was published under the title *Découvrons Henri Michaux*, in July 1941. It was yet another boost for Michaux's growing notoriety.[21]

Meanwhile, the first book Michaux illustrated with his own drawings was *Entre centre et absence*, published by Éditions Henri Matarasso in 1936. Although his interest in painting began in the mid-1920s with the discovery of Max Ernst, de Chirico, and most importantly Paul Klee, it was not until June 1937, after years of intense artistic activity, that the first exhibition of his own gouaches opened at the Galerie Paul Magné Ancienne, Paris. As he wrote in a letter to Superville that year, "I am in full fever of painting, I work at it for seven hours a day and am intending to have an exposition at the start of the school year, and this time there will no more 'drafts' (brouillons). You will be astonished at my progress." In November of 1938, Michaux had another exposition at the Galerie Pierre, Paris, *Peintures Nouvelles de Henri Michaux*. On the invitation card, a text: "UN POÈTE SE CHANGE EN PEINTRE. Always himself, the bizarre Michaux and his perpetual transforming invention."[22]

Apart from meeting him during World War II and at several casual social encounters,[23] Michaux had little apparent contact with Bataille, but

---

20. On the change in Michaux's life from being "Henry," a name he always detested as though it were a stamp of inferiority, to "Henri," the pen name he adopted, see Bernard Noël, "La ligne du pli," in *La Place de l'autre, Oeuvres III* (Paris: P.O.L., 2013), 525–32.
21. See Raymond Bellour and Yse Tran, "Chronologie," *OC* I (Paris: Gallimard, Bibliothèque de la Pléiade, 1998), cvxi.
22. Bellour and Tran, "Chronologie," *OC* I, lxxxviii, xcvii, cvii, cxvi, and cx.
23. See Jean-Pierre Martin, *Henri Michaux* (Paris: Gallimard, 2003), which notes Michaux's participation, along with a host of writers and painters including Matta, Miró, Masson, Picasso, Ernst, Tanguy, Bazin, and many others, in a charity event helping Bataille to acquire an apartment on Saint-Sulpice in 1961, just a year before his death in 1962, and a letter Michaux wrote to Bataille in April 1961 praising Bataille's "unique" and "capital" pages on ecstasy and laughter; "merci," as he wrote to Bataille (587).

he did acknowledge in 1940 having read an article, *L'Amitié*, destined for publication in *Mesures*, which was "the best thing I've read by him," he wrote to Paulhan.[24] Again, in 1961, there is another note praising what Bataille had said about ecstasy. Although he had a long literary and artistic career, he was never identified with any group. Critics sometimes like to link him with the Surrealists, but he was not amongst them. Nor was he associated with any of the groups or journals that Bataille and Klossowski were associated with, such as *Documents* or the Collège de Sociologie. Fiercely independent, often thought of as a mystic or a trailblazer in the world of hallucinogenic drugs like mescaline, he did attract the attention in the 1960s of the American poets Allen Ginsberg and John Ashbery, who described him as "hardly a painter, hardly even a writer, but a conscience—the most sensitive substance yet discovered for registering the fluctuating anguish of day-to-day, minute-to-minute living."[25]

Who was Henri Michaux, in his own words? In "Quelques renseignements sur cinquante neuf années d'existence"[26] he writes of himself as though he were writing of someone else, always in the third person. From 1900 to 1906, "he avoids life, games, amusements, and variation. Food disgusts him. Odors, contacts. His marrow does not make blood. His blood isn't wild with oxygen." Self-disgust seems to be a primary experience. "Secretive, withdrawn. Ashamed . . . of everything that surrounds him . . . ashamed of himself and for everything he has known up to now." The laconic "information" ends with two dates: "1956: First experiments with mescaline" and 1957: art shows in three countries, a broken right elbow, and discovery of the "left-handed man" ("l'homme gauche," or the clumsy man). "Despite so many efforts in so many directions all through his life to change himself, his bones, without paying any attention to him, blindly follow their familial, racial, Nordic evolutions."[27]

Whether or not he overcame those despondent feelings of his youth, Michaux's life and work prospered. Mainly through writing and painting about himself, his travels, his visions, his experiences, he seeks what makes him no longer belong to himself, all that loosens the grip of the "Je" (the "I"). Always a voyager to points beyond, he is summoned in writings and

---

24. Bellour and Tran, "Chronologie," cxv; and Martin, *Henri Michaux*, 331.
25. John Ashbery, quoted in *Darkness Moves*, ix.
26. Michaux, *OC* I, cxxxviv. Trans. by Ball as "Some Information About Fifty-Nine Years of Existence," in *Darkness Moves*, xxiv.
27. *OC* I, cxxxiv–v (*Darkness Moves*, xxx).

drawings by his memories and dreams, which arise like images from a world that comes before or beneath the "Je pense" ("I think"), emanations rising from a bottomless night. He learns to "prefer one reality to another." An early discovery in life that helped his turnaround was the discovery, around 1914, of the dictionary, where he noticed many words "that do not yet belong to phrases, to phrasemakers, masses of words, words he can use himself in his own way." Then the discovery of Latin, a language he loved and that set him "apart from others, transplants him: his first departure." This was his departure not only to the limits of both writing and painting but to the limits of himself, his own "clumsy self." What does it mean to say he was a "conscience" if not to say he was always on a voyage away from himself as an "ego" as a "true Self," which also implies he was a voyager within, "dedans," an explorer of the limits and the possibilities of himself as a conscience? And those limits are with his body. Indeed, his body is a constant presence in his writings. The body as a theater of pains and physical weaknesses—he had a congenital heart condition—but also the body as the sensitive "substance," as Ashbery calls it, a theater of visions, registering the "fluctuating anguish of day-to-day living."[28] The body as that substance not of the flesh Merleau-Ponty speaks of, but something darker, something from "the night," the "implacable night," the "night without limits"[29] where inside and outside have their folding point, their threshold, opening onto one another. He sought a "cure." He had wanted at one time in his youth to be a doctor but resisted the necessity of education because it always meant "accepting, accepting." Later in life, he pursued a science of the body by way of hallucinogenic drugs, mescaline, hoping to leave something from his experiences to science. But what could science know or say in the end?

Thus, we see how Raymond Bellour is right when he says that two words are essential for any introduction to Michaux's experience of writing: *guérir* and *savoir*. The force of these words, Bellour writes, are felt throughout Michaux's life as what frees him from any belief that his works would be accepted as "works," that his experiences would accept becoming a "work," a book, an autonomous thing, his life's completion and its "truth."[30] Alas, both guérir and savoir are impossible for Michaux: the body is finally healed only in death, and savoir ends in what Bataille might have called "non-savoir." Writing is always traversed by the "writing of the disaster," the point where

---

28. Ashbery, quoted in *Darkness Moves*, ix.
29. Michaux, "Dans la nuit," in *OC* I, 600.
30. Bellour, introduction to *OC* I, xvii–xix.

writing crumbles, changes form, becomes an animal—"animaux fantastiques," in Michaux's words—or an insect, not a "signifier," no longer a work but a thing, a substance of some sort crawling across the page. Could a universal language emerge from this cocoon?

He suffered, yet he lived on, a long life. Are his poems an "image of his life," which, as René Char writes, is what modern men—"les hommes d'aujourd'hui"—want? Is Michaux, such a "man of today"? Possibly, but as a poet of great consideration, coming from boundless spaces and tolerant of all that comes his way, he is the reverse of the sort of modern man Char evokes. Yet he too has written his own *poème pulverisé*, which, likewise, is the image of *une vie pulvérisée*, a pulverized life. "Dans la nuit," the space inside and outside, not where the light fails but where it begins, an emanation. How could he not have lived without always having "the unknown" before, *devans*, him, something without, *devans*, as much as it is within, *dedans, dans la nuit*? "Plunge into the unknown that cuts furrows. Make a point of spiraling," as Char writes.[31]

Three writers and painters from mid-twentieth-century French culture, each fiercely independent, belonging to no school, academy, or political persuasion: What do they have in common? While the three chapters in this volume do not initially set out to establish comparisons between these three writers, common ground emerges: each in their own "combat against culture" and in their conceptions of art and writing, pointing the way toward a nonrepresentational experience of art, one linked to ritual, to exorcism, and to healing.

---

31. René Char, *Feuillets d'Hypnos (1943–1944)*, in *Furor and Mystery*, 204. "The Leaves of Hypnos," in *Furor and Mystery*, 204–5. French original: "Enfonce-toi dans l'inconnu qui creuse. Oblige-toi à tournoyer."

Chapter 1

Apparitions

Georges Bataille, Lascaux, and the "Birth of Art"

The Unspeakable Beast

The Beast, unspeakable, brings up the rear of the graceful herd, a cyclopean buffoon . . .
From her hooves to her useless horns, she is sheathed in stench.
Thus, Wisdom appears to me in the Lascaux frieze, mother fantastically disguised,
Her eyes brimming with tears.

—René Char[1]

Ces oeuvres (at Lascaux) en aucune mesure, à aucun moment, ne furent des objets d'art: rien ne s'eloigne advantage, dans la production de tous les âges, de ce qui mérite le nom de chose. Leur sens se donnait dans l'apparition, non dans la chose durable, qui demeurait après l'apparition.

—Georges Bataille[2]

---

1. René Char, "La Béte innommable" [The Unspeakable Beast], *Lascaux*, trans. Nancy Kline, in *Furor and Mystery & Other Writing*s, trans. and eds. Mary Ann Caws and Nancy Kline (Boston: Black Widow Press, 2010), 359. Maurice Blanchot also quotes this poem in full on the opening pages of his *La bête de Lascaux* (Paris: Fata Morgana, 1982).

2. "La passage de l'animal à l'homme et la naissance de l'art," in *OC* XII, 274. ("Not by any measure nor at any time were Lascaux's paintings objects of art: nothing is further removed, in the production of all ages, from what can rightly be called a thing [*chose*]. Their meaning was given in their *apparition*, not in the durable thing, which remained after the apparition"; trans. mine.)

In many religious cultures, the holy is associated with the "high," with light and mountaintops. Lord Siva, for just one example, is a mountain dweller; Wat Phu, the name of one of the first temples dedicated to Siva in Southeast Asia, built in the fifth century, literally means "temple mountain." Likewise, Zeus is a sky god; his son Apollo is the god of the sun. For Christians, heaven and the throne of God is always said to be somehow "above"—Christ *ascends* to heaven.

But it wasn't always this way. Some 20,000 or more years ago, the holy sanctuary and the abode of the gods may have been deep in the earth, in the darkness of caves, in a labyrinthine "underworld." Such is perhaps the case at many of the most famous Paleolithic caves: Lascaux and Chauvet in France and Altamira in Spain. Chauvet is particularly striking in this regard. Only recently discovered, with only those doing research allowed in, Chauvet is particularly mysterious and enticing for modern explorers. The contemporary descent is facilitated only by the installation of metal ladders and walkways. The earthen floor of the cave must be kept pristine, all invasive bio-organisms must be cleansed from the researchers' clothing before they may even enter. The darkness that quickly engulfs the visitor may be momentarily dispelled by torchlight, but the silence can never be defeated. Thus, it is one of those rare archeological sites where the researcher can experience the site, the cave, in much the same way as did those who, at the other end of human history, at the "birth," at the origins of art itself, here painted, engraved, pressed their hands, stabbed at its rock walls, and communicated with their god(s). An altar-like stone was found in situ at Chauvet with a bear's skull placed upon it as though it were an offering. But to what? This darkness? This silence? A silence closest to the sacred, and a truest form of communication. Here, deep in this silence and darkness, something extraordinary happened that still resonates today, still poses itself as a question and a mystery. "Pourquoi l'art préhistorique?" "What is Paleolithic Art?" or "Why prehistoric art?" as Jean Clottes asks in a 2011 publication.[3]

Lascaux, Chauvet, Altamira: names that are often invoked to designate the places and times of the "dawn" or the "birth" of art. Do they fulfill the need to name a historical place and time for an origin of art that ever recedes in the silenced murmur of ancient things? Why is art always so intimately

---

3. *Pourquoi l'art préhistorique?* (Paris: Gallimard, 2011). Trans. by Oliver Y. Martin and Robert D. Martin as *What Is Paleolithic Art? Cave Paintings and the Dawn of Human Creativity* (Chicago: University of Chicago Press, 2016).

linked with the question of its irrecoverable origins? Denis Hollier, in his discussion of all the connotations of "labyrinth" in Bataille's writings, writes, "The question of the beginning, the 'commencement,' is itself already a labyrinth."[4] However essential it is to understanding art, the question of art's origins in human history is a question without an answer, for the origin, the time and place of the beginning and circumstances of art's arising, can never be established. The beginnings of things, the beginnings of art, like the beginnings of life itself, occur without leaving a trace, without a fossil, or a surviving witness. There is always a gap between the "origins" of art and its true beginnings in what can only be described as a "non-origin," a chance event, perhaps, without a precise time and place, an event remote, lost, unrecognizable. For generations of art historians, the beginnings of art were identified with the monumental art of the Egyptians or with the Greeks or the Romans. But the discoveries of Lascaux in September of 1940, by boys looking for a pirate's treasure, or of Chauvet more recently in the 1990s, of Altamira a hundred years before, also discovered by a child, overturned all of that. The discoveries of Paleolithic art at Lascaux, Chauvet, and Altamira, the scintillating gifts of serendipity, have pushed the place and time of the historical origins of art to a point in time quite beyond all recorded human history, if not all human memory. Lascaux has been dated to some 15,000 years ago, while Chauvet to about 30,000 years ago, suggesting a timeframe of some 25,000 years for the existence of a Paleolithic culture. That is several thousands of years longer in duration than all of recorded human history. Yet we know comparatively little about these places and the humans that left their signatures there. But even these ancient dates do not document the first beginnings, for art, most often identified in its infancy with painted or inscribed images or small portable statuettes, probably already had a long history before anyone set foot in the cave at Lascaux or Chauvet.

But what makes these ancient works so breathtaking is not only their great antiquity but also their remarkable state of preservation together with their often remarked upon "modernity." How did it happen that these works have come down to us as though they were painted or inscribed only yesterday? While the state of preservation for the paintings and engravings at these places is a miracle, no doubt, it only deepens their enigma. Why did these ancient people devote so much time and effort to producing images,

---

4. Denis Hollier, "La labyrinth et la pyramide," in *La prise de la Concorde: Essais sur Georges Bataille* (Paris: Gallimard, 1974), 111.

works of art as we might call them, in the bowels of the earth, works that could only be seen by torchlight, works wrapped in a seeming eternity of night and silence? The visitor senses that they are seeing these paintings and their cave environs much as did those who painted them thousands of years ago. But this sense of presence and immediacy, whereby time has seemingly come to a dramatic halt, only increases our sense of wonder, leaving us with a consternating mixture of stunned admiration and a desire to know the answers to so many unanswerable questions: "What does it all mean?" "Pourquoi l'art préhistorique?" ("Why prehistoric art?") as the expert Jean Clottes and others have asked.

The sciences of prehistoric cultures would like to find answers to these questions. Science is a discipline seeking answers that replace what was unknown with something known. Knowledge shall be the measure of all things. "Il faut render raisons," as Blanchot writes, "il faut que ce qu'il a à connaître, l'inconnu, se render au connu."[5] The scientist would begin by seeing these works as artifacts, things to be enumerated and described. But there is also and always something more. In the great Hall of Bulls at Lascaux, where the images of animals measure more than three meters in length, there is a stunning sense of "presence" that cannot be reproduced in the museum dioramas set up to depict the prehistoric world. What words or concepts, what "raisons" can account for this? Was this a sacred place, a place where early humans paid their respects, made their offerings, searched for a way to understand the world around them?

Georges Bataille's approach is quite different than that of the anthropological sciences. He remarked—in a rather unscientific way—on this sense of presence at Lascaux, linking it to the sacred and the "sovereign," an unsurpassed creation, an event like no other, calling it the double birth of art and modern human beings. Indeed, it is probably the case that while Lascaux may not in fact mark the ultimate historical origins of either art or humanity, it remains nonetheless true, in the words of Maurice Blanchot, that Lascaux "opened to man a unique abode within himself and the marvelous, behind which he had necessarily to remove and efface himself in order to discover himself," to configure himself and then to withdraw behind the concealing masks of "the majesty of the great bulls, the dark

---

5. Maurice Blanchot, *L'Entretien infini* (Paris: Gallimard, 1969), 61. Trans. by Susan Hanson as *The Infinite Conversation* (Minneapolis: University of Minnesota Press, 1993), 43. English trans.: "Reason must be given. What is to be known—the unknown—must surrender to the known."

fury of the bison, the grace of the little horses, the dreamy sprightliness of the stages, even the ridiculousness of the large leaping cows."⁶

And where the rare image of a human being appears, in sketchy, stick-figure caricatures, as it turns out, or as a sorcerer apparently masked in the garb of an animal world he has left behind, images traced in some of the most remote regions of the subterranean labyrinths, we find a different kind of origin, one that opened a destiny unfolding from the most distant past to an as yet unimaginable future, the origins of the enigma that humankind is for itself, the enigma of an initial plenitude, of a human sovereignty that left its signature, its self-portrait, in the "majesty," grace, and, yes, even the "ridiculousness" of animal faces. If not precisely the birth of art, Lascaux may mark the birth of a very human desire to always get beyond itself, to exceed the immediacy of practical needs and quotidian demands, to surpass what it is in the face of what it is not. If not the absolute origins of art and humanity, Lascaux and the other caverns that slumber beneath the mountains of southern France have bequeathed a treasure trove of images. We are free to make of them what we will, to describe them, to preserve them, even to forget them. How should we receive them, this gift of art? Is it posed to us today as something to be known, reducible to what is known? Or as something always irreducibly unknown, a birth of art and humanity beyond all remembering, linked with death and concealment, a birth whose mystery only deepens and resounds in every attempt to answer or to replace the poetry of perplexity with the logic of concepts and propositions?

The Scientific Accounts and What the "Poets" Say

So, our question is how to respond to this enigma of the animal paintings at Lascaux. We would prefer to frame this question not as "How do we explain the images?" but rather "How do they provoke our seeing and thinking?" and so remind us how reflecting on art is a reflection on reflection itself, something Merleau-Ponty referred to as a hyper-reflexion (*sur-réflexion*) "that would take itself and the changes it introduces into the spectacle into account."⁷ The burning presence of the animal images at Lascaux is an

---

6. Maurice Blanchot, "The Birth of Art," in *Friendship*, trans. Elizabeth Rottenberg (Stanford: Stanford University Press, 1997), 11.
7. Maurice Merleau-Ponty, *The Visible and the Invisible*, trans. Alphonso Lingus (Evanston, IL: Northwestern University Press, 1968), 38.

appeal to thinking, to thinking not just delimited to calculations of things but to the wonder of existence itself. The enigma of the animal images, and the labyrinth of rock, shadows, and silence in which they are situated, cannot be ignored or put at a distance, forgotten by being "understood," their enigma resolved. In this way, the ancient images at Lascaux or Chauvet present all the problems and questions we find in modern art today. How is the labyrinthine character of the cave so important to these images? How are the apparitions at Lascaux more than just a spectacle unfolding before us? How do they act on us, provoke our wonder, or allow us to discover more of our human world and its relation to animal being, to the animal being that a human being is in its very flesh? Are these images to be seen displayed before us as objects detached from us, put at a distance, as seeing and objective observation would require? Or do the animal images speak not just *to us*, addressing us as though from a distant beyond, but rather resonate from within, somewhat the way Merleau-Ponty suggested when he quoted Cézanne, "Nature is on the inside"—sensations, color, light depth, darkness, and silence "echo" in our body, "things have an internal equivalent in me," and "the body welcomes them."[8] Thus, the presence of these animal images, which Bataille so strongly remarked, would be something that strikes from *within* rather than being felt as a spectacle of which our eyes are merely the receptors. Between the animal images and those who painted them hundreds of centuries ago, as between those who see them today, spellbound, there is a system of exchanges, making it entirely appropriate to speak of "the animals and their men." "The animals painted on the walls of Lascaux," Merleau-Ponty wrote,

> are not there in the same way as the fissures and limestone formations. But they are not elsewhere. Pushed forward here, held back there, held up by the wall's mass they use so adroitly, they spread around the wall without ever breaking from their elusive moorings in it. I would be at great pains to say *where* is the painting I am looking at. For I do not look at it as I do at a thing; I do not fix it in its place. My gaze wanders in it as in the halos of Being. It is more accurate to say that I see according to it, or with, than that I see it.[9]

---

8. Merleau-Ponty, "Eye and Mind," trans. Carleton Dalleryn, in *The Primacy of Perception*, ed. James Edie (Evanston, IL: Northwestern University Press, 1964), 164.

9. Merleau-Ponty, "Eye and Mind," 164; Merleau-Ponty's italics.

Indeed, it was the animal that most preoccupied the painters at the caves of Chauvet and Lascaux. Human figures are rare in Paleolithic art, and those that do exist are often rough caricatures compared to the abundance and magisterial splendor of the animal images. But the very clarity of the animal images only deepens their mystery. That Paleolithic people invested so much time and trouble, working in such dark and difficult circumstances, to engrave and paint these animal figures testifies to the importance they must have had for their creators. But what can we say about the significance of these sensational figures? What desires propelled this creative activity? Was it a hunger for meat that drove them to it? Do the images of horses and reindeer represent the animals prehistoric people hunted? Was the painted image, then, not really a work of art at all, as we may think of it today, but merely a kind of tool useful for the hunting of such animals? Or was it a religious hunger that drove them, the desire to placate the implacable forces of the natural world that surrounded them? Do they represent spiritual gods or sensations? Are they signs, traces of myths? Do the animal images play a symbolic or semiological role, like the animals seen in ancient Egyptian art? Are they even representational? Could it be that there is more than representation at work here?

How, then, have the so-called human sciences, the sciences of Paleolithic art, responded to these animal images, and how has the response of the poets been so strikingly different, each giving us a not only a different Lascaux to see and experience but an entirely different conception of speaking and seeing? We shall proceed in the following pages through the interpretations of the animal images at Lascaux, presented first by the human sciences, and then, without abandoning this context, approach two more "poetic" responses, the first by Jean Rouaud and the second by Georges Bataille. Two key considerations shall be, first, how each of these different ways of encountering the mystery of Lascaux interprets both the animality and the images of that animality. What can be surmised about the relationship of the animals depicted in Lascaux's parietal art to the human world that created them? How has the anthropological sciences grasp of the art of Lascaux informed by their differing conceptions of the essence and purposes of art? Is art, or the marking of images, useful? Is it governed in its creation by considerations chiefly of utility?

For the more practical-minded of the human sciences, the images are first and foremost representations. They are images of animals representing the real animals hunted in the field. The images were therefore useful to the hunting magic probably practiced by the hunters who lived in the area around Lascaux. The animality brought to view here is an animality that is the object of a desire to eat. The animal is a thing both feared and coveted by the hunters' very own animal hungers. As such, it is the animal that is the Other to the community of human beings, an Other that, although on the outside, out there, so to speak, in the forest and field, is an Other that shall be brought inside, into the human community. Here serves the purposes of Lascaux's art: through hunting and the images produced by a "sympathetic hunting magic" to bring the animals to them, to gain a hold over them in the hazardous pursuit of their meat. Then, at a second, more formalistic level of interpretation—still within the purview of the human sciences—the images are not so much representations as they are signs, signifying elements comprising a "mythogram" spread out across the labyrinthine walls of Lascaux. The animals were "convenient to think with," and the labyrinth is conquered by mapping it, showing the precise placement of the images as signifying parts of a mythogrammatical text. André Leroi-Gourhan's reading of Lascaux transcribes the animal images from the domain of a very physical desire to eat and places them in a more transcendent realm of the metaphysical or the "religious." The shamanistic interpretation by Jean Clottes marks the limits of the traditional physical anthropology in other ways. The paintings are ritualistic for Clottes, modes of communication, places where the human world came to be possessed by a subterranean realm of spirits and forces incomprehensible to modern humanity. Animal being is spiritual, its image is an emanation or shamanistic visitation, making the caves less geological formations than places and events of contact between the human and the subterranean. For the writer/poet Rouaud, the images inscribe not only a deep brotherhood between animals and men but a cosmic turning of seasons that echoes their migrations, the howling of the winds, the decent and return of night, sun, and stars. They are the voices of the dead and all else that has passed into the night beyond. In this context, we turn to Bataille, for whom, as we shall see, Lascaux marks the "double birth of art and humanity." The key to this interpretation is the ever-changing relationship between the humans at Lascaux and the animal being that was both all around and within the humans who passed by Lascaux. The animal images are not things, not representations of objects coveted by a material hunger. They are apparitions, cuts, scarifications, and colors, the joyous traces of an enfolding of human and animal being. The images are a relatively sudden coming to appearance of animality, an apparition essentially linked, as Bataille claims, to rituals, dance, and sacrifice, times of play and a useless, festival expenditure of forces in which human beings celebrated a *sovereign animal being*, now otherwise inaccessible to them yet still desired, still admired and even envied by the human world of work and purpose that had to leave it behind. For Bataille, in short, Lascaux's animals are a sacred, visual, and poetic presence, a play of masks, not prayers for better food but a sovereign cry and an ecstatic binding of friendship between the animals and their men, the marks of a lost "intimacy," as Bataille calls it, between animal and human being that is here celebrated in all its fragile splendor and ferocity.

Shall this be an argumentative progression of some sort? Not necessarily. More of a way toward the dereliction of erudition and the fine ways of saying (*bien-parler*) what there is to see at Lascaux, more a "jamming" of the science of measures and maps as it approaches the splendor of the night at Lascaux, "une expérience intérieur" in the labyrinthine interiors of Lascaux, a darkness in excess of what can be seen, where words and linear sentences fail and fall silent within an unspeakable Lascaux.[10]

The Discoveries

Ever since their discovery in the late nineteenth century through the twentieth century, scientific and lay persons alike have wondered as to the "what" and the "why" of the ancient images and things found at places like Lascaux, Chauvet, and Altamira. In the second third of the nineteenth century, the first decorated mobile pieces were found: two harpoons engraved with geometric figures at Veyrier in Geneva and the small foot bone (the metapodial) of a reindeer with the engravings of two hinds at Le Chaffaud in France. But

---

10. See Bataille's 1935 essay on the labyrinth, "Le labyrinth" (*OC* I, 433–41), which was added in reduced form to *L'Expérience intérieure* under the title "Le labyrinth (ou la composition des êtres)," 1943, repub. in *OC* V, 97–110. Trans. by Leslie Anne Boldt (Albany: State University of New York Press, 1988), 81–92. See also Hollier, "La labyrinth et la pyramide," 110, where he notes how, for Bataille, "le labyrinth" is neither an object nor a referent, but first of all "the space where oppositions, (inside-outside, animal-human), unravel and become complicated, where diacritical pairs are misaligned, perverted . . . where the system somehow crumbles by itself, jammed by its own approach" ("l'espace où les oppositions se défont et se compliquent, où les couples diacritique sont désaxés, pervertis . . . où s'effrite le système en quelque sorte de lui-même, enrayé par sa propre démarche"; trans. mine).

these were only the minor preludes to the sensational discoveries of large-scale animal paintings at places like Altamira. These early discoveries came at a time when archaeology was in its comparative infancy. One can only imagine the common "natural attitudes" of the average European in those days. Precisely because they were so finely executed and accomplished, suggesting to some that they were not ancient at all but completely "modern," even more advanced in many ways than some of the art contemporary Europeans were seeing as true art, the discovery of Altamira in 1879 (by a child, as the story goes) so upset the traditional, perhaps religious frameworks of the day that the paintings were rejected outright as fakes, possibly an elaborate prank. It's been reported that the Surrealist André Breton scoffed when he saw the paintings at Lascaux, discovered in 1940 (again by children). "The paint isn't even dry," he allegedly observed. In the popular imagination of *fin-de-siècle* France, early human societies were thought to be bestial, crude, bereft of any acceptable religion—horribly uncivilized, in short—and so certainly too ill-equipped to produce anything of cultural value, especially not true works of art. At best, humans from the "reindeer age" were portrayed in a more romantic light, inspired perhaps by Rousseau, as living in a state of blissful nature, like children, unconcerned with property, ambition, or anything else identified with the ills of modern societies. Why would they have taken the trouble to paint such extravagant works of art? But the authenticity and a rough guess as to the age of the paintings were quickly established. Yet the vexing question "Why did they do it?" continued to hang in the air. Again, for the popular imagination, the animal images at best testify to a simple desire to decorate places of respite by hanging pictures on the walls, a kind of art free from any concern other than the pleasures of doodling on the walls, almost a kind of graffiti.

Today we know that these images are indeed very ancient. The images at Chauvet, for example, date from around 30,000 years ago; Lascaux is more recent, perhaps 15,000 to 20,000 years ago. They testify to the existence of a nomadic human society that was quite "like us." In anthropological terms, they were modern *Homo sapiens*, "man who knows," who has "taste." Accordingly, twentieth-century accounts of Lascaux's art are more appreciative than those of the late nineteenth century. Looming up from the darkness, an impossibly ancient cavalcade of line and color, parades of horses and bison mostly, leads the visitor into the darkness beyond. Such startling images are often said to mark the dawn or birth of art, or its historical beginnings. In all their radiant presence, these images are not a nocturnal art, defined by the darkness of their abode, but a brilliant dawning of art, the first morning light, the first breakthrough for a humanity rising after a long night of being confined to a world defined by work and tools, whose humble, mute testimonies were suddenly opened to the dazzling wonder of artistic creativity at Lascaux or Chauvet. Something new began there; something that had the force to open a new era in the way human beings experienced their world by leaving fragile traces of that experience. As Georges Bataille wrote in 1953, "What is striking about Lascaux is the way it reflects deeply in our eyes the first *sensible* sign that humanity has left of its irruption in the world."[11] Human beings may have created images for thousands of years before Lascaux and Chauvet. The possibility of the nomads tattooing their bodies or painting on bark or other surfaces in the open air cannot be excluded. There is no surviving evidence of this.[12] But Lascaux and Chauvet bear witness to a rather sudden takeoff, an explosion of activity on an unprecedented scale; a magnificence is evident, a flourishing that left its fragile traces in the cold and snowy mountains of ancient Europe.

The Science of the Prehistoric Images at Lascaux

The images found at Lascaux and Chauvet always seem to slip the net of the usual categories and nomenclatures we might adopt when trying to understand or to explain what it is that we see there. We can describe them with words, sort them out, classify them, count them and measure them; we can assign them to this or that significance. Yet their enigma remains, irreducible. We are always adjusting what we see and what we say about what we see, almost as though interpreting a dream. Is this not true of the study of human history as such?

Perhaps what we see at Lascaux can never be adequately said, making the experience of Lascaux something sublime. There is no evidential way of confirming any particular theory about the how, the why, or the what of these images. The culture that painted them thousands of years ago has vanished or been absorbed into later developments. Nothing remains of their language, their cultural traditions, their myths, their dreams.

---

11. "La passage de l'animal," in *OC* XII, 259.
12. The preserved body of a Chalcolithic (c. 4000 BCE) hunter, later nicknamed Ötzi, was found in 1991 in the Ötztal Alps in Italy. Well preserved, it had some sixty tattoos on its body, although most were lines rather than images.

Nomadic hunting cultures were replaced by agriculture, the wild bison by the domestic farm animal and the noisy flourishing of cities. Lasting for tens of thousands of years, nomadic Paleolithic societies had no written language that we know of. They were prehistoric in this sense. Mute. Even the natural environment has irrevocably changed today. The great glaciers have retreated, the magnificent herds of animals are gone, tourists now stroll where nomadic hunters once tracked their prey. We have no way of bridging the unfathomable chasm that separates those who painted these images or animals in their glory from those of us living today in a fully technologized and denatured society. No doubt the painters of Lascaux were modern human beings, like us, *Homo sapiens*. They are our ancient brothers and sisters. Yet today they are strangers to us, distant relatives with whom we are out of touch. For lack of any other reference, the modern expert can only resort to analogies with the present-day fragments of nomadic cultures that still manage to hang on to their traditions in the context of a modern world of atomic bombs, superhighways, and electronic communication. The most resolute scientific and cultural attempts to answer the mystery of the events at Lascaux or Chauvet would like to replace the shadowy questions of meaning and mystery with the light of scientific reason, to dispel the silence of Lascaux with the eloquence of explanations. But such efforts, often working on the basis of analogy, remain incomplete, stuttering, and unsatisfactory. As the researcher leaves the cave, the darkness and silence again closes in, impenetrable as ever.[13]

Thus, the sciences of Paleolithic art confront an insuperable problem: the sparce, ambiguous character of the remaining evidence results in a lack of corroboration for the claims the expert may venture about the meaning of the paintings. Prehistorians will say that they deal only in facts, but it always comes down to saying something about the meaning of the wall paintings and carved portable objects that have been found. By reducing the question of meaning to the questions of use and utility, it is easier to make claims that can be supported by empirical evidence. The question of a possible meaning or significance of these images would have to be addressed to living members of that society. "Ah, yes," we might imagine them saying, "this is what we usually mean by that." The culture that produced Lascaux's images has disappeared. But the ethnological sciences cannot proceed on the

---

13. The Lascaux community was no doubt aware of the acoustic possibilities of the cave's winding passages. Flutes and other devices found by archaeologists testify to the practice of music by Upper Paleolithic communities.

assumption that its scientific principles have any analogical value when it comes to establishing the meanings and functions of ancient social practices. What common ground does the contemporary researcher have with societies that flourished at the other side of human history? Can the contemporary ethnologist understand or explain, for example, how prehistoric human beings experienced time or their living in a cyclical mythical time, a time before history? As Merleau-Ponty writes in *The Visible and the Invisible*,

> It was evident to the man brought up in the objective cognition of the West that magic or myth has no intrinsic truth, that magical effects and the mythical and ritual life are to be explained by "objective" causes and what is left over to the illusions of Subjectivity. . . . The ethnologist cannot presuppose . . . that those societies have a lived experience of time like ours—according to the dimensions of a past that is no longer, a future that is not yet, and a present that alone fully is—and must describe a mythical time where certain events "in the beginning" maintain a continued efficacy. . . . To be sure, we have repressed the magical into the subjectivity, but there is no guarantee that the relationship between men does not inevitably involve magical and oneiric components.[14]

Nor are there documents that could verify contemporary ethnological claims. To find documents, one must look for—aside from the paintings and small sculptures—footprints, hand marks, the places where a child's fingers played across a wet surface. Hence, where the rubric of utility fails, many specialists would rather not hazard a guess as to the significance of the images. It's better to temper one's ambitions and limit oneself to describing them empirically. Any interpretation of meaning or significance risks going beyond the collected empirical data.

With analogical reasoning proving unsatisfactory, any mention of art, religion, or mystery is supplemented with empirical descriptions of "structures"—the dry inventories of artifacts, the counting and classifications, the physical analyses of the geology of the caves, and the chemical composition of the figures. Such workman-like efforts fulfil an essential need. They help assure the dates of the works and shed light on techniques, materials, and such, all of which are crucial in the creation of works of art.

---

14. Merleau-Ponty, *Visible and the Invisible*, 24.

Yet a certain sterility is often the result of such work. Empirical descriptions, which practice the scientific arts of measurement, leave the measureless enigma of the images untouched. Moreover, as has been noted by anthropologists such as Malinovsky and Steven Jay Gould, pure objectivity is a scientific myth. Descriptions are not neutral. For one thing, even the most objective definitions speak from an undeniable perspective: that of the specialist, the subject-qua-observer, an "objective" specialist, one who can know and say the verifiable "truth" about these images. For another thing, the specialist operates on the basis and from within the limitations of an implicit theory framework, which is often no more than what is generally accepted in the discourses of the community of researchers—what works for them—and so is allowed to go unquestioned as though it were self-evident. Scientific descriptions and the objective theories that claim to account for them without treading into the dangerous waters of the search for meaning are thus particular ways of seeing and defining the imagery. Of course, when blinded by their own zeal and self-certainty, the researcher can occasionally make mistakes in their descriptions: what they take to be arrows striking the flanks of an animal may actually be something entirely different. Jean Clottes, for example, describes how an Aboriginal guide in Australia told him about a university researcher who had claimed that lines seen on the flanks of a kangaroo depicted in some ancient cave images were spears passing through the animals' bodies. The "spears," as the Aboriginal guide said, are actually the lines of a path that suppliants must follow during initiation ceremonies.[15]

Scientific objectivity requires that the researcher be detached, observing at a certain distance from what they are describing. Scientific seeing must always assume a measurable distance between observer and observed. Objective description requires the researcher to stand apart from the object of investigation, resulting in what Merleau-Ponty called a *survol*, a "view from above." It is precisely the detachment of this observer that opens the way for a truly scientific, empirical way of phrasing or articulating these images, a way that objectifies them, sees them as countable things, reducing the density of their sensible materiality to numerical values. This objectivity is a way of rendering all disparate things as equal, equally countable and equally having a numerical, objectively assigned value. All can now be positioned on a scientific grid as they are the "facts of the matter." Their historical remoteness, their ineffable mystery, can now be set aside; they

---

15. Clottes, *What Is Paleolithic Art?*, 71.

become elements in a proposition and a propositional way of thinking. This is not necessarily a weakness in scientific accounts of Paleolithic images. Rather it is a necessary starting point. The researcher has no choice; they are scientists, not Paleolithic hunters. Science is their way of providing a best account, a "true" account, of the animal figures and the human culture that created them.

The best of them recognize that anthropology is not a hard, physical science. It may increasingly draw upon a diverse number of sciences—geology, chemistry, and statistics—but its methodology does not resemble these sciences. Anthropological research is not an experimental science, nor does it have a mathematical basis or demonstrable theorems. As Jean Clottes observed, its proofs are always "low-level," generally offering only the most plausible account, the one that is a "best fit" for the evidence obtained.[16] The sheer diversity of an artistic tradition that may have lasted for tens of thousands of years is far too diverse for any single theory to embrace it all. Yet, the quest to answer the questions of the purpose and significance of these ancient paintings must go on. An objective description, an inventory, can only go so far. A common idea is that the paintings are representational, that they refer to something outside or duplicate something apart from them, that they have a referential structure. But what do they represent? What is their reference?

There are three general types of images at issue here. First are the images of animals; second are the rare and enigmatic images of human figures, often shown wearing animal masks or disguises; and third are the mysterious, abstract signs, lines, and geometrical shapes sometimes sharply angular, sometimes more rounded, and sometimes nothing more than red dots patterned on a cave wall. These three categories have a common foundation: all assume a representational, referential conception of the imagery. The image thus becomes a sign. To what do these signs refer? What do they represent? Do they constitute a sort of map or guide, or are they a visual message? Do other lines observed near or on the bodies of the animals portrayed represent projectiles or spears? Do the human figures represent shamans, disguised hunters, perhaps the gods of the animals? Do the animal figures themselves represent real animals in the forests and fields? In any case, the image is always something referring to something else, belonging among things in themselves and referring to other things outside, in the world beyond them and their syntax. Perhaps the images were a way of

---

16. Clottes, 26.

getting a hold on the things to which they referred, somewhat the way a concept grasps at things.

Images Considered as Tools: The Sympathetic Hunting Magic Theory

Thus, many of the early scientific accounts of European Paleolithic images interpret the paintings of bison or reindeer as representing real animals in the forests and grasslands beyond, outside the cave, animals that are the objects of the hunters' attention, fear, and desire. A common argument might build from this assumption and go on to argue that those who created these images were first of all nomadic hunters; they had to hunt and kill to survive. Hunting such large animals as bison, horse, or reindeer—precisely the most common varieties depicted in Paleolithic cave paintings—had its risks. Success was not always assured. The naturalness of the animal in the Paleolithic paintings, the realism, may have been a way for hunters to gain an advantage over the animals they hunted. By painting the image of the animal on the cave wall, the hunter was facilitating the capture of the real animal in the field. The creation of the images was a kind of magical action at a distance. The hunters no doubt had a deep connection with their prey. Carefully observing prey in the field, and then transferring these observations to the production of images—a feat that anthropologists say was a significant accomplishment in human development, one that can be taken as evidence of a growing intellectual ability on the part of the Paleolithic painters—gave the hunter more than one advantage in the risky contingencies of the hunt.

Thus emerges a rough outline of the sympathetic hunting magic theory, first offered in 1903 by Solomon Reinach and famously prolonged by the abbé Breuil in his 1952 *Quatre cents siècles d'art parietal, Le Cavernes ornée de l'age du renne*. It is the creation of the images that is important for this theory, not their finished status as durable objects of aesthetic interest. Painting or engraving the image of an animal perhaps cast a sort of spell over the animal, and the hunter gains an advantage. Capturing the image of the animal in the field was moreover connected with rituals, ceremonial acts. This would explain why there is so much superimposition of one animal image on top of others, resulting in a palimpsest of imagery. It was the act and execution of the image that may have been essential, not the figure itself.

Accompanying the assumption that the Paleolithic images are representational is another assumption: that the images have a purpose, a telos or direction; that they have an appointed task; that they are useful. The old question of the significance of the imagery is conveniently reduced to utility. Why else would these ancient people have devoted so much time and effort to their production? The thorny question of significance, the reference, and the motivation for the images are all answered in a single stroke of interpretation. Everything falls into place once the human world is reduced to a world of work and the practicalities of sheer survival. The hunting magic theory thus rests on the bedrock of utilitarian assumptions. Utilitarianism is the theoretical framework that goes unquestioned here as though it were self-evident. The images have value only insofar as they accomplish an essential task: putting food on the table. They are certainly not works of art and have no religious or spiritual import. They are merely an extension of the spear and the arrow, tools tuned to the practical necessities of making a living in the rough and chilly times of the European Paleolithic.

On this point, the anthropologist interpreting the paintings at Lascaux might be compared to the Freudian psychoanalyst interpreting dreams, for whom the strange work of dreams is reduced to a single motivation: the fulfillment of a wish. If not to actually kill the animal in the field, the painted image of an animal might even be a way of ensuring the continuing fecundity of the herds, a way of contributing to their proliferation, or a form of atonement for killing them. Painted images double the size of the herds. On the other hand, and in a contrary direction, the depiction of dangerous animals such as lions can be explained as based on a fear of these animals and the desire to eliminate them. Despite its limitations, the hunting magic theory does fulfil the anthropologist's need for an economical theory that embraces a wide range of figures with the least number of terms and so seems to "best fit" the described realities and cultural contexts of Paleolithic life, just as the Freudian interpretation of dreams similarly reduces the tangled carnival of dreams to wish fulfillment. Both might be interpretated as ways of acting at a distance.

But if the representational and utilitarian hunting magic theory is to hold up, it must address some critical material and philosophical questions. For one, why were the paintings at Lascaux and Chauvet created deep in a cave, precisely where the light falls and darkness begins? Was darkness crucial to hunting magic? Projectiles decorated with animal figures and used in broad daylight may have served just as well, but why the need to paint such magnificent figures in deep darkness, only seen by torchlight? For another, are all the animals depicted at Lascaux and Chauvet the ones Paleolithic humans ate, or might they also have been "food for thought," as

Lévi-Strauss once suggested? While the paintings of reindeer might suggest a food source, there are yet many other animals depicted in the paintings—rhinoceros, for just one example, were not typically game animals for Paleolithic hunters. There are also the imaginary animals, the so-called unicorn that can be seen at Lascaux. There must be some explanation for that as well. But most importantly, what does the theory say about the relations between the humans and animals? Does it not say that they were essentially adversaries, the hunter versus the hunted?

When framed as a representational and utilitarian practice, the art of Lascaux is also fundamentally conceived as being essentially optical and narrative in nature. An optical art is useful for narrating events, for storytelling, as in cartoons and anime. While rare, there are isolated instances in which this narrational dimension is quite explicit, as in the famous scene depicted in one of the most inaccessible and remote areas of Lascaux, a place called the pit. The assemblage has the figures of a rhinoceros, a bison, and a human, plus some rows of dots. The animals are painted realistically, but the human is depicted as a stick figure, ithyphallic but with its face hidden by a bird's head, a mask possibly. This scene, as it is called, is said to be the narration of a hunting incident in which a large bison has been severely wounded; its entrails are spilling out. Possibly the broken spear, shown lying across its body, is the cause. Meanwhile, the rhino appears to walk nonchalantly away to stage-left in this mysterious drama. The human figure meanwhile appears to be dead. Was he killed in the action of the scene? Or is he in a trance or a state of ecstasy? As René Char wrote of this figure, this "dancer of chasms [*danseur d'abîme*]," his "long body . . . knew urgent exaltations [*l'enthousiasme exigeant*]."[17] All of this is indeterminable, an irreducible mystery, both veiled and unveiled by this particular assemblage, both inscribed and erased by the darkness in the deepest and most remote part of Lascaux.

But one of the most essential consequences of the referential theory of art is to install a distance between creator and spectator. Where the darkness and silence of the caves would tend to distance the images, burying them under earth and shadow, modern electrical lighting might seem to dispel distance and offer us immediacy. Just flick a switch and suddenly they are there. But in this case, the lighting of the images, even photographs of them, would replace the distance of time and obscurity experienced in the

---

17. Char, "Homme-oiseau mort et bison mourant" [Dead Bird-Man and Dying Bison], trans. Nancy Kline (English and French), in *Furor and Mystery*, 357.

caves with the immediacy of light and sight. Such immediacy is usually prescribed by a need for public accessibility. Lascaux is only a few hours' train ride from Paris. We can now easily and conveniently see the caves. But we cannot see them in the atmosphere, in the environs, in which they were both first created and experienced. An optic art is the correlate of an optical language, a discourse that sets its heart on seeing the truth, the "what is." Both tend to objectify and so open from the heart of immediacy other levels of distance, which in this case would not be just physical distance but might be the distance of alienation. Seeing the paintings as narratives, illustrated storytelling, or instruments of utility is to install three levels of distance in the paintings. First, it opens a distance between the images and what they might be images of: the animals in nature. This is an obvious consequence of the animal images being images, representations rather than real animals. Second, there is the distance between the paintings and the spectator, those who might have seen them 20,000 years ago. Were there spectators of these paintings or were they the secret domain of shamans only? If there were spectators, how did they experience the animal figures? It could not have been like the modern spectator going to see a Mickey Mouse cartoon. Did the prehistoric spectators experience the parade of images as representations of an animal world they were familiar with, the animals they ate? Did Paleolithic people see the animals like a person today would see a pot roast sitting on a supermarket shelf? Did these ancient people see them as the signs or symbols of territories—migratory routes—or as the symbols of ideas for which there were no words to name? Did they see them as scenes from a myth, a communal dream, or a tall tale visually unfolding before them? Such are questions for which there can be no answers. But contemporary material contexts have opened a third level of distance between the paintings and the spectator. The modern visitor's experience is mediated not only by the interpretations of the specialists or the guide that accompanies every step of the way but by the way they experience the cave paintings today. Today, one must settle for seeing the legendary paintings as reproductions in a movie-set cave built into an elaborate underground bunker, a kind of high-tech simulacre or museum diorama. First distinguished and so distanced from the original live animal, and then from the original paintings themselves, the Lascaux simulacre is a representation of a representation and thus twice removed not just from the physical animals but from the originating event of Lascaux. No doubt such technology is necessary to preserve the original paintings from the bacteria and mushroom spores the hordes of tourists would bring into the microclimate of the cave on their shoes, clothing, and moist breath. There is no way around it, but it does bleed the life out of the images and transforms the experience of Lascaux into something resembling an amusement park ride. Rather than the close encounter whereby the paintings would unfurl their original force, they are reduced to being something resembling a cartoon.

Again, the representational definition of this art sees these images as essentially an optic art. Optic art, as we have suggested, has the consequence of installing distances between work and viewer. Is there an alternative? Optic art can be distinguished from haptic art, from the Greek *haptesthai*, meaning "to touch," connoting contact and tactility. Haptic art is defined by proximity, not distance. As discussed by the philosopher Gilles Deleuze in connection with the paintings of Francis Bacon and Paul Cézanne, as well as Egyptian bas-reliefs, haptic art challenges or questions the subject—object distance between painter, viewer, and painted image. Haptic art does not presume a stage or a scene that a spectator watches from a distance. While there is evidence of a manual art in the Paleolithic caves (the imprint of hands, the casual doodling of fingers across a wet surface), Deleuze does not want to restrict haptic art to an art that manually explores a surface. Rather it is a multisensory art in which the sense of sight behaves like the sense of touch, having a frontal close-view in which figure and ground are experienced as though on the same plane. With haptic art, the images touch the viewer as much as the viewer, through vision, touches the painted image, connoting an intense point of contact between viewer and image. In Deleuze's pages on this, optic art is linked more to relations of value, the chiaroscuro of light and dark, whereas haptic art, or the "haptic function" as he calls it, bears on relations of color tones, the warm and cool colors that seem to "progress" and "regress" in a close view.[18]

But it is not, in short, simply a matter of vision being opposed to touch, but of two senses of "space" that compete with and complement one another in human experience, an optic space and a haptic space. For our purposes, where the color fields at Lascaux are more limited than those of a Cézanne painting and where it would be difficult to speak of an interplay between warm and cool colors, we would define the optic–haptic contrast as an opposition between seeing the paintings as theoretical constructs—whether as tools or texts, inhabiting the mind as much as the eye, so turning the viewer into a

---

18. Gilles Deleuze, *Francis Bacon: The Logic of Sensation*, trans. Daniel Smith (Minneapolis: University of Minnesota Press, 2002), 99, 107.

spectator who stands apart and does not participate in the games of art—and a visual experience of art that is closer to "touch" and thus more performative and participatory in nature, attaining a closer view in this sense. It all comes down to how one understands sensation. For haptic art, the subject–object relation is not primary. Sensation is not reducible to the subject–object bifurcation. Sensation, as the philosopher Henri Maldiney said, is communication.[19] Perhaps what is missing in the standard interpretations of Lascaux is a different understanding of the work of art. Its work is not to represent but to present. This is a fundamental declaration of such contemporary artists as Paul Klee and Henri Michaux for whom art is not representation but emergence, an apparition that works directly on the nervous system.

But how to go beyond the limits of these representational, utilitarian, and narrative theories of the Paleolithic paintings toward a view that would see emergence and communication as primary? The typical objective scientific view of Paleolithic art has the effect of reducing the paintings to something resembling a collection of extravagantly exotic insects desiccated and pinned in a glass box. Whence the original driving and communicative force of the animal images at Lascaux and Chauvet? Can we still approach them with the sneaking suspicion that they may have a spiritual or even a metaphysical dimension that envelops creator and spectator alike, bringing them in close proximity not only to the animal life they portray but to the human destiny they somehow foretell? Are there yet other ways to conceive of the relations between the animals and their men at Lascaux?

The Structuralist Account: André Leroi-Gourhan

Let's suppose that the animal images do not have their significance limited to their representational and referential relations. Likewise, when trying to determine the significance of the animal images, let us look not to their materiality, their chemical composition for example, that gives them their color; nor to their efficient cause, the maker or the technique; nor to their purpose, their telos, their utility. Let us look to their form.

---

19. Henri Maldiney, *Regard, Parole, Espace* (Paris: Cerf, 2012), 220. Maldiney writes, "*La relation Moi-Monde dans le Sentir n'est pas réductible au rapport Sujet-Objet. . . . La sensation est fondamentalement au mode de communication et, dans le sentir, nous vivons, sur un mode pathique, notre être-avec-le-monde*"; Maldiney's emphasis.

The word "form" has, of course, a long history in European philosophy, dating back to the Greeks, to Plato and Aristotle, who called it the *Eidos*, the "look" of a thing, its contour, its definition, its Substance (*Ousia*), its Idea. Form was always distinguished from matter, the *hyle* as the Greeks called it, resulting in a matter-form, a *hyle-morphic* conception of art. But for Leroi-Gourhan, the significance of form ultimately comes not from the way it might inform the matter of the image, nor from its referential relations or references to things in the world, but rather from the lateral relations that obtain between or across forms, the way signs have their meaning not so much in their reference to things but in their systematic, structural oppositions to other signs. On this basis let us sketch a formal and semiological account of Paleolithic animal imagery.

Leroi-Gourhan's magisterial work in the field of prehistory cannot be minimized. It was developed in France at a time when the structural analysis of everything from fashion to the human unconscious to works of art was gaining traction. In his two-volume *Le Geste et la Parole* (1964–1965), he actually begins by remarking how, especially since the eighteenth century, philosophy had expressed two opposing attitudes toward animality: on one hand, an unbridgeable disparity between animal and human, and on the other, an asserted identification. This distinction between animals and humans parallels the metaphysical divide between nature and culture, spirituality and materiality, or instinct and reason. Between the image of animality and the real animal there is the distance that obtains between the word and the tool, he writes.[20]

Gourhan would like to find a third way between these two attitudes by eliminating the animal as a material body and reinstating it as a "form," as a sign. Thus, linking figuration to language, Leroi-Gourhan observes that art's historical origins lie not in realism but in abstraction. Evidently, the Paleolithic hunter-artists never lost their preference for abstraction, regardless of the striking naturalism of the horses, bison, and reindeer at caves like Lascaux. Although this thesis sets up his preference for formalism, he also finds the beginnings of such formalism in the very materiality of gestures.

---

20. Leroi-Gourhan, *Le Geste et la Parole*, vol. I: *Technique et langage* (Paris: Albin Michel, 2022), 320. His pages show how the evolutionary development of hominids from getting around on four feet toward the development of a fully upright posture, erect stance, and bipedal mobility. This frees both the hands from being limited to more strictly motor functions and the mouth from more strictly alimentary functions—the chewing and processing of food—toward the development of more gestural functions creative of tools and the phonetic possibilities of language.

The engraved and painted images are the productions of a physical and mechanical rhythm of hands and arms that first echoes in the hammering of stone to make cutting devices. This rhythmic motoricity then became the basis for the gestures creating parietal images. Hence, while the art shall be read from a linguistic point of view, Leroi-Gourhan still insists on the muscular, physical, rhythmic, and decidedly nonformal basis for the animal images. The images are a "rhythmic device" (*dispositive rythmique*), he writes, having an "incantatory character."[21] Their incantatory character does not however challenge Leroi-Gourhan's primary thesis that figurative art is always, in its origins, directly tied to language and is much closer to writing than might be recognized.[22] "The submission," Leroi-Gourhan writes, "of graphic to vocalization and phonetics" brings about writing's "linearization." But Leroi-Gourhan resists the subordination of writing to phonetics; he insists on their "coordination." Yet a freedom obtains in painted images, or figuration, that is lacking in writing. The series of images introduces both a spatial and a temporal dimension bound together in a series of images that can be read from back to front, top to bottom, or vice versa. A rhythmic dimension is essential to the flow of image, with the oldest being a "naked expression" (*l'expression nue*) of "rhythmic values" (*valeurs rythmiques*). Leroi-Gourhan would like to distinguish the character of the images and their syntax from that of linear writing. The paintings do not progress from one end or beginning to another, like a narrative cartoon strip or a narrative sentence having a conclusion and a full stop. Perhaps myth becomes impoverished with repeated vocal recitation that uproots the myth from its context, not despite the importance of recitation to the Homeric myths. The myth vanishes with the recitation, as it only occupies the time of the recitation. Myth wanders with the poet who recites it. There is no place for myth in recitation alone. But this is not the case with the graphic, figural mythograms. Their context of the cave and its environs is always there as their place, their *fond*, their ground, their depth, their inner meaning. Across the visual images, "the richness of the world is integrated into—'reduced to,' some might say—a 'système de correspondences,' symbols,

---

21. Leroi-Gourhan, *Le Geste et la Parole*, vol. II: *La memoire et le rythmes*, 21. This emphasis on gesture influenced Bernard Noël's interpretation of artistic and poetic creation. He often cites *Le Geste et la Parole*.

22. Leroi-Gourhan writes that only four thousand years of linear writing have separated art and writing. *Le Geste et la Parole*, vol. I:324.

38 | Apparitions, Daemons, and Emanations

as it were, themselves having 'an extraordinary richness.'"[23] But was this richness always understood or seen in the same way? Was the correspondence of text and the richness of the world always fixed? The Paleolithic mytheme acquires a certain permanence, becomes fixed, in Leroi-Gourhan's mapping of Lascaux's images, with the same animal figures and the same semiological relationships symbolizing the same mythic referents over centuries and centuries. Myth becomes a monument. There seems a background assumption in Leroi-Gourhan's view here that myth does not evolve as it would with recitation but remains a fixed visual and spiritual referent for the Paleolithic cultures that once thrived in southwestern France and Spain.

No doubt, this is a consequence of the formalism and structuralism that remained the key interpretive tools for Leroi-Gourhan. His 1982 *The Dawn of European Art: An Introduction to Paleolithic Cave Painting* carries this forward by beginning with a morphology. The analysis of form has two interrelated tasks. First, the overall task is to show a mutual influence between form and content, the animals and the myth they allegedly communicated. Hence, a massive catalog; a classificatory system of forms, is presented as the visual body of a mythical if not metaphysical conception of the world. Another important task is to show the progressive scale, the evolution of these figurative states. Four such figurative states are listed: pure geometric, geometrical figurative, synthetic figurative, and analytical figurative.[24]

Let us now take a closer look.

Pure geometric forms are simply basic lines, the significance of which is undecidable for lack of any confirming oral or written contexts. These might be very ancient, some of the first engraved forms, dating from the Mousterian period circa 60,000 years ago. Geometric figurative forms allow at least a relative identification of the subject. Abstract signs, the rectangle or triangular geometrical shapes, or even the geometricization of animal figures (e.g., a "row of horses reduced to a line of saw teeth,") are included in this category. The synthetic figurative "expresses the form of the subject without representing the fine detail of the contours seen by the eye." The analytic figurative is a form shaded by the modulation of lines and proportions; it is more fleshed out, so to speak, more of a "total representation of the anatomically natural morphology."[25] Leroi-Gourhan assigns the analytic

---

23. Leroi-Gourhan, *Le Geste et la Parole*, I:325, 327; trans. mine.
24. André Leroi-Gourhan, *The Dawn of European Art: An Introduction to Paleolithic Cave Painting* (Cambridge: Cambridge University Press, 1982), 15.
25. Leroi-Gourhan, 17.

figurative forms to his "Style IV," which is characteristic of the Middle and Upper Magdalenian (12,000–20,000 years ago), the "classical period" of Paleolithic cave art, which would include Altamira, Font-de-Gaume, Les Combarelles, and Lascaux (Chauvet not having been discovered at the time Leroi-Gourhan's book was published in 1982).

Form is related to space, and here Leroi-Gourhan considers the disposition of forms across the spaces of the various caves and the "framing" of figures. Forms are characteristically adjusted to fit the space of the cave, what Leroi-Gourhan calls, "the manual field accessible to the artist without changing position."[26] Where space is compacted, forms can be bent or distorted to fit the frame allowed for them. Where the space is fairly open, there may be a large-scale juxtaposition of forms showing animals in lateral, parade-like formations. Superimpositions of figures or overlaps are often partial and might suggest perspective, suggesting in some cases a sense of depth to the parade of images, with one animal figure partially concealed behind another in front of it.[27] More extreme superimpositions show an incessant and repeated imposition of forms, one on top of another, resulting in a difficult to decipher tangle of figures. Les Combarelles and Lascaux are just two examples of sites that have panels like this. It is difficult to establish the chronology of such extreme superimpositions. How much time could have passed between the making of one form and the superimposition on top of it of yet another? It could have been decades or centuries. It could have been simultaneous or synchronic, suggesting thereby, a "specific form of representation," as though this is not accidental or simply due to a lack of space, but intentional. Whatever the case, Leroi-Gourhan claims that the particular groupings of different animals, horses, ibex, mammoths, and bison, where one image is superimposed atop others, might be significant rather than incidental. Do such superimpositions not reinforce the likelihood of a ritualistic context for these images?

The parietal ground or support of the images, the undulating, irregular surfaces of the cave walls, is also important for both its texture and configuration. The shape of a stalactite hanging from a low ceiling might suggest the head of a deer bending to take a drink of water, a stalagmite might evoke a phallus. Concavity of the surface could play a role in depicting body mass and shape. Movement of the figures could be suggested by the curvature and flow of a surface. In some cases, the figure–ground relation-

---

26. Leroi-Gourhan, 19.
27. Leroi-Gourhan, 21.

ship is ambiguous. Some of the figures seem to be missing their feet and appear detached from the ground, as though floating across the surface of the cave wall. Either imaginary lines or natural lines were used to establish the figure–ground relation. The alignment of animals shown following one another suggests an imaginary line, whereas a natural feature might provide a ground-surface, a natural horizonal line for the animal forms. This interaction of figure and ground and the way the natural surfaces and configurations of the caves were exploited in the creation of the animal forms were very important for Leroi-Gourhan, as was the precise placement of the forms in the context of the cave itself, whether near the entrance or deep in the more remote areas.

By working out the morphology and typology of the forms, by mapping the caves, showing precisely where each form was positioned, whether at the periphery or in the more central areas of the cave, by showing how each form was grouped and in association with what other forms, a syntax, a system of relations of the forms to one another and to space and time, comes into view. There is indeed a meaningful organization to the disposition of the animals and abstract signs in the caves. The caves were a "significant space." The paintings exhibit a signifying order; they are not random in placement or execution. Moreover, as a meaningful assemblage, it is the position of the animal sign-forms that is decisive, not their actions or "animation." Leroi-Gourhan's interest in the position of the animal forms in the caves marked a considerable progress over the earlier hunting magic theories, which tended to take the animal forms in isolation from one another. But again, it is the position of the figures in relation to one another, not "animation" that is decisive for establishing the significance of the paintings. The animal forms are nouns, so to speak, not verbs. "Animation," Leroi-Gourhan concluded, amounts only to "narrative license resting on essential representations."[28] A formal, rather static binary symbolic system thus ultimately emerges from Leroi-Gourhan's research in which the significance of the animal forms rests not in their reference to natural animals in the field but in their oppositional and signifying relations to one another. Leroi-Gourhan's original work in this area spanned a decade of highly regarded publications that appeared from 1958 to 1972 and drew much the same conclusions he drew in *The Dawn of European Art*, that the animals were not just good to eat but also good to think with. The figures "must have signified something," their assemblages imply an

---

28. Leroi-Gourhan, quoted in Clottes, *What Is Paleolithic Art*, 21.

"indisputable intention on the part of those who created them to produce something significant." There is a message here to be deciphered. Form is thus reduced to sign and symbol. The paintings "respond to the needs and means that man has had since the Upper Paleolithic to produce oral symbols in a material form by using his hands."[29] Perhaps, then, the signifying forms were related to the hand-tool-language connection Leroi-Gourhan elsewhere observed, a new order of abstract, albeit material, tools—a new order of symbolic communication.

Admittedly, the precise meaning of this message cannot be established, but its general function and form can be. This is where the use of statistical analysis is so important, for it documents the frequency of occurrence of particular forms in particular places of the caves. Essentially three numerically decreasing groups of animal forms are observed: equids and horses, which account for some 30 percent of all the figures, compose the first group; bison, cervids, caprids, and mammoths, another 30 percent, compose the second; and felines, ursines, and rhinoceros, the third. Fish, birds, insects, amphibians, and reptiles may be seen on portable objects but are either rare or missing in parietal art and so not included in any of these three major groups. These groups do not have a natural role to play, for they are now signs in a system of signs.

But since systems of signs are built on binary relations, what binary relation structures the panels of Paleolithic imagery? Leroi-Gourhan claims it is the binary sexual opposition between male and female: sexual difference. While the primary sexual characteristics of the animals are hardly ever evident, where the animal forms are not regarded as natural, biological beings but reduced to playing the role of signs, Leroi-Gourhan reads the animal forms as constituting a symbolic order based on oppositional groups having a sexual significance. Is it by chance that ancient humanity used animal forms to talk about sexuality? This seems to subscribe to the structural views of Jacques Lacan for whom sexual difference is nothing biological but pertains only to the way a subject is inscribed in a symbolic order. Even the cave itself may, symbolically speaking, be female. "Let us admit," he writes, that Paleolithic man practiced a generalized fertility cult through magic rites for both man and woman and that the animal forms were the "actors" or signs, the elements of a mythogram that may have played a decisive, communicating role in such a cult.[30] Hence, the horse

---

29. Leroi-Gourhan, *Dawn of European Art*, 43.
30. Leroi-Gourhan, 62.

or deer was assigned a male value and the bison a female value, and they were grouped accordingly. Likewise, the abstract signs had a symmetrical place in this system, with closed, rectangular, or triangular forms being female and the pointed, more phallic images being male.[31] Whether shown in relative isolation from one another or as "coupled" makes no difference to how they play their allotted signifying roles.

For lack of any surviving cultural context, it may never be known what the message of this Paleolithic symbolic system really was, but the structural, semiological presentation can show or suggest a possible answer to the enduring question "Why Paleolithic art?" The animal form was taken up, abstracted, and repurposed as semiological units communicating a conception, perhaps, of the way the world works. Leroi-Gourhan's analyses bring us closer to the possible spirituality of Paleolithic life. Was the message communicated by the assemblages of signs a religious one? Does it not suggest that Paleolithic humans had not only perceived something extraordinary, something exceeding or surpassing the brute materiality of everyday life, but that the animal forms and abstract signs were the communication of that vision? If so, this capacity for abstract communication of ideas through symbolic or semiotic forms was an important step in the development of human culture. Rather than try to interpret the figures one by one, we must read the animal groupings as signs comprising a text, signs established by systematic differences between signs, signs of sexual difference. The same binary codes that today instruct our digital world were already in play in Paleolithic art. We can now see Lascaux not as an ineffable mystery but as silently eloquent, a text we must learn to read across an entire cave's length, such that across its staging, across the grouping and positioning of forms, something significant comes into view. After Leroi-Gourhan's work, this is what we can now see and say about Lascaux: that it is one of the first great books of human history, a metaphysics for all we know, not written on paper or parchment but drawn, cut, or stamped deeply in the dark body of Mother Earth.

Perhaps this is what truly began at Lascaux and Altamira, certainly not just art as such, for Leroi-Gourhan was never really interested in the animal forms as works of art. Rather it is the dawning of a spirituality that, as the philosopher Heraclitus once said, the Lord whose Oracle is at Delphi "neither speaks nor conceals, but only indicates." Leroi-Gourhan's work, which broached the communicational dimension of Paleolithic art,

---

31. Leroi-Gourhan, *Préhistoire de l'art occidental* (Paris: Éditions d'Art Lucien Mazenod, 1965), 81–109ff.

was an important step forward. But his zeal for forms, for statistics and categorizations, the way he saw the art as a text to be read rather than a way of rendering visible, as a form of emergence, can never really touch or approach what truly dawns at Lascaux. *The Dawn of European Art* remains at a distance from that first light it seeks to grasp. Perhaps the key dimension to Lascaux is something that can never appear in a set of statistics or formalizations, something that bursts open in the light only to withdraw into darkness. Whether a work of art, a mythic code, or a language indecipherable to us today, the animal forms at Lascaux, Altamira, and Chauvet indeed have something irreducibly terrible about them that always slips between or under their staggering presence, a deforming force, an unnamable silence, a majestic silence, opening human beings to strange regions both beyond and within.[32] Thus, form is not only line and contour delimiting shape, it can also be a threshold where forces vibrate across a surface, a line of de-formation where inside and outside fold into one another.

Shamanism: Jean Clottes

The prehistorian Jean Clottes offers a third way of interpreting Paleolithic art. It is a way that emphasizes communication and the power of emergence while avoiding the pitfalls of structuralist abstraction from history and movement. He sees the paintings as shamanistic. This is indeed a fascinating alternative, but one that shall require a rigorous defense if it is to maintain its scientific credentials and not slip into a kind of new age mysticism.

The shamanistic interpretation of hunter–gatherer societies has had its predecessors: Mircea Eliade, Weston La Barre, and Joan Halifax, for example. Yet it has not enjoyed a great deal of influence among more the materialistic anthropologists. Clottes marshals support for his theory from two sources. First, comparative ethnography. The first chapter of *The Shamans of Prehistory* details the historical encounters of Europeans with hunter–gatherer societies that practiced shamanism across Australia, the Americas, Siberia, and southern Africa.[33] Ecstatic visions, tales of travels into spiritual worlds, dances that

---

32. Blanchot, *La bête de Lascaux*, 16.
33. Jean Clottes and David Lewis-Williams, *Chamanes de la préhistoire* (Paris: Seuil, 1996). Trans. by Sophie Hawkes as *The Shamans of Prehistory: Trance and Magic in the Painted Caves* (New York: Harry N. Abrams, 1998). Hereafter, citations refer to the English translation.

went on until the participants dropped to the ground exhausted, covered with the blood that poured profusely from their nostrils, were all reported and even photographed.[34] Guides from Australian Aboriginal peoples and American Indians were key witnesses and helpers to Clottes's anthropological work. While he recognizes that contemporary hunter–gatherer societies may bear only incidental or anecdotal comparison to Paleolithic hunters, that the differences in time, climate, and culture may be too great to draw irrefutable conclusions, it is true nonetheless that shamanism in one form or another has been a part of human culture from an early date and is widespread. A second source for his interpretation is neuropsychology and its experiments with hallucinations. Such states can be induced with psychotropic drugs or with pure physical efforts such as sleep deprivation. Current research has revealed the presence of gases in the caves that may also have induced hallucinations, as was the case with the Oracle at Delphi. Based on these experiments, Clottes develops a chart of the three stages of entopic figures marking the stages of an altered consciousness, beginning with a first stage in which visions of geometrical figures appear; a second stage with more clearly delineated, more naturalistic figures forming in the visions, a "down-the-rabbit-hole" transitional stage; and a third stage featuring terrifying full-fledged visions of half human, half animal beings that could speak to the visionary.[35] The first stage shown in Clottes's chart does indeed resemble some of the figures Henri Michaux drew as he recorded his hallucinations brought on by the consumption of mescaline.

Clottes goes beyond Leroi-Gourhan's structuralism by noting several criticisms that his shamanistic account shall address. First, while the structuralist interpretation of Paleolithic art is theoretically convincing, it did not address the question of why Paleolithic images were drawn in deep, dark caves, often in places very difficult to access.[36] Second, the apparent rigor of structuralist analyses is compromised by several subjective, a priori assumptions. If, for example, the paintings are a text based on signifying, semantic oppositions, how does it account for the necessity of the great number of animal figures painted in the caves? If we are only talking about a general symbolic value, why was it necessary to paint or draw so many figures requiring such elaborate inventories and topographical analyses? Moreover, is it supposed that the creators of these textual panoramas did their work all at once? If so,

---

34. Clottes and Lewis-Williams, *Shamans of Prehistory*, 11ff.
35. Clottes and Lewis-Williams, 14.
36. Clottes and Lewis-Williams, 75.

they could have provided a consistent presentation, eliminating the need to work around or incorporate earlier figures into the visual text. Where it is most likely that the paintings are not contemporary with one another but were made over thousands of years, was it not problematic for the creators to take stock of ancient work as they made new figures? Would they have had the same structural scheme in mind as their ancient forebearers when making new imagery? Finally, the structural account has little to say about panels and zones of imagery in the caves that are indeterminable because of considerable amounts of what looks like ritual superimpositions, areas where clear-cut oppositional relations could not be established because the figures cannot be clearly identified. Leroi-Gourhan called these "*panneaux à contours inachevés* (panels with formless outlines)."[37] These areas of formless outlines were the areas where the structuralist interpretation stumbled, not knowing quite what to do with it except to acknowledge that the superimpositions were intentional. For Clottes, they are significant areas of intense shamanistic rituals, perhaps marking areas where the world of the spirits was particularly close or accessible. In his discussions of structuralist interpretations of Paleolithic art, Clottes restricts himself to these practical matters and does not consider any of the many theoretical and philosophical objections that could be raised to semiotic theory in general. But he does seem to have reservations about a key idea in Leroi-Gourhan: the reduction of the images to "signs." As such, they are "the expression of concepts regarding the natural and supernatural organization of the living world."[38] Clottes would have them performing quite a different role than as representations, whether representing living animals in the forests and fields outside the cave or representing metaphysical concepts. In the shamanistic interpretation the images are neither utilitarian nor conceptual representations. Rather, they are points of contact and communication between the human and spiritual realms; they mark journeys and altered states of mind leaving the world of work and words behind.

 A first dimension Clottes takes into account is the context of the cave itself. The cave is not just the setting for the images but is itself an ensemble of different spaces that may have played varying roles in the ritual life of the Paleolithic people. The walls of the caves are important, and not just as providing the support for the images. Likewise, the ceilings and floors were also significant, even holes and cracks in the ceilings, walls, and floors were

---

37. Leroi-Gourhan, quoted in Clottes and Lewis-Williams, 109.
38. Leroi-Gourhan, quoted in Clottes and Lewis-Williams, 75.

significant. It may be a conventional and unquestioned assumption that the Paleolithic image makers regarded the walls as solid surfaces. But is this the case? Clottes suggests the fascinating possibility that the Paleolithic people regarded the walls, ceilings, and floors more as membranes or resembling a curtain, a surface that was porous, flexible, and penetrable, a surface that beings, whether human or spiritual, could pass through. The walls would be a zone of communication between the human and spiritual worlds, not a barrier. The walls would be a threshold between the human and spirit worlds, a line of passage, the cave as place and threshold for arrivals and departures, not a container. Rather than enclosing, the wall might open the space of the human world to the space of the spirit world. Thus, at a privately owned cave called Enlène, which is physically connected to the famous Grotte des Trois Frères caves, Clottes was shown a wall with many fractures. Animal bones and teeth, even spearheads, had been intentionally deposited in great numbers in these cracks in the wall. The leavings may have been gifts, offerings, or ways of communicating with the spirits beyond. At Enlène, there is also a passageway that can be accessed only by a single person at best. Yet the clay wall at the end of this passageway had been repeatedly stabbed by spears and marked by numerous fingerprints. Cave walls were extensively touched, Clottes observes, marked and imprinted by instruments, hands, or fingertips. Patterns of what are called "finger flutings" and animals crudely drawn by fingertips frequently scored these walls. His later book, the 2011 *Pourquoi l'art préhistorique*, continues to develop this important theme: touching was integral and important to painted images. The desire to enter into direct contact is in evidence with such touches. Were the Paleolithic people trying to capture the power of the subterranean world?[39] Hence, Clottes's interpretation is close to the manual version of the haptic art discussed earlier.

Other questions present themselves in this regard: Were these images painted or incised onto a surface, the way one applies oil paint to a canvas, or can they be seen as emerging from the surface, perhaps even emerging from behind it or within it, the way watercolor or ink washes often appear? Perhaps emergence can be seen here rather than inscription. Were the images emergences from the subterranean spirit world? Did the spirits take on animal forms in their visitations and participations in whatever rituals may have taken place in the depths of the cave? Perhaps the many painted handprints left on cave walls could be seen as reaching into the

---

39. Clottes, *What Is Paleolithic Art?*, 131.

spirit world, points of contact between human and spirit worlds. While the modern scientist may see the paint, derived from earthly materials such as carbon, sulfur, or iron oxide, as just a material used to make images, the Paleolithic image maker may have seen it differently. Is it a possibility that for them paint was a powerful magical substance that could actually penetrate the rock walls, making them porous and so facilitating human and spiritual contact?[40] We shall never know. But red ochre, a common material used in painted images, was also used in the burial of the dead. Even Neanderthals poured great amounts of it into their graves, suggesting that its use in images by Paleolithic *Homo sapiens* could have been a potent instrument for communicating with the dead and not just a color used to promote the realism of the image.

Another type of image very common in cave art is the human hand. The images of hands, commonly stenciled onto the walls using red ochre, often exhibit what interpreters most refer to as "mutilations." Some are missing fingers or have fingers that appear to have been cut off at the finger joint. Were mutilations part of shamanistic rituals? There is evidence for this in more recent shamanistic practices. Leroi-Gourhan supposed that these hands might not be mutilations at all. Rather the fingers may have been folded back, perhaps in order to display the sorts of signs hunters use to communicate with one another when quietly tracking prey. Clottes likes this interpretation, but he also suggests that the hand signs could be ways of greeting or otherwise communicating with the spirits.[41] In any event, the general framework of shamanism suggests that the images found in Paleolithic caves played an essential role in shamanistic journeys. Shamanism has both esoteric and communal elements. So the journey had both exterior and interior episodes. Areas outside the cave, where indeed animal figures cut into large rocks have been found, could have been the setting for communal activities involving larger numbers of people, while remote areas of the deep interiors of the cave, such as the famous pit at Lascaux, were probably visited only rarely and only by a select few. They may have been places of "vision-quest," in Clottes's words, places where sensory deprivation or the presence of gases may have been very conducive to hallucinations. The stick-figure of a man shown on the walls of the pit at Lascaux could indeed be interpreted as in an ecstatic or trance-like state of mind. Referring to the figures half-animal and half-human, as found at Trois Frères, Clottes

---

40. Clottes and Lewis-Williams, *Shamans of Prehistory*, 92–98.
41. Clottes and Lewis-Williams, 96.

even suggests that the shamans themselves are what is depicted on the cave walls, transformed into animals in their vision quests. "The general shamanic context of the art, however, suggests other possibilities. They may be images of shamans partially transformed, in their Stage Three hallucinations, into animals, as are comparable southern African or other shamanic images."[42] The shamanistic journey might have been from the world of light outside the cave into a dark, subterranean inside, and from that inside to another outside beyond the human world altogether. The cave itself would be a mobile folding of outside and inside.

Clottes's shamanistic interpretation does have the great merit of putting the whole question of the relations between the human and animal worlds on a new footing. The animals were not just the prey of the hunters. The animals were part of the human family, a brother or a sister. The Paleolithic societies were indeed hunting societies, but they were not trying to master or dominate the natural world, as is the case for the modern, technological world. The hunters ran alongside their animals and no doubt considered them to be spiritual beings, not just soulless mechanisms. Should one ask a Paleolithic hunter-imagemaker, "Who is painting the image? Are you the one creating that image?" the answer might be, "It is the spirit of the animal that guides my hand." This means that it is animals themselves, their spirits in this case, who are the primary creators of these images; the animals are the artists, not the humans.

This shamanistic theory of Paleolithic art opens a view of art as an art of intensity and metamorphosis, a voyage from one form to another, from one state of being to another, not an art of static forms—be they signs—placed on a cave wall and deprived of all movement, all animation, except a signifying movement passing between signs having opposed values. In Deleuzian terms, it is an art of "becomings," "becoming-animal,"[43] becoming an intensity, becoming imperceptible, becoming something more than a human being defined by utility. But becoming-animal does not imply resemblance. It does not mean putting on a mask or costume and imitating an animal being. Becoming-animal is not resemblance but contagion. Deleuze

---

42. Clottes and Lewis-Williams, 94.

43. See Jacques Derrida, *The Beast and the Sovereign*, trans. Geoffrey Bennington (Chicago: University of Chicago Press, 2009). The "Fifth Session," for example, discusses Deleuze on becoming-animal but especially on *bêtise*, not just animality but *bêtise* in connection with Deleuze, Lacan, and psychoanalysis, and especially in connection with political sovereignty, not just the ecstatic sovereignty in Bataille's writings on animality and Lascaux.

emphasizes the importance of the pack. Animals form packs, multiplicities, as seen in the herds and groups of animals in Paleolithic art. If the painter is a sorcerer, it is because the animal is the only population before which they are responsible, before which they must answer. Becoming-animal means becoming part of the pack. If the painter is a sorcerer, it is because painting, like writing, is a becoming. Painting is traversed by strange becomings: becoming bear, lion, bison, deer, bird, and so on. Becoming in this sense is what Deleuze calls an "affect," which is not a personal feeling or characteristic. Rather, in Deleuze's words, it is the "effectuation of a power of the pack that throws the self into upheaval, the violence of animal sequences that uproot one from humanity." If the painter is a sorcerer, working in a context of rituals, it is because the sorcerer, like the painter in this case, always travels the anomalous position of the borderline. They always dwell in the between zones, between inside and outside, between the secular and the spiritual, a point of passage between human and animal being. In fluid movements, they cross and recross the threshold between light and shadow, a threshold where alliances are opened with the underworld.[44] This is not a dream or a phantasm, but the work of art at Lascaux.

A Poet's Rendering: Jean Rouaud

We find parallels to this point of view not only in the work of other ethnologists working on sorcerer beliefs but also in the writing of the novelist Jean Rouaud, whose first novel, *Les Champs d'honneur* (1990), won the prestigious Prix Goncourt. In a recent publication, *La splendeur escamotée de frère Cheval* (2017), he continued and developed some of the themes we have been discussing in connection with the work of both Leroi-Grouhan and Jean Clottes. Like Leroi-Gourhan, he sees the Paleolithic paintings as telling us of the cosmology of the Upper Paleolithic. But he will not take the more cautious, calculating, and materialistic way of science. His book is an attempt to escape what he calls a "diktat matérialiste," where "a horse can only figure [*figurer*] a horse." Thus, he contrasts his own *pensée poétique* with a *pensée analytique*. The former, poetic thinking, proceeds by and through associations, correspondences, amalgams, analogues, and fusions. Analytic thinking, by contrast, dissects, separates, sorts, and classifies, as we

---

44. Gilles Deleuze and Félix Guattari, *A Thousand Plateaus: Capitalism & Schizophrenia*, trans. Brian Massumi (Minneapolis: University of Minnesota Press, 1987), 240–46.

saw in the work of Leroi-Gourhan. With poetic thinking, we communicate with the Paleolithic painters, and like them, we poetic thinkers reach for the beyond (*au-delà*) and its "obscurantist bric-à-brac."[45] Like shamans, "we poetic thinkers reach for the beyond."

Rouaud's text unfolds a captivating view of the Upper Paleolithic. Prescientific Paleolithic humans understood nothing of the true movements of the sun and the moon, of the passage between day and night, of life and death as understood by modern science. They could only observe and wonder. Their way of thinking was poetic, not analytic. They saw a rhythm of appearances and disappearances, the storms and clouds in the sky, always in movement, the miraculous shining of a rainbow, the living, once moving, changing into something else, something still, without breath, something gone from this world. They could observe how each day the sun would return following upon the darkness of the night; how, like the passage of stars across a night sky, the herds of reindeer would leave and return; how the plants, the leaves on the trees, the flowers of the field, would pass away and return. How the seasons revolved from warmer summer when life was abundant to colder winter when it seemed life would pass away, retreat deep into the frozen earth.

For Rouaud, this poetic and cyclic conception of the world implies a notion of limits. Not the sort of limits or prohibitions that Georges Bataille puts at the center of his interpretations of the art of Lascaux, prohibitions having death and sexuality as their concern. For Rouaud, the notion of limits is the more cosmic notion that the world is finite, a trap from which there is no escape, only turning and returning. The "whole system" of Paleolithic "representations depended on it," he states.[46] Trapped within the limits of the world, within the finitude of life, all of existence was thus caught up in a never arrested cycle of movement and passage. This was the rhythm of life and death, and it was the same rhythm that staked out the world of Paleolithic art. In the periodic going and returning of the sun and the moon, like the stars and the reindeer, might life, might the dead—who may dwell in the underworld—not also return? Might the dead one day come and sit once again among the living? Their art testifies to such a fateful cosmological view. They may have felt fear and incomprehension before these phenomena and wondered as to their place in it. They understood their place as analogous to that of the animal, a being caught up in the

---

45. Jean Rouaud, *La splendeur escamotée de frère Cheval* (Paris: Grasset, 2017), 19–20.
46. Rouaud, 90–99.

river of constant change and exchange, of the flow of life unto death. Life and death were, accordingly, experienced not so much as states and finalities but as movements, as repeated passages, a ceaseless rhythm of to-and-fro, like the exchanges of darkness and light, the moon and the sun. The Paleolithics might have been Heracliteans: for them, the sun was indeed "new each day." And the caves were, thus, the place where all of this could be worked out and carried forward in the forms of images, in the cavalcades of reindeer and bison, trapped in their restless migrations to the ends of the world and back again, coming and going in the shadowy passage of lamplight. Even the undulations of the walls suggested a moving, living yet nonliving animal. The caves were not just the belly of the world, they were the places where the ultimate exchanges of life and death took place. Thus, the fear of the painter upon entering the cave is likened to the fear of dying. The caves were the underworld, at once terrifying and welcoming, a dark and hushed domain where the ultimate migrations of life and death took place. The painter enters a domain apart as the place where he will leave his daily work behind, a place set deep in the earth where the bears go to die in winter only to be reborn again in the spring that follows. A domain of terrible miracles, yet linked with light and life. Is the radiance of the sun not reborn in the yellow bodies of the horses one sees at Lascaux? The hunter entered the cave in order to communicate with the invisible, Rouaud writes.[47] But he was always accompanied by his "brothers" in these journeys, the animals, fellow travelers on a journey into the unknown. Thus the animal was not just his prey, not just the object of his stealthy hunt. The animal was also his brother in the rhythm of life and death, a fellow traveler, companion, guide, spiritual force.[48] In the act of painting, it was the spirit of the horse that guided the painter's hand.[49]

The image thus attains a new status in Rouaud's text. Not a sign, but something closer to Clottes's interpretation, a mark indicating the point of separation and communication between spirit and matter, the living and the dead. Perhaps the paintings were closer to being divinations, a haruspex, not a static representation but a tool useful in the hunt. The great schema of life is there in these images, like the future glimpsed in the liver of a rabbit, the schema of becomings shivering across their contours, the movement of forces forming and de-forming all of existence. The painted

---

47. Rouaud, 113.
48. Rouaud, 122.
49. Rouaud, 99.

images are not static things but living forms, figures created and dissolved by powerful forces. As Rouaud writes, "Life is a song, a refrain." Is it a circular or cyclical return, an eternal return? "Not yet," Rouaud answers. There is not yet a great wheel of life, as in the Buddhist Dharma. The eternal return supposes a cycle. Life is more like a "ritornello," not so much a circle as a brief, repeated musical passage, back and forth. The bison are shown in face-to-face encounters, he writes, the horses line up back-to-back, the herds come and go; it is a "lateral ballet," like the movement of windshield wipers on a car, Rouaud concludes with a little laugh.[50] Perhaps even lateral movements such as this would have their circularity. A return is always a turning, a turning toward and a turning back. There is always a great curve in the movements of coming and going. Certainly, Paleolithic people had a deep, mythic awareness of the cycles and circles of nature, the passing arc of the sun in the sky, the turnings of the stars, the circular rhythms of the seasons. Their art is evidence for this. The circular conception of existence was certainly well established by Neolithic times, as one can see in the circle of stones at Stonehenge, for example.

Art was, at its "dawn," a part of the natural world; it did not stand apart and represent it, shaping it as a thing standing apart. Like all living beings, the painted image was in constant movement. In all the major images of animals, it is the powerful, physical movement of the animals that leaps forward, strongly contributing to the powerful presence of the images. The work of art and the animal world were not realms separated from one another but sustained in an intimacy, a belonging together, nearly unrecognizable today. Did the creators at Lascaux even have a word for what they were doing, a word for art? We can never know. In its force, the event that occurred at Lascaux, the famous dawn of art, reaches all the way, like a morning ray of sunlight, into the night of our modernity. We still marvel at the images, even when reproduced in color book plates, they seem so completely modern. But the artist who bequeathed them to us as our destiny could not have anticipated how posterity would transmogrify this event, this free creative force they brought to life hundreds of centuries ago as in a bolt of light. Not a movement, not a living thing, not the place for the occurrence, the apparition of the gods, the apparition of a divine world, the world has become dim and materialistic, and art a commercial thing, its value determined by the "culture industry." Lascaux's famous bulls are today's artistic livestock, art bought and sold like livestock on the

---

50. Rouaud, 91–92.

international art market. Yet the art at Lascaux retains its power, a force that works directly on the nervous system as on the imagination. This is perhaps one of the reasons writers on the Lascaux paintings so often use the word "birth," for the force of Lascaux is in its sense of radiant emergence, its "burning presence."

For the Paleolithic painter, the act, the event of painting itself, was always generative; the pulse of life fills every square inch of the great bulls at Lascaux; they are never degenerate in any sense of the word. Their world was divine, Rouaud suggests. But what conception of life and existence did Paleolithic people have? Did they believe there were gods behind the movement of the herds? Perhaps the very gestures of the painter convinced him something can be given birth from nothing, that from the blank wall there can surge forth a cavalcade of animality, that behind the curvatures of the surface that suggest the neckline or form the belly of the image of a horse there may be nothing but teeming life, or what later civilizations would call the Earth Mother. The Paleolithic painter was a thinker in Rouaud's eyes. There can be no resemblance of image and animal, no correspondence of charcoal outline with living creature without a *pensée élaborée*. But he did his thinking round the hearth, like Heraclitus, or in the grottos of Lascaux.[51]

Rouaud's book has this sense of loss and regrets for fallen worlds. The thinking of the Paleolithic creator becomes a Descartes taking refuge in his "Dutch oven" at La Haye-en-Touraine, the prophet of an enlightened world stripped of its "divine essence." Now the butchering can begin. The most strongly materialistic room, Rouaud says, is "a torture chamber" (La chambre forte matérialiste est une chambre de torture).[52] The bison that once thundered across the Paleolithic steppe were by Neolithic times already domesticated cattle, kept in pens or contained in fields, and the earth, the wild, dark earth, vast source and receiver of all life, had long ago given way to geometry.

Georges Bataille: Lascaux, Art, Festival, and Sovereignty

Shades of this sense of loss and lament color George Bataille's essays on Paleolithic painting, especially his "Terre inviable," dating from 1960 and composed in connection with a "world festival." "We know we have

---

51. Rouaud, 124–25.
52. Rouaud, 123–24.

fallen," Bataille writes, driven like Adam and Eve from paradise, from an ancient, half-paradisical world of intoxication, where, in Bataille's view, a festival meant the "exaltation . . . of great crowds, immersed in a tumult, danc(ing) and leap(ing) for joy, losing consciousness in their half-divine, half-daemonic intoxication." We live today not in a "world of intoxication" but a world of factories, machines, science, conflicts of interests, and mass slaughter made possible by our modern weaponry and atomic bombs. We are separated from this lost world where animals and men lived side by side, where the animal world had something of a perhaps sacred quality. Such a world seems an "incredible, marvelous, but inaccessible dream."[53] Yet while Bataille's biographer, Michel Surya, writes that certainly Bataille denounced the irremediable loss of the "intimacy" and "immediacy" of the sacred, he denies that Bataille had any "sense of origins" or nostalgia for beginnings since he had no nostalgia for lost ends or goals.[54] This seems an accurate sense of Bataille's feelings for what Surya calls "la malediction de l'histoire."

Putting two images snatched from the pages of Bataille's books side by side, we can see in the starkest of terms his indictment of our modern world. First, there are the images of the animals from Paleolithic sites published in Bataille's essays on prehistoric art dating from the 1950s, images communicating like an electric current the joy and exuberance he celebrates in such imagery. Put this alongside a famously disturbing black-and-white photograph taken by Eli Lotar featured in Bataille's periodical *Documents*, specifically with an entry entitled "Abattoir" published in his "Critical Dictionary" in November of 1929, showing the severed hooves of cattle carefully lined up against the outside walls of a slaughterhouse.[55] Bataille suggests a link between archaic religion and the modern slaughterhouse in that both the ancient temple and the modern abattoir were places where the blood of animals flowed in profusion, the first for sacrificial offerings to placate the anger and whimsy of the gods, and the second to placate the city dweller's appetite for animal flesh. Of course, there is a crucial difference: the archaic temple was, no doubt, the altar, the center of life and culture in the ancient

---

53. Bataille, "Terre inviable," in *OC* XII, 514. Trans. by Michelle Kendall and Stuart Kendall as "Unlivable Earth?," in *The Cradle of Humanity: Prehistoric Art and Culture* (New York: Zone Books, 2005), 175–76.

54. Michel Surya, *La mort a l'oeuvre* (Paris: Librairie Séguier, 1973), 381. English trans. by Krzysztof Fijalkowski and Michael Richardson (London: Verso, 2002), 383.

55. "Abattoir," in *Documents 6* (Paris: Mercure de France, 1968), 167. Trans. Annette Michelson as "Slaughterhouse," *October 36* (Spring, 1986): 11.

world, whereas the abattoir is a repulsive stench, baleful as a ship full of plague victims, and so delegated to the margins of city life. The photograph illustrated Bataille's definition of the term "abattoir," or "slaughterhouse," just as the images of Paleolithic paintings of animals accompanied his paean to ancient pagan life, and the contrast could not be more glaring. In both writings, it is not only a question of humanity's relation to animality. It is also, as we shall see, a question, for Bataille, of defining a new sense of the word "materialism." Always challenging and mocking the insipid materialism of our modern world, amorphous, "flabby," and shameful as it is, where nothing truly horrible remains except perhaps the countenance of a modern man, cursed, lazy, bored, unseemly in appearance, puny and bilious yet obsessed with his own cleanliness, Bataille celebrates a Paleolithic world to evoke, from the very midst of modernity's materialistic world, another materialism offered by another world, the materialism of the force and violent grandeur of a forgotten world of "animals and their men" (*les animaux et leurs hommes*).[56]

This questioning search for a new materialism began for Bataille in the late 1920s, in a series of articles comprising a "dictionary": entries where he presents another materialism, a "base materialism." One of his texts from this period, *Le bas matérialisme et la gnose*,[57] is suggestive for the way it shows how the masked, dancing, and ithyphallic figures of the subterranean Paleolithic cave had been transmogrified by fourth-century Gnosticism into the dreaded *archontes* depicted in small engravings: the Paleolithic shamans were now the rulers of a dark Christian underworld, demonic, indecent, and provocative. Like the Paleolithic images of the human figure, which in the case of male figures, at least, show ithyphallic humanoid figures with their faces replaced or hidden by an animal head and other animal features, so the Gnostic archontes are likewise depicted as acephalous, having the heads of ducks or of a solar ass. Are these two sets of images, the Paleolithic and the Gnostic engravings, linked? Across the unfathomable centuries separating them, does the same wild and subterranean force yet pulse in them both, a force that must be circumscribed, checked, and governed, if possible, by the

---

56. Georges Bataille, "Lascaux ou la naissance de l'art," in *OC* IX, 74. Trans. by Austryn Wainhouse as *Lascaux or the Birth of Art* (Geneva: Éditions d'Art Albert Skira, 1980), 125.
57. In *Documents 6* (Paris: Mercure de France, 1968), 93. Trans. by Allan Stoekl as "Base Materialism and Gnosticism," in *Visions of Excess: Selected Writings 1927–1939* (Minneapolis: University of Minnesota Press, 1985), 45–53. First published in *Documents, deuxième anné* 1 (1930): 1–8.

imposition of stern prohibitions? A deceptive and superficial concordance of appearances and topographical situation (both are dwellers of an underworld) might prompt the comparison of the Paleolithic and Gnostic images, but this is quickly defeated on closer examination. The most insuperable gulf separating them is the gulf created, at least in the European consciousness, by the advent of Christianity, with its transcendental gods and morality of good and evil. Heretical though it may have been, Gnosticism, as Bataille notes, was a dualism between a supreme and hidden god who offered the hope of salvation and a lesser, malevolent deity, a cursed god, "sometimes associated with Jehovah, or Yahweh, of the Bible," who is responsible for the creation of matter.[58] The leitmotiv of Gnosticism was its conception of the creation of matter as an "active principle having its own eternal autonomous existence as darkness," revealed in the monstrous archontes. Evil was not merely the absence of good but a creative force, albeit a force condemned to darkness. As with the Paleolithic hunter societies, there is also a Gnostic obsession with darkness, a "sinister love" of darkness, a "monstrous taste for obscene and lawless *archontes*." It has, in its "licentious" sects, an "obscure demand for an irreducible baseness, respect for which was exercised through rites that inspire today's 'black magic.'"[59]

Gnostic materialism, the base materialism that is the subject of Bataille's essay, suggests a revision of the sorts of modern, philosophical, and cultural materialism in that it does not imply an ontology whereby matter is rendered a thing-in-itself. The base materialism Bataille evokes in connection with Gnosticism is "external and foreign to human aspirations, and it refuses to allow itself to be reduced to the great ontological machines resulting from those aspirations."[60] Bataille's base materialism uproots philosophical egoism and solecism. It is the invocation of a dimension opposed to all and any idealism, or transcendentalism, a dimension that contests both the idea of a "myself" as a thinking cogito and its ideas of reason. Matter, in this transformed view, is not limited by reason. Had reason the power to limit such a materialism, circumscribing it in the futility of interdictions, reason would be transposed into a superior principle. While such a promotion of reason, as Bataille puts it, would certainly please a "servile reason" by exalting it to the status of an "authorized functionary," it is precisely this

---

58. Bataille, "Base Materialism and Gnosticism," 47–48.
59. Bataille, 47–48.
60. Bataille, 47–48.

sort of promotion and exaltation of servile reason that Bataille decries.[61] Resembling "stupefied scarecrows," the artistic forms produced by Gnostic hands—deformed, one might say, insofar as they are penetrated and imbued with monstrous yet creative forces—defy the regulated manner of the classical style.[62] The far shadow of all idealisms, they are the expression of an "intransigent" and irreducible materialism and so steadily compromise the "powers that be in matters of form," replacing a crude, almost laughable grandeur—the grandeur of a scarecrow—for the cool sobriety of traditional entities.[63] This is a defiance, in other words, of artistic forms that would like to be as specific and meaningful as language itself, a defiance that allows something subterranean and unspeakable to break forth into the light, an accursed, dangerous emanation.

Bataille's writings from the 1950s on the dawn of art at Lascaux in the Upper Paleolithic are still informed by the same desire to articulate this conception of materialism first articulated in the 1920s and 1930s, a base materialism, powerful and creative yet irreducible to either the metaphysical opposition of matter-form or any idealism or ontology. Base materialism becomes the labyrinth at Lascaux and other places. It is a force from the outside, so to speak, folded into the inside of societal and artistic forms, a materialism that would be quite the opposite of the insipid and "flabby" materialisms that lend a false pride to much of the modern philosophy Bataille had encountered: the inverted idealism of existentialism, or the totalizing idealism of Hegel, an idealism that had the power and the audacity to stand up to death and put it to work in the production of reason's triumph. From within the very terms of such a philosophy, Bataille brought to light a base yet sovereign materialism defined by its intransigent refusal to serve whatever alleged superior principles, be it Truth or Beauty. He sees this base materialism embodied not only in Paleolithic art but also in laughter, in festivals, and in the "big toe": gross and unseemly though it may be, it is the secret, the repulsive key to the erect posture of that idealizing

---

61. Bataille, 51.

62. This parallels a similar distinction Bataille draws between the "barbaric" horses of pre-Roman Gaul and the classical forms of horses in the Greco-Roman period. We return to this in the postface. Bataille, "Le cheval académique," in *OC* I, 159–63. First published in *Documents 8*, 1930. Trans. by Krzysztof Fijalkowski and Michael Richardson as "The Academic Horse," in *Undercover Surrealism: Georges Bataille and DOCUMENTS*, eds. Dawn Ades and Simon Baker (Cambridge, MA: MIT Press, 2006), 237–43.

63. Bataille, "Base Materialism and Gnosticism," 51.

machine called modern man. Where the specialized scientific discourses on Paleolithic art sought to frame a plane or zone of conceptual operations, intent on establishing order and clarity in what must have seemed a tangled savagery of lines and forms, Bataille's writings open a zone of effacements and showings, of sensations and forces, not a plane of representations but a plane for the presentation of a base materiality, a zone of prodigious desires, a plane for the apparition of rhythms of prohibitions and transgressions that constitute the life blood of the animal imagery. Let us now see how this materialism unfolds in his writings on prehistoric art.

The Paradox of Humanity Adorned in the Prestige of the Beast

This is a paradox that too often goes without the emphasis it requires, Bataille wrote.[64] It is a paradox because it marks the threshold between humanity and the "beasts" as first of all associated not only with tool making and internment of the dead but equally with ritual adornments, the wearing of the masks—the prestige—of the Other. It is a paradox of showing by not showing, putting on a mask so as to reveal not something on the outside, but something on the inside; it is the paradox of apparitions that are the place for a rhythm of revealing and concealing.

How is our humanity portrayed at Lascaux? In his review of abbé Breuil's *Quatre cents siècles d'art pariétal*, titled "Les Cavernes ornées de l'age du renne" (1952) and published in the journal *Critique* in April 1953,[65] Bataille turns to the images of human beings that have been found at sites like Lascaux and Trois Frères. In these images, engraved on the walls of the caves, Bataille observes a striking ambiguity. The human figures have masked their heads and faces with animal forms, yet their genitals—their real animality—are revealed. This is an obvious reversal from the postures of modern man, who would prefer to conceal the genitals and show the face. Why this ambiguity, repeated as it is throughout the Upper Paleolithic?

---

64. Bataille, *Lascaux ou la naissance de l'art*, 63 (Trans., *Lascaux or the Birth of Art*, 116). "Ce paradoxe, celui de 'l'homme pare du prestige de la bête,' n'est pas formulé d'ordinaire avec l'accentuation qu'il exige."
65. Bataille, "Les Cavernes ornées de l'age du renne," in *OC* XII, 259–77. Trans. by Stuart Kendall as "The Passage from Animal to Man and the Birth of Art," in *Cradle of Humanity*, 57–80.

Abbé Breuil does pause to describe these humanoid images at length, but he does not exactly linger over them either. He notes an image of a "dead man" at Lascaux, childish in execution; perhaps it is the image of a "God," he states, that presides over the animal world, or perhaps they are hunting disguises or misadventures. "Horrible anthropoids" with "grotesque faces," having "knock-knees and arched feet." Their postures lowly, they resemble a monkey, or at best, something only half-human. Perhaps there was something magical at work in them, the magic of the hunt, many were likely the "products of fancy."[66] Strange that he does not note the many displays of male genitalia on display. No doubt this was part of their horror, their grotesqueness.

Bataille sees something very different in these rare images of the human being: he envisions an astonishing "effacement of man before the animal, at the very moment when the animal within became human." This, Bataille says, is "the greatest effacement that can be conceived"[67] and the most remarkable paradox about the art of Lascaux: that human beings had attained a virtuosity when it came to realistic depictions of animal being, but this virtuosity collapsed or was set aside when it came to depicting the human figure, as though the human figure must not share in the same compelling realism as the animal figures. The Paleolithic painter, in Bataille's words, "disdained to portray his/her own face." The painter may have confessed to having a human form—this was evident in the hand that shaped the animal form. But at the same time, he hid it, as though ashamed of his own face, "as though when wishing to designate himself he had instantly to put on the mask of another." During the Upper Paleolithic, humankind left its signature, marking the completed birth of humanity as *Homo sapiens*, but they did so by "adorning himself in the prestige of the animal."[68]

Hence, another way of conceiving the human–animal imagery: not just in terms of tools, or forms, nor as representing wild beasts running in the fields, but as something *interior* to humanity, an animality now interiorized, and the human being as masked in its presence, its human visage subjected to an effacement. Such animality is one aspect of the base materialism Bataille sees at Lascaux, a materialism essential to our humanity but a materialism covered over, transformed by subsequent idealism. For Bataille, animality is not only a base materialism; it is also a sovereignty.

---

66. Quoted by Bataille, in *OC* XII, 266–68 (*Cradle of Humanity*, 60–69).
67. *OC* XII, 262 (*Cradle of Humanity*, 60).
68. Bataille, *Lascaux ou la naissance de l'art*, 62 (Trans., *Lascaux or the Birth of Art*, 115).

Why this ambiguous "effacement" of humankind before animality? What was the power of animal being that so impressed this early hunting society? The study of Paleolithic art in the 1950s was dominated by the hunting magic interpretation, as discussed earlier. Not tempted by the incipient applications of structuralism to human cultural manifestations, he agrees with abbé Breuil's interpretation: hunting was the dominate way of putting food on the table. The animals were powerful and swift. Hunting them was a risky adventure. Could a little magic have helped? Doubtless, the images of animals played a necessary role in this enterprise. Yet there is more to the images than this unimaginative utilitarian outlook. The images go beyond utility in abundance of what Bataille calls joy, grace, and exuberance. Where schematic figures of the animals might have sufficed, had they been reduced in advance to playing but a formal, signifying role in a mythogram, the paintings are instead astonishing in their power. Great effort was risked and expended under difficult circumstances to bring them to life. Some have almost monumental proportions, prompting Lascaux's comparison to the Sistine Chapel ceilings. Lascaux's paintings are a festival celebration of animality, not just tools for the hunt. The animals were hunted by Paleolithic humans, certainly they killed them, but the way they were portrayed on the walls of Lascaux testifies to the fact they also loved them, admired them, as though they marked a threshold that once crossed could never be recrossed, the threshold of the passage between animal being and a human being. A threshold inscribed in works of what we call "art" for lack of anything better, where a way of return was momentarily opened to something lost, to something left behind, an animality left behind that had not yet been cursed and demeaned by triumphant reason. Rather, animality was held to an incalculable prestige. The paintings are high praise for the elegance and physical power of the animals. The Lascaux painters withheld attributing such elegance and power from their depictions of the human figure. A human being perhaps did not seem to compare in their regard with animal being.

Lascaux's paintings no doubt marked and opened something we might call the destiny and the fate of both humans and animals, a destiny that has now become our modern world. This destiny, this "fate," in which the darkness of ancient caves was supplanted by the darkness of modern times, as during the horror of mechanized war and world conflagration, was depicted in Franz Marc's apocalyptic painting *Fate of the Animals* (1913). Painted just three years before he himself was killed at the Battle of Verdun, it portrays the animal elegance and nobility celebrated at Lascaux as swept away in a nightmare, a catastrophic flight of animals, the blinding horror of war descending all around them.

But there's little or no romance to Bataille's glory-tinged view of animality. Certainly, the animal world was one of intimacy and immediacy with its natural environment. The animal has no sense of a world, a world of objects, things set apart from itself. The animals do not serve, they are wild and free. They do not have to work in order to live. The animal world, in other words, is a world without transcendence. While their lives may be instinctive, they have no goals, no ideals or desires to fulfill, as humans do. The human world of work, by contrast, has ruptured that immediacy and intimacy with animal being. The human world is a world of transcendence, of higher truths, of gods, of ultimate purposes and goals. The tool hammered out in rhythmic gestures shatters all intimacy and immediacy and introduces such transcendency. Nature becomes an object, a force to be reckoned with, conquered, mastered through work.

But Bataille's essays do not compose a song mourning a lost Eden. Bataille knows that animal being is savage, remorseless, merciless. It has none of those moral or ethical values that characterize human ideals, not animal realities: ideals of remorse, mercy, and kindness. Lascaux's animals are adored, but they are not adorable. But Lascaux's paintings manifest a celebration of an animal world that must have inspired in them equal shares of dread and awe.

With its unequalled celebration of animal being, the human figure is indeed rare in Paleolithic art. Never portrayed equipped as a hunter bearing spears and arrows, the human figure had another crucial role to play, a festival, ritual role moving between the human and animal worlds, belonging to both. Bataille's book on Lascaux[69] documents a half a dozen such figures found in caves throughout Western Europe: at Hornos de la Peña in Spain, a cave that has evidence of both the last of the Neanderthals and the first of the *Homo sapiens* to live in Cantabria, there is the outline of an ambiguous humanoid figure, looking almost spectral, having, in the words of the abbé Breuil, "the bearing and look of a monkey"; at Peche Merle in France, at Combarelles near Les Eyzies, and at Marsoulas, too, other spectral figures seemingly suspended between life and death, human

---

69. This refers not only to his *Lascaux or the Birth of Art* but also to his *Les larmes d'Éros: Nouvelle édition augmenté* (Paris: Société nouvelle des éditions Pauvert, 1981), 17–23, which has photo documentation for many small sculpted female figures, dating from the earliest periods of Upper Paleolithic art.

and animal states of existence can be seen. The abbé Breuil described them as "elementary figures, with gross and infantile faces."[70]

But whereas the genitalia were proudly displayed, we hardly ever see their actual faces as they were generally masked or have the heads of animals. Wearing an animal mask seems to have liberated the human figure from utilitarian postures. Such mysterious figures were usually portrayed as though dancing or in a trance. This suggests the possibility of the figures having an important ritual role, not as hunter of flesh but as a hunter of spirits, as a shaman or sorcerer who may have communicated with animals, spiritually traveling with them rather than hunting them. At Trois Frères, the striking "dream-begotten" figure of an ithyphallic man dressed in the mask and horns of an animal, a painting mentioned earlier, was thought by abbé Breuil to be a "god." Perhaps no other interpretation seemed possible to him. Whether a god or not, whether a being with governing, conquering powers or not, Bataille saw this figure's evident sovereignty not as god-like but as communicating a "remarkable negation of whatever has to do with man's everyday life."[71] The shaman is a human transformed, wearing the garb of an animal, his humanity has journeyed to a dimension closer to that of a sovereign animality than to the conventional cares of the human world. What could account for the rather sudden arrival of this visual theater of animals and men that seems to have burst forth, a dawning, from eras of relative cultural darkness? What, for Bataille, was the key condition for the "double birth" of art and modern humanity he celebrates at Lascaux and other sites?

A Double Economy of Work and Expenditure, Taboo and Transgression

"Our effort to penetrate into the secret of Lascaux shall not succeed unless from the first, we behold Lascaux as a world bound together by the idea of prohibition, pervaded by taboos."[72] This introduces an important theme in Bataille's interpretation of the Lascaux paintings: they are situated within and constituted by a double economy of transgression and prohibitions

---

70. Abbé Breuil, quoted in *Lascaux or the Birth of Art*, 134.

71. Bataille, *Lascaux or the Birth of Art*, 121.

72. Bataille, *Lascaux*, in *OC* IX, 32 (*Lascaux*, 34). ("Le monde de Lascaux, tel que nous nous efforçons de l'entrevoir, est avant tout le monde qu'ordonna le sentiment de l'interdit: nous ne pourrions le pénétrer si nous ne l'apercevions sous ce jour dés abord.")

(*interdiction*), an economy of profane work doubled by an economy of sovereign, sacred expenditures. This is not just a "grid of concepts" in which Bataille is "trapped," as Roger Laporte has claimed. These terms name not concepts. Rather they are the least inappropriate way of naming the forces that shaped the crucible for the emergence of Lascaux's art. They are the keys for penetrating its "secret."

Whether in the sepulture of the deceased or in the limitations imposed against incest, such prohibitions seek to contain, to proscribe, the disturbing, baleful power unleashed by the experiences of death and sexuality. Bataille suggests how early human beings gradually came to an awareness of death. For a million years, hominids made stone tools. While their stone tools survived seemingly forever, the stuff that shaped the tools—their flesh and bones—did not. An awareness of death led to death's striking fatality and the sentiments it inspires being wrapped in taboos and prohibitions. Such a reign of prohibitions brings stability to human life, makes purposes and achievements possible. Human life stripped of prohibitions would thus be "unthinkable," Bataille concludes.[73] This economy of prohibitions, generally directed at death and sexuality, is the most essential difference, the uncrossable threshold between the human and animal being.

For the images to be possible, for their appearance to arise, the human world—a world of work defined by prohibitions—must already be active. Human prohibitions effectively transform death and sexuality. Such a transformation is the key, in Bataille's view, to the crucial passage between human and animal being. Whereas for an animal, avoidance of death and the impulse to procreate are matters of instinct, not culture; they are certainly not restricted in any way. The human reign of prohibitions changes all that. Death and sexuality now become terrifying or provocative forces that must be contained, restricted; their threatening power sublimated or set aside in privileged and darkened locales. For the world of human work to be possible, for human survival to be possible, such prohibitions are a necessity. They perforce regulate the difference between what *can be* seen, what is allowed or accepted, from what *should not* be seen, said, or done in human society. For the animal, by contrast, nothing is prohibited, there are no perceived limits. This is the defining difference for Bataille that sets forth humanity in all its frailty and possibilities.

The enactment of prohibitions is always drawn against the animality within a human being, those dimensions of sexuality and death, that shape

---

73. Bataille, *Lascaux or the Birth of Art*, 32–33.

our humanity. But the force of prohibitions also transformed the animal being from being a mere natural thing, a profane being, the object of the hunt, into a sacred being, embodying all that is greater than the human world of toil and work. The animal, thus, was both on the *outside* of human culture, in the forest and field, ferocious or desired, and on the *inside*, deep inside the caves where human beings celebrated in the extravagance of paintings large and small the animals they both hunted and adored.

The imposition of prohibitions and taboos drawn against the animal dimensions of human life is charged with, doubled by, the intransigent force of transgression. To prohibit is to inflame a desire for precisely what has proscribed. Prohibitions comprise a threshold that incites the transgressions of those prohibitions. Shamanistic rituals, the practice of sacrifice, is one such enactment of transgression. Bataille defines it as a way of bringing the prohibited—death's terrible force—to appearance. In the practice of animal sacrifice, for example, the human sacrificer seems to identify with the animal sacrificed, thus re-creating a sense of the intimacy not only with the animal world but with the terrors of death as well. Sacrifice for Bataille, is a sacred act. "In the etymological sense of the word, 'sacrifice is nothing other than the production of *sacred* things."[74] But the sacred is thus not just a thing or an object, not a sacred cow so to speak, but first an act of destruction, a violation of the prohibitions enveloping the human experience of death and eroticism, a transgressive encounter with the void of irrevocable death. Even poetry is an act of sacrifice, Bataille believes, in which words are the sacrificial victims.

Perhaps they are a key to the human desire to go beyond what is merely possible. The animal does not know either the rule of prohibitions or the incited flame of transgressions. The animal is forever locked in place, a natural being. It can only be what it is once and forever and cannot desire anything more. For the animal, there are no such possibilities. Perhaps they do not have a "world" at all. Prohibitions thus open and make possible a human world in which something more is always glimpsed or tasted in every limitation. With their restrictive force focused on dimensions of human sexuality and death, such prohibitions tear the human from animal being. But if their reign made possible the world of work and regulated, purposive activity, festival transgression offered yet another possibility: the possibility of a simulacral return to animal being. Not just accessories or decorations

---

74. See Bataille, "La Notion de dépense," in *OC* I, 306. Trans. by Alan Stoekl, with Carl R. Lovitt and Donald Leslie Jr., as "The Notion of Expenditure," in *Visions of Excess*, 119.

for this, the animal images were full participants. What was once put at a distance, foreclosed as impossible, thus became momentarily possible, a community, a friendship, and a communication between "the animals and their men," as Bataille phrases it.[75]

In festival, sovereign joy, humanity transgresses, surpasses, or oversteps the profane limits that contain and define that humanity. It is, however, important to note in this context that the transgressions that Bataille refers to and calls "authentic transgressions" are not the isolated and low-level sorts of transgressions that come with a want of sensibility or with an ignorance of the law. Transgression is not unbridled savagery. There is no act more circumscribed by rules and regulations than ritual sacrifice. Rather, they are done knowingly and in a state of profound distress. Transgression thus does not destroy the law. Whether as sacrificial slaughter or joyous laughter, as dance, festival, or as works of art, transgression actually intensifies the rule of law, lighting it up, so to speak, like a camera flashbulb at a crime scene.

The images of animals in their glory and of human beings in their strange animal guises, the "scene in the pit" (or "well") for example, are all inscribed within this double economy of work and festival play. They illuminate the threshold between the profane and sacred worlds. They are at the limits of what can be seen and said in images. We can experience Lascaux's sheer extravagance in the colorful grandeur of its paintings, but it is also evident in the human, material resources expended in order to make it all possible. Paintings flow from the cave's entrance to its darkest recesses and there seems no letup in their vitality. Such extravagance must flow from a delight in making visible, a festival delight in images and the possibilities they unleash that exceeded the limits of what had been possible before the "birth" of art at Lascaux.

Bataille's remarks on prohibition and transgression from the 1950s and early 1960s[76] find their most enigmatic evidence in this most famous painting of a human figure, painted in a place called the "pit," perhaps the darkest and most inaccessible part of Lascaux's labyrinth. Certainly, no crowds could gather here. This was a place set aside, remote, no doubt sacred, a place of visitations. Here, in this inaccessible gloom, a scene was portrayed, one of the few scenes from Paleolithic art suggesting an indecipherable exchange of

---

75. Bataille, *Lascaux*, 125.

76. Across three important books, the 1955 *Lascaux ou la naissance de l'art*, the 1957 *L'Érotisme*, and the 1961 *Les larmes d'Éros*, Bataille returned again and again to this mysterious set of images, offering slightly different adjustments to his interpretation.

animals and men. Once again, the side-by-side contrast between the reduced, schematic manner of depicting the human being and the accomplished realism and virtuosity of the portrayal of animal being is striking. Where the human figure is a childish, stick-like caricature, the realism of the animals is quite accomplished. A large bison is shown with its viscera spilling out, the animal's "menace" compounded by its "anguish."[77] A human figure lies nearby, face-to-face with the eviscerated bison. The figure is ithyphallic: a stiff posture suggesting a state of ecstatic trance. He wears the mask of a bird. A staff lying nearby has what appears to be the sculpted figure of a bird perched at its top end.

How are these figures related? Is this a hunting scene? Does it show the shamanistic sacrifice of animals?[78] Bataille's later work on the scene in the pit at Lascaux, composed after *Lascaux or the Birth of Art*, does come to a tentative hypothesis that the painting shows death and eroticism side by side, the "scene of original sin, "la mort liée au pêché, liée à l'exaltation sexuelle, à l'érotisme, (death tied to sin, tied to sexual exaltation, to eroticism.)" He then asserts that the paintings could also show a shaman's dying in expiation for the murder (sacrificial?) of the animal.[79] Whatever one surmises, we must settle for conjecture at best. Denis Hollier suggests that Bataille sees this scene as a form of "Minotauromachie," the killing of the minotaur in the labyrinth.[80] But to kill the minotaur—as in the antique myth of Ariadne and Theseus—is to escape the mortal, monstrous dangers of the labyrinth. Does Bataille acknowledge the possibility of such escape? Whatever the case, the essential relation of the image and whatever scene it evokes is highly ambiguous. The pit is not a sacrificial altar. Regardless, the ecstatic energy of the image, the way it brings death and eros together in what may or may not be an actual sacrifice of the animal, strongly suggests its being an important part of shamanistic rituals. Such scenes most importantly suggest to Bataille the presence of powerful prohibitions particularly concerning death and sexuality, the prohibitions and taboos that

---

77. Bataille, *Les larmes d'Éros*, 43.

78. Bataille does refer to a German anthropologist, H. Kirchner, whose *Ein Beitrag zur Urgeschichte der Schamanismus* argues in favor of a shamanistic sacrificial interpretation. But he is basing his research on an analogy with more modern Siberian hunter societies. *Les larmes d'Éros*, 15.

79. *Les larmes d'Éros*, 23 and 27. See also his 1957 *L'Érotisme* (Paris: Minuit, 1957), 83.

80. Hollier, "La labyrinth et la pyramide," 115. Hollier's reference is to the Greek myth of the famous labyrinth at Knossos, Crete and its minotaur, half-man, half bull.

define the human world, that set it apart from the animal world by making possible both the human world of work that takes place in the light and the journeys of a shaman that traverse the night.

Rather than seeing Lascaux's most famous image-scene as in any way connected to or governed by "utility," or work, Bataille sees the figures of masked man and dying animality as images of death and ecstasy, side by side, as it were. Do they also tell us that the power of the image brings death to the animal? In any case, Bataille cannot be satisfied by reducing them to being but the profane illustration of an actual event, a hunting scene. Bataille seems to prefer to read "the scene in the pit," as it is called, in terms of ritual, ecstatic experiences, a sacred surpassing of work and utility. In this way, the images combining death and ecstasy are poetic, where death and animality rise in the apparitions of images. Whether it is an actual sacrificial scene or not, Bataille cannot say. But, as in ritual sacrifice, these images made visible what could never and should never appear, namely death's terrible darkness, here brought to an appearance in the midst of life, as in the moment of ritual sacrifice. Does the moment of the creation of images in one of the darkest and most forbidding locations in the labyrinth of Lascaux parallel in obscure ways the gripping power of the sacrificial death of animals? The cuts of the tool in the flesh of the wall, the marking of figures across the body of the cave, are they something close to a sacrificial cut? Here, artistic creation, the masked figures, embodied a force that could confront faceless death. The secret to art's force is in the power of prohibitions that try to distance death's unapproachable terror. The work of art, its alleged "purpose," is not to come magically to the assistance of the hunter but to approach the unapproachable, death, now wrapped in prohibitions and wearing the guise of animal being. What could not and must not be seen is here brought to visibility in images, works of what we today call "art." Art is thus equally the child of prohibitions and of transgressions. Of course, nothing truly dies in a work of art portraying death, yet Lascaux's images do not in any way stand apart from death. The work of art, the famous scene in the pit at Lascaux, for example, thus seems wedded to an expenditure of life. It shines in its chasm of darkness, portraying a moment or an occasion now lost in time, a moment in which what can be seen, the priest and the animal, and what is impossible to see, namely death's terrifying agony, are brought together in images as though in a metaphorical transposition. Thus, the scene in the pit is not the mere *representation* of ritual practice for Bataillle. This would only install a conceptual gap or a distance between the ritual acts and the work of art. Not a representation, then, the scene in the pit would be for Bataille but the *apparition* of mortality, now brought to its simulacral appearance, wrapped in the guises that the net of human prohibitions would seem to require, guises that make death visible while at the same time withholding it from the glaring light of profane visibility.

Bataille's interpretation emphasizes the festival, sacred force communicated in and by the work of art, not its representational employment. A transgressive act pulses in the work, is communicated through it like a contagion, as though the terrifying emotional and psychological force of the act also animates and shudders through the work of art. Art thus shares in the act of ritual sacrifice that both summons forth and is summoned by the engulfing power of what cannot—should not—be seen, death's shudder, here seen *as* this image, *as* this agony portrayed. Death, what cannot be seen or named or seized, is here seen and seized *as* this dying animal agony. For Bataille, such images, such "apparitions" as he calls them, such "simulacra," are the unequalled inscription of the passage from animal to human being. Humanity, looking back at the animal world it has left behind, now carries an unfulfilled longing for meaning and for an answer to life's riddles and passions, the longing for a chance illumination, in other words, of its ultimate destiny. And this longing here found its least inappropriate expression in the making, the *poiesis*, of animal forms, a *poiesis* that emerges from its base materiality. We may say that the images at Lascaux for Bataille are not so much static figures on an ancient wall as they are an experience that he, too, participates in. What is here enclosed in the darkness of caves and their pits is, thus, an experience that Bataille's prose-poems will famously evoke as the *l'expérience intérieure* of humanity, an experience he adorns with the rubrics of sovereignty, the tears of laughter, death, and éros.

The passage between animal and human being is a passage never completed. Without telos or finality, it is a fold rather than a linear, chronological narrative. This passage, this folding of human and animal being and its connection to works of art, is not taken into account by the specialized anthropological disciplines, Bataille claims. They "confine their thoughts to the evidence at hand" and do not attempt to pose the problem of the passage from animal to man, he writes.[81] Is this because the key conditioning dimension to this passage—and for the creation of works of art generally—is the self-imposition of prohibitions, particularly those pertaining

---

81. *OC* IX, 33 (*Lascaux or the Birth of Art*, 30–31).

to death and sexuality? Apart from graves and in such portable figures as the famous Venus de Lespugue, it is indeed hard to treat that empirically or find physical evidence for it. Nor is it but a metaphysical opposition between two states of being, the human and the animal, two different ways of existence in being. The gap between human and animal being for Bataille is always one of passage, of movement, of transposition. It is a threshold, in other words, marked in Bataille's view by prohibitions that necessarily and irrevocably incite transgression, and a simulacral return to animality. It is a threshold that can be crossed, transgressed, and recrossed, but only in and through what sets aside the utilitarian concerns of everyday life, as in dance, ecstasy, ritual celebration, sacrifice, and works of art.

For Bataille, this passage from or between animal and human being is a passage essentially inscribed or marked in such images, paintings, and inscriptions, what we would call works of art. The animal being celebrated in these images is thus nothing natural but something now cultural, transformed as the unapproachable *physis* of animality becomes an animal image, its simulacre. It comes to appearance in all its exuberant glory only in and through images. The images capture and simultaneously dissimulate animality. Appearing in the image, its living contours illuminated only by a passing torch light, what appears briefly in the light vanishes back into darkness almost as quickly as it appears. This is the humanity of their creation, the way the double economy of work and expenditure is also a doubling of appearance and disappearance. As such, they inhabit the ever-changing threshold enfolding what Merleau-Ponty called the visible and the invisible.

Art and humanity are thus essentially linked in Bataille's view. Lascaux's images not only promote the human being, the ones who left the signature of their passing in animal images, but they also bring to appearance a more generalized animality: animality as a sovereign, sacred force of nature and culture, a force that comes to appearance, that emerges, in the apparitions of horses and bison shown running wild and free across parietal surfaces, as though weightless, their colors emanating from the sun. They no doubt had a place and a role to play in a whole context of images, rituals, and religious beliefs, a context we shall know, never hear or see. In that way they are cultural and in that capacity no doubt productive of value. But as the simulacra of an exuberant animal being, they also overflow productivity. For Bataille, they are the apparitions of sovereignty, where sovereignty connotes an incalculable excess of the profane world of work and culture, an excess of being dissimulated in images, simulacra for an animality that is sacred in some sense, and so more than can be seen by a hunter's eye.

70 | Apparitions, Daemons, and Emanations

Compared to the world of human work, always restricted by its purposes and cares, the animal world must have seemed a sovereign and sacred world. In excess of any utilitarian value, the animal images brought a sovereign, measureless value into the measured, work-a-day human world. They communicate a joy and a sense of wonder that lifts the world of everyday cares and concerns. Of course, animals may not experience such "joy," yet the walls of Lascaux communicate that joy, communicate an exuberance that does not know death, a way of being mortal that is paradoxically in excess of mortality. In comparing themselves to a perceived animal sovereignty, nascent humanity suffers and chooses to efface itself. In glorious cavalcades of horses and bison, in the mysterious scene in the pit where an animal is shown dying, its viscera spilling into the earth from which it arose, a feast of images unfolds, marking a doubling of appearance by disappearance. "Animal being" is also a force or a chaos[82]—a "base materialism"—that can be seen but not said, experienced but not mapped except in and through the metaphoricity of simulacra. Ancient images, fading in the darkness, are a threshold, the place, the wall, the event, the folding of visibility. They mark a coming to appearance, a metaphorical "carrying across"[83] of astonishing natural force into the force of images, a lighting up, so to speak, a transposition into appearing. Folded into this

---

82. As Bataille writes elsewhere, "Au coeur même de l'existence, nous trouvons une sorte de chaos, peut-être un vide béant, que dissimule un délire chaotique. Au coeur de l'existence, nous trouvons l'art, et nous trouvons la poésie; nous trouvons encore la multitude des religions. Mais il n'est personne qui n'ignore ce'qu est l'art. Ou la poésie." And, a bit later, he continues, "l'apparition de l'animal ne fut pas, devant l'homme qui s'emerveilla de le faire apparaître, celle d'un objet définissable, comme l'est, des nos jours, à la boucherie. . . . Ce qui apparaissait avait d'abord un sens peu accessible, au-delà de ce qui aurait pu, virtuellement, être défini. Précisément, ce sens equivoque, indéfinissable, értait religieux." *La religion préhistorique* (1959), in *OC* XII, 494. ("At the very heart of existence, we find a sort of chaos, perhaps a gaping void, concealed by a chaotic delirium. At the heart of existence, we find art, and we find poetry; we still find the multitude of religions. But there is no one who is unaware of what art is. Or poetry." And, a bit later, he continues, "The appearance of the animal was not, before the man who marveled at making it appear, that of a definable object, as is, nowadays, [meat] at the butcher's. . . . What appeared at first had a meaning that was not very accessible, beyond what could, virtually, have been defined. Precisely, this equivocal, indefinable sense was religious"; trans. mine.)

83. "Metaphor" is here being used in its most basic connotation derived from the Latin *metaphora* and the Greek *metapherein*, where *meta* is "across" and *pherein* is "to bear," "carry," or "transfer."

very appearing and essential to it there is also a disappearance, a withdrawal from visibility into a chasm of night.

In their world defined by prohibitions, in their world sheltered by work and a fear of death, the Lascaux painters might have felt almost ashamed when looking upon the exuberance of their animal brothers. The images they created paradoxically communicate both their pride and their humility before the animals they left on the walls of Lascaux. They celebrate an exuberance that, for them, is now something that can only be poetically evoked, precisely because it can no longer be lived as an animal lives. This is why ritual sacrifice, dance, laughter, communal joy, and the glory of art all play such an essential even religious role, for they are all modalities of transgression, facilitating an impossible, masked return to animal exuberance. The sacred festival days and nights were the only restricted occasions in which this generalized transgression of the profane could be tolerated, its destructive force carried over into the beauty of images. Thus the images both tamed and released what we might call a second order of animality, an order in which the terrors of the forest and field were given some free play in the context of human culture, as was also the case with the Dionysian festivals of tragic drama in ancient Greece, songs sung on the occasion of the sacrifice of a goat or bull.

Today's modern work of art, by contrast, is transformed. Whether by "AI," secular globalism, or the mechanics of commercial mass reproduction, art has become a key player in a global "culture industry," as it has been called. Endlessly multiplied, proliferated, and commercialized, art's imagery, whether it be of animality or not, has been domesticated and has lost much of its provocative power. The sacred, morning-of-the-world joy that Bataille evokes in connection with the art of the Upper Paleolithic has been largely stripped away from today's art. In this capacity, art is most importantly productive of accrued monetary values, not *gaspillage* or *dépense*, the expenditure or squandering of value, unless this would mean the squandering of money. No doubt, it is important to art's commercial and cultural value that it be ironically defined in some way as "countercultural," as "edgy," and as a "conversation starter," perhaps, but it can no longer be a part of an economy of expenditure, no longer an essential act as it was in an ancient shamanistic society, where the work of art brought a force from beyond to be there, to be visible in this world. Art can no longer be "transgressive," an act in which a force appears, takes, or makes—as in a *poiésis*—form. The essential links between art, transgression, and the sacred have been broken in art's modern, secularized configuration. The masked shaman has been replaced by the auctioneer, and the animal being that once stood by his side is now replaced by the ghastly corpse of a large shark floating in a glass tank full of formaldehyde, an artwork by Damien Hurst.[84] Art today is ever hungry only for the new, not the transgressive. This modern predicament is not to be found at Lascaux where nothing had commercial value and where centuries would pass without there being anything new in the fundamental structures and rhythms of life. Lascaux's art seems completely—at least in Bataille's view—identified with transgression and the sacred. Work made it possible, but work and the world of money it implies are not the truth of the art at Lascaux. Hence, we may see Bataille's interpretations of Lascaux as also having a critical thrust directed at the cultural condition or situation of art in the modern world.

Homo Ludens

Beautiful and troubling, Bataille's writings on Lascaux evoke a world in which work, profane cares, and the sheer need to survive all gave way to something else, something more. It gave way to a festival of rituals and expenditures that suspended the time of labors and fears. Such ritual play may have already been practiced by earlier human beings, but at Lascaux it was not allowed to vanish unremarked back into darkness and forgetting once its ecstatic moments had expired. Rather the perishing of dance and joy was transformed into the permanence of mural paintings, a celebration of the belonging together of the animals and their men, here inscribed and handed down to posterity. Art's sovereignty shines at Lascaux in the torsions of these double economies of prohibition and transgression.

His essays on prehistoric art also make something else indelibly clear: the capacity for thought and reason possessed by Lascaux's painters did not yet carry with it a more modern contempt for animal being. Rather than expressing a desire to dominate nature, a spear-pointed desire to kill and eat animals, why not see the paintings as evincing a desire for a becoming, a becoming-animal, if only in the context of the event, the apparition of prodigious and ambiguous works of art. Desire always measures the distance between desire and its object. A possible desire for a becoming-animal

---

84. I refer to just one example of his work, entitled *The Physical Impossibility of Death in the Mind of Someone Living* (1991).

would thus begin with a love for the distance separating, dissociating and associating animal being and human being.

Becoming-human commences with the metaphorical, poetic becoming-animal that art makes possible.[85] Strange becoming this is, its ambiguous footprints trace the emergence of modern man, *Homo sapiens*, the human who knows, as one who knows not just this or that but its own fundamental and intrinsic animality. Would such knowing be first and foremost a remembering? Becoming-animal as a path of recollection? The collecting again of an animal force *Homo sapiens* still feels stirring in his blood and hears echoing in the silence of the dark labyrinths of Lascaux, Chauvet, or Trois Frères. Is it a becoming also identified with knowledge, (*sapiens*)? And a strange species of knowledge this would be, a knowledge, or a "taste"—*sapiens* also means "taste"—that gives way to non-knowledge, a *sapiens* that gives way to *ludens*, to a taste for a different way of being, a taste for the animal play of dance and festival. Thus, Lascaux also marks the birth of animality as a figure and a force in art, a force too often betrayed, compromised, or subjugated in the subsequent rise of civilization, but that springs to life here, from these half-forgotten prehistorical times, in these striking, powerful images that mark both the limits of the possible for humanity and an impossible transgression of those limits. Such a humanity that emerges here would thus be not only *Homo sapiens*, the human who knows, who is wise, but even more sovereignly, *Homo ludens*, "human who plays."[86]

From the Figurative to the Figural

Bataille's interpretation thus proffers a different perspective on Lascaux's paintings. Unlike Clottes or Leroi-Gourhan, and certainly unlike the sym-

---

85. Again, "metaphor" is being used in the most basic sense of the word, from the Greek *metapherein*, "to carry across, to transfer." Here, it is animal being, a force unknowable, unseen, that is carried across, rising to its apparitional coming to appearance in and as the image of an animal, seen *as* this herd of reindeer, *as* this cavalcade of horses. Such metaphor does not *represent* but *transposes* animality. As such the animal image is a "hyperbate" in the sense of being both associative and dissociative, conjoining and disjoining humanity and animality, showing and dissimulating humanity and animality.

86. *Homo ludens* is a term by Johan Huizinga, quoted in Bataille, *Lascaux or the Birth of Art*, 35.

pathetic hunting magic theory with which he even expressed some concordance, Bataille is not asking, "What do these paintings mean?" or "What do they narrate?" or "What were they useful for, what purpose?" The effort to isolate the levels of signification or narrative function is restricted to seeing the paintings on a purely figurative level, whereby interpreting the images becomes a project of hooking them up or linking them to what they represent—the external object or living animal—or to the useful functions they might have facilitated in prehistoric societies. Seeing the images as signs likewise reduplicates the basic metaphysical structure that subtends the utilitarian interpretations: the essential relationships between art and life are representational, they are relations of a representing subject and a represented object. The structural account is not far from this when it says that structural relations establish how the fascinating linkages between signs is but a way of representing a quite possibly metaphysical conception of the world, in the way a tool is essentially linked to its particular purpose.

Certainly, one of the positive outcomes of such scientifically inclined analyses is to open a viable link between what can be seen and what can be said about Paleolithic painting, to establish a level of discourse that can be verified and so establish an epistemological threshold for Paleolithic art, helping us to answer some of its mystery. But Bataille's essays on Paleolithic painting proceed in a different direction. He avoids the narrative and illustrative dimensions that constitute what Deleuze and Lyotard call the figurative dimensions of painting. For Bataille, Lascaux's paintings are more than figurative. There is also a level of what we shall call, after Lyotard and Deleuze, the *figural*, a level of forces and desire that both forms and deforms Paleolithic painting—a sheer prodigious force that shimmers through the great bulls at Lascaux, just as it does in the "knock-kneed" dancing figure that abbé Breuil described. At the figurative level, they are put to work in an epistemological enterprise, seen as objects of an investigation. For Bataille, there is more: they are first the apparitions of the rhythm of life, powerful becomings, not fixed substances, a level of "apparitions," as he calls it, lacking fixed contours or established signifying relationships. This other level beyond the figurative is what Deleuze calls the Figure and Lyotard before him called the Figural or figural-space. Everything we have been presenting in terms of joy and sovereignty obtains at this level that Bataille calls the "desire for the prodigal."[87] While Lyotard says that figural space "shuns sight and thought," and that "it indicates itself laterally, fleetingly, within

---

87. *OC* IX, 42 (*Lascaux or the Birth of Art*, 39).

discourses and perceptions, as what disturbs them,"[88] the artistic problem remains: How can sensation be the apparition for the figural, the site for its occurrence, using color, contour, and the undulating surface of the cave wall not to represent the animals but to present the forces and intensities of animal being? It is a problem of apparitional presentation, not representation. The emphasis is on sensation, not signification. The question is not, What do the images mean? The question is, How is sensation—the base materiality of color, line, and texture—here the conductor and communicator of forces, rather than meanings or signification? The figural is a different level of materiality; it is a base materiality of forces and intensities irreducible to playing the role of signs linked to signifiers. The figural transforms not only the form of images, the figurative level of art, but also the forms of discourse that would seek to establish the significance of their sensations. This is the role of the figural: to ever contest and open the limits of the possible for language and sensation. No longer limited to the propositional form, no longer freighted with the task of framing the paintings in terms of signification and narration, Bataille's writing becomes poetic; poetic being the form of language that is always in revolt against the limits of language, and the poet, "that part of man rebellious to calculated projects."[89]

Analogous to the double birth of art and man, Bataille claims, as we have seen, that Lascaux's images evoke a double economy of work and expenditure that parallels a double economy of the figurative and the figural. There is another way of saying this: the transgressive doubling of figurative values and work by the forces of figural expenditure, a rhythmic movement linking profane purpose and sacred joy that overflows the frame of art. Lascaux's paintings are in this way limit figures, doubled by both eloquence and silence, both figurative and figural. Their base materiality is the figural level of intensities that draw us into what might be termed inhuman becomings, animal-becomings, even into the nonorganic life of things where silence and the rhythms of light and darkness are encountered as a preorganic germinability common to animate and inanimate being. Beyond or in excess of the materiality that informs their paint and their lines, they embody the materiality that becomes life, that becomes the life that spreads itself through all matter. It is this silence, the silence of art, that cannot be

---

88. Jean-François Lyotard, *Discours, Figure* (Paris: Klingkssibeck, 1971). Trans. by Antony Hudek and Mary Lydon as *Discourse, Figure* (Minneapolis: University of Minnesota Press, 2011), 129.

89. Char, "About Furor and Mystery," trans. Mary Anne Caws, in *Furor and Mystery*, 35.

tamed, as Lyotard claimed, a silence that precedes speech and figuration. And just as the Lascaux paintings show how impossible it is to return to animal being, they also show that it is only from within language, only from within words and the limits of the figurative, that one can approach the figural, that one can turn toward the silence of art.[90] There is no ineffable beyond of language and painting that would, like an ideality or a play of Reason's hidden hand, somehow shape their destiny and their power.

It is in this marvelous transformative power of what Deleuze is here calling the figural that we find the explosive energy that opened the passage between the animal and modern humanity. The figural shows that the overleaping of animality was not experienced in humanity's degradation but in the very gestures by which its prodigality is celebrated: in the rhythms of dance, in painting, poetry, songs, and "tears of eros." A sovereign becoming-animal? Such a rubric only names what is perhaps unnamable; beneath or within the figurations of animals, from within the representational and the narrative, there is a play of desire, a level of force, of intensity and creative joy that bursts the figurative, that bursts the human world into new forms and shapes and so opens the passage to new worlds, a new level of humanity: the human being as a work of art.

Thus the paintings discovered at Lascaux show more than a draftsman's skill. They have a silent power that can dissolve form—even the form of the human face—and impose the existence of an indeterminable zone, a zone of "savagery" in which it can no longer be known which is animal and which is human. A zone in which what was once clear and distinct, the distinction between the human and the animal, for example, becomes indistinct. Lascaux's forms opened the way for the greatest undertaking: to mark the dawning of a beauty, that first light, that gives birth to itself from the depths of night. Is this not the *fond*, the grounds, the inner sense, for that beauty? A chiaroscuro-spiraling folding of human and animal being brought to an impossible presence here some 15,000 years ago, a presence dissimulated in simulacra, apparitions, irreducible to any final determination or interpretation; traces of a muted joy, a gift lost and wrapped in darkness for another age—our modern age—to discover and bring to light once again, a communication from prehistory now broken off and regarded as a curiosity.

We have already set aside the possibility that this is a nostalgia on Bataille's part for a lost beginning. Writing in the 1950s when it might have seemed there would be nothing more in the way of miracles or the marvelous

---

90. Lyotard, *Discours*, 7–9.

in the world, Bataille encountered them in the miracle of Lascaux, not in the glare of modern life but deep in a darkness our modernity has forgotten. But he is not suggesting an impossible forsaking of our modern humanity, risking an impossible return to illusory origins, reentering a night now dispelled by the dawn of our science and objective cognition. For Bataille, it is always a question of what we are as human beings, here and now, today, a question that scientific cognition might approach but that it always misses in its enthusiasm for explanations rather than irreducible enigmas. Animal being is not the night, not an amorphous Other, an outside or beyond, an inaccessible origin. It remains part of what we are, a divine-like power namely to determine ourselves, to mark the passage from animal to human being, to arise from a bloc of indetermination like a flash of dawning light.

Thus, the paintings at Lascaux are not just a "dispositif," a text to be read, not a message spelled out in opposed syntactical values, nor are they merely utilitarian representations, tools, nets, traps useful to the hunt. They come down to us from a vanished world, a visual poem found as though in a bottle left on the strands of history. How to respond to the resilient enigma that is Lascaux? So as to hear that world, to see its enigmatic presence loom up in the torchlight from the abyssal night of the cave, one perhaps must be chosen, as Henri Michaux wrote of Paul Klee, one must be of the elected, "having kept and protected an awareness that one is entering upon a world of enigmas, for which enigmas are the best reply, or way of 'writing back' (*répondre*)."[91] There is indeed something shamanistic about them, the way they portray the "animals and their humans,"[92] images crossing a porous threshold, surface, or screen through which a sacred communication occurs. The images on these silent, ancient walls, wrapped in darkness, are a wonder for the way they anticipate what the modern painter Paul Klee has famously said about painting: they do not reproduce the visible, but "make visible." No doubt Lascaux's paintings make animal and human beings visible in their outward appearances. They also make an awareness of death and desire visible, the "unnamable animals" of Lascaux, a "wisdom, fantastically disguised," its eyes "briming with tears." Thus, they make visible that seeing can be something more than a power to calculate, a power that measures and works; seeing can also be a rhythm. Seeing that gives birth to astonishment, perplexity, and wonder can also be a joyous dance in which we are more than what we are.

---

91. Michaux, "Aventures de lignes," in *OC* II, 362.
92. Bataille, "Les animaux et leurs hommes," in *OC* IX, 74.

> Que signifie la verité, en dehors de la representation de l'excès, si nous ne voyons ce qui excède la possibilité de voir, ce qu'il est intolérable de voir, comme, dans l'extase, il est intolérable de jouir? si nous ne pensons ce qui excède la possibilité de penser.
>
> —Bataille, *Madame Edwarda*, preface

[What, apart from the representations of excess, what does truth signify if we do not see that which exceeds sight's possibilities, that which is unbearable to see, as, in ecstasy, it is unbearable to know pleasure? If we do not think that which exceeds the possibility of thinking.][93]

---

93. Bataille, *Madame Edwarda*, in *OC* III, 7–32. Trans. by Austryn Wainhouse in *Madame Edwarda* (London: Marion Books, 1989), 135–60 (trans. altered).

Chapter 2

Diabolo scilicet

Pierre Klossowski: The Work of Art as Demonology

La rupture du quotidien par quelque chose d'apparemment quotidien. (Something seemingly mundane that interrupts the mundane.)

—Pierre Klossowski, *Ressemblance*

The phenomenon of painting in the traditional sense is in no way the reflection of a dead star in the heart of our industrial universe—or rather in this absence of "world" or of the "world" as perpetually taken to pieces as industry signifies—painting in the traditional sense has precisely the prestige of a persisting reflection, the source of which is nowhere else than in our own psyche, occulted in its breath and its rhythm and this occultation gives birth to legions of phantasms desperately seeking their own images where they can lodge.

—Pierre Klossowski, *La Différence*

Write in order not simply to destroy, in order not simply to conserve, in order not to transmit; write in the thrall of the impossible real, that share of disaster wherein every reality, safe and sound, sinks.

—Maurice Blanchot, *The Writing of Disaster*

What a storm of controversy and criticism Klossowski's drawings and novels might incite in today's culture. If the April 2020 exhibition *Titian: Women,*

Myth & Power, at the Isabella Stewart Gardner Museum in Boston, consisting of six monumental paintings by Titian—scenes from mythology, including the famous *Rape of Europa*—can provoke an essay in the *New York Times*[1] asking whether the "greatness" of Titian's art isn't clouded in the eyes of the contemporary viewer by its brazen and often violent treatment of women, what would be said of Klossowski's drawings and novels? For here too, from *Le lois de l'hospitalité* to *Le bain de Diane*, the theme of women, myth, and power is certainly prevalent. Indeed, although it is women who hold all the cards in these *récits*, there's no denying the objectionable violence of the scenes Klossowski gives us to see in his large mural-sized drawings, images "having the ambiance of old theatre posters."[2] Many of these poster-sized paintings show the misadventures of a fictional woman named Roberte, the star of *Robert, ce soir*, or the baleful theophany of the Greek/Latin goddess Diana, as in *Diana at Her Bath*. Because of their size, they have an immediate effect, captivating both the imagination and the body of the viewer. The classical idea of the nude, as seen in Titian for example, accomplished a neutralization of the violence of the act of the gaze. Sleek, classical nudes aroused only to neutralize the "primitive violence" of a gaze, the "profanatory contemplation" that beholds and so appropriates a woman's imaginary body, of which the picture is only a simulacre.[3] Klossowski's images are not nudes of "the classical type" (*R*, 70). They are in open rebellion against any such "idea of the nude" and oppose any such ideality that would effectively neutralize the violence of the gaze. Far from being a "profanatory contemplation" intent only on a salacious and violent rendering, Klossowski's simulacra are at once "below and beyond violence."[4] For the violence neutralized in and by the idea of the nude is the violence of the nude itself, the violence of the appropriation and domination it may inspire, and these are not Klossowski's motivations. Can one argue, however, that there is another even more "primitive" violence at work in Klossowski's simulacra, a violence that seduces, that composes the lure and trap for a gaze unto death?

---

1. Holland Cotter, "Can We Ever Look at Titian's Paintings in the Same Way Again?," *New York Times*, Aug. 12, 2021.

2. Pierre Klossowski with Rémy Zaugg, "Simulacra," in *Phantasm and Simulacra: The Drawings of Pierre Klossowski*, eds. Paul Foss, Paul Taylor, and Allen S. Weiss (Melbourne, Victoria: Art & Text, July 1985), 48.

3. Pierre Klossowski, "The Decline of the Nude," trans. Paul Foss, in *Phantasm and Simulacre*, 20.

4. Klossowski, "The Decline of the Nude," 20–21.

His images emerge directly and aggressively from their support, as Zaugg notes.[5] The large formats seem to fly in the face of censorship, which may be one reason Klossowski rather insisted upon it. One shows a woman tied to a set of parallel bars in a basement room while being assaulted by two grotesque men. In another scene, there are images of the same woman being accosted on a flight of stairs by schoolboys armed with flashlights. And in yet another text, another suite of drawings, we see images of a woman who bears a striking resemblance to the one seen on the parallel bars, but this time she is a goddess, the goddess Diana, being assaulted by a figure half animal and half human. The surprising precedent for these images can be found not in the bestiary of the Marquis de Sade but in the *Ecstasy of St. Theresa* (Bernini, mid-seventeenth century), as beautifully described by Klossowski in his 1965 novel *Le Baphomet* (B, 78/108–9). Does ethics here not clash with "aesthetics" and beauty? As the *New York Times* essay asked, "Is great art exempt from moral scrutiny?" While Klossowski is certainly no Titian, it is nonetheless an open question as to whether or not a public exhibition of his hand-drawn images would be possible today, especially because he is no Titian. Such an exhibition, were it convened in an American city, might garner not only official state censorship, and not only an essay in the *New York Times*, but quite possibly the censorship of an outraged public much like the one that greeted Manet's *Olympia* in 1865, when police were summoned to protect the painting from attack. A hundred years later, in 1956, when Klossowski mounted his first exhibition of four large format pencil lead drawings of scenes from his novel *Robert, ce soir*, in consideration of the strict censorship that was current at the time, he chose a private venue for the exhibition, an empty studio belonging to his brother, Balthus, and invited only a hundred guests.[6]

Unlike the Titian exhibition, Klossowski's novels and drawings are not presenting scenes from mythology or even a meditation on modern, bourgeois love. Instead, is there a revolution in how we see art, "un revolution de regard" as Alain Jouffroy has claimed, bringing us a new "look" that comically, ironically, upends Western conventions of artistic creation and reception?[7] Klossowski's art does not transmit a message or ideality, does not illustrate primitive fantasies, and does not seek to destroy or even to conserve, but,

---

5. Zaugg and Klossowski, "Simulacra," 54.
6. Zaugg and Klossowski, "Simulacra," 56.
7. Pierre Klossowski and Alain Jouffroy, *Le Secret pouvoir du sens* (Paris: Écriture, 1994), 63.

in the words of Blanchot, it is an art "in the thrall of the impossible real, that share of disaster wherein every reality, safe and sound, sinks."

While Klossowski denies that his drawings have any overt intention of ensnaring a naive public by producing spectacular cultural shocks, they certainly do have a moral, ethical edge: they offer the viewer not an object of detached contemplation but scenes in which the viewer actively participates, is "morally" and physically solicited and made implicit in the scene beheld. These are images, scenes, situations, movements to which the viewer/reader must respond. Writing "in the thrall of the impossible real," Klossowski is asking, along with Nietzsche, What is a moral value? What is the role such cultural values play in estimating the inestimable value of a work of art? He questions the role and place of art not in relation to culture but to life, to desire, to libidinal drives, to ever mobile intensities, not static essences. Klossowski's art is writing at the limits of the possible as he experiences it, yet in sentences that seem classically composed, submitting to the censure of classical syntax, that is to say, to its logical rigor (R, 11). Like the physiognomies of the characters in his novels and drawings, they hardly grimace at the moment of their violation. A revolution in thought occurs here that does not revolt against culture through real violence, but only through "pantomime" and "simulacra." Simulacra of what? Of the intensities in a moment suspended between space and time, the time and space of a death-bound theophany.

Introductory Notes on the Art and Literature of Pierre Klossowski

What is happening, what is given, suspended in the gap between seeing and saying in the drawings and writings by Pierre Klossowski? Set aside any notion that the drawings are merely illustrations for the written text. Set aside notions of narrative function between the two, writing and image. See instead the spectacle they stage.

Two key elements shall be considered: the theatrical character of Klossowski's work and the structure of the gaze that comprises the ropes and pulleys for this theater of desire. But more so, it is a matter of situating Klossowsk's work, situating or placing his unplaceable art in its betweenness, between bodies and spirits, humans and their gods, life and death, or, in the words of Maurice Blanchot, "between the meaning of existents and the being forever where sense is lost (*s'abime*) . . . (in) that region called Literature or Art."[8]

The settings and the characters of Klossowski's novels, his emphasis on "seeing" or the "gaze," underscores the strong theatrical character of his work. Klossowski once described himself as more of a playwright than a novelist. "For me, the film and the drawings are a type of spectacle. I would also like to make this claim for the writing in my books. . . . A script or book with me is always a succession of scenes and moments which I describe, which I imagine according to the words I use to express them."[9] So, an event or situation is first *seen*, is first of all a *scene* with its own spatial-temporal dimensions, an interiority, a "phantasm," as Klossowski often says, arising from a "monomania," which is then described, written or drawn and so exteriorized, thereby invoking different spatial-temporal parameters pertaining to signification. His 1960 novel *Le Souffleur* is subtitled "Le théatre de société," the first sentences of which describe a theater, portrayed as though the reader were sitting in that theater waiting for the "petite scene" to begin: "Soudain la lumière s'éteignit, les chuchotements se turent dans la salle, le rideu se leva sur la petite scene."[10] Thus, there is an incessant drift, one might say, of Klossowski's work from the interior vision, a "cinéma intérieur" in Jouffreoy's words,[11] to the written page, and from there to the drawn images and on to the theatrical, and inevitably to the cinematic and sculptural media. All the while the intention of this drift is to seek more effective ways of involving or implicating the viewer as much as possible in the scene at hand, to make the spectator an actor and composer of a scene rather than just its passive viewer. There is a tactile dimension in his images as well. One of his images shows phantom hands reaching out, disembodied, to grasp Roberte: these hands could be those of the viewer. More so, in addition to the novels, the philosophical essays, *Nietzsche and the Vicious Circle* (1969) for example, also have an undeniable theatrical component.

---

8. Maurice Blanchot, quoted by Klossowski in *Une si funeste désir* (Paris: Gallimard, 1963), 86. Trans. by Russell Ford as "On Maurice Blanchot," in *SDD* (Albany: State University of New York Press, 2007), 85–98.

9. Zaugg and Klossowski, "Simulacra," 65.

10. "Suddenly the lights were extinguished, whispers hushed in the room, the curtain rose on the small stage"; trans. mine. Klossowski, *Le Souffleur, ou le theatre de sociéte* (Paris: Jean-Jacques Pauvert, 1960), 7.

11. Klossowski and Jouffroy, *Le Secret pouvoir du sens*, 62.

Klossowski himself stresses this, describing his work as a "pantomime of the spirits," or in a reference to Nietzsche and the "Vicious Circle," a theater of the Eternal Return, rather than a mode of more traditional philosophical thinking. He also described his works as "machines," a word he says can be used interchangeably with simulacra and has a theatrical sense as in a deus ex machina. Again, the emphasis is that his drawings are not "disinterested trinkets" but "an instrument," a "materialization," which "once arranged in a particular manner, expresses or acts."[12] With their constricted, closeted settings—the drawing room, a flight of stairs, an altar, a quiet pond in an enchanted glen—we, readers and spectators of these texts and images, are invited into more interior, intimate, theatrical scenes far from the noisy glare of the outside modern world. Rather like the limited stage settings in Bacon's paintings, the action always seems somehow confined, yet in such a way that its power or its intensity is more concentrated.

Fables of hosts and hostesses, of nephews and their tutor aunts, of priests and spirits in modern dress—let us first consider their strangely anachronistic theatrical settings. While Klossowski insists that this "point of view of the epoch and all that accompanies it is a false problem," and that "one creates an epoch," his choice of a dated costume style and physical setting has an important impact on his novels and images. The contrast of his settings with the contemporary world seems essential to their dramatic force. It may be one way of evading censorship by simulating what may have gone on in past ages, when naughty aunts would educate their beautifully naive nephews in the privacy of their homes, as an arcane practice, erotic, perhaps, but laughable at the same time. An autobiographical element also suggests itself, which would concern Klossowski's own tutelage under André Gide.[13] But he always felt somehow out of his own time, a living anachronism. As Klossowski asks rhetorically through a character perfectly resembling his fictional character Octave (or is it Klossowski himself?) in the 1965 novel *The Baphomet*:

> Is it his fault if he was born too soon or too late, at the time of the Antichrist rather than in the age of idols, at the time when Christ Crucified and the idols of nations and of all eras merely serve to enrich the merchants, after the abolition of serfdom rather than during the slave-trade, before or after the age of

---

12. Zaugg and Klossowski, "Simulacra," 60.
13. Zaugg and Klossowski, "Simulacra," 50.

arena games, of mystery plays or of the silver screen, the age of barter or of the holidays with pay, of palfreys or sleeping-cars, of zoos, zen or insecticide spray, in 1264 or 1964? Like it or not he must accept the inevitable. (*B*, 154/216)

Indeed, what is the date and time for the setting of *The Baphomet*? Is it in 1264 or 1964? Although the specific historical context for *The Baphomet* dates from the early fourteenth century, and however this context—that of the Gnostic traditions, the influence of Islam and the Christian Crusades—seems essential to anchoring or positioning Klossowski's fiction, the narrative's ambiance is an indefinite day and time that cannot be situated on a chronological scale, a time and place situated between earth and sky, a time outside of time, a "immense abolition of time," and "an image of the Eternal return."[14] This immense suspension of time is also the case in the novel *Diana at Her Bath*, set in a mythical space-time, a suspended moment when time seems to have bent back upon itself, seems to have come to a stop, where past and present meet on the stage of an eternal moment.

The characters that populate these strange little tales thus seem to have stepped not from the modern world but from an antique one. In the novel *Robert, ce soir*, for example, they pantomime a return of the belle époque, figures from an age gone by when gentlemen always wore ties and a woman would never go out without her hat and gloves. This curious context makes the outrageous situations in which they find themselves all the more striking. Whether they appear in novels or drawings, the characters inhabit interior settings only summarily sketched, implied rather than fully represented. There is a drawing room sparsely furnished with antiques; there is also a curtain, and in another setting, a set of parallel bars in a basement room off the Galérie de Beaujolais. These are placid, almost inert backdrops for the disturbing scenes he depicts. Another story is set in a mythical space amongst a clutch of willows on the banks of a mythical pond. A fantastic drama of seeing and saying, of desire and the transformations that accompany the daemon's work of desire. But the setting is from an age of gods and goddesses long absent—or are they returning?—briefly making their appearance in a death-bound theophany.

From Klossowski's point of view, the personae in his drawings and novels are not representations or even imaginations. Rather, they are "intensities," simulacra that appear to us, the reader/spectator, as a daemon would have

---

14. Klossowski and Jouffroy, *Le Secret pouvoir du sens*, 46–47.

them appear. These characters are simulacra much as the ancient Roman statues of the gods and goddesses were likewise regarded as simulacra. They are the way an intensity is given a body, that of a Roberte, or a Diana and her Acteon, whereby the materiality of lead pencil and heavy paper are transubstantiated—a literary Eucharist—and become something more, a "glorious body." All this to stage the unfolding of intensities at the moment, a suspended moment, when they turn back upon themselves and interpret themselves. His essays and interviews leave little doubt that he found such images to be better than words for communicating a certain intensity of soul, as he calls it, where to communicate would be to communicate not concepts, not a message as such, but a contagion, a daemonic solicitation of the body by the text and of the viewer by the picture. The picture would be a daemon's work, in short, something dramatic, theatrical, and even comic, the other side of its violence.

As such, Klossowski's personae establish themselves not as fixed or eternal archetypes but as a mobile field of forces neither confined nor defined by the once-and-for-all of fixed identities. His characters are multiple, a restless exchange of bodies and spirits where nothing is named such that it is fixed in its identity. They drift, nomads, wandering from setting to setting, from novel to novel, more Deleuzian rhizomes than single-fiber taproots. There are gender ambiguities, as well, with the youth Ogier portrayed in *The Baphomet*, for example, having a strikingly resemblance to the female heroine Roberte from the earlier novels. Roberte, one of Klossowski's most recognizable characters, especially reappears in other guises and other situations in several of Klossowski's novels and images. She stars in his most famous novel, *Robert, ce soir*, but in other stories, *The Baphomet* for example, she cameos, once again named, "Roberte has wildly beautiful eyes" (*B*, 151/212).

The question, then, is not how to portray but how to exorcize an intensity by lending it a human form. How to bring not an ideality to appearance, not a classical nude, but an enigma? Klossowski's Roberte, modeled after his wife, Denise, is always a woman of a certain austere maturity, stiff-lipped, dressed like a modern-day nun in her business suit and high heels, always wearing a hat and gloves—always gloves—which, as they conceal the open palm, are the objects of an irresistible scopic passion when removed with salacious ceremony. She is an official state censor by profession, the party to verbal lucubrations by day and laughable yet silent seductions by night.[15] Her husband, Octave, hardly lays a finger on her,

---

15. In an interview with the *Nouvel Observateur* (Feb. 1982), Klossowski says that Roberte's demonstrations and arguments are her silence, her way of being silent; she

preferring the role of a voyeur.[16] From behind a curtain, his gaze possesses his wife only by dispossessing her to the company of strangers. Such are his "laws of hospitality," laws of seeing, laws of almost priestly rituals of sacrifice and a hosting of the spirits. A retired professor of theology, Octave is already an anachronism in an age defined by the death of God and the "twilight of the idols." A caricature of the French bourgeoisie, he is, in his simulacral role, also a foot soldier in a "combat against culture." The dry, dusty, and doting husband of a much younger woman, he beholds his wife not so much as a person he loves but as an enigma he wishes to resolve. Accordingly, his only preoccupation—his "monomania"—is obsessively focused on seeing what he supposes to be her secret inner self, the one she hides in her role as state censor; a silent, secretive one that hides behind pure public speech, speaking of virtues and vices. But Octave's methods are hardly conventional. His is almost a religious quest. He wants to see her soul as God would see her, which requires a strategy of spying on her with the aim of seeing her when her hidden desires are no longer hidden, when she is in the transports of erotic desire. This means he must play games that will enable this monstrous gaze, games of "hospitality" games of hunter and huntress.

There's also a nephew in the family story *Robert, ce soir*, Antoine, who is young, naive, and straitlaced but also bursting with curiosity. Devoted to his aunt, Roberte, he apparently has nothing very urgent on his agenda except satisfying his curiosity about what really happened to her that day her dress caught fire while she was giving a lecture. This event is marked by a barely discernible ambiguity: Did Aunt Roberte intentionally fall into the hands of the gentleman who immediately ripped off her burning skirt? One of Antoine's roles is to intensify the enigma of the gaze that is thematic in these narratives. As they gaze together at the photographs Octave took that day of the enigmatic and decisive moment when, her skirt afire, Roberte fell into the arms of a gentleman who had ostensibly leapt to her

---

refuses to "deliver" herself except in gestures. In the silence of gestures, she is eloquent. "There is a moral barter (*troc*) produced only in silence." Quoted in A.-M. Lugan-Dardigna, *Klossowski: L'homme aux simulacres* (Paris: Navarin Éditeur, La Collection du Studiolo, 1986), 28.

16. Arnaud challenges the notion that Octave is a "voyeur" on the grounds that the voyeur is solipsistic and prefers not to be seen, no other gaze is active but that of the voyeur. Klossowski, on the other hand, partners with the spectator or viewer and prefers to be seen, as in the films and photographs of the scenes from *Les lois de l'hospitalité*. Alain Arnaud, *Pierre Klossowski* (Paris: Seuil, 1990), 72.

rescue, he asks, "What do you see, Antoine, in the pictures I took of that event, photographs of the decisive moment?" We might wonder why Octave just happened to have a camera on that day. Was he somehow anticipating Roberte's skirt catching fire, as though this apparently random and spontaneous incident concealed a level of preplanning, as though it were set up to be a spectacle? Antoine, who had been looking to his aunt for an education and a career, must now see her in a different light in this scene of calamity and seduction. But he gets more than a little tutoring from his uncle Octave, who not only wishes to educate his ability to see and to say what he sees in this scene flashing at the edge of indiscernibility but who also secretly guides the naive nephew into situations where he too will become a participant in Octave's stratagems. Antoine's curiosity will lead him in his own pure and unwitting way to witness Roberte showing herself both to him and to Octave as she is, "this evening," her hidden desires now a spectacle, caught as in a snapshot.

The counterpart to all of this can be found in our author's treatment of the theophany of the goddess, Diana, when she is at her bath, fatally witnessed by her nephew, the hunter Acteon, hiding at the edge of the pond, behind a curtain of leaves, waiting for his chance to see and touch the goddess's naked flanks. A daemon plays the role of the husband, Octave, setting up the scene, including how the main actors will appear both to themselves and to the viewer.

With all the emphasis on character and setting, it is thus seeing rather than conceptualizing that is the predominate motivation in Klossowski's works. Regardless of the different stage settings in *Robert, ce soir* or *Diana at Her Bath*, there is a structure that recurs as a mobilizing force from drama to drama whereby the "laws of hospitality" find their counterpart in the theophany of the goddess after her hunt. This structure is that of the gaze, carried on, carried away, driven to its own destruction.

Le regard

For Klossowski, to see is to think (*regarder est penser*), but this is not to say that seeing becomes an exercise of conceptualizing. Seeing, for Klossowski, is "to gaze," or "to give to see," as in a spectacle (*donner à regarder*), to enter through the gaze into a forbidden (*interdict*) domain, difficult to penetrate, of thought, life, and desire.[17] Klossowski often insists that his novels and

---

17. Klossowski and Jouffroy, *Le Secret pouvoir du sens*, 57.

drawings are more concerned with seeing, in this sense of *le regard*, than conceptualizing, emphasizing the role of the spectator rather than the speculator. But can *le regard* be "thought"? Or is it somehow below, before, or beyond thinking? Does it obtain more at the level of desires and sexuality than to cognition? Can the philosopher think of it not as a mechanism but as an intensity having a certain armature or structure repeated across several narratives?

Le regard, translated as "seeing," is more than seeing. Seeing, as in the perceptual experience of the world, must be distinguished from the gaze. It may be that what Klossowski refers to as seeing actually bears a greater family resemblance to what Lacan and others have called the "gaze." Perhaps, but Klossowski has his own way of articulating his experience of the gaze, which is not identical to the Lacanian formulations of the gaze in *Seminar XI*. Klossowski himself uses the word *regard* in his written texts, which, while it can be translated as "look" (or even "manhole" or "peephole"), it is most often rendered by "gaze" in English language translations of Klossowski. Moreover, where seeing, by contrast, is bound to the intentional apprehension of objects in a field of vision, the gaze stems not from intentionality but from intensities, libidinal intensities. Where seeing is perhaps more Cartesian, representing the Cartesian "cogito," the "I-think," the gaze stems from, the "desidero," "I-desire," as the commentator Hanjo Berressem puts it. Whereas seeing maps the visual structure of a field of vision, the gaze maps the position of the subject within that field.[18] This distinction may not be so clean-cut, especially if you read Merleau-Ponty's late phenomenology *The Visible and the Invisible*, where "seeing" in the sense of visual perception is developed as a direct critique of Cartesian "optics." Nonetheless, so crucial was the role of seeing, or the gaze, in his work, together with its essential bonding with images and the power of images, that Klossowski gave up the role of writer after 1975 for that of the visual artist, exchanging words, sayings, for images.

But there's more to it than this change of career path. The drawn picture, even more so than the written text, permits a suspension, or a solecism, of the essential moment of vision, a suspension of the gaze precisely at the moment where the action reaches its zenith, where something happens, something ambiguous—a skirt catches fire—something that draws the viewer in, deepening their involvement in the image. Antoine cannot

---

18. Hanjo Berressem, "The 'Evil Eye' of Painting: Jacques Lacan and Witold Gombrowicz," in *Reading Seminar XI*, eds. Richard Feldstein, Bruce Fink, and Maire Jaanus (Albany: State University of New York Press, 1995), 175.

quite know, cannot see or say fully what happened. A photograph of the event, taken by Uncle Octave at the desired moment, a *moment voulu*, has no before and after, no sequence, no beginning or end. It stands on its own, structured by ambiguity and mystery. In the picture, time, like language, seems to come to a stop, arrested, an instant of the Eternal Return frozen on the ever-moving wheel of time. This double movement of the opening of the gaze and its suspension in an essential moment, a *moment voulu* as Klossowski calls it, forms the structure shared between the novels *Robert, ce soir* and *Le bain de Diane*.

Let us develop in what follows these aspects of Klossowski's work: the combat against culture with which Klossowski opens his book on Nietzsche and the self-description of his work as a work of theater, of simulacra, a "pantomime of the spirits." That and his emphasis on seeing, *le regard* or the gaze, showing how, in relation to the exigencies of seeing, Klossowski conceives the exigency of a semiology of intensities.

A Combat against Culture

We begin with his book *Nietzsche et le cercle vicieux*, published in 1969. As we read this text, the main actor is Nietzsche. But, reading attentively, we can also see how Klossowski develops his own ideas through Nietzsche's text. Was it not Nietzsche who first pioneered some of the very ideas and perspectives that became the heart of Klossowski's art and thought?

Taking Nietzsche's notebooks from the 1880s as his main text, not the great books that Nietzsche also wrote in those years but the background notebooks, the personal remarks that Nietzsche jotted down for himself and that were later transcribed by Peter Gast, one of the few who could decipher Nietzsche's handwriting, Klossowski developed a most original and forceful interpretation of Nietzsche. From the first pages of *Nietzsche and the Vicious Circle*, Klossowski isolates two abiding guidelines for his reading of Nietzsche's notebooks. First, where the notebooks speak of Nietzsche's "complot," his "conspiracy," it must be understood that this is not a conspiracy directed against his class or his country but against the human species in its entirety[19] (*NVC*, xv/12). This shall be the combat against culture,

---

19. In 1888, on Dec. 26 or 27, just days before his collapse on Jan. 3, 1889, at Turin, Nietzsche wrote to Overbeck "about his plans to incite the powers of Europe, by means of a *Promemoria*, to form an anti-German, anti-Hohenzollern league. In general, an intense

and the overturning of man into something he calls the Overman. The second point guiding Klossowski's reading is the centrality of Nietzsche's "delirium," not only in his immense physical suffering, his loneliness, the transgressive grandeur of his thoughts, but also in "the irresistible attraction that Chaos had for him" (xv/12). Nietzsche's thought revolved around an axis of delirium, and as Klossowski notes, the more Nietzsche studied the phenomenon of thought and the different behaviors that emerged from it, the more the modern world provoked reactions from the individual, and the more Nietzsche studied these reactions, "the closer he drew to this chasm" (xv/12). The second point is related to the first in that chaos and delirium, intensities, or "tonalities of the soul," as the Nietzschean formulation has it, are incommunicable through cultural instruments of declarative language and the institutions of teaching and research. Delirium is already a combat against culture. Delirium is written off as madness and so culturally marginalized. Nietzsche's thought may have touched the limits, but whatever the delirium of his thought, it is not "pathological."[20] Migraines and a possible syphilitic condition are put forth by the professors of ideas and psychiatrists alike as good biological and pathological reasons to reject Nietzsche's thought as the blathering of an irrational voluntarism, unintelligible, possibly dangerous but eminently quotable. In his single-handed conspiracy against humanity, Nietzsche is unable to communicate. At the summit of lucidity, he falls into delirium, like the madman in the parable, crashing his lantern in the midst of an indifferent humanity, proclaiming the "death of God," and, through all the intensities, the rising and falling tonalities of his "soul," rejecting both the principle of reality and the principle of identity, the twin pillars of communication and knowledge. He falls into "mutism," the other side of his strident proclamations. In another text, Klossowski similarly refers to a "conspiration du silence" with regard to his Roberte, an ambiguous, two-sided silence: both a sign, a way of communicating akin to the gesture of

---

concern with 'grand politics' marks these days." See David Farrell Krell and Donald L. Bates, *The Good European: Nietzsche's Work Sites in Word and Image* (Chicago: University of Chicago Press, 1997), 240. Klossowski's final chapter of *NVC*, "The Euphoria of Turin," refers to Nietzsche's "transfiguration of the world at Turin," completed by "a final transfiguration of history" (248).

20. Klossowski writes, "Lucid thought, delirium and the conspiracy form an indissoluble whole in Nietzsche. . . . This does not mean that, since it involved delirium, Nietzsche's thought was 'pathological; rather, because his thought was lucid to the extreme, it took on the form of a delirious interpretation—and required the entire experimental initiative of the modern world." *NVC*, xvi/12.

her open palm, and a solecism, a discontinuity, a break in the discourse of Klossowski's narrative. For Klossowski's Nietzsche, silence was also ambiguous, both a "mutism" that is "the obstacle" against any teaching—he could not say what he had seen—and something taken by culture as "merely speech," Nietzsche's way of eloquence. Inner silence, outer eloquence. These first pages of Klossowski's text thus establish the parameters not only for his reading of Nietzsche but for his own work as well: the doubling tension between speech and silence, between lucidity and delirium, between what culture gives us to see and what is forbidden to see, between the body and language, the tensions in short that frame Klossowski's own combat against culture. As with Nietzsche, so too Klossowski's combat against culture asks what is hidden in language, whether it be the language of speech and writing or the language of the body and its gestures. "*What is lucid and what is unconscious* in our thought and in our actions?—a subterranean question that disguised itself outwardly in a critique of culture and that intentionally made itself explicit in a form that could still be integrated into the speculative and historical discussion of his time" (xvi/13).

The opening pages of *Nietzsche and the Vicious Circle*, from a chapter entitled "The Combat against Culture," provide a long quotation from Nietzsche's notebooks. "Is the 'philosopher' still possible today?" Nietzsche asks. Perhaps there is too much to know; perhaps the known is "too great," or the philosopher's knowledge would always come too late, like Hegel's owl, taking flight only at dusk when the day has passed. The role of the philosopher is damaged today, degraded and degenerated, "so that his judgement no longer means anything" (1/19). Having lost the "great pathos, his great respect for him/herself," the philosopher is left to become something other than what they have been in the past so that they can become what they are today in the modern world: nothing but "a dilettante with a thousand antennae," a "great actor, a kind of Cagliostro philosopher" (1/19).

What, then, is left for the role of the philosopher with regard to the great questions of life and culture? With the "true world" having become a "fable," as Nietzsche said, the philosopher's role has likewise diminished. Is the philosopher the one who sees that philosophy has become cut off from life, that it has become a purely cultural artifact, leaving the philosopher with nothing to do but be a "lucid and impotent spectator?"[21] In Nietzsche's case, if he is even to be called a philosopher, the philosopher must become not an artifact of culture, not a speculator about life, but one immersed

---

21. Nietzsche, quoted by Klossowski in *NVC*, 3/19.

in life and one who combats against culture, specifically against culture's growing conceptualization of and alienation from life. After Nietzsche, the philosopher is no longer a contemplator of truth or even one who listens to the call of being but one who engages in a combat of all that stands against life, all that brings on human suffering and crime against humanity, a humanity that, as Nietzsche claimed, is yet something to be overcome. This combat against culture shall have profound consequences for philosophical work. It shall inveigh new criteria in its combat against culture: not moral criteria, "good" and "bad," but criteria of health and sickness, strength and weakness, the strength of a particular individual who can resist the gravitational pull of gregariousness and the language of stereotypes, who can have the strength for the "highest thought" and the greatest vision, that of the Eternal Return, the Vicious Circle.

What does this phrase name? Such a terrifying name, at once trivial and imponderable, foreshadows the challenges that lie ahead. Not "knowledge," then, the philosopher in Nietzsche's case has a great vision, an ecstatic lived experience in which they witness an event that could "break the history of humanity in two": the death or disappearance of a unique God, perhaps the return of multiple gods, and the bending of time back upon itself, forming a Vicious Circle in which the "once and for all" character of life is overcome and all identity of a unique Self is uprooted by a vision of its incessant and multiple return. But how to communicate this vision? Is a scientific formulation possible? Can conceptual language succeed? Or must the philosopher first *mime* this shattering experience? (*NVC*, 4/23) Mime it and develop along the "gestural semiotic of the Soothsayers and Prophets" (4/23).

Thus, Nietzsche's combat against culture and the metaphysical philosophies that were its armature and justification is not just a conceptual or dialectical combat but one that overturns by returning philosophy to the body and its flow of pulsions. There is such a powerful contrast on this point between Nietzsche's unutterable vision of the Eternal Recurrence, pulsing like a shockwave through his body, bringing immense terror and suffering, and Descartes's transcendent vision of an indubitable God, conceived as he was napping by his fireside. At the beginning of the modern era in philosophy, Descartes journeyed inwardly, seeking the indisputable grounds for a unified science of nature in the immediacy of self-certainty and identity of a cogito, the "I-think," and its object of thought, its noema. The journey begins by bypassing the body and putting perceptual experience in question. Descartes's meditations begin by passing through the dreamworld and the confusion of lived experience with fanciful imaginings, touching upon but pulling back from madness, only to end up being seized by a vision of God as the basis of all certainty. Abstracting from the shadowy world of bodily perceptions, Descartes had to seize upon the Idea of a perfect God as a luminous counterweight to that shadow-filled world of dreams and perceptions, for only the ponderous weight of such a vision could counter the daemonic pull of flickering appearances. Perfection—at least the Idea of perfection—the icy perfection of a diamond, became the primal, foundational Guarantor of the value and integrity of knowledge. Here lies the abstraction of philosophy from life, from existence, and its withdrawal into mathematics and science. Looking out his window, what did Descartes see walking on the streets below? Machines, robots dressed in overcoats. Such formalism, in Nietzsche's eyes, would leave a deep and lasting mark on modern philosophy, climaxing in the total spiritualization of philosophy and truth in Hegel's *Phenomenology of Spirit*.

Writing at the close of the modern era Descartes helped to open, Klossowski likewise journeys inward but discovers not the indubitability of an immediate self-relation, the unmediated and so undeceived firm foundation of thought in the identity of a cogito (the "I-think"), but the rising and falling of intensities, an incessant movement he calls a chaos. Not the indubitable cogito and the unquestionable perfection of God as guarantor of identity and self-certainty, Klossowski inhabits a world from which God has withdrawn, where the self is divided and multiple, where there is neither a True World nor an Appearing World but only a world of doubles, a labyrinth of differences, multiplicities, and absence, desire and death.

Klossowski's little dramas, his own theater of the Eternal Return, together with his remarkable philosophical essays, have tried to pull inside out the whole mechanism of philosophy and theology that has provided the foundations for Western European culture since the times of the late Roman world, since the reign of the Scholastics up until the revolution enacted by Descartes's *Meditations*, the so-called first book of modern philosophy, whereby the primacy of the cogito is established. The quiet, duplicitous violence of their scenes is not just sexual, it is also a form of combat Klossowski wages especially against all the metaphysical forms of identity: the identity of the Self, the identity of God, of language, time, and world. The Nietzschean experiences of the death of God and the Eternal Return are keys to this effort. It is his own combat against culture, which he saw outlined in the work of his forebearer, Nietzsche.

Pulling inside out Descartes's revolutionary journey inward, a journey recorded in his *Meditations*—which is also very much a drama, with its staged sequence of scenes—Klossowski's journey reaches not the bedrock of certitude and identity but an embodied, inexpressible play of forces, a war of force against force in which forces, or intensities, rise and fall, like waves on a vast sea. These forces are given many names and faces in the course of Klossowski's and Nietzsche's writings. They are spiritual forces, a "tonality of the soul," somatic forces, forces of desire, unconscious forces known only through their effects. Are they libidinal pulsations or intensifications, as in Lyotard's *Économie libidinale*? They are all of these and more. This is a combat without dialectical resolution, as in the Hegelian *Phenomenology of Spirit*, but only temporary equilibriums, as described in Nietzsche's notebooks, momentary respites from continuous suffering and torment as recorded in *Nietzsche and the Vicious Circle*. Whatever the case, this encounter with intensities shall entail a prolonged meditation on the powers and limits of language and communication. How can an "intensity" be communicated? How can it attain signification? This question is most acute in the case of Nietzsche's "highest thought," the occasion of a "highest tonality of soul": the ecstatic vision of the Eternal Return, an intensity that Klossowski has discussed at length in *Nietzsche and the Vicious Circle*. When the bedrock of the cogito has been shattered, and, with the death of God, who or what can communicate this ecstasy? Does such a vision not challenge the limits of language? Can an intensity that has the power to break the history of humanity in two be communicated in words? Can it ever be rendered unto signification? What is the role of concepts, ideals, values, norms in society? How does this question become a part of Nietzsche's and Klossowski's own combat against culture?

With the death of God and with Nietzsche's "highest thought" of the Eternal Recurrence, the foundations of all certainty and identity have been swept away in a torrent. Henceforth, the artist, the poet, the thinker all find themselves in a much altered, indeed, inverted environment. Where Tertullian, for example, quoted by Klossowski, says, "If representation resides in the image of truth, and the image itself in the truth of being, the thing must exist for itself before serving as an image for another," then for the modern thinker, for Maurice Blanchot, this is pulled inside out: "Representation may well reside in the image of truth, but truth is only ever an image and the image is itself only an absence of being, thus a presence of nothingness."[22]

---

22. Klossowski, *Une si funeste désir*, 159–84. ("On Maurice Blanchot," in *SDD*, 85–98.)

Certainly not all of modern French thought subscribed to this line of thinking, especially where it concerns language. In his 1947 essay on Perain,[23] Sartre expressed his reservations and objections: "things"—forces?—"do not clash, only words do." Klossowski's reply to this might be that words are themselves the effects of intensities and forces. Sartre sees matters quite differently. Upholding the synthesizing activity of the cogito in its relations with others, Sartre condemns the route many modern French writers, particularly those who were linked with the surrealist circle, have taken. Here, the clash of words has resulted in a catastrophe of language. He quotes Bataille's proclamation: "Poetry is a holocaust of words." And, on the subject of Maurice Blanchot, he writes, "The latest arrival, M. Blanchot, betrayed the secret of his attempts when he explained to us that *the writer must speak in order to say nothing*." Perhaps Sartre was thinking of passages from Blanchot where he articulates his philosophy of language. As Klossowski quotes one such passage, "for in order for a thing to be able to serve as the image of another, it must cease to exist for itself. Language, as the image of a thing, designates nothing but the absence of this other thing."[24] From this absence, Blanchot claims that the function of language is the function of death. It is these terms that Klossowski confronts anew all the problems and questions of the communicability of intensities he experiences in this inward journey and so, surpassing the notion of a cogito as the basis of language, he surpasses the Sartrean critique.

Returning to the vision of the Eternal Return, does this highest tonality of soul, this highest thought, spring not from the words of a cogito but from the rising and falling of the intensities of a soul, or a Self? Self (*Selbst*) has a double meaning in this Nietzschean context that distances it from the Cartesian notion: on one hand it has a moral dimension, the *Selbstsucht*, selfishness, the hubristic avidity of the *Soi*, of the *Selbst*, translated erroneously as "egoism." On the other hand, it is "force," unconscious to cerebral consciousness, that obeys a hidden reason, *un raison cachée* (*NVC*, 58/32, Klossowski's footnote). The term Klossowski uses in his *Nietzsche and the Vicious Circle* is *suppôt*, translated as "agent," a term he revives from the Scholastic tradition and applies to the Nietzschean context. It designates not a substantial Cartesian cogito but only a fragile, organic membrane suspended

---

23. Jean-Paul Sartre, "Departure and Return," in *Literary and Philosophical Essays* (New York: Collier Books, 1955), 150.

24. Klossowski, "On Maurice Blanchot," in *SDD*, 85 (*Une si funeste désir* [Paris: Gallimard, 1963], 160).

between birth and death, nothing more than a grammatical unity, a fiction, really, a phantasm, a phantasmatic "I," where that first-person pronoun, as in "I-think," names not an enduring, necessary identity but only a fortuitous interpretation of the impulses in terms of a hierarchy of gregarious material and moral social needs.[25] He will also speak of "la conscience sans suppôt" in connection with a "vacance du moi" (*R*, 23). Hence, as Nietzsche continues, the *Selbst* becomes identified with the body rather than with consciousness: "The body is the Self, the Self resides in the midst of the body and expresses itself through the body"[26] (*NVC*, 32/58). The body is not one but a multiplicity of "millions of vague impulses," which the "brain" interprets and bestows a meaning upon (33/59). The body is the source for every creative impulse and every evaluation, and "it is from their cerebral inversion that mortal specters arise, starting with the voluntary ego (*moi*), and even the other person (*le prochain*), the neighbor. All of this is "nothing but a projection of the Self (*Soi*), the 'you' having no more lasting, necessary reality than the me (*moi*)." Thus, the Self is in the body only as a "prolonged extremity of Chaos," the chaos of the multiplicity of impulses that defines the body (58/32). Attempting to interpret this multiplicity, attempting to interpret the highest vision of the Eternal Return that arises in and through the body, Nietzsche always comes up against the limitations of the gregarious means of communicating this vision, the stereotypes that he must fall back upon as he struggles with the necessity and the impossibility of communication. Culture always assumes the unity and identity of persons and their bodies, always assumes the function of language as the communication of ideas, conceptual realities, rather than impulses or *Stimmung* (moods) of the body, Self, or soul. The combat against culture would bring into view the pulsional multiplicity of the body; against the culture of identity of persons and their bodies, it would evoke "la conscience sans suppôt." It would be a combat with and against the very language used to talk about and to think about the body only by abbreviating it, abstracting a unit by reducing the play of discontinuities and multiplicities, producing thereby a phantasmatic unity of body and mind, the oneness and identity of an individual.

But language, the language of signs arising from the body's pulsional field, seems to fail as it reaches to interpret and so to name the highest vision of the Eternal Return, the most elevated *Stimmung* of the soul as

---

25. Daniel W Smith, "Translator's Preface," in *NVC*, xiiff.

26. French original: "Le corps étant le Soi, le Soi résidant au sein du corps et s'exprimant par le corps." *NVC*, 32/58.

Nietzsche also calls it, which cannot be described as a calm and luxurious contemplation of eternal truths but only as a deep-seated, death-bound intensity. The Eternal Return marks the triumph of multiplicity, difference, and repetition. How can it ever attain the coherence and the terms and structure necessary for it to become a teachable experience? Such an experience is not thinkable in the confines of the metaphysical systems of philosophy. For Nietzsche and Klossowski, the difficult work of philosophy is not to be the architect of a system of thought, as were so many from Descartes to Hegel. Philosophers may construct vast, heroic systems of thought, they may seek a unified science of nature, but, in Nietzsche's view, they are only talking about themselves, they only interpret their strongest, most dominant impulses and put only what is communicable of that into their systems. "The philosopher is only a kind of occasion and chance through which the impulse is finally able to speak." Speaking of truth, the philosopher speaks only of themselves, as Nietzsche writes in another passage quoted by Klossowski (4–5/24).

Nietzsche and Klossowski both reject the role of the philosopher-teacher, whose job would be to articulate the foundations and guarantees for the continuation of a gregarious and productive society. Philosophers, artists, even scientists, Nietzsche claims, were, in a "bourgeois" society, to establish the moral justifications for society, to reintegrate society, to contribute to its continuation. But the vision of the Eternal Return is a thought that would shatter that equilibrium, not only of society but especially for the individual who was possessed by it. How could it ever be a teachable doctrine, the subject of erudite lectures? This highest thought was not the serene and divine-like experience advocated by the ancient Greeks but was a physical and spiritual ordeal for Nietzsche. The intensity of the experience made him tremble when he spoke of it. Klossowski quotes Lou Salomé's account of Nietzsche's attempt to confide his vision to her: "Unforgettable for me are those hours in which he first confided to me his secret, whose inevitable fulfillments and validation he anticipated with shudders. Only with a quiet voice and with all the signs of deepest horror did he speak about this secret. Life, in fact, produced such suffering in him that the certainty of an eternal return of life had to mean something horrifying to him" (95/145).

This intensity of thought and experience Klossowski links to Nietzsche's physical suffering, his insomnia, his massive headaches and problems with his eyesight, his fits of despair and joy. Suffering is eloquent where garrulous words seem to fail. The highest thought resists the registers and codes of everydayness and sinks into the silence of the suffering body; it trembles like an earthquake in the flesh as much as it does in thought and language. But however incommunicable, this vision beyond all vision must yet be communicated. It requires its "unique sign" by which its communication would be concentrated and facilitated. Perhaps Nietzsche found that sign in the pyramid-shaped boulder he encountered on the shores of Lake Silvaplana, near Sils-Maria, which is where he experienced his traumatic vision of the eternal recurrence. Or the sign of the Circle, the Vicious Circle, is the "unique sign" for the inexpressible whole of this vision. But lest it be forgotten, passed over as just a fortuitous hallucination, the incommunicable must take some kind of form, it must attain significance, must take flight as a moving signifier in Nietzsche's oeuvre. However, the experience of the Eternal Return is ostensibly a remembrance; forgetting was its active force. Even naming this highest thought of the Eternal Return constrained it and committed it to forgetting. Forgetting occurs each time the vision of the Eternal Return is called the Vicious Circle, whereby the ecstatic experience is called back to the quotidian languages and stereotypes of the "herd" and is duly transformed, de-formed, and forgotten in and by all such names. Naming the Eternal Recurrence is not a matter of expression here, but of objectification, the way an impulse, the way a blinding vision, becomes the neutralized object of a proposition. The "highest vision" sinks to the level of being the object of commentary where it is captured on a conceptual scale ranging from highest of all metaphysical ideas to a mere lunatic's delusion, a "Vicious Circle." The French *Vicieux* connotes "depravity"—the vision becomes typecast as a baseless theory of existence, nihilistic, life as pointless and morbid, offering no way out from the ceaseless and senselessly circular return of the same blindly suffering material world. The sole point such a doctrine of the Vicious Circle would seem to be exhausted in showing how any notion of a beginning and an end and any notion of God, Truth, or Self are but illusions to overcome. But so long as this remains but a doctrine, an assemblage of words and concepts, nothing is ever overcome. Conversely, the vision—communicated to Nietzsche one dark night by a daemon, a "spider"—can degenerate into a new age mantra, "affirm life," which only trivializes the horror of Nietzsche's vision. Illusions are simply reinstated in new stereotypical forms. In the vision of the Eternal Return, Nietzsche surpasses the limits of all that can be said or seen, yet as soon as he had to come down from his mountaintop in order to communicate his experience, his visions, he could only do so in the terms of the codes of everyday signs. This *höchste Gefühl*, Nietzsche's original, indelible, and maddening experience, thus becomes reduced, neutralized by culture to formulae, the "Vicious Circle," where it withers as the very image and prize of nihilistic modernist despair. Thus, seeing is betrayed by saying. Perhaps such unsustainable moments of lucidity find their means of communication not in words or concepts but only in laughter, the laughter of the gods who die of laughter whenever any one of them would assert itself as the one, supreme god.

The experience of the Eternal Return compares with Acteon's seeing of the goddess Diana at her bath: a seeing that renders, that tears to pieces. "Is there any vision more mad than the one that greets Actaeon's eyes through the parted foliage?" Or, Klossowski asks, quoting the goddess, Diana, "Now you may tell you saw me here unclothed / If you can tell at all."²⁷ How, like Acteon's vision of the goddess Diana, can the solitude of Nietzsche's highest thought of the Eternal Return be communicated, be seen and said, without being trivialized in and by the gregariousness of everyday signs? Phrased differently, if significance requires, as in the very structure of a sentence or a proposition, a beginning and an end, then what sentences, what memories, can say what *is* without beginning or end, the Eternal Return? In his "On Maurice Blanchot," Klossowski situates Blanchot's work in terms of a "remembrance" that is also at the heart of his own work: "the Remembrance (*Souvenir*) of what in itself is only the absence of all memory, therefore forgetting: being, this perpetuity that supports neither beginning nor end."²⁸ Is this experience of the Eternal Return not the impossible experience, the limit experience of language, as of all seeing and saying, where both seeing and saying, where the identity and unity of any Self or "I" that may be said to be the ground or the subject—the *sub-jectum*—of the experience, breaks down, is experienced as an absence by a consciousness that is itself this very absence? (*R*, 23). Like Acteon, torn to pieces, blind and stammering. But with the rising and falling of intensities, like waves on the sea, so too does the highest vision give way once again to the lowest of the codes of everydayness. In his readings of Nietzsche's experience of a highest tonality of soul, through the myth of Diana and Acteon, Klossowski approaches the extremes of language and human life. He approaches the unknown. To what tricks, traps, and strategies does he resort in order to communicate this limit-experience? What would such a communication consist of that could see and say such a death-bound theophany? Would it

---

27. Pierre Klossowski, *DB*, trans. Sophie Hawkes and Stephen Sartarelli (Boston: Eridanos Press, 1990), 63/80.
28. Klossowski, *Une si funeste désir*, 159–84 ("On Maurice Blanchot," in *SDD*, 85–98).

be a message embedded in a system of signs? Or would it be a mirror play of sameness and difference, of humans and the divine and the daemonic play of simulacra that passes between them? Would communication in this instance not communicate concepts but instead be more like a contagion, a daemonic solicitation of the body by the text and of the viewer by the picture? It would be a daemon's work. Must Klossowski not have the inventiveness of a daemon in order to bring to words and to vision what cannot but must be seen? His work, whether written or drawn, with its simulacral plays, comprises a philosophical-mythological theater that has its secret operator, its secret stage manager and designer, a daemon, a being between the human and the divine. Klossowski's art likewise must be seen as situated daemonically between the language of everydayness and the silence of intensities, between the beginning and ends of words and signification, and the "being forever where sense is lost,"[29] between art and life. His work is above all but "a pantomime of the spirits," as he himself describes it, a philosophical theater of death and desire, a theater of the Eternal Return.

But before we consider this theatrical dimension, there is yet another matter in play in the combat against culture. For Nietzsche, the combat against culture is a combat against the modalities of servitude and so a combat against the guilt that comes with it (*NVC*, 10). Culture is a "slave morality." What does this mean?

As Klossowski shows, although Nietzsche had little knowledge of Hegel's famous passage from the *Phenomenology of Spirit*, the Master-Slave dialectic, it can be a useful interpretive tool for understanding Nietzsche's notion of a "slave culture." Hegel's dialectic shows how a confrontation emerges between two initially autonomous consciousnesses, a life-death struggle through which the distinction between a Slave and a Master arises as a Gestalt or one of the shapes or figures in Hegel's *Phenomenology of Spirit*.[30] Death's melting power plays a key role in this confrontation. In Hegel's dialectic, a slave mentality is born out of the insuperable fear of death that overwhelms but one of the two consciousness confronting one another in this struggle. The struggle between these two consciousnesses is a struggle for recognition. One of the consciousnesses in this struggle is willing to give its life: recognition or death, it proclaims. But the other balks; it shrinks before death. It would

---

29. Klossowski, "On Maurice Blanchot," in *SDD*, 85.
30. G. W. F. Hegel, *Phänomenologie des Geistes* (Hamburg: Felix Meiner Verlag, 1952), 146ff. Trans. by A. V. Miller as *The Phenomenology of Spirit* (Oxford: Clarendon Press, 1977), 111ff.

rather live and so submits to the other's demands for recognition. Thus, the consciousness that desires the recognition of the other more than life itself becomes the Master. The other, clinging to life, melting with fear in the face of death, relinquishes its freedom to the other. Contrary to an ancient view, Hegel shows that slavery is not a natural condition but something created, something that arises in and through the dialectic set forth in his *Phenomenology*. The slave mentality is created when a fear of death drives consciousness into submission. This basic, instinctive and insuperable fear becomes the basis for its bondage and for its seeking security in the comfort of the herd. In Nietzsche's terms, a herd mentality, a herd morality, here arises that becomes the basis for culture. Hegel's Mastery, or "Lordship," consists in idleness. Basking in the recognition of its Slave, it only consumes the labor of the Slave. While the Master is idle, a consumer, the Slave, works, setting the Master's table. Through its work and self-denial, it produces the culture that the Mastery consumes and enjoys. It may be that work "makes free," but in this case it is the freedom that is the truth of bondage. The culture that emerges, the culture that is to become the truth of Mastery, is thus a Slave culture, the culture of the herd, a culture that Nietzsche sees in everything from art to religion, in all the cultural forms that assuage and mollify the terrors that strike the heart of the Slave.

Klossowski notes how Nietzsche remained foreign to any notion of a consciousness mediated by another consciousness (*NVC*, 12/31–33). Nonetheless, Nietzsche might agree with aspects of the Hegelian dialectic: slave culture is a guilt culture, a culture of fear, the culture of Christian morality, in other words, the culture that finds its salvation in work and self-denial, in the steady hand that turns against the dark, irrational pulsions and desires of the body in order to produce what is necessary for salvation and so to maintain its place in the huddled safety of the gregarious herd. Nietzsche is himself the beneficiary of this culture. He lives in it and benefits from it. Yet, it was also the culture against which he rebelled, recognizing that culture exists only for those who are able to enjoy it, namely bourgeois Christian culture and morality. It is largely through art that this historical and cultural world is produced as a monumental legacy of holy books, churches, towers, and prisons.

What Klossowski and Nietzsche recognize is that a cultural manifestation such as art is produced as an *affect*; it is rooted in a field of intensities of which it is an interpretation and a reproduction. Art arises not from spiritual inspiration or from the necessary logic of a dialectic, as in Hegel, but from the chaos of the forces and pulsions of the body. By becoming a cultural pastime, art silences or contains these intensities by reducing them to the polite chatter of bland, blunted images. Art might thus disappear by having its affects swallowed or absorbed—not just in and by Hegel's dialectic of Spirit but by the world of commerce, making it but another exchangeable product in a global industrialized world. This is a possibility even Nietzsche recognized. So long as art remains a cultural, commercial form of idleness, the idleness of masters and museums, it draws upon the servitude of a large number of people, as in Hegel's dialectic. As it is for Nietzsche and Klossowski, so much of what passes for art today is the product not of intensities but of a garrulous slave culture, a culture of guilt, a culture that would prefer to look away. It even becomes something "criminal," its sanctity resting on the suffering of the masses that sustain it. Art, in summary, rests upon the prevalence of inequalities, and these inequalities made life unbearable for Nietzsche. This questioning of art and language, the combat against its cultural modalities of naming and forgetting the pulsions at its core, is also at the core of Klosswski's own combat against culture.

Nietzsche's vision of the Eternal Return, his highest and most intense experience of its incommunicability—greater even than the shadow of death—brings with it a series of ruptures that characterize his own combat against culture and that Klossowski continues to pursue in his own writings and drawings: the rupture of the principle of identity; the rupture with principle of communication; the rupture with any principle of goals, of *sens*, direction, purpose (time as circular, nondirectional); and the rupture with the principles of exchange, exchanging the unexchangeable, and the ever renewed combat against the stereotype by which culture and cultural gregariousness are maintained. And this combat is never ending. It must be recommenced again and again, ever recommencing with the movement of the Eternal Return, a movement ever embraced by the twin forces of remembering and forgetting.

The first crucial pages of *Nietzsche and the Vicious Circle* show the consequences of this combat against culture for the philosopher. The thinker, the poet, and the artist shall have new roles as "actors," participants in a daemonic "pantomime of the spirits." In the pages that follow upon this in *Nietzsche and the Vicious Circle*, Klossowski, through Nietzsche, develops a semiology of intensities and so addresses the question of what, in art and language, survives these ruptures, which are not really "breaks" but more a way of turning inside-out the bourgeois culture Klossowski both lived within and struggled against.

Where the philosopher is an artifact of culture, any combat against culture would have as its consequence an extensive overhaul of the role of the philosopher. The first sentence of *Nietzsche and the Vicious Circle* asks, "Is the 'philosopher' still possible today?" No longer able to play the role of the sage who proffers the Truth, the philosopher now seems damaged, degraded, degenerated. With no absolutes to contemplate, the philosopher is reduced to being "just a dilettante" with a "thousand antennae," stripped of any capacity to "direct or command." What's the philosopher to do? Klossowski-Nietzsche's[31] response: no longer at home in the institutional discourses of knowledge, might the philosopher invent a semiology of intensities or "become a great actor, a kind of Cagliostro philosopher," as Nietzsche says, or a "mime," as Klossowski suggests? An actor, the philosopher would also be a *daemon*, a fluid point between humans, agitated by their passions, and their impassive, simulacral gods, between the cultural stereotypes, the institutional languages, and the infinite chaos from which they emerge. But there is still one more role left for the philosopher to assume, one more mask to try, discovered so long ago and never quite abandoned: the double role of the daemon and the priest, the role of one who can, at the Eucharist of art and writing, transform a body into something spiritual.

Klossowski's combat against culture will be a combat against the bourgeois morality that makes of that culture a slave culture determined to silence the uproar of affects that emerge from the body, the physical, human body, as well as from the body of language and art and all that links both with death and desire. What emerges from this combat against culture will be a new adventure, a new role for the philosopher, the poet, and the artist, those three whose vocation it is to combat against the prevailing cultural stereotypes, stereotypes that ossify and turn against life. A new adventure in the imbrications of writing, painting, theater, and philosophy begins between Nietzsche and Klossowski, a new situation for art and the artist: henceforth, their work shall not be the classical work of resemblance, laboring in the work of producing identities and differences, but shall be the daemonic play of simulacra bearing no reference to fixed identities or transcendental ideals, as in the classic Platonic schema, being instead the juncture where an intensity turns back upon itself, designates itself, and as so becomes a "sign," a unique sign, by which the incommunicable is communicated.

---

31. Regarding "Klossowski-Nietzsche," I am here identifying the two positions as actually one. Klossowski is not just writing a commentary about Nietzsche, he is identifying with what Nietzsche says about the philosopher being a "mime," something Klossowski shares.

A Semiology of Intensities:
Signs, Phantasms, and Simulacra

> The simulacre is never that which conceals the truth—it is the truth which conceals that there is no truth. The simulacre is true.[32]
>
> —*Ecclesiastes*, quoted by Jean Baudrillard

Henceforth, philosophy will escape the institutional modalities of "savoir" by becoming a pulsional semiotic, a "semiology of intensities," essentially an act of resistance against everydayness, against the stereotypes and conventions of culture, here called the "codes of everyday signs." This semiology might take a variety of modes of presentation: poetic, artistic, contemplative, and so on. This new work, the work of the artist, the poet, and the thinker, will reconnect thinking and culture with life.

When Klossowski asks, what, for Nietzsche, is thinking, he finds the answer in Nietzsche's account of thought as a fluctuation of intensities, which means describing life in its fundamental incommunicability.[33] Elsewhere, he writes that thinking, arising from the fluctuation of intensities, itself becomes but a product of the code of everyday signs by which the agent (*sûppot*) thinks, makes statements, or remains silent. This general and always fluctuating code establishes itself in the identity of the thinking agent. It is useful, perhaps necessary to life, for it resists the incessant flows of intensities and so fashions a state of relative lucidity. But with lucidity comes forgetfulness, the forgetfulness of the life of intensities, a life beyond all remembering. The codes of everyday signs are modes of forgetting insofar as they give birth to a reign of stereotypes, as when a phrase or a look is repeated through images, songs, and words. Forgetting is the neutralization of intensities, their reinvestment into strategies of useful work. The stereotype has this effect: just like an intensity, it is a counter-intensity. The effect of the stereotype is to neutralize intensity by reducing it, stabilizing it, making into an exchangeable thing, and so returning intensity's outburst to the limits of what Freud called "the pleasure principle" whereby intensity can be resisted and contained. Klossowski on Nietzsche: "The thinking

---

32. *Ecclesiastes*, quoted by Jean Baudrillard, "La précession des simulacres," in *Le simulacre*, TRAVERSES/10 39 (Paris: Minuit, Centre National d'Art et de Culture Georges Pompidou, 1978), 3.

33. Pierre Klossowski, *Du signe unique: Feuillets inédits* (Paris: Les Petits Matins, 2018), 81.

agent exists only because of the greater or lesser resistance of the impulsive forces—which constitutes the agent as a corporeal unity with respect to the code of everyday signs" (*NVC*, 37/65–66).

Yet however Nietzsche may combat against it, he recognizes how we are all also and always dependent on this code precisely because it shelters the absence and forgetting necessary to life. Human life drifts within it, almost floating, like the dust on a mirror, over the void of chaos that lies beneath, the chasm of a "hidden inner depth," something unexchangeable, unspeakable, monstrous, one might suppose, because it does not signify anything, does not stand for or represent anything, the void of "Chaos" (40–41/71–72).

The code of everyday signs is, then, but the abbreviated form, the simulacra of the impulsive movements of intensities and bodily gestures. In the form of personal names, the code establishes the agent's identity by which they become an agent, having a recognized exchange value. The code establishes itself in every person's inner monologue of thinking and is the source for its own illusory identity and sense of personal necessity. What is outside, namely the social codes of language that define our world, then becomes the agent's "interior," by which the chaotic, disruptive flow of impulses can be resisted and the supposed unity of the agent be maintained, or interrupted, by silence. Inner life is just the outside, the code of everyday signs, speaking within us. As Klossowski writes, quoting Nietzsche, life's origins may lie in chance combinations, but it must maintain itself and believe in its own necessity. The truth of such necessity is, however, only a belief, articulated in and by the code of everyday signs whereby "truth becomes an error without which life could not live" (45/76).

Abandoning the speculative realm of traditional German idealism, Nietzsche's combat against culture is thus a combative assertion not of an "I" (*Ich*) but of a singularity against the reign of gregariousness and the cultural stereotypes that protect and nurture such gregariousness. It is a combat against the morality of the herd, whereby the impulses that seek safety in numbers and established ways of seeing become dominant. Against this, Nietzsche and Klossowski simulate the "preliminary elements of a conspiracy," which is that of the mutism, or silence of the body, the body as the "obstacle" of the singular individual, mutely opposed to culture's loquaciousness, the disruptive force of a singular silence that interrupts the constant chatter of the code of everyday signs.

A paradoxical "semiology": Would it not be both a science, a cultural form of knowledge and teaching, and at the same time the rejection of such a science and a combat against it as a cultural form? What is the source of these signs Klossowski invokes? How do they come about? What do they communicate? How are they related to the act of thinking and to moral judgments, the kind of judgments that frame, inform, and even determine the way we look at art? Are these signs a combat against such a domain of judgments?

Nietzsche's notebooks from the 1880s, the trouble-stalked years contemporaneous with his *The Gay Science* and *Human, All Too Human*, provided Klossowski with not so much a doctrine but a vocabulary, an inspiration and an orientation for articulating his own conception of creativity. Klossowski is, of course, an erudite student of Nietzsche, as he was of Sade, but he is neither a commentator nor an acolyte. Through Nietzsche, and in a compassionate act of thinking and reading Nietzsche's notebooks that detail his wanderings, his sufferings, his ecstasies and insights, Klossowski finds a way to communicate the aim and meaning of his own art, be it in writing or drawing, as an art that paradoxically denies any ultimate aim or meaning. Klossowski's art emphasizes discontinuity, differences, and repetitions. It presents, in images and writings, the ruptures that the "conspiracy" of a "mutism" introduces into the declarations of the code of everyday signs. Phrased otherwise, the Nietzschean-Klossowskian semiology sketches the breaks and discontinuities that the "real" of somatic impulses and intensities introduces into the symbolic order of culture and language. This, then, is the thrust of Klossowski's semiology of intensities: to double the cultural forms, institutions, and authorities of knowledge and teaching with a conspiracy of a disruptive silence and to show that the obverse, the underside, the reverse side of these cultural forms, institutions, and authorities is the silence and chaos of intensities, not the lucid universals of speculative reason. What semiology is this that does not fall back upon or even refer to the classical conceptions of a sign? It will show, reflected as it were in the mirror of Nietzsche's texts, how signs become stereotypes and how the disruptive play of simulacra is a bold, ever moving counterweight to the dominion of the stereotype.

Nietzsche's famous parable, "How the True World Became a Fable," from his 1888 *Twilight of the Idols*, concluded that with the True World becoming just a fable, the metaphysical distinction between truth and appearances collapses. There is no True World, a realm of eternal truths, nor are there "appearances" that would conceal this True World. This collapse of such metaphysical oppositions informs Klossowski's semiology of intensities. He rejects, for example, the distinction between the conscious and the unconscious, which can be found in Nietzsche but not in a way that directly anticipates the Freudian conception of the unconscious with its attendant apparatus of castration and repression, displacements and condensation. What we call the unconscious is just a designation of the everyday code of signs, a product of the cultural domain of knowledge, teaching, and declarative language (*NVC*, 37/65). "The terms conscious and unconscious," Klossowski writes, "are therefore applicable to nothing that is real. If Nietzsche made use of them, it was only as a 'psychological' convention, but he nonetheless let us hear what he did not say: namely, that the act of thinking corresponds to a passivity, and that this passivity is grounded in the fixity of the signs of language whose combinations simulate gestures and movements that reduce language to silence."[34]

So, the first thing we learn is that the semiology of intensities shall be a semiology of somatic impulses and that this shall constitute in the rhythm of its risings and fallings, a domain of inner silence—source from which the obstacle of mutism arises beneath the loquacity of everyday signs.

Rejecting the conscious-unconscious distinction as just a product of the cultural domain of everyday signs and corresponding to nothing real, Klossowski nonetheless establishes two parallel levels in constant exchange with one another: the level of intensities and the code of everyday signs, the reign of the cultural stereotype that Klossowski and Nietzsche would like to combat and disrupt. Other texts, *The Laws of Hospitality*, *Diana at Her Bath*, or *The Baphomet*, for example, continue to upend any conception of there being two hierarchical levels in the agent (*suppôt*), an unconscious and a consciousness. Abandoning the hierarchical conscious-unconscious distinction, Klossowski posits a doubling that recalls the Catholic doctrine of the "communication of idioms," which refers to the double nature of Christ, a singular being but possessing two natures in a hypostatic union, one human, another divine.[35] Thus the doubling of Roberte, who is both an official of the state censorship board and a woman who conceals and resists—who self-censors, as it were—the upsurge of her own tumultuous desires. Or the doubling of Diana, both untouchable goddess, pure divine spirit, and, in her epiphany, an irresistible woman, or the Baphomet in Klossowski's novel, both an androgenous young boy and one inhabited by the pure spirit of Teresa of Avila. All of these characters must fight off the importune ravages of those

---

34. *NVC*, 43/72. See also, "Ni conscience ni inconscience," in *Du signe unique*, 92–93.
35. See Pierre Klossowski, *Roberte, ce soir*, 126. Trans. by Austryn Wainhouse as *Roberte Ce Soir* (New York: Grove Press, 1969), 32; and Arnaud, *Pierre Klossowski*, 94ff.

who would like to possess them sexually by possessing their "properties," or attributes, while at the same leaving the purity of their divine nature untouched and untroubled.[36] This theme of the doubling of the *sûppot*, of the agent, is just one of many such doublings and foldings that run throughout Klossowski's work, both written and drawn, as we have seen: the doubling of consciousness by the unconscious, of speech by silence, of the body and flesh by the spirit, of writing by drawing, of lucidity by chaos, of "the inside and the outside," of what can be seen and said with what cannot.

Meanwhile, let us now return to Klossowski's reading of Nietzsche's semiology of intensities. Here too the theme of doublings and discontinuities returns. A sign is the doubling of an intensity, its "reproduction," albeit in an abbreviated form. It is the trace of an intensity, a "residue," something left behind in and by the movement, the upward or downward movement of an intensity.

Recall a question posed earlier: How can a tonality, a *Stimmung*, of soul, at its highest pitch of intensity, the *höchste Gefühl*, become a thought? In the postface to *Les lois de l'hospitalité*, Klossowski asks, "Isn't it strange that intensity can designate itself as thought?" (*LH*, 338; trans. mine). At that highest pitch of intensity, it would seem that the lucidity of thought is excluded by this intensity. Yet Klossowski's claim is that thought is most coherent with itself at this highest intensity, when at the same time it is most incoherent to everyday quotidian life. Hence, the incommunicability of the thought of the eternal return. For Klossowski, the signs of quotidian life are essentially "signs of being and having." But the intensity of thought at its highest *Stimmung* excludes these. The coherence of thought is silence, not the linkages of signs of being and having.

Let us summarize this paradoxical situation. First, a *Stimmung* is a fluctuation of intensity. It seems that intensity always seeks to communicate itself, as though it cannot remain with itself. Does communication fan the flames of an intensity, so to speak, bringing it to new heights? Only by a reflexive movement of turning back on itself and designating itself, interpreting itself, doubling itself, does intensity actually fade, diminish, fall away such that its former incommunicability is now designated by a *sign*. Silence is shattered. An intensity is now communicable, its constraining power expelled by being transformed in and by intensity's reflexivity.

Let's explore this reflexivity a bit. In the postface to *Les lois de l'hospitalité*, Klossowski writes that this reflexive movement, the movement of

---

36. Klossowski, *Du signe unique*, 96; trans. mine.

intensity's turning back on itself, is a movement of self-interpretation. There is a priority here: intensity's reflexivity first designates itself before being designated by a sign, even a unique sign (*LH*, 338). Interpreting itself, or designating itself, here means that the intensity divides itself (*se partage*), separates from itself and comes back together (*se disjoigne, se rejoigne*), and in doing so becomes a "counterweight" to itself (*NVC*, 60/96). The rising and falling of pulsions, their "*impulse* and *repulsion*, is already interpretative" (47/77; Klossowski's emphasis). The act of self-interpretation is here a doubling of intensity as it folds back upon itself in a movement of impulse or repulsion. These moments of interpretation are the moments of the rise and fall of intensities, likened to waves on a sea, rising and falling, forming and breaking again back into the depths. Klossowski recognizes that this is just a "simple observation" and carries little weight in answering the abiding question of how signification can arise from what has no meaning. Again, the "*agent* of meaning" (Klossowski is not using the term *sûppot* here) is intensity, which is only an intensity—by itself it has no meaning. If intensity is to constitute meaning, it must do so in this reflexive, almost Hegelian dialectical movement of separating from itself and returning back upon itself and so moving, as though in a Hegelian *Aufhebung*, to rise above itself and so become not just an intensity but the "agent of signification." Is signification the counterweight here? Again, an intensity becomes or acquires a meaning; meaning is a repetition of intensity that is also a reduction of intensity. Klossowski: "How then does it," (an intensity), "acquire a meaning, and how is meaning constituted in the intensity? Precisely by turning back on itself, by *repeating* and, as it were, *imitating* itself, it becomes a sign"[37] (61/98; italics mine). The key terms here are "repeating" and "imitating": the becoming of a sign is an imitation that is first a repetition of intensity. Is this reflexivity of intensity also a kind of rudimentary mimesis? Mimesis would be a repetition, not representation, a "*ressemblance*" that, more than a mere resemblance, would be the repetition of an intensity, the attempt to make it signify something, to make it eloquent.

We could say, perhaps, that Klossowski's "*ressemblance*" is something like a metaphor in the sense of its being a "transfer," a transposition, a repetition, a reactivation of the force of an intensity, but not a mere resemblance of intensity. Intensity is there in the *ressemblance*; it is not just imitated but

---

37. French original: "Comment alors lui vient un sens et comment se constitue le sens dans l'intensité? Mais justement, en revenant sur elle-même, même dans une fluctuation nouvelle! En quoi, se répétant et comme s'imitant, elle deviant un signe." *NVC*, 61/98.

reactivated, albeit abbreviated. Klossowski's mimetology is "metaphorical" in this sense. An intensity springs from chaos and so cannot be copied, duplicated, but only mimed. A sign or a simulacre mimes an intensity. Imitation, mimesis, mime: there is a role and play of the mime at the level of intensities. Thus the "imposter-philosopher" as "mime" reactivates what has already been occurring at the level of intensities.

The key term here, in Klossowski's book on the Eternal Recurrence, is "repeating" (*répétant*), repeating as doubling. Through the eternal repeating of the Eternal Recurrence, doubling will go to infinity. But always as a doubling, a repetition, in which something of the original force of an intensity is dissipated. Reflexivity, repetition effects the dissipation or "abbreviation" of intensity and so is the essential force in the production of signs and simulacra in Klossowski's pulsional semiology. Through repetition and imitation, an abbreviation of the constraining impulse occurs such that the impulse can now be led back to the coherent unity of the agent (*sûppot*). Thus a repetition, an imitation, and a reduction of the intensity facilitates the success of the abbreviating system of signs, enabling it to reduce the impulse or repulsion of the intensity to an intentional state of the agent and so to acquire signification.

> The agent now thinks or believes it is thinking. Intellect is nothing more than a repulsion of anything that might destroy the cohesion between the agent and the abbreviating system. . . . Fluctuations always oppose their reduction in and by the abbreviating system. Thought emerges as the result of a momentary relation of power between impulses, those that dominate and those that resist. . . . A combat of impulses conditions the agent, yet the agent is ignorant of it. A new cohesion results that is beyond that agent, between the body and Chaos—a state of tension between the fortuitous cohesion of the agent and the incoherence of Chaos. (*NVC*, 49–50/79–80)

And as for Roberte, where does she stand in this "state of tension between the fortuitous cohesion of the agent and the incoherence of Chaos?" Is she not just a bit of a stereotype? As a simulacre, as a "unique sign," her persona is a doubling repetition, the imitation of an intensity. But by also thus being the diminution of intensity she is essential in so far as she makes the life of implacable intensities livable. As a sign, a simulacre, a "type," Roberte is the form taken by a formless intensity, an intensity that was unlivable until it could be reduced to a sign, "Roberte," and signed by Pierre Klossowski.

Moreover, let us note in passing Klossowski's preference for the word and the concept of a "sign." How does his account of the sign depart from other contemporary formulations, those of Saussure and Lacan, for example?

A sign, as conceived by Saussure, has two essential components: a signifier and its signified. The signifier is the phonological element of a sign, not the actual acoustic sound but the mental sound image, a mental "acoustic image," in Saussure's words. The signified, meanwhile, is composed rather than given, composed of other signifiers. Of course, Klossowski's sign does not refer to an "acoustic image" but only to the silent chaos of inner intensities. Saussure's account of the acoustic image makes no such mention of any underlying impulses or unconscious dimensions.

Lacan, on the other hand, does assert the importance of the unconscious for his semiology. But he differs from Saussure not only on this point but also in his emphasis not on "signs" but on "signifiers" that float free from their anchorage in a phonic "acoustic image." Lacan's signifier has a structuring, constitutive role in the unconscious, something not found in Saussure. Lacan's signifier is famously defined as representing something for another signifier. Lacan thus privileges the signifier over both the subject and the sign. Lacan's "subject" is not a primary, substantial reality but a product of the symbolic order. As such, it is divided between consciousness and unconsciousness, a division that is constituted and revealed by signifiers. "The fact that the signifier reveals to the subject his own division should not make us forget that this division stems from nothing other than that very same play, the play of signifiers—signifiers, not signs. Signs are polyvalent: they may represent something to someone but the status of that someone is uncertain whereas the signifier always represents a subject to another signifier," and this is "the structure of all unconscious formations: dreams, slips of the tongue, and witticisms, and it explains the subject's original division."[38]

In this elementary and constitutive role, might Lacan's account of the signifier also suggest itself to Klossowski, giving him pause to reflect on his unchallenged use of the term "sign"? Does Klossowski's "sign" have a similar function as the "signifier" in Lacan? Does the signifier help explain, as Lacan suggests it does, the subject's profound and constitutive division within itself? Such a division, it seems, is the subject of *Roberte, ce soir*. But

---

38. Jacques Lacan, *Écrits*, trans. Bruce Fink with Héloïse Fink and Russell Grigg (New York: W. W. Norton, 2002), 712–13 (French in *Écrits* II, 320).

the division in Klossowski's novel differs from Lacan's account. For Lacan the division is more unconscious, a function or effect of the inscription of the "symbolic order" onto the "subject," thereby subjecting it by giving it a name and an identity. Lacan's "subject" is always thus "subjected."

Where Lacan's "subject" is divided between conscious and unconscious registers, Roberte's division is otherwise inscribed as a "duality of idioms." Klossowski's account of the division between what Roberte says in public (as she argues and debates and performs her role as state censor) and what she does privately and secretly is a different division. Lacan's notion of the divided subject is much richer than the simple duality of a split personality. The question could be posed in this way: Are Roberte's divisions between her public and her private personae, between what she says in discourse with Octave and what she writes to herself in her diary, between the stiffness and chastity of her daily dress and the ease with which it all comes off in the secret places of stairwells and basements, is all this the effect of the imperative inscription of the symbolic order—the "Big Other" as Lacan calls it, the domain, in other words, of language and of phallocentric institutions like marriage and the state censorship board or the Catholic Church—onto her body and desires? Are her desires—and even her name, Roberte—all products of that inscription and the decisive cut, the cut of castration, that constitutes Lacan's divided subject? Such may be the case. On the other hand, can Roberte's actions be seen as ways of resisting and undermining this largely phallocentric symbolic order? But to experiment with the function of the signifier in this Lacanian sense, Klossowski would have to subscribe to Lacan's notion of the unconscious, structured, as he famously says, by signifiers, "like a language," and so distinguished from consciousness, the realm of the ego and the quotidian codes.

Contrary to Freud and Lacan, Klossowski also claims that the distinction between conscious and unconscious actually presupposes rather than challenges the unity and identity of the subject. Whatever unity the "I" maintains in the midst of all such divisions, any such unity of a self, Klossowski writes, is but a "flickering memory, maintained exclusively by the designations of the everyday code which intervene in accordance with changing excitations, upon which they impose their own linkages in order to conceal the total discontinuity of our state" (*NVC*, 38/67). Rather than the Freudian distinction between conscious and unconscious, Klossowski insists upon the distinction or the discontinuity between silence and the declarations or enunciations of the everyday codes of signs (37/66–67). Klossowski's firm response to the invitation of psychoanalysis denies any role of the Freudian unconscious in his work. Impulses, obsessive forces, or phantasms do not comprise "unconscious formations." "Our inner depth, *le fond*, is not exchangeable because it does not signify anything" (40/68). This is a major departure from Lacan's account.

Klossowski's reading of Nietzsche claims that signification arises almost as a transfiguration of materiality into spirituality. Signification arises from a materiality, from a movement of differences and repetitions, self-imitations and doublings, not from a preexisting unity or ideality that is the referent of a sign. Meaning, signification, identity, and the "reality principle" are seemingly suspended over chaos, haunted by it from within. Everything that conditions signification, identity, and relations of being and having is also its undoing. Meaning arises as a reflexive fluctuation of meaninglessness. The continuity of meaning, the continuity of a sign, if there be such continuity, arises from discontinuity, from the flux of chaos. This, then, seems to be the sign's function at this point: to introduce, to mark within chaos the limit-point of difference where signification both arises and falls.

Intensity repeats, imitates, and interprets itself, thereby producing the nullity of signs that congeal into stereotypes and the everyday codes of signification whereby the stability and continuity of gregarious everydayness is grounded and assured. The pulses of intensity are subject to a decay, or a fading. Stereotypes are but decayed, "abbreviated" intensities.

But intensity can also double back upon itself to constitute a "unique sign," where, however abbreviated, intensity's force is still quite powerful and gripping. A unique sign, the sign of the Eternal Recurrence, for example, a unique vision, Roberte or Diana, a "tonality of soul," as she is *ce soir*, at her bath. A vision that could break the world in two, the vision of Roberte or the Eternal Recurrence would thus be the breaking points for the everyday codes of signs. A sign is "unique" in this sense: it is a singular sign in which intensity has not faded away but has become an obsessive, constraining, breaking force.

This seems an extraordinary claim. Everything rests on the primacy and the power that Klossowski invests, like Nietzsche before him, perhaps, in the role that intensities, "tonalities," play in the constitution of signs and signification. The highest point of an intensity cannot be contained in any codes of signs. It can only break the world of signification in two. In and through its movement of self-differencing and return, from this self-alienation and coming back to itself, intensity can thus bring forth a "higher level," an irreducible level of signs whereby a highest tonality, in a crushing circularity back upon itself, becomes, or is carried across into a sign, the sign of the Vicious Circle, for example, or that of Roberte. Klossowski calls these "unique" signs, the explosive sign of a highest thought, a singularity of the greatest intensity. We shall be returning to this.

In sum, in Klossowski's more generalized doctrine of the sign, a sign—the "unique sign," as well—is but the "trace" of a fluctuation of intensity. Like the froth or the crest atop a wave, it marks the highest point of the afflux and so marks the point where it begins to fall. Marking the highest point, the point of greatest intensity, it can also mark the absence of intensity—and for this, "*encore*, a new afflux is necessary if only to signify this absence!" (*NVC*, 61/98). The encore resounds again! What does the sign inscribe? What is its tone, its sound and its resounding? A sign marks—"encore!"—the identity of the highest tonality of soul; its "encore" resounds, as Blanchot writes, in "in the thrall of the impossible real, that share of disaster wherein every reality, safe and sound, sinks."

Whence the "phantasm," the defining image that is so crucial to Klossowski's art and writing, and the simulacre? Are these also signs? A phantasm functions somewhat like a sign in that it is a representation, but, more than a sign, it is also an obsessive *image* for Klossowski. His monomania, as he calls it, circulates around this image, the product of intensities, the form given to impulsive, irrevocable forces. The master phantasm at work in Klossowski's work is the phantasm of a woman, of a type. The phantasm becomes an obsession, a constricting and containing force upon his soul, which can only be communicated—and communicated it must be, for there is an "exorcism" at work here—by and through a simulacre. The phantasm seems to require the simulacre, for it to be communicated, its restrictive, obsessive, daemonic chains broken, exorcized. The simulacre both *reproduces* and *reduces* the phantasm. It is not a sign considered as an agent of signification. A phantasm can become a sign, a "unique sign," whereby it reproduces the extremity of an intensity. Klossowski's practice and concept of the simulacre springs from his readings of Saint Augustine, where he describes the Roman tradition of the *theologia theatrica*, as well as from the writings of Tertullian and Hermes Trismegistus. A mingling, then, of classicism and early Church Fathers, of late paganism and early Christian doctrine. But it is Nietzsche who provides the initial vocabulary and guidelines for Klossowski's treatment of the phantasm. Summarizing Nietzsche, Klossowski writes,

> Every living being interprets according to a code of signs, responding to variations in *excited* or *excitable* states. Whence

> come *images*: representations of *what has taken place or what could have taken place*—thus a *phantasm*, which makes a discharge necessary. . . . The attraction of the phantasm is produced from the relation between impulsive forces of varying intensity. . . . A phantasm, or several phantasms, can be formed in accordance with the relations among impulsive forces, some of which will be codified when these forces intensify this or that signifying trace. (*NVC*, 47/77)

Whereas a phantasm can take the form of an obsessive image or the persistence of a name, Roberte, it does not, however, make up for a "lack," or anything missing or cut away from the subject as a result of its having been inscribed in the symbolic order. If anything, a phantasm is the index of an unbearable excess of intensity, not a lack. Klossowski's account of a phantasm thus strongly differs from the semiology on finds in Lacan or Freud.

Is there an implicit nihilism at work in Klossowski's account of the phantasm? Lyotard suggests such a possibility. Intensity's reflexivity, he suggests, is not just a "turning back" of intensity upon itself, but a "turning away" of intensity, its self-denial, as it adopts the form of a phantasm.[39] Klossowski's notion of similitude and the simulacre might appear to subscribe to an Augustinian theology of *Similitudo*, except for the exceptional influence of Nietzsche on his thought. Is Klossowski a "nihilist?" A last metaphysician, therefore? Does his account of the phantasm constitute a turning away, a turning against the life of intensity? Does it resound or echo an early Christian rancor against the life of the body? The sign, the simulacre, the phantasm, all the terms Klossowski uses instead of the word "representation," are to be understood as repetitions; similitude is a doubling. Chaos is one of the names for dissimilitude. The diminution, the discharge of an

---

39. See Lyotard's discussion in *Économie libidinale* (Paris: Minuit, 1974), 84–90. Trans. by Iain Hamilton Grant as *Libidinal Economy* (London: Bloomsbury Academic, 2021), 81–86. Lyotard writes of the phantasm: "What Klossowski understands by the name *phantasm* (is) an object fabricated out of pulsional force *turned away* from its 'normal' use, as a generator." Lyotard, *Économie libidinale*, 87–90 (*Libidinal Economy*, 86; italics mine). Lyotard furthermore writes of this phantasmic "turning away" of the pulsional forces that it evinces a nihilism, the "same nihilism we have . . . denounced in the theory of the simulacre, and therefore the persistence in Klossowski . . . of a theology of dissimilitude belonging necessarily to the Augustinian theology of *Similitudo*." *Libidinal Economy*, 81–86.

intensity is not a nihilistic way of saying "no" to intensity but of affirming it as the very life of all signification.

Nor are phantasms the products of a will. They are not produced by consciousness or practical reason but by the rising and falling of pulsional forces. When the phantasm is reproduced, it becomes a simulacre, which is, in Klossowski's words, a "willed reproduction of a non-willed phantasm, born from the life of the impulses" (*NVC*, 133/196). The phantasm can also be a "residue," something left over or left behind by an action, event, or gesture, a trace, in other words. The residual phantasm can itself in its turn take on the value of a gesture, action, or event either already completed or yet to come.

And art, Klossowski writes, "essentially reconstitutes in its own figures the conditions that have constituted the phantasm, namely the intensities of the impulses. The simulacre, in relation to the intellect, is the license that the latter concedes to art: a *ludic* suspension of the reality principle" (*NVC*, 134/197). If personal identity, as well as a clear distinction between what is true and what is false, together with the distinction between moral right and wrong linked with a perhaps naive acceptance of reality as an objective self-evident given, are all constitutive of the reality principle, then art, as the ludic suspension of this principle, acts on the basis of an incommunicable combat and chaos of intensities, the forces of pulsion and repulsion, the libidinal forces that undermine personal identity and the reality principle. The ludic work of art must occur between chaos, the field of pure forces—a chaos without signification for it is without beginning or end—and the world opened by work, the world where the reality principle holds sway, where there is always significance because there is always a before and an after, a beginning and an end, an irreversible course of things, of bodies and lives and worlds, that can only be managed for better or worse—the world, in short, where an the illusory truths of self, art, and reality are all necessary for human life to sustain itself.

Art, like the daemon, like the phantasm, dwells in the between of the human world of work and the chaos of intensities; between the combat of forces without beginning or end and the world of more or less stable, existent things; between the extinction of the individual and the world where the individual, possessed of the idea of its own necessity, is committed to doing whatever it can to ensure its own survival.

Art's position seems more precarious than that of science, for the latter is singularly committed to ensuring and working for the survival of the species. Art, by contrast, is always double, always "between"—between production and expenditure, between the clarity and distinctness promised by science and the dark tumult accessed in the gestures of the artist. This "between" of art obtains between the play of simulacral images circulating in culture and their *fond*, their chaotic substrate of intensities. The simulacral images of art are doubled as it were by their *fond*, the folding of the intensity back upon itself. The chaos of intensities surfaces for example not just in the image but also in the rhythmic gestures of the artist's hand, Klossowski's hand in this case, gripping its pencils and crayons, manically producing drawings of a woman suspended on parallel bars.

Art is the place, the scene, the screen where an intensity, a "virulence of phantasms" imitates and so repeats itself, doubling itself in *ressemblances*—the fold of a mime, the crest of a wave. This between position propels the ludic dimension of art, denying it any sense of enduring substantiality or monumentality. Klossowski's images have a delicate semitransparent quality, something he consciously pursued, which makes them more like the flickering images of a movie or a dream than the thick oil canvases hanging in museums. Which would imply, of course, that the work of art, as a work of culture, must serve two masters: both the chaos of intensities and the world of the gregarious, acculturated herd, both the sovereignty of a ludic ruin of identities and the servitude of work. Art is between the ludic collapse of substances and identities and the world of work and steady progress. On account of its need for efficacious gestures, regular and repeatable gestures and operations, the servitude of work—of artistic work—demands the discipline that circumscribes and confines the ludic. As far as the world of work is concerned, the only pleasures allowed are those that create their own reality principle, not the suspension or transgression of one as sometimes seems promised by art. While art may arise from work, from the rhythm of gestures, it is also more than work. Art is not restricted to work productive of or representing meanings and higher goals. It also has a sovereign dimension of expenditure and loss. Certainly, art must partake of the labor, as in the servile work of Hegel's bondsman, but it also irrupts in sovereign gestures and a sovereign burst of laughter. Art's "between" both supports and embellishes the world of work while at the same time, in different gestures, strikes against it, combats it, undermines it, opens it to a ludic dimension it cannot contain. Klossowski's daemonic art must be both a ludic play and the suspension of that play. We can see this doubling, this between, of art in Klossowski's characters Roberte and Diana and his famous "laws of hospitality," of which Roberte is both the defiled victim and the clever operator of that defilement.

Roberte: The Unique Woman, the Unique Sign

> Au sortir d'une période où je fus ramené trois fois de suite au même thème dont résultèrent trois variations, le phénomène de la pensée me revient, tel qu'il s'était produit avec ses hausses, ses chutes et ses absences, lorsqu'on jour, ayant cherché à relater quelques circonstances de ma vie, il m'arrive d'être bientôt réduit à un signe.[40]
>
> —*Les lois de l'hospitalité*, postface

Les lois de l'hospitalité, published in 1965, is indeed a case where the pleasure principle creates rather than defies its own reality principle. And that reality, that dream theater, has but one law: the law of hospitality, established by Octave, the principal male character in *Les lois de l'hospitalité*. In this comedic little drama on the bourgeois institution of monogamous marriage, everything turns on the interplay of revealing and concealing, like a magic show. The action is comedic with its curtains, its flashlights, its sudden outbursts and apparitional arrivals of seducers in Roberte's *salle de bains*.

First, let us give a preliminary sketch of the players in this drama and the tensions between them.

Octave is a seventy-year-old reactionary and admirer of General Patain, whose aesthetic proclivities are evident in his collection of the erotic art of one Frédéric Tonnerre, a fictitious nineteenth-century painter invented by Klossowski. He is also a professor of canon law and a happily married man, perhaps too happy, for he is sick from being so happy in his marriage. Thus, from the outset, we see on stage a heady mix of Scholastic argumentation, home economics, and bourgeois marriage, together with a most ludic play of desire.[41]

---

40. Klossowski, *LH*, "Postface," 333. ("At the end of a period when I was brought back three times in a row to the same theme from which three variations resulted, the phenomenon of thought comes back to me, just as it had happened with its rises, its falls and its absences, when one day, having tried to relate some circumstances of my life, it happens that I am soon reduced to a sign"; trans. mine.)

41. In the "Avertissement" to the *Révocation de l'Édict de Nantes*, Octave/Klossowski writes, "Je me suis borne à déduire du sacrament de marriage la réaction par chaîne à partir de l'anneau conjugal." Wilhem, who also quotes this passage, comments at length on the importance of "l'anneau conjugal" for Klossowski's laws of hospitality. But he does not see this: the marriage ring is a torus, a circle around a hole, a bit like a Möbius strip in the Lacanian topology, a continuous curving surface with both an inside and an outside turning around a center that is an absence, a void, a hole. It is, thus, the

Roberte, on the other hand, is more problematic. She is the pivot, the verb in Klossowski's *récit*, the crucial point of action in this theatrical piece. Who is Roberte, ce soir? Her persona is suspended between the parallel bars of a double life: both austere wife and sensuous, promiscuous woman. She could be easily defined by her day job outside the closed Hôtel Longchamps. An attractive, precocious woman in her thirties, she is the president of the board of censorship at the government ministry and a radical socialist who has no belief whatsoever in God. On the surface, or in accordance with the quotidian codes of her daily life, she is a highly respectable woman. At home, she is the quotidian mistress of the house, the Hôtel Longchamps, its hostess, that is to say, the one in charge of the home's economics. She is a double Roberte, a Roberte turning back upon herself with ever increasing intensities. When not a hostess, when not grooming her guests, she is armed with her sharp red pencils, her Légion d'honneur medallion pinned to her lapel, busying herself by censoring her husband's demented manuscripts. But there is always that moment, that private moment when she must put her red pencils down, as she must one night during her evening toilette. In the privacy of her dressing rooms, she is reading and censoring passages from Octave's writings. Then, the very writings she would like to destroy with her red pencils suddenly turn back on her. Reading them incites her desires and summons her spirits, her phantasms, the Guardsman and the dwarf, the personifications, the phantasms of her desires, and she is again carried away. Both censor and seducer, Roberte is a lure and a trap for desire.

Octave always wants more from his wife. It's not enough that she is hostess and government censor. He wants to know her "identité veritable."[42] A professor of theology, Octave suspects that somewhere beyond this formidable and publicly recognized epidermis there is another hidden and mute side, one more fluid and inclined to sexual adventure. For Octave, she is a woman who is not one, for she is multiple, held, as Octave might suspect, in a hypostatic union. She seems to present something of a theological problem to him: the duality of her being and her "communication of idioms," a Catholic notion referred to earlier. Is she not concealing beneath this stiff masquerade of respectability a sensuous being who responds to the language

---

very image of marriage for Octave, with its double logic of matrimonial monogamy and polyandry. Klossowski, *Les lois de l'hospitalité*, 7; and Daniel Wilhem, *Pierre Klossowski: Le corps impie*, 10/18 (Paris: Union Générale d'Éditions, 1979), 154.

42. Pierre Klossowski, "Protase et apodoses," in *l'Arc* 43 (Paris: Librairie Duponchelle, 1990), 12.

of touch and sexual desire? Octave is curious about this other dimension of her being. Certainly she lectures and debates, but does Roberte also shelter a hidden, mute essence? Does she have two or more hidden sides to her private inner life? Is her quotidian side, which is quite prolix, not doubled by this other side? A *Roberte absolue*? Roberte as phantasm? This question and this quest sparks Octave's curiosity, which is fueled no doubt by his erudition in Scholasticism and Catholicism that provide the working vocabulary and the perspective he needs to accomplish his desire to see Roberte as she absolutely is, to see her hidden, sensuous essence that lurks behind the quotidian facade, to see her as God would see her. Thus Octave is not a rake, not a libertine, but a man who wants to know. He wants to know more, where to know is to see more, perhaps too much more, like Oedipus, who also wanted to know who the woman he married really is: a being doubled, the public folded onto another face, another phantasmic life, hidden beneath the censorious public face. Octave's quest for knowledge is, of course, laughable rather than horrifying as it was with Oedipus.

So it is not jealousy "or suspicion that drives Octave in his obsession to be the eye of the voyeur, but his curiosity.[43] As Hervé Castanet also points out in his essay on Klossowski, Octave's curiosity actualizes, gives body and form to, what had been but an absence, a mystery to him. But his role as curious host consequently overrides his role as master of the house, for a master would never allow the games Octave's curiosity animates.[44] Yet by making himself a pure curiosity, and so a voyeur in his pursuit of the "absolute Roberte," as in *Les lois de l'hospitalité*, Octave does not grasp that he is not the cause of the arrangement of the laws of hospitality, but its effect: as Hervé Castanet writes, "Cependent, en se faisant objet regard, en se faisant pure curiosité, ce que ne peut saisir Octave, c'est qu'il n'est pas cause de ce qui s'agence, mais son effet."[45] Thus, this theologia theatrica is

---

43. "Si l'essence de l'hôtesse demeure ainsi indéterminée, parce qu'il semble à l'hôte qu'il lui échapperait . . . l'essence de l'hôte se propose comme un homage de sa curiosité à l'essence de l'hôtessse" ("If the hostess' essence remains thus indeterminate, because to the host it seems that something of the hostess might escape him . . . the essence of the host is proposed as a homage of the host's curiosity to the essence of the hostess"). *Roberte, ce soir*, in *LH*, 111 (English trans. from *Roberte Ce Soir*, 14).

44. Hervé Castanet, *Pierre Klossowski: La pantomime des esprits* (Nantes, France: Cécile Defaut, 2007), 134.

45. Castanet, 135. ("However, by making himself the object of a gaze, by making himself pure curiosity, what Octave cannot grasp is that he is not the cause of what is arranged, but its effect"; trans. mine.)

dominated by the desire to see. Is this a "scopic drive"? But can one say what one sees? Is speaking not seeing, and seeing not a saying?

Now for a closer inspection of these unique "laws," the entangling web in which these characters are caught.

The laws of hospitality are Octave's way of dealing with his insatiable curiosity and his intolerable situation vis-à-vis Roberte. He is terribly stuck, tormented by the curiosity he has concerning his wife's ultimate, real, and absolute essence, which always seems hidden from him. This hiddenness delights him, drives him, pushes him to want to see more. But because Octave cannot see or experience, because he cannot "actualize" Roberte's hidden essence directly, described as it is in the Scholastic terms of a theologian as an *inactualité*, he devises his laws of hospitality as a way out of this aporia. The laws are a desiring machine that produces a spectacle for Octave, a stratagem by which this hidden *inactualité* can be actualized, Roberte's non-present essence brought to presence, made visible, and, as though in a moment of catharsis, curing Octave of his torment.

Accordingly, the laws of hospitality arrange little theatrical sketches and variations of a situation in which Roberte, as austere hostess, shall end up in the intimate company of a stranger, in which situation she will let herself go and her hidden and presumably promiscuous essence be thusly manifested. In each of the little plays in Klossowski's *récit*, this scene is repeated: Roberte, the Stranger, or the sudden arrival of an apparition, the Guardsman, while she is at her bath. First, she is hostess for a dinner party of three consisting of Roberte; the guest, who is an outsider, a single male stranger hosted for dinner; and the host, Octave, who uses the dinner party as a pretext for ultimately "sharing" his wife's physical attributes with his guest. Octave's strategy, his role, is to be the voyeur on the scene as it unfolds, both a character seen by the reader/spectator and one seeing, or gazing, from behind a curtain at his wife in the arms of their guest. From the arms of their guest, or her assailant as the case may be, the ambiguous language of Roberte's physical gestures, the ambivalent language of her body, both denying and inviting, communicates her mute essence to Octave's hidden gaze. He is to discover "dans le fond," when Roberte is in contact with strangers, with the other, that her true identity is not "one" but multiple, "une pluralité de natures," which are revealed on each occasion she is in the arms of a stranger. Each time, her response is different. Octave senses that he will indeed know his wife only when she is "dans le fond," with "the unknown" (*l'inconnu*). He will experience the jouissance of his "inalienable good" (*bien inaliénable*) only when he alienates her, gives what cannot be given to the other. In this coded economy of desire, the other, the guest that looks at her and desires her, magnifies or increases Roberte's value for Octave. To desire Roberte is one thing, but to have her is another, and this is possible only through the embrace of the other. Roberte herself realizes that her fidelity to Octave depends on her betraying him with a stranger. Thus, the laws of hospitality are the laws of a paradoxical home economics, a paradoxical notion of value, which springs from this highly coded interplay of desire.[46] The laws introduce a moment of suspension into the temporal haste of the mundane. All is, generally, comedic rather than lascivious. It is laughter, coupled with eroticism, that pulls the reader/spectator in.

In a variation, described by Antoine on the very first pages of *The Laws of Hospitality*, when Octave would take Roberte in his arms, "one must not believe that he was the only one 'taking her.'" He has left their room's door slightly ajar, for a "guest" might soon arrive. But Roberte, completely given over to Octave's presence, is unaware that the guest has already arrived, is in the room where she is in Octave's arms, and is already looming up behind her, watching, just as Octave makes "his entry" (*mon oncle qui entrait*) "just in time to surprise my aunt's satisfied fright at being surprised by the guest." All of this accomplishes a virtual reversal of roles: the host, Octave, is suddenly able to feel that he is now the guest: it is his arm that quietly opens the door, it is his gaze that beholds the couple in bed together (*LH*, 11/109)—a voyeur through the eyes of another.

But this law of hospitality, like any law, must presume the principle of noncontradiction for it to be communicable and thereby command and have the force of a law. But there is a contradiction at its heart that grounds the "incommunicability" of the laws of hospitality. For this law commands that a host give or exchange what cannot be given or exchanged, namely his wife, Roberte. She is unique, and so unexchangeable. She is all the women in the world but she is unique. Something can either be exchanged or it is unexchangeable, but it cannot be both at the same time. The contradiction also shows up in the way Roberte, the unexchangeable, must betray Octave in order to be faithful to him. This could be a way of saying that the stereotypical laws of monogamous matrimony are confirmed in and by the very customs they prohibit, namely polyandry and polygamy. Monogamy thus conditions polygamy. But this contradiction places the laws of hospitality outside the rituals and practices of both mundane promiscuity, or libertinage, and prostitution, insofar as they still presuppose

---

46. Klossowski, "Protase et apodoses," 12.

the identity of a responsible ego or self—the one who enjoys—and so seeks merely to transgress rather than confirm the laws of matrimony. A "vaine liberté," Klossowski would say (*R*, 11). Rather, as in Bataille's account of transgression and the limit, the laws of hospitality must presuppose the integrity of the quotidian codes and what he elsewhere calls "la censure de la syntaxe classique" that they violate.[47] The laws of hospitality maintain the principles of proprietary monogamy, "without which the practice itself of this particular hospitality would be deprived of meaning (*sens*)."[48] The "laws" are not out to destroy the principles of monogamy but perhaps to pantomime their transgression. Again, transgression maintains, highlights, the very laws it only appears to violate.

The sanctity of the unexchangeable is confirmed in the exchange. The everyday codes of language and morality might respond by censoring the experience and the phantasms of Klossowski's laws of hospitality but they cannot understand them. The laws of hospitality, mundane though they may be, will displace the mundane everyday rituals of Octave's happily married life by introducing into the rituals and routines a wild card in the form of the stranger, the guest, an unpredictable play of chance and fortune. It will be the cure for the misery of his all-too-predictable conjugal happiness.

A similar situation obtains between Octave and Antoine. Antoine sees his aunt as a severe and austere elder sister who is also very desirable, perhaps due to her severity and austerity. Octave sees her icy austerity as an enigma, and especially this incites his erotic curiosity. Is there a lava flow of passion beneath this austerity? In the course of a conversation between Antoine and Octave—a conversation that pantomimes a Scholastic debate—Octave presents the enigma of Roberte's dual nature in the dusty terms of the theological doctrine of a "hypostatic union" of a pure, divine, unexchangeable and incommunicable essence with the flesh of an animal, a flesh defined by its human, all-too-human desires.[49] The enigma lies in the way the flesh can also dissimulate its desires under a glaze of austerity. Is her austerity just a costume? Does this glaze not melt away when she is alone in her bath or walking down a lonely avenue followed by a stranger? Where is the "true" Roberte? Is her essence lascivious while her body resists? Or is

---

47. Klossowski, "Protase et Apodose," 15; and *R*, 11.

48. Klossowski, "Protase et Apodose," 14. Klossowski writes, "*Les lois de l'hospitalité* mainiennent le principe de propriété monogamique, sans lequel la pratique même de cette hospitalité particuliére serait dépourvu de sens"; trans. mine.

49. *LH*, 126 (*Roberte Ce Soir*, 32).

it the other way around? Roberte's essence is enigmatic because it is ever a mute inactuality that is generally hidden, a "potentiality"—as the language of Scholasticism would say—ready to erupt when the time, the place, and the act are momentarily aligned. It is actualized only in and by its acts, its encounters with the other, with the stranger, the guest, or the pure spirits to which Octave has denounced her. In acts he witnesses, Roberte's essence is actualized for Antoine, but not for Octave, acts that surprise, that suspend Antoine's superficial perception of her. But these are always acts or situations that also somehow escape Antoine. He cannot describe, cannot say exactly what he sees, as in the scene when he and Octave are regarding the photo Octave took of Roberte at the moment her skirt caught fire, causing her to leap in a surprised fright into the arms of an apparent stranger. It is the same surprised fright—a fright so crucial to Klossowski—Octave wished to see in the bedroom scene described by Antoine on the first pages of *The Laws of Hospitality*. Antoine, like Octave, also wants to know—wants to see—these "frivolous" aspects, wants to see the surprised fright of Roberte at the moment she is seen or seized by the guest, the other.

Thus, the dinner guest and the curious nephew are both essential players in this drama. Are they but "screens," enabling Octave to see what his scopic curiosity drives him to see? There are others that must be mentioned, having a similar role to play. There is Victor, chosen by Roberte to be Octave's tutor, and who, incidentally, was the same stranger at the villa of Madame de Watteville into whose arms Roberte leapt the moment her skirt accidentally caught fire while she was giving a lecture. There are also the "spirits," to whom Octave has "denounced" Roberte, spirits that will come to her at night, muscular apparitions who actualize themselves in and through her body. All of these players intercede between Octave and Roberte, like a screen. Or somewhat like the mediating role of labor in Hegel's *Phenomenology*, the dinner guest, Antoine, Victor, and the spirits all set the table for the host, Octave.

The climax of this stratagem is not the close moment of touch, of skin on skin, but the moment of seeing, the spectacle that takes place at a distance, so to speak. Octave hides behind a curtain or a door watching his wife maneuver their guest into position. The "laws" make Roberte's promiscuity a spectacle and Klossowski's book more a sculptural or pictorial play than a written discourse.[50] This produces a moment crucial to

---

50. Wilhem, on "the beauty of the simulacre," where the simulacre "gathers and saturates [rassemble et sature en lui] not things, not traces, but human beings, those of the *tableau*

the narrative, a moment repeated, both written and drawn in Klossowski's book. This intensity of the act of seduction leads not to a quicker pace of the narrative but to its sudden coming to a halt, as though an intensity causes the figures to freeze in ambiguous poses: Roberte, her skirt aflame, seen falling ambiguously into the arms of a supposed "stranger" or Roberte suddenly seized on a darkened flight of stairs. A flashbulb or a flashlight illuminates the decisive moment but only for a second, lighting it up in a blinding, brief light. The book's sculptural quality thus communicates this "suspended moment" in which the figures are suddenly frozen at a moment of climax in the action. Suddenly the narrative breaks off, the time of the narrative comes to a sudden stop as though in a *syncope*, a moment of frozen climax, a heart-attack stop, as in a photograph of a sequence of action, or in a sudden, climatic halt in the spellbinding movement of a dance.[51] At this moment, a moment desired, the curtain of visibility is suddenly drawn closed once again, the figures left standing in the positions they had assumed at the decisive moment of a "syncope." Time and visibility are bound together. The suspension of one is the suspension of the other. At the moment of climax in a sequence of action, as when, Roberte, in the middle of a sentence in her lecture is suddenly aflame and falling into the ready arms of a stranger, a moment Octave just happens to photograph, there is a sudden stop. One can no longer say or see for certain what has happened. Or the moment Octave is gazing from behind a curtain onto a salacious comedy of desire as it unfolds. Suddenly, the narrative comes to a stop. At the breaking moment of an excess of intensity—the intensity of laughter?—seeing suddenly reaches its scopic climax, and the time of writing, the time of the narration, likewise, suddenly stops. Suddenly, in a moment, in a *syncope*, time and seeing are suspended (*basculé*). There is a suspension of the book, a suspension of time's before and after, a sudden halt of the narrative, a break in what can be said and seen as an intensity bends back

---

vivant," making the Klossowskian *récit* "more pictorial or sculptural." *Pierre Klossowski*, 69; trans. mine.

51. Referring to the syncope, Clément writes, "Soudain, le temps bascule" ("Suddenly, time shifts, rocks, or seesaws"). Clément further relates the syncope to dance, with its rapid, rhythmic movements punctuated by a sudden coming to a stop in which case the dancers are suddenly "arrested," "fixed" for an instant, reversed, suspended. "There is no dance without syncope," she writes. The movements and turnings that pass between the characters in Klossowski's *Robert, ce soir* could be seen as dance movements with syncopes. Catherine Clément, *La syncope: Philosophie du ravissement* (Paris: Bernard Grasset, 1990), 11–12.

upon itself. Everything in the drama must lead up to this crucial moment of seeing, a moment when visibility's intensity bends back upon itself in blindness, a moment not only of visibility but also when the lights go out, so to speak, and there is nothing more that can be seen or written. Such a moment of intensity, suspending the mundane codes not only of matrimony but also of visibility and writing, thus disrupts the mundane from within the mundane. *Les lois de l'hospitalité*, in both writing and drawing, presents an impossible, impractical, or condemnable custom on the stage of the customary world we live in, namely the adulteration of a wife by her husband. Such is Klossowski's own "combat against culture." A maddening, ludic situation spirals ambiguously and paradoxically throughout Klossowski's books, its tricks and enticements draws the reader/spectator in as a participant from behind the curtain of the printed page, inviting them to partake as well in this combat.

Not only are the characters double, but language itself is double, both a language of verbalisms and a mute language of the body, a language of gestures, glances, and pantomimes, each reflected in the mirror of the other. Gilles Deleuze insisted upon this in his essay on Klossowski: "Klossowski's work is built upon an astonishing parallelism between body and language, or rather on the reflections of one in the other."[52] As Alain Arnaud argues, the body is a "crucible of signs" in *Les lois de l'hospitalité*.[53]

Roberte's body is a body of desirable flesh and bones, a body of physical pains, suffering, and desires, but it is also a body that writes and is written upon, a body of signs, a "somatic semiotic." This makes her not only a manifold of desires and apprehensions but also a "unique sign." The body writes texts and emits signs, gestures, and other readable traces. Certain of Roberte's gestures are unique and overdetermined, such as the open palm, the gloved hand, the gesture of removing the glove, the bended knee. These gestures can be seen repeated throughout Klossowski's drawings. They are the gestures that inflame Octave's curiosity, that mark a moment of highest intensity. There is a reversibility and a parallel between the body considered as a topos of pulsions and libidinal drives and language considered as a semiotic system, as though, in Lacan's terms, the "symbolic order" has already penetrated the "Real." There is a somatic semiotic, as we have seen. For Klossowski, the body both writes—in its repetition of

---

52. Gilles Deleuze, *The Logic of Sense*, trans. Mark Lester, with Charles Stivale (New York: Columbia University Press, 1990), 280.
53. Arnaud, *Pierre Klossowski*, 136. Arnaud also quotes Deleuze.

gestures, in the characteristic glance, or the way a glove is removed from an open palm—and is written upon in the drawings of bodies, a way of writing on the body, touching yet not touching the skin. In the customs that govern its gestures, in the uniforms and fashions that adorn, conceal, and reveal its flesh, in the signs that style its femininity or masculinity and that constitute its social-sexual identity, the body is written upon in many ways. It is thus, a kind of palimpsest of signs, symbols, and signifiers that the gaze of another must interpret and decode.

Similarly, language or signs can also become flesh, the words/signs being like "shreds"' (*lambeaux*) or pieces of skin. The words of the Gospel of St. John, "Et Verbum caro factum est," are central not only to Christianity but also to Klossowski's novels. The word of the Gospels is understood and communicated in and by the body, incarnate in Christ.[54]

What word is conveyed in the body of Klossowski's writings and drawings? The word that names a woman, a physiognomy, a repertoire of looks and gestures, and a way of arguing, of speaking, of asserting her authority. A look, a physiognomy, but also a theological problem, perhaps: Roberte, like the word or the name "God," is, for Klossowski, the unique sign. Roberte also names a pivot or a topos in this drama, a place within the mundane where it folds, the instance of its reversibility. She is a doubling, a folding of an intensity back upon itself that is outside or on the margins of the mundane, a "mutism," a silent play of simulacra. But she is a mutism that also speaks to the mundane world if not through her role as hostess, then through her diaries, the supposedly secret written recollections of her adventures. Published in Klossowski's novels, the privacy of her diaries is thus betrayed as it becomes a public archive and open confessional of her hidden transgressions, showing to her reader and the mundane world what she might want otherwise to remain private, obscure, her secret. But is this not Klossowski's own doing? Is he not the author of these diaries he attributes to his Roberte? Roberte's double character makes her the unique sign for Klossowski's own passions. Whether in writing or drawing, Klossowski's hands bring her to light, his master-phantasm, his own guiding secret, hushed on the surfaces of a printed page, traveling with him between the daylight of mundane public life and the private nights of discreet unnameable passions.

Thus, Klossowski's unique sign is a folding within the mundane world of his everyday life, a little blind spot in its midst. This is how she

---

54. Arnaud, *Pierre Klossowski*, 136.

is, "ce soir," how Klossowski wishes her to be seen and known, as his own double, his other self, so to speak, a woman and a sign, a body of flesh and a body of writing, the icy eloquence of a stride doubled, tripped up by a sudden moment of passion. Mundane, she is also a woman carried away. Bundled into a basement by two brutes she has both fled and subtly provoked, she vaguely resembles Europa in Titian's painting being carried away on the back of Zeus, disguised as a bull. Her business suit unbuttoned, her Légion d'honneur pin still in her possession, the accoutrements of her mundanity dangle about her in a state of deshabille as she is tied up and assaulted in a moment of terror mingled with erotic passion. Does she not strangely resemble Acteon at the moment he is transformed into a deer, his hunting horn and tunic still dangling uselessly from his arms? This is how Klossowski wants her to be seen and read: a woman and a sign that "stands for everything that takes place in the world,"[55] unique in the way it both maintains and interrupts the mundane, a syncope for the mundane, the disturbing other side of the Légion d'honneur.

As a unique sign, Roberte stands apart from the noisy rage of the world outside the cloistered scenes of her seductions. Perhaps this is Klossowski's purpose, to bring to the stage of his secret theater a little something, almost nothing, that darkens the glare of lights, that causes a hush to spread amongst the whispers and clamors of his audience and raises the curtains on a discreetly charming bourgeois scene.

Roberte thus embodies the structure and incommunicability of the very laws of hospitality in which she is situated, laws that define her role on the little stage of Klossowski's theater. The so-called laws of hospitality are as incommunicable as the insults and jouissance that await on the parallel bars in the basement of the Galérie de Beaujolais. Such curious laws and signs these are, suspended between the parallel bars of the communicable and the incommunicable.

Both the name and the physiognomy of Roberte are the signs for a coherence of thought with itself that, while it can be named, cannot be

---

55. Daniel Wilhem writes, "Le signe unique fait coïncider une intensité, un nom, et un physionomie. Cette coïncidence cache un continuité et une discontinuité, un mouvement donnant-lieu et un mouvement oubliant-lieu" ("The unique sign brings together an intensity, a name, and a physiognomy. This coincidence conceals a continuity and a discontinuity, a movement giving place and a movement forgetting-place"; trans. mine). The unique sign casts a "shadow" over reality, and by that Wilhem means *le quotidien code*. Wilhem, *Pierre Klossowski*, 62–66.

contained within language and the laws of desire, a coherence that requires communication, that must be communicated if it is to be livable, but that is always slightly more than can be communicated. As we saw in our discussion of Klossowski's pulsional semiotic, such a unique sign occurs when, at its summit, intensity turns back upon itself and designates itself with a name, and the name thus evokes the extremity of thought's intense and incommunicable coherence with itself. Such an extreme coherence of thought with itself has an unlivable constraining force for Klossowski. The phantasm, the image, or the name "Roberte" all have this constraining force. The constraint of the name "Roberte," in its binding with an intensity of thought, is the incommunicability of thought in relation to the world. For the world, Klossowski says, such intensity is the contrary of its everyday coherence, its *basculé*. The coherence of the unique sign, the coherence of thought with itself, thus appears in the midst of the everyday world as an incoherence, as a madness, no doubt, while from the perspective of the unique sign and its coherence with itself, the coherence of the everyday world is likewise experienced as an incoherence.

The incoherence that we are in the world is an incoherence that is the necessary outcome of our requiring the code of everyday signs, the symbolic order, defined as it is by breaks and differences, by solecisms; the incoherence of the world also lies in the chains of memories that come and go, in our expectations, our projects, in all the work that could not get done if it were likewise constrained by the intensity of thought and the unique sign. The incoherence of the world is covered over and made livable by the ruse of the gregarious codes.

The unique sign thus seems to straddle what Lacan called the domains of the Symbolic, the Imaginary, and the Real, marking the point of their overlap. But the absolute coherence of the unique sign and the culmination of an intensity—the way it plunges into the Real—make for an unlivable situation. Such coherence renounces the clamor of the world and falls into the madness of isolation. "To . . . remain in the coherence of a unique sign is to renounce living in the world constituted by the incoherence that reigns in the code of quotidian signs. Thus, to accept the constraint that thought exercises through the coherence of a unique sign is to accept madness (*la folie*)." No doubt this must be escaped, "exorcised," and perhaps writing or drawing are the escape routes. Escaping the madness of coherence only returns the writer/drawer to the madness and incoherence of the code of everyday signs. But even at that level, at the level of everydayness where forgetfulness reigns, the unique sign still "watches" and asserts its compelling force. As Klossowski writes, "To renounce the unique sign in order to live in the world is no less to submit to the perpetual constraint of the unique sign in so far as the thought of this sign watches us (*nous épie*): be it as madness."[56] This force of the unique sign, the force of its very mute coherence, compels Klossowski to write.[57] Writing or drawing assuages the terror of his mania and offers a way out, albeit only temporarily. The suffocating weight of his mania, its constraining force, is strong enough to force an abandonment of writing in favor of drawing that has yet other demands: the striking disparity between the large formats of his images and the diminutive pencils used to realize them becomes the formula for an obsessive, minute, and time-consuming attention to manual technique and details of structure and shading, gradually filling the space of the empty page, composing an equivalent to his passion, a way of externalizing it in a work that would be the means of "convincing us that we have not fallen into madness."[58]

Les lois de l'hospitalité, taken as a book, would be this equivalent and the way in which Klossowski can on one hand elude madness by creating a literary equivalent, and on the other give a place for a custom practiced at the heart of the lived incoherence of the world and maintain it through the very quotidian codes that sustain the incoherence of the world. The incoherence of the world and its quotidian codes are the stage upon which Klossowski's strange play of marital customs are both illuminated and censored for being an aberration that should not be seen. "Turn off the lights," Roberte says to her two attackers as she is strapped into a set of parallel bars in a nameless basement along the Galérie de Beaujolais.

The book, *Les lois de l'hospitalité*, becomes the stage upon which Roberte shall play her roles in the privacy of her home as well as in the stairs of a public building, or in the basements of the world of quotidian codes along the Rue de Rivoli. Roberte, a woman, a wife, a censor, and a sign, not just as a persona in a comedy but also as an absolute and unique sign. She is absolute in her desires, unique in that, as a sign, she also marks an act or juncture where the *sens*, the meaning and direction of the polite

---

56. Klossowski, "Protase et apodoses," 10–11; trans. mine.
57. See also the postface, where we return to this theme.
58. Klossowski, "Protase et apodoses," 10–11.

everyday world of quotidian codes and signs, breaks down, "passes out" so to speak, loses bits and pieces of itself, a syncope. She is, as a unique sign, as a syncope,[59] a sudden coming to a stop, a disruption of the paradoxical coherent-incoherence of the quotidian work-a-day world.

In the repeated scenes of her dishonor, and in her own ultimate suspension of good manners, in the scandalous impracticality and incommunicability of her situation, it may seem she is the victim of Octave's laws of hospitality. But she is also the maker, the spider that weaves these laws forming the strands of the web in which she keeps her Octave/Klossowski, trapped like a desiccated fly. Keep this in mind: Roberte is not a person. She is a phantasm, a simulacre, arising from Klossowski's "mania," the creation not of Klossowski, the author and consciousness that writes such good books, but of Klossowski's obsession, his inconsolable mania, the Chaos of pulsions that subtends his identity as author and artist. "Roberte"—not by day, when she has her red pencil and her stiff suit of clothing, her Légion d'honneur rosette in the buttonhole of her jacket, but "ce soir" ("this evening"), when she is at her bath or in a scene she records in her diaries, strolling through the Palais Royal followed by a man encountered on the city bus who will soon see her suspended, tied to the parallel bars that await her. Roberte tries to summon the darkness that will clothe the "ob-scene" (what must be kept off-scene or out of sight) act taking place beneath the mundane world of the closed shops and basements of the Galérie de Beaujolais.[60]

Klossowski's incommunicable laws of hospitality would have Roberte be communicable in more than one sense of this word, not as a concept or a figure having a meaning to communicate but more as an intensity, a shudder passing from the author through the hand that writes or draws, through the body of text and its images, and on to the nervous system of his reader/spectator, establishing thereby a magnetic field of intensities. *Roberte,*

---

59. Clément, *La syncope*, 11, where she writes, "La syncope: une absence du suject. Une 'eclipse cérébrale', si semblable à la mort qu'on l'appelle aussi 'mort apparente.' . . ."

60. I refer to the famous scene related in *The Revocation of the Edict of Nantes*. Suspended, bound to the parallel bars, a hunchback at her feet, her skirt unhooked, another man licking her tied, open palm, Roberte "abandons herself, 'Get rid of those lights' ('Éteignez donc!'), she commands, in a voice that is not hers anymore. But the lights stay on so she closes her eyes, 'unpenting,' (opening) herself before the lascivious stares of her attackers" ("le soulagement que j'éprouve alors à m'ouvrir enfin, à sortir de mois sous leurs regards dans cette impossible position"). *La Révocation de l'Édit de Nantes*, in *Les lois de l'hospitalité* (Paris: Gallimard, 1965), 42–44. *The Revocation of the Edict of Nantes*, trans. Austryn Wainhouse (New York: Grove Press, 1969), 138–39.

ce soir: each and every time the reader opens its pages. And this, indeed, is what Klossowski sought, to involve his reader/viewer in this drama, making them participants in this pantomime of desire.

Thus, as a unique sign, Roberte is far from having a passive role in this drama. She is not just a victim. She is also the key to putting this hidden domestic comedy into play.[61] Is her often praised beauty not the siren's call that Octave cannot resist? The lure and the trap for Octave, who will slip on the banana peel of desire, the Scholastic theologian whose predicament is enough to incite the laughter of the gods. Does she not also draw the reader/spectator into this comedy? Is the reader/spectator not also dimly reflected in the mirror before which Roberte pauses to admire herself? Does she not help set the stage for the scene involving the two men and the parallel bars? The gaze, Octave's own gaze, by which he hoped to see Roberte's mute, hidden side as God would see her, will be returned, will seem to look back at him. He is the one who will be torn to pieces—like Acteon—as he looks to see what cannot be seen and said.

Les simulacra

Before turning to *Diana at Her Bath* and its sadly all-too-human story of the hunter, Acteon, and his impossible dream, let us first consider Klossowski's earlier, 1950 essay on Bataille, "The Mass of Georges Bataille,"[62] ostensibly a review of Bataille's 1950 novel *l'Abbé C*, then his 1963 essay on Bataille, "Du simulacre dans las communication de Georges Bataille," reprinted in *Ressemblance* (1984). His reflections on Bataille more than touch upon the very distress Klossowski himself experienced as an artist and writer: not just the stereotypical problem of the inadequacy of a language of notions, of a gregarious code of signs to communicate the solitude of an experience,

---

61. Blanchot insists on the comedic dimensions of Klossowski's narratives. Klossowski "brings to literature what since Lautréamont it has lacked . . . the hilarity of the serious" (*l'hilarité du sérieux*) "a humor that goes much further than the promises of this word, a force that is not only parodic or a force of derision, but calls forth a burst of laughter and point to laughter as the ultimate meaning of theology." Blanchot, "The Laughter of the Gods," in *Friendship*, trans. Elizabeth Rottenberg (Stanford: Stanford University Press, 1997), 170; "Le Rire des Dieux," in *l'Amitié* (Paris: Gallimard, 1971), 193. Passage also quoted in Wilhem, *Pierre Klossowski*, 56.

62. Pierre Klossowski, "La messe de Georges Bataille," in *Une si funeste désir*, 123–32 (*SDD*, 65–70).

of an intensity that seems to open beings and notions of identity beyond themselves, but rather the question of how transgression is not just an "ethical transgression," a matter of right and wrong, of the proper and the improper, but "a violence done to the integrity—the purity—of a being" (*SDD*, 69). Transgression in this extra-ethical sense consists in the "need to make what is beautiful ugly, or to profane or corrupt what is pure." Transgression as "profanation." And, in a surprising reversal, profanation becomes a "spiritual force" (69), not the desire to destroy. Klossowski shows how profanation violates the "integrity of a being," its purity, whether that being is the flesh of the body or the flesh of language. Integrity carries profanation within it since it is the "menacing relation to the disintegrating act of profanation that the mind conceives of integrity." For Bataille, it is through the act of profanation that the mind conceives of integrity. As he writes in *l'Abbé C*, "The only way to atone for the sin (la faute) of writing is to annihilate what is written. But that can be done only by the author; destruction leaves that which is essential intact. I can, however, tie negation so closely to affirmation that my pen gradually effaces what it has written."[63] Thus, Klossowski writes, the presence that emerges in Bataille's "inverted transubstantiation" is a presence beyond death that yet does not have a transcendental reality: "In relation to that menace of profanation" that fixes the mind, it is nothing more than an immanent reality (69). To profane is to violate a heavenly purity——the purity of what Bataille called "heavenly flesh"—to profane the purity of its silence through carnal acts described in the violence of words.

This is what occurs in *l'Abbé C*, as Charles and his lover, the whore Eponine, attempt to reveal the weakness of the libertine hiding falsely under the priest's cassock his brother, Robert, wears. "I still shudder today at the thought of that mixture (*mélange*) of vulgar gaiety and unction."[64] Charles and Eponine succeed, but only by profaning and so destroying Robert, the twin brother and priest. But profanation also brings to presence what it seems to be violating. Profanation, sacrifice, and sacrilege, especially when the profanation of the purest and most noble name in existence, are the transgressive acts that bring that name to presence. This increases the value of that name all the more. Thus there is a consecration at work in the act

---

63. Georges Bataille, *l'Abbé C*, trans. Philip A. Facey (London: Marion Boyars, 1983), 128; *OC* III, 336.

64. Bataille, *l'Abbé C*, 128/*OC* III, 336.

and violence of transgression, a consecration in which the priest-writer-artist converts the flesh, converts the material realities of language and draws into something spiritual, making them a "spiritual force" (67–68).

Thus, in the violations of Roberte's "purity," the purity of her words and her profession as a state censor, in seeing her violated, whether in the arms of a guest or a stranger, her hidden essence, her many other silent and hidden identities, come into view, under the gaze of Octave. But he cannot say what he sees. Profanation then becomes a "consecration," a spiritual force making it possible "to see her as God would see her." If it is the so-called integrity and purity of language and notions, the purity permitted by the quotidian codes that are transgressed rather than the flesh of a woman, then transgression—profanation—becomes a transgression of language by language, a way of opening language beyond itself but from within itself. Such a violation, the profanation of purity, is directed at the "theological" problem that Roberte, or Robert in *l'Abbé C*, presents: their dual nature. Klossowski's Roberte, like Bataille's Robert, are both severe censors and sensuous bodies. But in *The Laws of Hospitality* for example, the transgression of flesh is something that takes place in language or in the mechanics of drawing. "There is nothing more verbal here than the excesses of the flesh." A "transgression of language by flesh and of the flesh by language" is what makes the carnal act attractive. The transgression of the carnal act, reproduced retroactively in a reiterated description, is not only an account of transgression, but it is also a transgression of language by language. Bataille intensifies the identification of language and transgression (*SDD*, 67). Such a transgression of language Klossowski finds in Bataille's novel *l'Abbé C*, but it is also the very subject of Klossowski's own books and images. They enact a violence that is an excess of language, bringing forth a presence, the presence of an absence, pure silence. This is the violence and the consecration of a profanation whereby the transgression of language by language brings to a terrible presence the deeper, pure silence that the impurity of words would violate. Enter the simulacre. "Heavenly flesh," Roberte's body, the inverted transubstantiation are but simulacra of language.

Klossowski's account of the simulacre is expanded in the later, 1963 essay on Bataille and the simulacre. A language of notions is a language built upon principles of identity and noncontradiction. Klossowksi, summarizing Bataille, says: "Le langage manque parce que le langage est fait de propositions qui font intervenir des identités et a partir du moment où, du fait du trop plein des sommes à depenser, on est obligé de ne plus dépenser pour le gain, mais de dépenser pour dépenser, on ne peut plus se tenir sur le plan de l'identité. On est obligé d'ouvrir les notions au-delà d'elle-mêmes"[65] (*R*, 27). Propositional language, which proffers the intervention of identities, the "I" or the *Je*, as Klossowski writes, the subject of the enunciation, this unique sign that is the ego, the "mine," the master of the house so to speak, opens "beyond itself" in an act of expenditure, or even of *gaspillage*, of waste or squandering, "dépenser pour dépenser." It is at that moment, that moment suspended on the threshold of transgression, that identity, as a notion, the identity and integrity of beings, is opened beyond itself.

Klossowski writes that for Bataille, the "dépenser pour dépenser" resembles a Heideggarian flight from being. Expenditure, loss, gaspillage, the general ontological catastrophe Bataille names, are but the obverse of the summit of being, what Bataille calls "the sovereign moment." Sovereignty, as flight from being, is a flight from the being of the world of work and utility in sovereign moments of "l'ivress, le rire, l'effusion érotique et sacrificielle, expériences que caracteréisent une dépense sans compensation, une prodigialité sans mesure" (*R*, 29). The sovereign moment, as the experience of the discontinuity of being, cannot be communicated in a notional discourse defined as it is by continuity, or logical, syntactical continuity. Of course, Klossowski will reverse this equation. Bataille's sovereign moment is a moment of highest intensity, of greatest continuity with itself in a going beyond itself, whereas the discourse of everyday codes and notions is a discontinuity, always a before and an after, always a discourse of means and ends. How can such sovereign moments that have no place in such a discourse be communicated? If the sovereign moment is the transgressive opening (*ouvrir*) of notions beyond themselves, it is also the collapse of identity. Bataille writes an "a-théologie" that commences with the experience of the emptiness of the place and role specifically taken by the name "God," God as guarantor of personal identity. Thus a-théologie is also the experience of the emptiness of the place and role of the ego, the *moi*, the "me and mine,"

---

65. Klossowski also quotes Bataille from the *Discussion sur le péché* as published in *Dieu vivant* 4 (1945). See Bataille's discussion with J.-P. Sartre in *Discussion sur le péché* (Paris: Gallimard, 1973); and Nouvelles Éditions Lignes (Paris, 2010), 126ff; and Bataille, *OC VI*, 315–58. (My trans. of Klossowski's text from *Ressemblance*: "Language fails because language is made up of propositions that involve identities, and from the moment when, due to the overflow of sums to be spent, one is obliged no longer to spend for gain, but to spend in order to spend, we can no longer stand on the plane of identity. We are obliged to open these notions beyond themselves.")

"la vacance du moi," a vacance—the presence of an absence—experienced in and by consciousness, which in order not to be this ego is itself a vacance, pure silence, pure emptiness (*R*, 23).

Again, as Klossowski asks of Bataille, can the intensity of such a sovereign moment—an expenditure that is pure loss of all such identity—be communicated where there is no topos for the enunciation? Any enunciation would always come after the so-called sovereign moment, and so would be descriptive, metaphorical rather than experiential. If the sovereign moment is a moment of silence, even when it is a moment of laughter, then any enunciation would be a violation of its pure silence. And in what language now free of any interventions from the notions of identity could one communicate a sovereign moment? Does the sovereign moment, as the "summit of being," not dwell in silence? Is an intensity, what Bataille is calling a sovereignty, the violent opening to a mutism, to a silence? And is this silence, which is its own combat against culture, a combat against the world defined by work and notions of utility? But if communicated in the gregarious codes of everydayness, or in a propositional language, will that not make the intensity of a sovereign moment into just another notion that must now be opened beyond itself once again? And this silence—is it too not just another word? Another sign? Another notion?

Thus, Klossowski writes that for Bataille, the sovereign moment of silence is also where the simulacre comes into play. Because a propositional language of notions (grounded as it is on the law of noncontradiction) would make contradictory any study or research into the "moment souverain," inaccessible as it is to all such research due to its sudden surging forth (*son surgissement*), its lack of all objectivity, its expenditure of names and naming. What is left? Mutism. Silence. Not a silence simply beyond language but a silence beyond the distinction between language and silence, a "pure silence," which can never be pure if "words break its continuity with acts" (*SDD*, 65). There, at the moment of the *surgissement*, in a rising, surging intensity, silence imposes itself, but in the same stroke the simulacre is also imposed[66] (*R*, 31).

But how is a sovereign moment of "pure" silence also the source of the simulacre and even the reign of stereotypes, which are but faded simulacra?

---

66. French original: "Ainsi, parce que le langage (notionnel) rend contradictoire l'étude et la recherche du moment souverain, inaccessible par son surgissement, là-même où s'impose le silence, s'impose du même coup le simularcre." *R*, 31.

The answer to these questions is in Klossowski's notions of a stereotype, and its doubling in the simulacre: both the trace of the stereotype and a going beyond the stereotype. The simulacre is the phantasmatic, metaphorical form—or *ressemblance*—assumed by a formless, intensity. Words, concepts, even propositions are also simulacre and the only way an intensity can be communicated. It is this structure, the relation between an intensity, the summit of being as flight from being, and the simulacre, the relation between an intensity as phantasm and its simulacre, that puts the action in *Diana at Her Bath* into play.

Diana, Acteon, and the Daemon: The Work of Art as Daemonology

> (Démonologie) ne considère pas la possession comme une maladie, mais comme un fait spirituel. L'ame est toujours habitée par quelque puissance, bonne ou mauvaise. Ce n'est pas lorsque les âmes sont habitées qu'elles sont maladies; c'est lorsqu'elles ne sont plus habitables. La Maladie du monde modern, c'est que les âmes ne sont plus habitables, et qu'elles en souffrent![67]
>
> —Pierre Klossowski, *Ressemblance*

Turning now to the role of the daemon in Klossowski's *Diana at Her Bath* brings us to a closer look at Klossowski's visual imagery. Although the images, whether drawn with lead or colored pencils, seem to be but mere illustrations accompanying a written text, Klossowski always insisted on the great divide between writing and drawing. In the mid-1970s, a gallery prompted him to try color. When he did, Klossowski saw, in contrast with writing, the more direct power of an image, especially a color image, and this provoked him to abandon writing in favor of making color images. Where writing entails logic, the steady flow of persuasion and demonstra-

---

67. *R*, 108; trans. mine: "Daemonology does not consider possession as a malady, but as a spiritual fact. The soul is always inhabited by some power, good or bad. It is not when souls are sick that they are inhabited; they are sick when they are no longer habitable. The Malady of the modern world is that souls are no longer habitable, and they are suffering from it!"

tion, the visual work of art is all about the spectacle; it is all about the life of the eye that can take on the roles and capacities of the other bodily members: the eye can see, but the eye can also touch, grasp, engage. The eye—*le regard*—can be both the topos for a pathophany and the topos for a cure in the form of an exorcism. Is such a conception of visual imagery a cultural contribution, or is it a form of combat against culture? Is this where the violence of Klossowski's images is situated?

Perhaps Klossowski is using the traditions of Western artistic culture to wage his own combat against culture, turning its well-heeled classical statements into something bordering on parody. At first, the stereotypical amateurism of the images pops out at the viewer. They are exhibition works, but they are not as accomplished as the images one usually sees in galleries. There is an evident depth to the images. They have a stiff, sculptural quality, suggesting without optical tricks the full dimensionality of space. In the 1990s, sculptures were made of Roberte on the parallel bars and of Diana and Acteon. Awkward as they may appear, Klossowski recoils at any suggestion that his drawn images resemble dolls or that they are wooden in appearance. His color schemes, poses, and arrangements of figures resemble the murals from Pompeii and the early Italian Renaissance. Klossowski saw many such works while traveling in Italy in 1963 (Tivoli, Hadrian's Villa, Rome, and Lake Nemi, "Diana's Mirror," where he saw the ruins of a temple dedicated to Diana). From the French classical and neoclassical traditions there are quotations, both stylistic and thematic: from David, the open hand, and from Ingres, the tradition of the classical nude. Courbet is present, the realist, as is modern cinema, technology, and mass entertainment. The list could go on. But how do we situate Klossowski's work more fundamentally in relation to the great classical traditions of Western art?

First, the great classical statements on art situate the work of art in terms of an absolute, objective, and transcendental Truth and Being. Plato's *Republic* is a most striking source for this characterization of art in its relation to a transcendental Truth, which was something rather new in the context of mid-fifth-century Greek culture. While the critical literature on these points is vast, the reader is especially referred to an essay by Jean-Pierre Vernant, "The Birth of Images," where he argues that with Xenophon, while the artwork is a mimesis, it is oriented toward the spectator and so becomes a *mimeisthai* (to mimic), with the mime as both genre and actor. Plato made the artwork turn more on the artisan–model relationship, which then introduced the strong relation between art and truth. From the fourth to the fifth centuries, this promoted a devaluation of images, cutting them off "from the real and from knowledge."[68] But the Eleatic-Platonic opposition between Being and Seeming, in which the image is a *faux-semblant*, is a legacy passed down to the Latin and Hellenistic theories of the simulacre that were so decisive for Klossowski.[69] The opposition Being/Truth and Non-Being/Seeming does situate the image as between Being and Non-Being, ontologically and pedagogically ambiguous. This too echoes in Klossowski's images, in their own striking ambiguities. Art occupies a low rung on the great Platonic ladder of Truth and Being. Compared to the radiance of Truth, which Plato compares to the Sun, visual art is *pseudos*, more a false pretender to truth, more shadow in its pretenses of light. The work appeals to the human eye, which is hungry for images, but returns only a play of shadows. The real concern amongst the Greek philosophers following Plato was the effect of art, how it turned the soul away from the pursuit of Truth only to be satisfied with the shadow-play. Plato's cave was a theater of lost souls, chained to their fixed beliefs and stereotypical conceptions, believing that passing shadows were realities, their "knowledge" amounting to no more than a guessing game. Art charmed the prisoners in Plato's allegory of the cave into believing that something they could see with their eyes rather than think with their intellects—namely a passing sequence of shadows, like writing on paper—was True Being. Badiou calls this "the charm of art," its aesthetic, the way art can act upon and move the human soul.[70] Plato saw a danger in art's charms. Like the Sophist, painting makes claims to truth, largely on the strength of the realism of its images, but its "truth," the truth of a sensuous representation or a semblance, misleads. The charm of images, the seduction of images, draws the soul away from its difficult ascent to transcendent truth and pins it to the delights of an earthly, sensuous representation of things that is so convincing they appear as though seen through a window. But such reality is but a shadow-play for Plato. Thus the danger of art for Plato was that it would have a corruptive effect on the soul, potentially causing it to become ill, in profound disharmony, due to its attachment to such shadows. Art is therefore condemned in Plato's educational state. Plato, the great dramatic artist himself, allowed only

---

68. Jean-Pierre Vernant, "The Birth of Images," in *Mortals and Immortals: Collected Essays*, ed. Froma I. Zeitlin (Princeton, NJ: Princeton University Press), 165, 180.

69. Vernant, 181.

70. Alain Badiou, *Handbook of Inaesthetics*, trans. Alberto Toscano (Stanford: Stanford University Press, 2005), 2–4.

disciplined art, militaristic art into his state, the "Republic," that Socrates and his interlocutors invent one night in their speeches. Even poetry was condemned. Where art, untamed art, could unleash movements in the soul that would have a destabilizing effect upon it, upsetting its health, its inner harmony, Plato's Socrates claimed that only education in philosophy and geometry—celebrants of balanced proportions—could be the cure for this.

Klossowski's art is hardly about restoring a well-balanced, harmonious soul. Nor is it harnessed to transcendental idealities. It is an art suspended from a subterranean "Real," not the real of Truth and Being (ultimate reality), not Substance (the real that is Rational), but the Real named by Blanchot or Lacan, the "impossible real, that share of disaster," the incommunicable and unexchangeable Real, incommunicable because it cannot be exchanged. Nothing can represent it to another signifier, as it is outside—or the other side of—any system or economy of exchanges, called the incommunicable *fond*, that point of pulsions, overflows, excess on the other side of language. Dissimilitude. Not the contrary of Plato's radiant Truth but its blind spot, the pupil of its eye into which signification collapses. Is the "Real" death? Is this what the violence of Klossowski's images brings to presence insofar as he says his art is an art of revelation in which death is brought to an appearing, mimed in the theater of desire? The Real, in any case, is always already there, indivisible, without fissure, like the smooth surface of an egg or a Möbius strip where a side doubles into its other without a rupture or break.

Klossowski carries forward this classical Greek concern for the effects of a work of art, the way it solicits and charms the viewer. Art, especially dramatic, poetic art, is given a slightly different, slightly improved treatment in Aristotle. The purpose of art, especially tragic drama, is not speculative, as in Plato, a shadowy reflection of absolute Truth, but cathartic, performative, "the disposition of the passions in a transference onto semblance," in Badiou's words.[71] Aristotle's treatment of the work of art largely focuses on the dramatic arts and is not so much concerned with knowledge as it is with purging the soul of its illnesses by generating images, dramatic action sequences that produce a cathartic experience in the audience of viewers. The context for this purging would have been a huge festival, days of poetry, dances, Dionysian abandonment, and animal sacrifices that more than prepared audiences emotionally for the terrors they would witness in Euripides's *Bacchae*, for example. Klossowski's art likewise is a crucible

---

71. Badiou, 2–4.

for mingling the passions and gazes of artist and spectator, soliciting them both to set aside the mundane and enter his theater of unholy rites. Like the ancients, Klossowski well understood the power of the work of art to solicit and change souls.

Does this compare with the work of psychoanalysis? In an interview with Alain Arnaud, Klossowski is asked if his work, considered as a "daemonology" in its practice and methods, can be compared to the work of psychoanalysis, which seems on the surface to be the modern equivalent of this ancient, Aristotelian doctrine of the cathartic effects of art. Klossowski explains that his art is a true *pathophanie*, an art that provides a place or topos traversed by unlivable tendencies and conflicts of the soul: Klossowski's "monomania," in this case. Arnaud suggests that this is similar to psychoanalysis, "which also considers pathos as a topos" (*R*, 106). But Klossowski considers the analogy between "therapy" and his "daemonology" to be too facile and leads to confusion (107). Therapy and daemonology differ in both aim and methodology. For one thing, daemonology and psychoanalysis have differing conceptions of *inside* and *outside* and their roles in purging the soul. For the analyst, the patient is incapable of getting out of their own interiority and can find no salvation except in the therapist. The therapist leads their patients to see the phenomena, the memories, the sterile manias that are choking their lives, casting them out of a troubled interiority, effectively purging them by objectifying their troubles in speech acts. The notions of the unconscious or an occulted consciousness equate interiority with the limits of individual subjectivity and the exteriority with a progressive objectification brought about by the return of the reality principle. This means that the cure is effective only by creating another new alienation. The patient recovers normality—and it is normality that can be truly alienating—"only by rejecting the events of his/her own *interiority*, which he/she experiences afterwards as realities that were *external to him/herself*."[72] Daemonology, on the other hand, does not consider "possession" (by spirits) as a malady or illness but as a "spiritual fact" not to be rejected, and the life of subjectivity to be a folding of inside and outside, and therefore not opposing dimensions of an interior unconscious and an objective outside represented by the science and knowledge of the analyst and the role played by the reality principle. No doubt Klossowski's conception of the work of psychoanalysis and its notions especially of the "unconscious" seem rather

---

72. *R*, 107; italics in original; trans. mine.

naive or simplistic. Is this perhaps because he is actually closer to certain aspects of psychoanalysis than he thinks or would admit?

But don't expect the analyst to play the part of the daemon, traveling between gods and humans. In his 1955 lecture "The Freudian Thing," Lacan sees Freud more in the role of Acteon, that stealthy hunter of the truth of desire, "perpetually set upon by dogs that are thrown off the scent right from the outset."[73] Diana, "chthonian Diana, the damp shade that confounds the cave with the emblematic abode of truth, offers to his (Acteon's) thirst, along with the smooth surface of death, the quasi-mystical limits of the most rational discourse the world has ever heard, so that we might recognize there the locus in which the symbol substitutes for death in order to take possession of the first budding of life."[74] Is this also Klossowski's connection with "truth"? Incommunicable truth. Unexchangeable. A unique sign: Roberte, pure even when her flesh trembles, always concealing and revealing, a locus of darkness and light, that "symbol substituting for death in order to take possession of budding life."

Klossowski often insists on the fact that Roberte's physiognomy is always the instance of a specific "type," androgenous and severe, that solicits Octave's desire. She is more the type Octave sees in work by his mythical artist, Tonnerre, more a nineteenth-century sort of woman as seen in paintings by Courbet, for example, an archaic type of beauty, not the slick pin-up girl or the "vamp-vedette," the movie starlets that have supplanted these classical beauties. His Roberte is a type that still appears from time to time in certain social settings, the product of the breeding grounds of High Protestant Society ("H.S.P.").[75] Klossowski's Roberte and Diana are instances of this type, this physiognomy.

Across a portfolio of images, Roberte is portrayed in a seeming variety of undesirable situations that turn out to be rather the same situation. Dating from the 1950s and across three decades, we see not only the same self-taught artistic style but the same subject matter: a woman, a physiognomy, the same facial expressions, upturned palms, ambiguous gestures, bent knees, and such, gestures springing from a sudden fright through which the ambiguity of her essence is revealed. Roberte, multiple, yet the same, the

---

73. Lacan, *Écrits*, 334–363 (French in *Écrits* I, 398–33).
74. Lacan, 343/409.
75. See Klossowski, *The Révocation de l'Édict of Nantes*, 15 (English trans., 98).

bearer of repetitions and differences that are the key to the work of art's solicitations. Not just the language of limbs and flanks disposed in certain provocative poses, there are also the hat and gloves, things she wears that both cover and can be removed to reveal. In *Robert, ce soir*, for example, she wears a hat, even while she is being molested by a colossal fiend. The hat reappears quite symbolically in *Diana at Her Bath*: Roberte/Diana, too, wears a hat, the crescent moon as her divine insignia. In the 1990 sculpture of Diana and Acteon she is nude except for wearing practically the same hat she wore in her apparition as Roberte. The hat is her attribute, in the sense of being an object that helps identify deities or daemons, an essential part of her theatrical persona. Across a suite of such images, this repetition, this recurrence of obsessive forces in figures, drawings, works of sculpture, and even film produces an effect, a jouissance, acting "morally" on the viewer, making the work of art, the image, the classical statue, for example, an invocation of the daemon. The work's "*ressemblance*," the type, the physiognomy and its idioms, the gestures and the situations it invokes, all solicit the daemon.[76] Art then circumscribes a daemonic force, capturing it, containing it so as to exorcize it. Enter the simulacre, plaything of a daemon.[77]

In a 1982 essay "Du Simulacre," Klossowski quotes Hermès Trismégiste, who furnished him with his basic conception of both the simulacre and the role of the daemon in the work of art. The ancient, Hellenistic statues of the gods were regarded as a way not of merely representing the gods to the imagination but of actually bringing them to presence in and as simulacra, as simulations able to act morally on the viewer.[78] Trismégiste: "Faced with

---

76. Castanet, *Pierre Klossowski*, 162.

77. On the simulacre, Wilhem writes, "La function du simulacre, coutumier donc, est celle du piège" ("The simulacre, as a custom, functions as a trap") and the "domaine du simulacre," meanwhile, is the ritual. Wilhem, *Pierre Klossowski*, 67–69.

78. In his short essay, "Du Simulacre," Klossowski writes, "Mon propos reste toujours de solliciter les reactions du contemplateur: choisir dans ses dispositions celles qui, matérialisée par les moyens les plus conventionnels, surgiront dans son propre espace et l'envahiront. Le contemplateur se retrouve face à cette region de lui-même qu'il ne peut reconnaître que representee à l'extérieur de lui-même." He then quotes Hermès Trismégiste (*TV*, 142–43). ("My purpose is always to solicit the reactions of the viewer: to choose from his dispositions those which, materialized by the most conventional means, will arise in his own space and invade it. The viewer finds himself face to face with this region of himself that he can recognize only if it is represented as exterior to himself"; trans. mine.)

the impossibility of creating a soul in in order to animate the simulacra of the gods, one could invoke the souls of demons and angels and one could enclose them in the saintly images. At last, thanks to these souls, the idols had the power of doing good and evil" (*TV*, 143; trans. mine). The simulacra would come to life under the power of the daemon; they could know the future and announce it through dreams, songs, divinations.[79] They could solicit the viewer. It is this conception of the simulacre, in conjunction with the daemonic, that informed Klossowski's way of looking at art: Could a modern work of art—not just a work of writing but the kind of imitative paintings and the scale of such paintings that one sees in the museums—a modern work of this sort, take its start from the same principles as ancient Hellenistic statuary? The conception of art is then very traditional; it is imitative, but its effect is active, not contemplative or reproductive; it is a "spiritual force," a way of acting with and on the viewer, making the viewer participate in the scene. In his adoption of this ancient principle for his own production of simulacra, Klossowski writes that Trismégiste's conception concerns him only in the way it is grounded on the impossibility of creating a soul for the sculptural simulacre that would be able to animate an inert object such as a stone sculpture of the god/goddess. Therefore, he denies the artist "the means of acting by and through his subjectivity alone and attributes to the complicity of a daemonic force the very moral action of the visual object produced by the artist" (143–44).[80]

The status of the daemon is troubling for Klossowski. His daemon is always in movement between scenes and dimensions. A mediator between the gods and humans, the daemon traffics in desire, either the desire of the gods for a mortal human or a human's desire to see and touch the heavenly flesh of the gods. In classical Greek times, although a daemon was a spirit operating between gods and humans, it had few negative connotations. Socrates was said to have been guided by such a daemon, a female named Diotima. Plato's *Symposium* introduces the notion of a daemon (202d–203a) as traveling between the gods and humans. An evil daemon is argued for

---

79. Foucault writes that while Klossowski's world is "sparing of objects," it is well populated by human bodies, the "Simulacral Men." "The point is that humans are simulacra much more vertiginous than the painted faces of deities." Foucault, "The Prose of Acteon," in *The Baphomet*, xxix.

80. English trans. mine. French original: "donc qu'il dénie à l'artiste le moyen d'agir par sa seule subjectivité et n'attribute qu'à la complicité d'une force démonique l'action morale d l'objet visuel produit par l'artiste."

by Xenocrates, Plato's pupil. This carries over into Neoplatonism, through Plutarch, Porphyry, Iamblichus, Trismégiste, and Tertullian. The daemon's role was most often to be a mask of the gods, a mime that plays the part of the gods, simulating them, even when they withdraw into their impassibility and especially when they engage in a game of trying to test one another's impassibility (*DB*, 36/48). "The daemon, neither god nor man but the reflection of one in the other," Klossowski writes (*DB*, 45–46/60). The daemon's hidden gaze "simulates Diana in her theophany and inspires in Acteon the desire and mad hope to possess the goddess. He becomes Acteon's imagination and Diana's mirror" (*DB*, 35/46). The daemon's troubling in-betweenness always moves between the obsessive phantasm and the simulacre of that phantasm, between the artist and the viewer, a moving spiritual force, neither human nor divine, something conjured that can be mischievous or malevolent, good or evil. A daemon does not inhabit so much as it possesses a creature. Especially the human soul is a playground, a topos, for the daemon, where its spiritual force is most active. That a daemon must be exorcised is a view filtered through Christianity and Renaissance magic and occultism, and it is still active in Klossowski's twentieth-century texts: write and draw so as to exorcize a daemonic obsession.

What is a daemon in a demythologized world?

Le bain de Diana, a book possessed by a daemon, was first published by Jean-Jacques Pauvert in 1956 during an international arms race to build, deploy, and use atomic bombs and during the golden age of capitalism that cemented the domination of the principle of the exchangeability of all goods. This did not stop Klossowski from creating and deploying his own daemons. He had lots of company: the twentieth-century artistic worlds of Bataille, Michaux, Blanchot, and Klossowski, just to name a few prominent examples, dwell in a realm between life and death, day and night, human and divine. In this respect, the artist too is a sort of daemon. In Nietzsche's *Gay Science*, it is a daemon that announces the Eternal Recurrence. While some may be tempted to say psychoanalytically that the daemon is just the hypostasis of an obsessional force acting through a plastic work of art, as in Freud's interpretation of Michelangelo's *Moses*, this hypothesis "matters little to the artist," in Klossowski's view, since it is not always successful in helping the artist to produce their work or affect (*TV*, 144). But the hypothesis of a daemonic world—and this is all it is, a hypothesis, something quoted from the ancient literatures—as "*analogous* to obsessional forces," to the point of regarding any and every movement of the soul as the correlate of a daemonic movement, is, Klossowski writes, the "*imperative même* of visual suggestion"

(144; emphasis mine). The "movements of soul," the daemonic movements, analogous to the obsessional forces, become the artist's interior model. The simulacre produced is but a counterfeit (*contrefaire*) of the movement of the soul, the counterfeit of an intensity. Taking the position of the sign in the semiology of intensities (*le sémiotique pulsionnelle*) discussed earlier, the sign-simulacre is the folding back of intensity upon itself, repeating itself, a *similitudo*, an intensity diminished, not denied but falling away from within the rising and falling of pulsions. Diana's theophany is thus a simulacre, a counterfeit of the daemon's making.

In Klossowski's account, the figure of the work of art, the beauty of the statue of a goddess, seduces the daemon into the work. Again, this is the charm of art that works even on the daemonic. The statue or the painting then circumscribes this daemonic intensity. Its resemblance (*ressemblance*) to the artist's emotion empowers the simulacre to act daemonically on the viewer. A daemonic circuit is thus established, linking the obsessive phantasms of the artist to the work of art and through it to the viewer. Klossowski quotes Tertullien: "The daemon was at once in the thing that he made visible and in those who perceived what the daemon had made visible." There is an important side effect for this approach: the artist experiences the daemonic as an exterior force that provokes in the artist's interior an "obsessive vision," exorcized only in and through the creation of the simulacre, the work of art. The resemblance of this obsessive vision to the figure in the work of art seduces the daemon, conjures it, and circumscribes it. But, as we shall see, the daemonic is all about seeing, making visible: the daemon is the source of the image, of the phantasm; the daemon is there to make possible an impossible vision. This is Klossowski's mythological vision in *Le bain de Diane*.

As was the case in his earlier novel, *Robert, ce soir*, so too in *Le bain de Diane* that vision is focused on the figure of a woman with two natures united in a hypostatic union. Like his Roberte, Klossowski's Diana evinces a strikingly and alluring duality of severity, austerity, and sensuousness. She is both an impassible, "unexchangeable" virgin, possessing a divine essence, and a woman having the passibility, the exchangeability, of a mortal human. This monstrous union of the human and the divine is a lure and a trap for mortal desire. Far from discouraging the hunter, Acteon, Diana's fleshy divinity only serves to incite and incense him.

Again, it is the daemon who is the key player here. *Le bain de Diane*, or the Book of Artemis as we Greeks might call it, has a very active daemon whose job it is to make visible, to push visibility to the point of blindness.

"Look not at Artemis face to face," the daemon warns Acteon, and the reader as well, "or you will vanish beneath her gaze. For it is I myself who envelop her essence; only her gaze I cannot veil: for the rest of you, it means death (to look upon her face to face)" (*DB*, 39/52). Diana's lacerating union of the passible and the impassible provokes Acteon, leading him to his horrifying destiny. Diana is the image of his own impossible desires, desires culminating in death. "Diana makes a pact with a daemon who intercedes between the gods and humanity, in order to appear to Acteon. Through his airy body, the daemon simulates Diana in her theophany and inspires in Acteon the desire and the mad hope to possess the goddess. He becomes Acteon's imagination and Diana's mirror" (*DB*, 35/46). The dance of death and desire that goes on between Diana and Acteon is all put into motion by the daemon who stands in the middle, between the visible and the invisible. It is the daemon who makes Diana appear to Acteon just as he would like to see her or has already seen her in his imagination, his hungry expectation. It is the daemon, who, and at the "same time"—recall that we are situated in a timeless mythic space here in Klossowsi's mythic vision, where time has come to a theatrical stop, a syncope in time—makes Diana appear to herself, for the gods always loved to see a spectacle of themselves, which is why they arranged the *ludi scaenicae*, the "stage games" described by St. Augustine in *The City of God*. (See *DB*, 33, and translator's note.)

Does the artist/writer partake of these powers described above to make Diana visible by making an image of her, drawing a body to suit her unapproachable, unpossessable, and invisible essence? Is the "making visible" the work of the artist at all, or is it the work of a daemon? The gods, in their essence, are all one, a unified force of nature having different dimensions. But, in order to appear to embodied humanity, they must take shape, usually in and as works of art, as statues, images, and the like. Thus they are individuated by becoming—only seemingly—embodied in the forms that humans would admire and call divine. And the gods themselves delight in this, for once embodied they also become a spectacle to themselves. The work of art facilitates and participates in this divine narcissism. Does the artist make visible not only the body but also the desire buried in its flesh?

> Under the mask of this daemonic body she can surrender herself, or experience incognito the emotions that her immutable principle precludes, including the emotions of chastity. In this way, without prejudice to her essential and invisible body, inseparable from her divine principle, impassible because impalpable, through

a spectator (for Diana, more than the other gods, has a taste for spectacle), she witnesses her own adventures—adventures in which her chastity is put to the test. (*DB*, 38/50)

This may be one of the senses of the notion of the pantomime in Klossowski's writing and drawing. Klossowski himself characterized his work as a "pantomime of the spirits." In creating images of Diana, by envisioning her face, her limbs, her costume; by putting words in her mouth, does Klossowski not also pantomime her spirit? Through the simulacre, through the pantomime, the writer becomes many, becomes other, becomes woman, goddess, hunter, and stag; through the pantomime, he moves at other velocities, on other planes of existence and through different times, becoming mythic. In becoming something else, he overcomes himself, his manias, his self-obsessions, his suffocating intensity of thought. Through the pantomime, the artist not only makes the goddess visible but in doing so transubstantiates the materiality of his art into something spiritual. Is the pantomime Klossowski's answer to the "allure" of art, which for Plato worked in precisely an opposite direction and had an opposite effect, leading the spirit away from the spiritual and deeper into materiality?

A pantomime in classical times was an erotic, effeminate dance. In Roman times, it was a dance accompanied by what is known as a *fabula saltica*, a "dance story." The pantomimic dance, accompanied by a song, was sometimes sung by the dancer himself, with the audience encouraged to participate and sing along. In Greek, a *pantominos* is a dancer who plays—or mimes—all (*pan*) the parts. This mimesis is not mere imitation but "an 'authentic' mime" that "gets inside the skin of the character one imitates, by donning his or her mask."[81] Thus, where Klossowski's writings and drawings are a pantomime of the spirits, this might suggest that Klossowski himself is to play all the parts in his novels and drawings as he gets "inside the skin" of his characters.

This introduces a Deleuzian perspective, as in *Milles Plateaux*: a zone of indeterminacy, zone of the becoming-woman, becoming-animal, becoming-daemonic spirit, which is not just trans-gender but trans-desire. This is the zone haunted by the artist where he lays down a plane of composition, as Deleuze calls it, onto chaos. In this way, the writer/artist takes on the role of the daemon, who is also a "mask" and "mime" of the gods.

---

81. Vernant, "Death in the Eyes: Gorgo, Figure of the Other," in *Mortals and Immortals*, 125.

Klossowski's pantomime enacts the many forms of desire, but especially the desire, the drive as Lacan would call it, to see. He too, in a sense, must dwell in this zone of indeterminacy, in this zone of "becomings" that the pantomime, the simulacre of writing and drawing, establishes at the edge of chaos. He ultimately pantomimes the attraction, through desire, to chaos and the dissolution of the subject, as we shall see in connection with the myth of Acteon's desire for Artemis. No doubt this notion of the pantomime affirms the connection between art and life for Klossowski. Life's true subject, its incommunicable *fond*, can only be suggested, approached, and distanced through the pantomime of art, through the simulacre, in other words, drawing upon and upending the play of the stereotype in art and communication as it does.

Diana's coming to visibility mirrors the way an intensity becomes a thought. In becoming visible, in becoming a phantasm in the daemonic mirror-play that confirms her theophany, a divine intensity, like a wave, folds back upon itself and designates itself as a body, as an individual, as a deathly desire. For her to appear as the virgin temptress hunting in Acteon's imagination, she must look into the daemon's mirror. And as she mirrors herself, her "idiom," her essence, joins with that of the daemon. So there is this fascinating and rather Freudian interplay between Diana and her mirror. Instead of looking into a mirror and seeing a fully integrated, threatening body as does the child in the Freudian myth, the goddess Diana sees herself as an individual rather than in a union with the twelve gods. And she especially sees herself as a desiring and desired body, miraculously having the flesh that no goddess could ever have, and without giving up her divine impassibility. Diana is a written body; writing is her mirror. In mirroring herself, her divine impassibility assumes the passibility of the daemon. She becomes chaste, yet equally palpable, her divine femininity now reflected in mortal flesh. Now, as she looks at herself in the mirror of her pond, she has a body that delights, that has its jouissance in making itself visible, something seen, the object of a desiring gaze. This making visible is the daemon's work. The daemon even invests her not only with a voluptuous appearance but with his own "lasciviousness" as well. Only this way, as the hypostatic union of divine impassibility and the passibility of mortal flesh, can Diana enjoy what her divine impassibility forbids (*DB*, 37). Thus commences her theophany, in which divine nature mirrors its essence, comes to appearance in the form of what it is not, a "contrefaire." In this daemonic mirroring—a mirroring of gazes—divine purity is doubled with the impurity of flesh. She becomes the intertwining of light and darkness, the intertwining of two spaces, two times, divine and mortal. She hunts, she bathes in a divine, mythic space-time, but in her theophany she travels as the huntress into the world of humans and animals, a palpable world of desires that she cannot know as a disembodied goddess. The daemon enables Acteon to see her, Diana, beyond death, beyond the transgressions of the flesh. "Does the gaze survive its abolition, posthumously?" the daemon asks (*DB*, 47).

In the space of Klossowski's mythic world, this question is out of place. In the space of the mythic world, Diana proffers the eternal recurrence of her feminine cyclicality: the crescent moon, her insignia, and the movement of circular progressions; the hunt; the bath; the theophany; the return to Olympus. Through her body, borrowed from the daemon, Diana submits to the linear time of desire and reflection, the time of beginnings and ends. She then becomes a spectacle, as though the very linearity of time was her illumination. She enjoys this herself in her own narcissism, just as Roberte enjoyed looking at herself before her dressing mirror. But in submitting herself to visibility, language, and desire, she also holds something back, something invisible, impassible, and impalpable. Just as Acteon looks, Diana escapes into invisibility, into the betweenness of time and myth, into the visible and the invisible: language and silence. Echoing Antoine from *Robert, ce soir*, therefore, Acteon says of what he sees when he beholds the nude Diana at her bath: "What I saw, I cannot say what it was" (*DB*, 51/69). He sees but he cannot say, and what he says he cannot see because the object of all such seeing and saying would be always "a flight from being." As he beholds what the daemon has given him to see, Acteon thinks he beholds the goddess, nude, at her bath. But what he sees is only the simulacre, the phantasm of his own desire. And this moment of insight and silence, this moment between time and myth, between time and the eternal return, is to recur eternally. In the ever-recurring cycle of the hunt, the bath, the baleful theophany, and the eventual return to Olympus, this collapsing, passing, transitory moment will find its eternity.

Mirrors and Gazes

Diana and Roberte are doubles of one another, and both are modeled after Klossowski's real-life wife, Denise Marie *Roberte* Morin-Sinclaire, a resistance fighter in World War II. Acteon is the double of Octave and Antoine. But insofar as the daemon is also described by his author, Klossowski, as a voyeur, it is tempting to see the link between this daemon and Klossowski himself: after all, this is his passion on display, his phantasy. He is the one who ultimately makes all this appear to us in his images. In his interview with Pierre and Denise Klossowski at the Galerie Beaubourg in Paris, Alain Jouffroy asked Denise if she identified with these images. Denise replied, "Not at all. It's Pierre's *fantasme*."[82] The *fantasme* is pantomimed in the theophany, whether of Diana or Roberte.

But it is especially the gaze (*le regard*) that relates these two stories of "hospitality," the gaze in all its links with the becoming visible of Diana/Roberte. A visibility in which a phantasy is enacted, pantomimed, that of a woman—a goddess—stripped bare, like truth itself, as in the drawings and sculpture dedicated to the scene of Diana and Acteon embracing in a dance of death. The gaze, *le regard*, structures the stories.

The scene that describes Diana at her bath is dominated by the exigencies of the gaze. It is a Baroque palace, a "panopticon"[83] of mirrors and reflections with its sacred pond, a massive, glassy mirror, the reflection of the goddess floating dreamlike on its surface. Diana sees another reflection as well, the reflection of Acteon. She senses his lust lurking nearby, the hunter's eyes greedy for what they cannot see. As he sees, he is both solicited by the goddess, desires at the behest of the goddess, and simultaneously denied by her, Diana, who denies mortals the privilege of ever seeing let alone touching the divine body, which, in truth, is nothing physical or mortal at all. She is pure spirit, which cannot be known by the human world of time, language, theophany, desire, and death. Diana's flesh is unmoved by desire or death. It is heavenly flesh. Its very desirability guarantees its unexchangeable chastity. From across an infinite distance yet so close, Acteon looks. He expects to see heavenly flesh, but Diana cups a hand of water from her sacred pool and splashes it on him, the hapless hunter hiding nearby. At the moment he looks, Acteon does not see, cannot see, for the moment of his seeing is also the moment of his metamorphosis into a stag, into an animal, and he is quickly attacked and torn apart by his own hunting dogs, which no longer see their master but their prey. Seeing is linked not only to desire but to death and destruction. Acteon becomes animal in this zone of indeterminacy opened by the daemon, between the human and the divine, between the animal and the human. Acteon's gaze attempts to cross that zone, driven by

---

82. Klossowski and Jouffroy, *Le Secret pouvoir du sens*, 79–80.

83. Alain Arnaud uses this term in his account of the gaze in Klossowski's novels. Arnaud, *Pierre Klossowski*, 68.

the desire to see. But the bath, the sacred pool, restores Diana's invisibility, her essential body. O vicious circle, for an eternity Acteon's gaze spies upon her, and for all eternity she feels the need to wash herself of the defilement that gaze brings. Klossowski quotes his translation of Ovid's *Metamorphosis*: "Now you may tell you saw me here unclothed / If you can tell at all!"[84] The provocation: say it, then, describe Diana's nudity, her charms. "That, no doubt, is what you're waiting for, what your fellow men would love to know!" (*DB*, 63/81). The irony: "If you can tell at all." Diana's last and only words to Acteon abolish language because they are part of "the game that is the sole expression of myth itself." And because this game is myth itself, it is the game whereby the sacred words abolish a profane language (*DB*, 64/81).

Thus, the myth, the fable of Diana and Acteon is about the simultaneity of divulgence and the impossibility of divulgence. Acteon is a man who "hunts with his eyes," a man possessed by the desire for truth and a desire to communicate that truth, where truth is equated with what one sees and says. Could he thus say what he sees, if anything, from under the mask of stag? Is he not condemned in advance rather than exalted? Condemned but not made manifest in his condemnation? Thus he does not enter the light he seeks, for all that is made manifest is light: the goddess is pure light, like Zeus, a pure pulse of energy, a pure intensity, incommunicable as it is in its surging forth (*DB*, 64, trans. altered). But, on the other hand, as Klossowski continues, "The words of the goddess, by way of irony, invite him (Acteon) to describe the scene of Diana naked before the stag-man by means of indiscreet or profane language, and to find an intelligible mystery by other means than the spectacle in which the mystery is realized" (64). Diana herself moves in silence. She bathes. She senses Acteon nearby. She cups the water, splashes the hunter, silencing him and blinding him in the same gesture. She does all this in silence, in the silence of a pantomime enacting the myth joining human, animal, and divine natures. Letting Acteon draw near to her, Diana is ready to receive him, to subject him to the rite of the stag. If Acteon heard those words in his innermost heart, it is because he deliberately excluded himself from the mystery, acting only upon "You may tell." But by then nothing remained except the mocking words of the goddess floating over the ruin of the man Acteon: "If you

---

84. Klossowski quotes his translation of Ovid, *Metamorphoses*, III: "Nunc tibi me posito visam velamine nares // Si poteris, licet." *DB*, 3/7. The above quoted passages are from DB, 63–64/80–81).

can." Abolishing language, Diana also abolishes desire, death and life, truth and communication. She could even abolish all seeing and saying.

Alain Arnaud speaks of Klossowski's panopticon as having but one rule, one law: to see and to see incessantly. Arnaud quotes Octave's last words, a cry of victory, as he lay dying from the poison administered by his Roberte: "Je vois encore, je verrai toujours."[85] Thus, a dramaturgy of the gaze in Klossowski's novels and paintings, a theater with its own rules of hospitality: here, actors, spectators, and the writer exchange roles, intermingle, each participant being invited to abandon their illusory personal identity, the identity established by names and by the "I," that floating signifier, in order to borrow the mask of another. Klossowski's dramaturgy is a play with a triple regard, or gaze: Arnaud quotes Klossowski who says he doubles or even triples himself in the gaze. Hence, there is the regard named by St. Augustine, the *"image inadmissible*, the enigma *du fond inéchangeable* and his solitude," an enigmatic and unexchangeable essence or ground, a groundless ground, that can only be communicated in stereotypes of language and discourse. Even as the writer reaches for this incommunicable, silent ground (*fond*), the constraint of the "classical syntax" must be obeyed. The second level of the gaze, *le regard*, is that of Klossowski doubling himself from writer into painter, a doubling of text and image used to communicate an obsessive force in the classical syntax and the stereotypes of culture. Finally, Klossowski offers his spectacles to the gazes of others, the reader and viewer (*contemplateur*) who receives them, gazes upon them from their own universes and according to their own experiences and tastes. But this triple gaze is all a ruse: through its artistic clumsiness, through its many reflections and doublings, through all its ruses, Arnaud argues that purpose of the gaze is to solicit, to insinuate, and to suggest.[86] They form a lure and a trap, drawing the spectator in until it is the spectator who gazes and is gazed upon, whose eyes are those behind the curtain, one who "hunts with his/her eyes, one who wants to see 'encore' et 'toujours.'"

These remarks are fine as far as they go. Other dimensions of the gaze lurk unseen. Diana's gaze into the mirror surface of the pond has been mentioned, but it is not named among Alain's tripartite gaze. The God's-eye view must also be considered—the eye unseen that never closes, that never

---

85. Arnaud, *Pierre Klossowski*, 68; Klossowski, *Les lois de l'hospitalité*, 86. English trans., *Roberte Ce Soir*, 192: "Ah, between her spread slender fingers I was able to see, nevertheless, I still see, I shall always see."

86. All quotes in this paragraph above from Arnaud, *Pierre Klossowski*, 69.

blinks, that sees all, that can see Roberte's essence, hidden from Octave. A gaze suggested in the writing. But is it already there in other forms? Octave would wish to ascend to its capacities, but he is restrained by materiality. He must be satisfied with his tawdry position behind the curtain. The God's-eye gaze requires no curtain, for it sees all but is itself unseen.

There is also the "indiscreet" male gaze named by Chantal Thomas. Where is this gaze? Is it subjective or objective? Is it incarnated, the gaze of the spectator, of Octave, or of his creator, Pierre Klossowski? This is the gaze that "unveils in a woman what she is striving to disavow, her pleasurable being," that arouses only if it is linked with surprise, and that therefore sees how a woman reveals herself "despite herself." However, Thomas concludes, "What the eye unmasks is always a masked woman, forever impregnable to the game of truth." Unless, of course, truth is a woman, always hiding, concealing and revealing in the same eternally recurring suspended moment.[87]

There is also the objective gaze of the picture itself, the gaze that looks back at the viewer. Manet already made such a gaze a focal point of his paintings, or what Roland Barthes might have called its "punctum." *Olympia* (1863), *Le Déjeuner sur l'herb* (1863), and *The Balcony* (1868) are obvious examples. Bataille's monograph on Manet, published in 1955, just a year before *Diana at Her Bath*, mentions another work, *Woman with a Fan* (1872). He insists on an "absence of meaning" in Manet's canvases; the "real subject" slips in a "surreptitious way into the ambiguity of *The Balcony*, or, in other portraits, into the tremor of their suspended animation, or stranger still, in between the spokes of an outspread fan through which nothing is visible but a pair of mysterious eyes. "If it is true, as I (Bataille) believe, that Manet's initial secret is to be discovered in *Olympia* . . . there is a deeper secret perhaps, whose hiding-place is hinted at by the outspread fan that conceals it."[88] This is the secret of the gaze, which, as Bataille writes in his closing sentence, "modern painting offers up to our gaze."[89] Is this, too, the "hidden secret" in Klossowski's drawings?

The gaze must be considered first as a function, not a concept. Not "What does it mean?" but "What does it do?" In this case, the gaze is doubled: it is both a look and a blindness, both a subject and an other. As Sartre wrote in *Being and Nothingness*, the "look" (*le regard*) is first on the

---

87. Chantal Thomas, "The Indiscreet Gaze," in *Art & Text 18*, 107.
88. Georges Bataille, *Manet*, trans. Austryn Wainhouse and James Emmons (New York: Skira, Rozzoli International, 1983), 114–15.
89. Bataille, 114–15.

side of the subject, and then, in the moment of being looked at, the look also becomes identified with the subjectivity of the other, the other person. Sartre's notion of the gaze also emanates from the side of the object. It is in the "rustling of branches," or the "sound of a footstep followed by silence," "the slight movement of a curtain." But the subject is always implied in these scenarios, and the gaze seems in these cases to be more the trace of a passing presence, and so it is still identified with the subject.[90]

Where Sartre identifies the gaze and the subjective look, making the look its function, Lacan takes the gaze out of subjectivity by taking it out of the act of looking and makes it into the *object of the act of looking*, the object of the scopic drive,[91] especially the gaze of the other. The term "drive" translates the French word "pulsion" and Freud's "Trieb." But Lacan points out the insufficiencies of these terms, for a drive is not an animal instinct (a Trieb) but rather an energy in the sense of being a constant force, tireless and unstoppable. Klossowski's rhythmic rising and falling of pulsions and the cyclic, feminine rhythms of the moon connected with the myth of Diana/Artemis thus differs from the Freudian "drive," for a drive is not a pulsion in this way, nor is it a "pulse" despite its being translated as "pulsion." Nor is a drive natural or dictated by laws of nature, not cyclical or rhythmic as in animal sexuality. It is cultural, which is to say acquired and so completely inscribed in the "symbolic order."[92] The drive is also multiple—Lacan calls it a montage—and so defines the immense varieties of human sexuality, whereas instincts confine and define an animal's sexuality. Moreover, a Lacanian interpretation of the gaze would be based on the unconscious, "structured like a language," the folding inscription of the symbolic order that defines the subject and would be defined, therefore, as the seat of desire. Such notions and structures are all rather alien to Klossowski, it would seem, as he insists on the disjunctions of silence and speaking, not unconscious and conscious. There are passing references to the unconscious already in play in Klossowski's work. But when he uses the word "unconscious," Klossowski usually does not have any technical meaning in mind, certainly nothing to

---

90. Jean-Paul Sartre, *Being and Nothingness*, trans. Hazel E. Barnes (New York: Philosophical Library, 1956), 257.

91. Jacques Lacan, *The Four Fundamental Concepts of Psychoanalysis*, trans. Alan Sheridan (New York: W. W. Norton, 1978), 75ff. Also see Dylan Evans, *Dictionary of Lacanian Psychoanalysis* (London: Routledge, 1996), 72–73.

92. Jacques Lacan, "On Freud's 'Trieb' and the Psychoanalyst's Desire," in *Écrits*, 722–25 (*Écrits* II, 331–34); Evans, *Dictionary*, 46.

do with repression. It seems rather to indicate an interior "field of forces" of which a person is not aware but which are active in every one of their desires. We may also detect the unconscious in its syncopes: the ambiguous gestures and their repetitions evident in Klossowski's paintings that bring time to a sudden stop or break. Such repetitions may be another most important symptom of an insatiable force, a drive, a "death drive" at work in Klossowski's writing and painting. If, indeed, all drives are ultimately reducible to the death drive, then the scopic drive, the gaze, would also belong to the death drive, the gaze into death. Nonetheless, Klossowski's "gaze" cannot be subsumed so easily under the Lacanian notion of the scopic drive even though it retains some of its aspects, its implacable insistence, its force, and so on, and how it is knotted up with death.

Relating the predominance of "seeing" and "making visible" in Klossowski's visual imagery to a Lacanian notion of the gaze would certainly be adventurous yet also strikingly suggestive. Aspects of the Lacanian teaching are indeed propitious to our reading of Klossowski. While one may say, for example, that the presence of the voyeur in Klossowski's stories already entails the active presence of the gaze in Klossowski's work, a Lacanian reading of this situation would entail looking not at the voyeur in his act of seeing but at the object: what he sees. The object of the gaze, is the gaze of the other (Roberte/Diana). It is this that so captures the voyeur, Octave/Acteon. For the Lacanian formulation, desire is the desire of the other's desire, as in a desire for recognition, demonstrated in Hegel's Master-Slave dialectic. Hence, the object of Octave's desire is the desire of the other, Roberte/Diana, and this he sees looking back at him and not just in her eyes. Roberte's gaze also dwells in the form of her ambiguous gestures: in the skin of her palms and fingers, in the whiteness of her flesh. Octave is enraptured by the pure whiteness of that gaze. Hence the open palm is repeated in image after image. This is her "weak spot," the daemon reveals (*DB*, 40). Is this what Acteon is also looking for as he hunts with his eyes? Does he hunt for the gaze of the goddess, the object of his desire, looking back at him? But what he desires is not what he shall want. He could not know, however, that he is trapped in his own phantasy, which, although no doubt the work of the daemon, haunts him *from within*. Nor could he know that Diana's gaze, which illuminates her desire for Acteon, and which Acteon so ardently seeks, is nothing real, but only the little *objet a*, the object of his phantasy, as Lacan called it, and what triggers Acteon's own desire. The mythic time of the action is the mythic time of the phantasy. This is the truth Acteon sought, the truth of his desire, which, as Lacan said again and again, can only be "half-said" (*mi-dire*). This is the object of his gaze, Diana's desire gazing back at him, a phantasy that leads him through desire to destruction and death. "Look not at Artemis face to face," the daemon warns Acteon, "or you will vanish under her gaze. For her entire body is visible, it is I myself who envelop her essence; only her gaze I cannot veil" (*DB*, 39). Only the gaze cannot be veiled; only the gaze is not a part of her theophany, the gaze that is not of her fleshly appearance, that comes from pure mythic time, the Vicious Circle, the gaze that is the terror of gods and humans. What is behind this gaze? The Real. Nothing. Silence. Thus, the lure and the trap of phantasmic beauty is in the gaze, not the profile, not the flesh, not the naked body but the veiled gaze that leads unto death.

A drawing, which enacts the structure of the gaze, can be a little machine, a desiring, gazing machine. There were several such image machines produced in connection with the 1956 publication of *Le bain de Diane*. There was even a full-color sculpture in the round made in 1990, complete with a scenic backdrop. But let's take a look at one such drawing, a simple drawing made in lead pencil and published with the text. The drawing is entitled *Le bain de Diane*, and it is also published in the 1980 edition of *Le bain de Diane*.[93] The drawing, probably dating from the mid-1950s, is quite like the 1990 sculpture. The scene in the drawing takes place, has its topos, in an enclosed, idealized space of reflections located in mythic time. There is no before and after of this image. It shows a moment where time has come to a stop, a timeless moment on the wheel of the Eternal Return, the circularity of time. But in terms of the myth's narrative, it depicts the moment in which the hunter tries to seize Diana, the purported object of his desires. Acteon, the mortal intruder, is trying to seize what he is forbidden to see. Perhaps the viewer's sympathies—their fear and pity—for Acteon are solicited by this image, where the hero of the tragedy is about to suffer a fatal fall. Forbidden, denied, yet destined in advance to risk the impossible and to see Diana in her nudity, in her "possessability," Acteon is trapped in the spiral of desire and death that unfolds in the mirror of the image. The duplicity and fatality of his situation is already anticipated in the duplicity of Diana's hands. As Acteon approaches, one of Diana's hands has withdrawn from the space between her thighs, uncovering her

---

93. The 1990 English translation of *Le bain de Diane* has yet another drawing of this scene, with variations in its opening pages. A color version (1973) of the drawing in the French text is on the cover of the English translation. It is entitled *M. de Max et Mlle Glissant dans le role de Diane et Acteon*.

"vermillion vulva," those "hellish lips," and by this gesture so ending her theophany. Her other hand, meanwhile, with its divine white palm, cups the water from her bath and splashes Acteon. Diana has thus taken the sight from human eyes, but at the same time and in the same gesture, has opened the eyes of the stag he shall now become, thus initiating him to her "final rite." The drawing shows Acteon thus transformed into a stag-man, half human, half animal, no longer able to see as a human what he craves to see, nor able to say what he has already seen, the hidden, undefilable, unpossessable purity of the goddess.

Klossowski's drawing brings this moment to visibility. The narrative has Acteon wearing a hollow stag's head mask over his own face, a disguise he had hoped would allow him an easier approach to the spring and to see Diana at her bath. Diana has upped his game by transforming him into a real stag, a transformation that confuses his hunting dogs, who now see their master as their prey. The metamorphosis, Acteon's becoming-animal, has closed Acteon's human eyes and allowed the eyes of the dying stag to open. This opens Acteon's animal lust and propels him to his destruction. The drawing allows us to see what no human could ever see, a stag-man trying to assault a goddess. Depicted in mid-metamorphosis from a human into a stag, Acteon has caught Diana from behind, as in several other of Klossowski's drawings of Roberte. There is a contrast: the male principle in this image, Acteon, is not satisfied hiding behind a curtain, but is masked and in active pursuit of Diana, who looks quite like Roberte, even wearing the same hat. A crescent moon, Diana's insignia, floats overhead and reminds us that this is Diana, huntress of the night, a night goddess, a goddess of the moon as well as the mistress of the animals. Acteon's right arm, now the extended leg and cloven hoof of a stag, is gripping Diana at her waist. Her image, the simulacre of her pure, feminine goddess, is now shown enveloped in animality. Acteon's right leg, changed into a stag's leg and hoof, supports from behind. His hunter's tunic clings to his shoulders, and his hunting horn still dangles from his right shoulder. His left arm and hand—still human—grips Diana's right arm and holds it up, exposing her armpit. The stag-man's long snout is pointing into Diana's exposed right armpit. Her left arm is bent across her left leg toward the stag. Her left hand turns up, displaying an ambiguous gesture, its opened naked palm close to the stag's encircling right leg and hoof. Her gesture signals alarm, flight, resistance, and at the same time, an invitation. The stag's right hoof reaches toward her naked crotch, now exposed to the curiosity and little tongue flicks of one of Acteon's hunting dogs. Diana's shudder is noted in

Klossowski's text, but her pleasures are all just "appearings," elements of her theophany, all a part of Acteon's phantasm, no doubt the doing of the daemon, and not arising from the purity of her godhead, which remains unshaken, uncompromised, unexchanged.

No doubt it is just a coincidence that this image of a human dressed as a stag was made about the same time as Georges Bataille's descriptions,[94] of the "sorcerer" stag-men, dating from the Upper Paleolithic, found on the walls of caverns in France and Spain. A man wearing the mask of an animal suggested to Bataille a portrait of human sovereignty signed under the face of an other, the face of an animal. Klossowski's image shows a variation on this theme, a twisting, dynamic balance of figures and forces human, animal, and divine, frozen in their embrace in a moment of mythical time. Like the Paleolithic image, Klossowski's drawing is also a time machine of sorts, transporting the contemplator into the eternal recurrence of a mythic time, into a moment that both never occurred and shall recur eternally, time-become-space, the space of this little machine. We stand before such images unsure of what we are witnessing but compelled, perhaps by nothing more than "curiosity," to see more. This shows us just how much these drawings are desiring machines, productive of desire and the violence of desire. Of course, the figures are also stereotypes, having the expected physiognomy, the "type" one associates with the ancient Roman simulacra, which were also statues. But the stereotype is a machine designed to capture and contain the pulsion, the force of the originating intensity and its phantasmic image, capturing it and releasing it to the gaze of the viewer who participates in this scene via the daemonic circuit of forces, desires, and images.

Is all of this, the simulacra, the pantomime of spirits, all just narcissism? Are Klossowski's "machines" facilitators of his narcissism? Narcissism is usually regarded as a psychological notion. But there is a "narcissism of vision and touch," remarked upon by Merleau-Ponty:

> Thus, since (the seer) is caught up in what he sees, it is still himself he sees: there is a fundamental narcissism of all vision. And thus, for the same reason, the vision he exercises, he also undergoes from the things, such that many painters have said, I feel myself looked at by the things, my activity is equally passivity—which is a second and more profound sense of the

---

94. Georges Bataille, *Lascaux or the Birth of Art*, trans. Austryn Wainhouse (Geneva: Éditions d'Art Albert Skira, 1980), 120, 136.

narcissism: not to see in the outside, as the others see it, the contour of the body one inhabits, but especially to be seen by the outside, to exist within it, to emigrate into it, to be seduced, captivated, alienated by the phantom, so that the seer and the visible reciprocate one another and we no longer know which sees and which is seen.[95]

As regards Klossowski, who is not developing, as was Merleau-Ponty, a philosophy of vision or of the visible but who is concerned with his own particular situation, one could point to the self-referentiality of the intensities and the signs they produce through their "chutes," (decreasing intensity) and "hausses" (increasing intensity)—one could point to Roberte/Diana. These are Klossowski's obsessions, his own monomania that is the focus of his work. Do a painter's images not also put the artist on display? Are they inverted forms of exhibitionism? Do they show images of other people? Or are these the images of the author/artist and his obsessions, like Roberte admiring herself in the mirror or Diana enjoying her appearing body in the mirror-play of the bath? Roberte/Diana—identified with a certain physiognomy, with certain ambiguous gestures and situations—if she is indeed the pivot of the writer's narcissism, "perhaps marks the opening between consciousness and the unconscious," their division and folding of one upon the other. We ask Klossowski, Is writing and drawing a substitute for the sexual act, a way through the memory of touching while not touching? Is his Roberte/Diana not modeled after a type of woman he saw as a young boy? Are his androgenous images of young boys, for example Ogier in *The Baphomet* or Platonic scenes featuring Socrates and the young Charmides, not also modeled after the boys of Klossowski's youth? The images and writings are bound with the circularity of repetitions, just like the cycles of the moon and the rhythms of the natural world. Michèle Montrelay has argued something like this with regard to *Robert, ce soir*. Klossowski's books and drawings are the machines that put the circuits of narcissism, both primary and secondary narcissism, into play. "The narrative (*récit*) becomes our gaze"; its principle of perception and thought becomes our gaze, our thought; the images and narratives speak from the structure of the unconscious. They "model the gaze" for both Klossowski and his reader/viewer, becoming routes for our own narcissistic pleasure. "Klossowski want

---

95. Maurice Merleau-Ponty, *The Visible and the Invisible*, trans. Alfonso Lingus (Evanston, IL: Northwestern University Press, 1968), 139.

us to enjoy ourselves."[96] Is all of this is, however, not a pleasure arranged by the narrator/author of Klossowski's books on Roberte and Diana? Is our enjoyment but the reflection, the circuits of his own narcissism? The role of the narrator generates this interplay of gazes and so opens the question of a possible narcissism driving Klossowski's work. As we close, let us now turn to this last interpretation of Klossowski's work.

Who Is This "I"?

The first word of *Diana at Her Bath* is the first-person personal pronoun "I": "J'aimerais vous parler de Diane et d'Actéon" (*DB*, 3/7). "I," the subject of this enunciation, would like to speak to you, to "us," its readers, about the myth of Diana and Acteon. This is similar to the first words of *Robert, ce soir*, where it is the nephew who names his uncle, Octave: naming and denouncing him to the spirits in the same breath. Who is this narrator who so announces his topic in *Diana at Her Bath*? Who is this narrator who says, "I would like to talk about Diana and Acteon"? (3/7). Is it Klossowski who uses the narrative structure of a myth handed down to us through who knows what textual legacy from a vanished humanity?

Klossowski here uses a pagan myth and not a Christian formulation to cloak the frame of his obsession, his phantasm of a woman surprised, carried away, like Europa in the Titian painting, riding Zeus, disguised as a golden bull. Classical mythology is full of stories like this. They were popular. They were staged in Roman times in a theological theater of cruelty and hanky-panky.

Did the classical myth displace Christianity in Klossowski's work as Catherine Backès-Clément claims?[97] Why, in other words, the change in Klossowski's books from a language heavily infused with Christian Scholasticism to one embracing pre-Christian myths? Such a displacement would have to be explained. There may be many reasons for this. Was the light and amorous adventures of the ancient myths a more appealing, more flexible vocabulary than the dark, dour confession booths or the stilted Scholasticism of Christianity for the exorcism of his mania? Aren't the classical myths more playful, more relaxed in their treatment of fleshly desires than

---

96. Michèle Montrelay, "'Les Lois de l'Hospitalité' en tant que lois du narcissisme," in *l'Arc* 43, 63–72. Quotations from 69.

97. Catherine Backès-Clément, "Incarnation fantastique," in *l'Arc* 43, 28.

their Christian counterparts, not freighted by the Christian doctrines of sin and redemption? Was mythology not closer to life? Did the twelve gods of classical mythology not walk amongst their human counterparts, unlike the single Christian God, who is more remote, judgmental, and severe? Did the classical myth not also have the crucial and playful role of the Daemon, something one will not see in the Christianity? Christian arts—replete with images of death on the cross—did not offer him what the old Roman myths could, an archive rich in imaginative texts and images for his own doctrine of the simulacre.

Whatever the case, the ultimate displacement here is that of the author/artist himself. Regarding Klossowski's narratives, there may not be a displacement at all if one considers how both the more Scholastically intoned story of Roberte and the Romanized Diana myth are both subtended by the geometry of the gaze. The two narratives share much in common: the emphasis on the gaze, on the desire that gazes to see and to touch the forbidden; the importance of mirrors; the ambiguous idioms of gestures. Diana also has a role similar to Roberte's. As Catherine Backès-Clément writes, Diana too is the pivot in the narrative. Like Roberte, who poisons her Octave, so too Diana leads Acteon to his death. She too is a verb, the carrier of the action, seizing our hunter-author as he reaches to seize her, his prey, leading him unto his ultimate encounter with human finitude. Although Backès-Clément says the displacement of Christianity by the classical myth displacement must be "explained," we ask if can it be better understood as a variation on a theme rather than a displacement, a myth offering a different setting, a different vocabulary, a slightly different situation in which to explore the same obsessive manias, a different way to unfold the structure of the gaze and the structure of a phantasy that "really is the 'stuff' ("*étoffe*") of the *I*."[98] Do both narratives, in short, Roberte's and Diana's, unfold in different but complementary ways the same structure of the gaze and the same overriding narcissism?

Narcissism is studied by psychoanalysis in connection with ego development, the development of the "I." In his 1914 essay "On Narcissism: An

---

98. Lacan, *Écrits*, 691 (*Écrits* II, 297). Emphasis in original. English trans.: "That fantasy is really the 'stuff' of the *I* that is primarily repressed, because it can be indicated only in the fading of enunciation." The *I*, as Lacan says, is submitted to the symbolic order, submitted to or subordinated by signification and so becomes the "I" that can speak. "Fading" can also mean "eclipsed" (see *Écrits* II, 296): the "I" is eclipsed in and by the enunciation, the "saying," the symbolic order.

Introduction," Freud writes that the narcissist is a person whose libido is invested in their ego, a person whose "libidinal development has suffered some disturbance, such as perverts and homosexuals, such that, in their later choice of love-objects, they have taken as a model not their mother but their own selves. They are plainly seeking themselves as a love-object, and are exhibiting a type of object-choice which must be termed 'narcissistic.' "[99] This is characteristic of the male, although Freud does see a similar type in women who are in love with being loved (Is Diana such a woman?). This may stem from the child's primary narcissism, which is then "transferred onto the sexual object," constituting secondary narcissism.[100]

Montrelay sees this in the circuits Klossowski describes in *Les lois de l'hospitalité* of the sign that forms when (quoting Klossowski) a "circuit closes itself" (*se refermait*) to such an extent that it becomes an immobile circle, the "intensity of the sign," an absolute self-relation, an absolute and absolutely suffocating self-coherence. The exigency of thought to designate itself is experienced as a constraint. The cut of naming and designating has yet to arrive. Constraint, the binding necessary for coherence, also ultimately both excludes and requires the *Je* of thought. Primary narcissism in Klossowski's narrations and images is a subject-less self-relation that only an external sign, that of the floating signifier *Je*, can designate. However, it would designate not an enduring self but only an absence of self, lost as this self is in its own *imago*, its own self-image, reflected back to it. There is no self–other configuration here. This narcissism, where a powerful coherence establishes itself, maintains itself, projects itself through the gesture, which Montrelay calls an "inflexion of substance."[101] Gestures are physical expressions hurled against the limits that would censor them. Some gestures are permitted. Others are not. The gesture is exhibited and repeated not only in the image—the open palm, the exposed armpit—but also in the artist's motions as he draws the image, using lead pencils or pastel-colored crayons, just as Roberte used a red pencil to censor Octave's writings. The gesture is the graphism of Klossowski's work, constitutive of his secondary narcissism, the projection outward of self-love onto a love object, the figure and face of Roberte/Diana. In the pantomime of the spirits, the one singing

---

99. Sigmund Freud, "On Narcissism, An Introduction," in *The Standard Edition (SE) of the Complete Psychological Works of Sigmund Freud*, vol. 14, trans. James Strachey (London: Random House/Vintage, 2001), 89.

100. Freud, 88.

101. Montrelay, *l'Arc* 43, 64.

the song, the *fabula saltica*, plays all the parts. The circularity of this narcissistic self-relation is in tune with the circular harmony of seasons and the stars, Montrelay writes,[102] thus linking or folding outside and inside upon one another. Klossowski's secondary narcissism, then, is the projection of this self-love onto external objects, the objectification of intensity in forms, simulacra. Seemingly external to the ego, seemingly in the "real world," they are forms that are actually the subject's own phantasms, its own creations. This is the secondary narcissism of the gaze.

The Lacanian version sticks closer to the original Greek myth of Narcissus, of a young man falling in love with his own image reflected in a pool of water. In his 1936 address to the Marienbad Congress, Lacan presented his theory of the mirror stage. His study showed the behavior of an infant, at about six months of age, taking delight in its own image in a mirror, suggesting to Lacan an "identificatory capture by the imago," the specular image in the mirror of the child's body.[103] What is more, delight turns to aggressiveness when the fragmented, uncoordinated body of the infant feels threatened by the complete and unified image it beholds in the mirror. The *imago* seems to then threaten the child with destruction, tearing it to pieces. The myth of Narcissus, Lacan reminds us, is linked with a suicidal tendency. This suicidal tendency is what Freud sought to situate in his metapsychology as the "death drive" and "primary masochism" and that Lacan locates in the traumas of infancy: birth, physiological prematurity, and the trauma of weaning.[104]

For an alternative reading of this myth of Narcissus and of narcissism, we can turn to Blanchot's *The Writing of Disaster*. "What Ovid's account forgets," in Blanchot's reading, is that Narcissus,

> bending over the spring, does not recognize himself in the fluid image that the water sends back to him. It is, thus, not himself, not his perhaps nonexistent "I" that he loves or—even in his mystification—desires. And if he does not recognize himself, it is because what he sees is an image, and because the similitude of an image is not likeness to anyone or anything: the image characteristically resembles nothing. Narcissus falls 'in love' with

---

102. Montrelay, 65.
103. Jacques Lacan, "Presentation on Psychical Causality" (1946), in *Écrits*, 150 (*Écrits* I, 184).
104. Lacan, "Presentation on Psychical Causality," in *Écrits*, 152 (*Écrits* I, 187).

the image because the image as such—because any image—is attractive: the image exerts the attraction of the void, and of death in its falsity.

The teaching of the myth is that one must not "entrust oneself to the fascination of images which not only deceive but render all love mad. For distance is necessary if desire is to be born of not being immediately satisfied." As Narcissus/Klossowski might have said, Possession dispossessed me. What is mythical in this myth is death's practically unnamed presence.

A few pages later, Blanchot continues, "The water in which Narcissus sees what he shouldn't is not a mirror, capable of producing a distinct and definite image. What he sees is the invisible in the visible," something "without presence . . . without a model . . . a nameless one. . . . It is madness he sees, and death."[105] Is this the truth of the gaze and of Klossowski's narcissism, that he does not fall in love with his own image, is not captured by his own *imago*, captivated by it or its simulacre, the image of a woman surprised? Nor is he contained by it, for it is also a stereotype whose tyranny must always be broken and resisted. What gazes back is not his own face, the object of his own desire; rather, in Blanchot's words, touched by the gaze, Roberte's or Diana's gaze, he is in the thrall of the impossible real, that share of disaster wherein every reality, safe and sound, sinks.

This connects with what Lacan writes in "The Freudian Thing," that truth, "complex in its essence, humble in its offices and foreign to reality, refractory to the choice of sex, akin to death, on the whole, rather inhuman, Diana perhaps . . . Acteon, too, guilty to hunt the goddess, prey in which is caught, O huntsman, the shadow that you become."[106]

Acteon's gaze, what he sees, he cannot say, but he does see it, wordless, gazing back at him from Diana's position in his phantasy, his own truth, the inhuman truth of his desire, the purity of death dwelling within the glorious body of the goddess. This is what he reaches out to touch when he reaches for the flesh of the goddess. Not just this body, this flesh, but the invisible, the unsayable—the incommunicable *fond*—the intensity and the calamity she conceals in her showing. The gaze brings the impossible union of the human and the inhuman, to which Klossowski's spectator is initiated.

---

105. Maurice Blanchot, *L'Écriture du Désastre* (Paris: Gallimard, 1980), 192–94, 204–5. Trans. by Ann Smock as *The Writing of Disaster* (Lincoln: University of Nebraska Press, 1986), 124–26, 134.

106. Lacan, *Écrits*, 362 (*Écrits*, 433).

Let us conclude with a rather long citation from our author, whose role in this drama is quite ambiguous. Acteon, wearing the mask of a stag, leans out over the mirror of the pond where Diana is preparing her bath,

> and, as he takes on bit by bit the transparency of the pool, then in the dark night of his mind, Diana . . . but never was a stag's head more replete with thoughts; for even the thought most generously inclined to fade to nothing remains no less watchful of its progressive nothingness, and however deep it may plunge into the night, it remains no less a *gaze* peering into the night—a supreme temptation to interrupt this *Bath*, to suspend, if only for an instant, the separation of Diana from her daemon, of Diana from her visible body . . . poor hunter in the *dark night*, false ascetic in *the light of day*—for Diana never ceases to reflect her chastity in her apparent body: O vicious circle! . . . It is thus for all eternity that she suffers the defilement of his gaze, for all eternity that she feels the need to wash herself of this defilement—and no stag's mask will ever enable him to contemplate Diana at her Bath with a pure gaze, unless Diana herself, from without, opens within the hunter the eyes of the dying stag.[107]

Who, then, is this "I" that narrates the myth of Diana at her bath, whose all-seeing presence is announced on its beginning pages and who, playing the role of the daemon that he is, also drew the image, wound up the little machine, that accompanies the written text? Who is this "I"? An "I" that is multiple, not a simple unique identity but the folding of multiplicities: spectator, artist, the goddess, all the playthings of a daemonic animality. Have they too not always and already died and lived to return again, countless times and time again, to this moment suspended by this enchanted pool, with its mysterious atmospheres? "O vicious circle"—this unique I, this unique sign. Have the gods not yet died from laughter?

---

107. Pierre Klossowski, *BD* (Paris: Gallimard, 1980), 73. DB, trans. Sophie Hawkes and Stephen Sartarelli (Boston: Eridanos Press, 1990), 55; Klossowski's italics.

Chapter 3

Emanations

The Painting and Poetry of Henri Michaux

> Longing for more, for better, for what lies beyond, beyond the known, the expressible, the representable, the thinkable, the admirable, beyond everything imaginable.
>
> —Henri Michaux, *Miserable Miracle*

> L'inconnu est son seul point commun avec tout et avec tous.
>
> —Alain Jouffroy, *Avec Henri Michaux*

Michaux's art famously incorporates two related but distinguishable techniques. First, there are the line drawings, *le lignes*, the *traits*, the strokes, black calligraphic images marked on a white surface, images that bristle, break, swirl, and begin again, images constituted of discontinuities, gestural intensities. Second, there are the "tachist" images, often in color, created by dropping drips or splotches of watercolor paint onto an absorbent paper. Unlike images produced in the application of paint *to* a surface, as in conventional painting, these forms emerge or emanate from *within* the paper. Emerging from the whimsy of color drops on paper, they are the children of a chance operation. Michaux created many images of heads and faces in this manner. Images that seem almost formless, unformed, or as though still emerging into form from a formless background. Thus, our problem and our question: the relations between form and formless, between seeing and saying, between the finite and the infinite in Michaux's texts and images.

At the limits of language, where the inexpressible and the inexhaustible are manifest in visions, feverish, formless splendors beyond the reach of quotidian, profane language (the languages of knowledge, the university, science, authority, and religious doctrine), there comes into view a sacred language, simulacre of the divine, a sign or signs, registering a tonality or intensity of soul that can neither be taught nor learned but that could be the basis for a universal language.[1]

Here They Come . . .

> Darkness, lair from which everything can leap, lair in which we need to seek.
>
> —Henri Michaux, *Emergences/Resurgences*

Here they come, the heads, the *personnages*, apparitions emerging from within or perhaps from behind the paper, from the darkness of black paper as though the paper is a thin membrane or screen, all that separates the world of spirits from the human world. They emerge from a formless background, from an indeterminable state of matter. Some with and some without bodies. Spectral life forms, ill-defined, shifting, with soft, aqueous contours. Some have faces, others only seem to. The most magnificent of all, *Le Prince de la nuit* (1937): we see a red skull with something appearing to emerge from the top of its cranium. His body is a rag pile of color: orange, blue, purple. A rustic, rigid, rust-brown throne supports the Prince, whose body seems at once ponderous and weightless. The Prince extends a vaguely colored hand,

---

1. One of Michaux's lifelong projects was to show the basis for such a "universal language." A note from 1938 announces three projects, one of which is the "rudiments of a universal ideographic language having nine hundred ideograms and a grammar." "Chronologie," in *OC* I, cix. As he writes elsewhere, "As a child I did not understand other people. And they didn't understand me. I found them absurd. They were foreigners. Since then, this has gotten better. Nonetheless, the impression that we don't really understand each other has not disappeared. Oh, if only there were a universal language that absolutely everybody could understand! Dogs, men, children—and not just a little, not with things being kept back. The appeal and the mirage of a true, immediate language—the longing for it—has survived in me despite everything." Michaux, "Le Rideau des rêves," in *OC* III, 458. Trans. by David Ball as "The Curtain of Dreams," in *Darkness Moves: Henri Michaux Anthology 1927–1984* (Berkeley: University of California Press, 1994), 229.

a wooden hand, Michaux calls it, that almost resembles the profile of a crocodile. Is it a welcoming gesture? Or is it expecting a gift, offering, or tribute? Another disembodied, skull-faced figure floats nearby, its toothless jaws open, empty eye sockets filled with darkness. "Prince of the Night," of all that is formless. Prince of Death. The Prince's kingdom, his palace and the setting for this scene-macabre, is a bottomless night flecked with a spermatozoon of colored stars and planets, a chaotic cosmos without center or limit, lacking constellations and the force of gravity. Black all around. "Arriving at black. Black brings things back to fundamentals, to origins," Michaux writes.[2] The scene is divided by a thick gray line on the right side that almost seems illuminated by a source somewhere outside the frame, behind the backs of the viewer and the painter, perhaps. Is it a piece of architecture? There is nothing in this scene that requires any support. This is the land of the insupportable. So what is it? There is no way of knowing. Michaux himself calls it "the useless column, of the supreme questioning."[3]

And here, on other pages, hundreds of pages, here are the *traits*, flicks of ink on paper, the trace of a gesture, the scar left where the tip of a pen or the stroke of a brush touched the page, the black ink revealing all the more the white, formless background of the empty page. These gestural lines vaguely resemble a script of calligrams. Flushed with spontaneity and not guided by any concept, they float in an almost prelinguistic world where the relations anchoring signs to signification have not yet been born. Other lines form images that look like both signs and bodies in motion, as though indistinguishable; movements, always movements. Nothing ever stands still. Nothing at rest. Nothing one can read or identify except through the imagination. Imaginary worlds that have emerged from what Michaux calls "l'espace du dedans."

But Michaux is first, since his youth, a poet. The images would come a bit later.[4] The author of many books, he writes against books. In a prose work entitled "A Dog's Life," he writes, "Books bother me more than anything. I can't let one word keep its meaning, nor even its form."[5] The book

---

2. Henri Michaux, *Emergences/Resurgences*, trans. Richard Sieburth (New York: Skira Editions and The Drawing Center, 2000), 14.

3. Henri Michaux, "Le Prince de la nuit," in *OC* I, 712.

4. See the biographical notes in the introduction of this volume.

5. Henri Michaux, "Une vie de chien," in *OC* I, 469–70. Trans. by Anne McGarrell as "A Dog's Life," in *Someone Wants to Steal My Name*, ed. Nin Andrews (Cleveland, OH: Cleveland State University Poetry Center, 2003), 35.

may be impossible, as Roger Laporte has said, "but the white page is no less so, because everything passes as if, between writing and silence, there is an infinite pathway, as if the absence of the book demanded the infinite movement of writing."[6]

This recalls the following lines from Maurice Blanchot, who once remarked how close he felt to Henri Michaux,[7] and it also marks the beginning of the paths, the "infinite pathways" we shall seek through the work of Henri Michaux: "To write is to produce the absence of the work (worklessness), unworking (désoeuvrement). Or again, writing is the absence of the work as it produces itself through the work, traversing it throughout."[8]

Blanchot distinguishes a "book of knowledge" from a "work." Whereas a book of knowledge hardly exists as a book, as a "volume unfolding," the work differs in its claims to be "singular, unique, irreplaceable . . . almost a person."[9] The work of Henri Michaux, such as *Misérable miracle* (1955) or *L'Infini turbulent* (1957), and especially *Un certain Plume* (1930), are works of that description. Yet such works by Michaux have a vexing, impossible double life; they are both science and poetry. These dimensions do not stand apart from one another. They interweave, they combine in a volatile tension. The book of knowledge and the works of poetry are folded one into the other, a writing and image-making that produce an "absence of the work." Strange "works" that work to produce their own absence.

In the course of his life, Michaux became a renowned poet and painter. In part, this renown is due not only to the enchantment of his writings, at once mystical, playful, and vehement, but above all to the numberless visions, the sheer optical spectacle his books contain, drawn from his experiments with drugs, especially mescaline. Such writings, collected for example in *L'Espace du dedans*, *Misérable miracle*, and *L'Infini turbulent*, have a visionary, hallucinatory character that seems far from anything conceptual or scientific.

---

6. Roger Laporte, "Une passion," in *Deux lectures de Maurice Blanchot* (Paris: Fata Morgana, 1973), 71. In the "new version" of this essay, "Maurice Blanchot: Une passion, nouvelle version," in *A l'extrême pointe, Proust, Bataille, Blanchot* (Paris: P.O.L., 1998), the line quoted above is retained, 66.

7. Henri Michaux, "Letter to Raymond Bellour," quoted by Blanchot in a footnote to his article "L'infini et l'infini," in *L'Herne: Henri Michaux* (Paris: l'Herne, 1966), 88.

8. Maurice Blanchot, *l'Entretien infini* (Paris: Gallimard, 1969), 622. Trans. by Susan Hanson as *The Infinite Conversation* (Minneapolis: University of Minnesota Press, 1993), 424. These lines are also quoted in Laporte, "Une passion," in *Deux lectures*, 71.

9. Blanchot, *L'Entretien infini*, 623 (*Infinite Conversation*, 424).

It is surprising to see that there is also something vaguely resembling a scientific project at work in these writings and drawings. Science and poetry interweave in an essential mission, already sketched in the 1936 *Recherche dans la poésie contemporaine*, to create "a new optic," to be the "eye, the witness" to a "psychopathological research," to make an account of the dangerous states of the self (*soi*) (*OC* I, 971–78).

This is carried forward in the mescaline adventures of the 1950s and 1960s. The mescaline adventures are not just intoxicating, they seek "knowledge" (*savoir*). Indeed, they began as clinically observed experiments. The problem is how to stabilize the mescaline visions, how to capture them, objectify them and so be able to retain in some form the images that appear to him, whether when he was on mescaline or locked in the cold arms of death, spending his moments looking "for the last time" at beings, "profoundly." He concludes, "I searched for them, wanting to retain something of what I'd seen that even death could not take away" (*OC* I, 930–31). Translated into books such as *Miserable Miracle*, Michaux organizes his experiences into a taxonomy, listing the effects and visions the drugs produce in his brain.[10] Drawn from what he calls the powder keg of inner experience, these books are the translation of an experience of limits at the frontiers of the unknown. But they are also books charged with the task of stabilizing the mental images he has seen, working them up into forms that can offer the possibility of not just amorphous spectacles but also knowledge (*savoir*) of these interior mental images. The images then become something published, seen in the form of images, read in the form of texts, seized in and through concepts.

Moreover, within the signs and images he produces on the heels these experiences, Michaux also seems to be in pursuit of a universal language that would arise not from writing and drawing but from something before, something more ancient, more archaic, a language of "gesture-signs." "C'etaient des gestes, les gestes intérieurs, ceux pour lesquels nous n'avons pas de membres mais des envies de membres, des tensions, des élans et tout cela en cordes vivantes, jamais épaisses, jamais grosses de chair ou fermées de peau."[11] His 1946 *Peintures et dessins*, for example, presents a table of

---

10. See *Connaissance par les gouffres*, in *OC* III, 3–153, which details a wide variety of drug-induced experiences but also discusses hallucinations of taste and smell; see also, "Chaos: Tragèdie de l'intensité, visions intérieures. Visions hallucinatoires," in *Connaissance par les. gouffres*, in *OC* III, 97–101.

11. Henri Michaux, "Signes," in *OC* II, 431. ("They were gestures, interior gestures, those for which we have no members but only the desires for members, tensions,

signs that suggests an alphabet. In an entry entitled "Alphabets," Michaux seems on the verge of inventing perhaps a universal sign system, the basis for a new language (*OC* I, 930). What is particularly striking about this project is that it would also first be a language by which, or through which, humans and animals could communicate, "une langue commune aux chiens et aux hommes."[12] Conceived during Michaux's dreams, such a universal language between humans and animals immediately throws into question the traditionally conceived decisive difference, the limit, between humans and animals: animals do not understand or use spoken languages. Now, as Bataille remarks in 1953, "La Fontaine's fables are of no avail in helping us to recall that, in distant yesterdays, animals could talk."[13] If we do not need a La Fontaine to remind us that animals do talk, nor do we need Michaux to tell us, in what he describes as an important revelation, a "most major discovery about Nature," the same thing, namely that animals talk, "parler des chiens" (not talking *about* dogs but the "talking *of* dogs"). All of this, as with much else in these pages from Michaux, written as they were from the other side of the "curtain of dreams," cannot be taken as scientific propositions but rather as pieces of wit, the fragments of broken dreams. Nonetheless, animality, as a literary and figurative motif, is important for Michaux. It returns in his collections of written signs: many are the outlines of animal forms, some resembling the painted animal forms one can see at Lascaux. Michaux visited the Lascaux caves in 1946, just a few years after their discovery. Likewise, his alphabet of signs is his connection to another world, a world in which animals play an essential role: they are the connection to a forgotten world, a world before the writing of history, in which images of animals may been used to communicate between the human and the spirit worlds. We shall be returning to this in pages that follow.

We have then these two contrary trajectories in his writing and drawing. First, the production of books of knowledge devoted to his mescaline experiences, books having taxonomies and descriptions, books that would be devoted to the search for a universal language, books that would have both scientific and mythic components. Second, more than a book, there are the "works." In Blanchot's quoted sense of the word, "works" of drawings

---

impulses and all this in living cords/bonds, never thick, never thick in flesh or closed in/by skin"; trans. mine.)

12. Michaux, "Le Rideau des rêves," in *OC* III, 418 ("The Curtain of Dreams," in *Darkness Moves*, 229).

13. Bataille, "Passage de l'animal à l'homme et la naissance de l'art," in *OC* XII, 273.

and poetics that produce not just concepts but the shredding of writing and drawing, putting it into motion—discovering its hidden rhythms and undercurrents—what Blanchot might call writing "the absence of the Book." In the most general terms, these two trajectories are instances of the two fundamental thrusts, *une poussée duelle*, that drive Michaux's writing: a movement toward concentration and unification, which Bellour calls "definition by absorption," the movement into the entire being of a thing—as Michaux wrote in *Connaissance par le gouffre*: "Je me suis uni à la nuit"; a "union with the night" and—not quite on the other hand—the shattering movements of fragmentation, Bellour's "indefinition by dissemination into the flux."[14]

How, then, do we find these two pulsions in Michaux's writings: a pulsion that seeks "peace" and another that undergoes a "breaking?" Is Michaux's ultimate destination to find "peace in the breaking" (*paix dans les brisements*)?

Another way of framing the notion of the double pulsion (*une poussée duelle*) active in Michaux's work would be this: a pulsion toward unification is doubled by a pulsion toward shattering. Writing a book of knowledge (*savoir*) proves impossible for Michaux, given the tumult and flux of the initial experiences. The book of knowledge gives way to the work of poetry and poetry in turn gives way to images. The book of knowledge, of a science Michaux planned concerning his experiments with mescaline, is always upended by another "work" at work, a *désoeuvrement*, a putting-out-of-work, an anti-writing that tears and shatters the writing of knowledge. Michaux could not communicate in propositional forms of knowledge, or even in the form of drawings, the unification he experienced with mescaline. Concentration is always doubled by shattering, by dispersion, by "dissemination into the flux." Beneath, within, perhaps even before the writing that gathers knowledge into linear propositions, there is another writing seemingly freed from the rigors of form, a movement of fragmentation that upends propositional forms, producing not knowledge but "scraps of writing" (*déchiquètements d'écriture*), a "shredded writing," an "indefinition" of writing, anticipating what Blanchot has called a "writing of disaster." How, then, between the seeing of the mescaline visions and the writing and the drawing of those visions, how in the pursuit of a scientifically inspired project concerning the effects of mescaline is there also a *désoeuvrement* at work? A book of

---

14. "Notices to Plume," in *OC* III, 1468. Original: "Indefinition par dissémination dans le flux du divers." Bellour is speaking especially of *Misérable miracle* and *Paix dans les brisements*.

knowledge never completed because always put out of work by a dual pulsion (*une poussée duelle*) that belongs to no author, the pulsion toward unification and concentration—a pulsion toward the "book"—doubled by a pulsion toward the poetic "work," a pulsion that tears writing to pieces, and that equally arises on a blank page as a floating head, leaving behind not knowledge but only the fragile scraps of words and, images. Tracings that are all that remains of a language that has hurled itself against the great wall of the unknowable, the unsayable, and the unseeable.

Phrased otherwise, how have the writings and drawings of Henri Michaux in their doubling of "book" and "work" marked and transgressed the limits of writing and images, writing a dissemination and "indefinition" of writing and speech, folding the established forms and limits of modern European languages, its grammars, vocabularies, and syntax, into those of lost, ancient, half-forgotten forms, writing a language of the Other, an ancient language of animality? Writing at the limits of writing, writing a *des-astre* that "de-scribes," that is "beyond the pale of writing," in Blanchot's words. Michaux's writing de-territorializes writing, pushing it away from the "stars" (*astre*) that might illuminate the Night, toward a night "delivered of stars."[15] His writing pushes toward an encounter from the inside (*dedans*) of writing, from within the book or the work. But driving deeper into writing, into language, also drives his writing toward an *outside* of writing, neither "book" nor "work," for it produces nothing, signifies nothing. Michaux discovers that this "outside" is already active from the inside of language and writing. Silent scribbles disseminated into the flux, not toward a beyond of language, writing, or the visible but toward a "disaster" that is neither inside nor outside, the folding of outside and inside at a point where the difference between them is indiscernible, no longer at work or in play. From the inside of writing, from where it generates signification, there is a *désoeuvrement* at work. From inside of language, where, in the trembling of a voice that speaks or in the hand that writes, a threshold is approached and marked, a limit between the inside and the outside, between life and death, where they overlap and enfold into one another. This is a threshold Michaux always approaches but from which he must turn back. In every attempt he makes to name, to draw, to define the infinite movement of what he has seen, a double pulsion that both summons his work toward a limit beyond which there is nothing more to be said, where language shatters,

---

15. Marie-Claire Ropars-Wuilleumier, "On Unworking: The Image in Writing according to Blanchot," in *Maurice Blanchot: The Demand of Writing*, ed. Carolyn Bailey Gill (London: Routledge, 1996), 138.

and that equally drives him to seek a center of unification, of peace and concentration. But the center sought is also an absence of center, both a unification and a "dissemination into the flux."

This interplay between the private visions Michaux claims to have experienced and the translation of those visions into a more universal and published writing or drawing produces a tension that pulses throughout his books and drawings, shaking them, keeping them in movement, helping them to resist every attempt by commentary to define and reduce them to established academic categories and meanings.

What is the relationship of the visions, the writings, and the images that seem linked together? Are Michaux's writing and drawings the true representations, visual recollections of what he has seen and what it is like to be under the influence of mescaline, like snapshots from the edge of madness itself? The problem is how to stabilize the image, how to objectify it, how to capture it, how to retain in some way the images that appear to him, as when he was locked in the cold arms of death and spent his moments looking "for the last time, at beings, profoundly," he concludes. "I searched them, wanting to retain something of what I'd seen that even death could not take away" (*OC* I, 930–31).

Yet he disdains art as representation. From his earliest works, from the experiments with ink and watercolor, even in his use of line in pen and ink, he sees the images produced on paper not as representations but as emanations. Emanations are emergences. This shall be our theme, our passport through the writings and drawings of Henri Michaux: such emanations are the emanations of "disaster," the writing of disaster, an emergence that is also a disappearance.

Between Center and Absence

Let us consider four books and their visions that Michaux published beginning in the 1930s, visions of heads and of the "infinite" from which they emerge. The first, from *L'Espace du dedans*,[16] first published in 1938 in *Lointain intérieur*: "Une tête sort du mur" ("A Head Comes Out of the Wall").[17] Tired, presumably alone in his room, the narrator, Henri Michaux (?), turns out the light. He waits, hoping to be approached from out of

---

16. Henri Michaux, *L'Espace du dedans* (Paris: Gallimard, 1966), 204–5.
17. Henri Michaux, "A Head Comes Out of the Wall," trans. Richard Ellmann, in *Henri Michaux: Selected Writings* (New York: New Directions, 1968), 195–97.

the dark, hoping to speak to some creature. Suddenly, an "enormous head," emerges, "about six feet across, which after suddenly forming, dashes upon the obstacles which separate it from the open air." He attributes the whole affair to his solitude, a solitude that weighs on him and that he subconsciously tries to escape. "The head is alive, of course. It possesses *its* life"; Michaux's emphasis.

This text foreshadows a second book, *Émergences-Résurgences*, commissioned in 1972 for Éditions Albert Skira: "In all unfinished things I discover heads. Heads, the gathering points of moments, of probings and anxieties, of desires, of whatever drives things forward, where everything combines and appreciates . . . including drawing. Once it has come to rest, everything fluid becomes a head. I recognize all imprecise forms as heads."[18]

These heads are alive, of course. But where are they? Where is this "life?" A dark room, much like a scene from the walls of Paleolithic art, like a setting in one of Blanchot's novels, or a room from Kafka's *Metamorphosis*, a room that exists in a text. Is this a real vision or is it an invention, a textual animal, a textual head emerging from the wall of language? What are the links here between the seeing, the vision, and the saying of it in the form of a writing? One could extrapolate endlessly, so it seems. The point is that such emanations come from "the space inside," yet they are also outside: they are writings. They are also "out there," in the night. Michaux really experiences these mental visions. But he does not experience them as mere projections of subconscious states. They do not live on a life borrowed from their beholder. The head comes ferociously from the wall, from the unseen other side of the wall. It has its own life and even wrestles with the visionary who beholds it. Michaux's vision seems shamanistic. His solitude has come to life in the form of a head now dashing at top speed and in a thousand ways throughout his room. Meeting it head-on shall require extreme measures. The vision transforms the writer's body into a contradictory, impossible state of being, both hard and fluid but "infinitely more mobile" than his own natural body. Movement is its essential attribute. As a new phantasmal body, he is able "to dash impetuously," passing through walls and doors. Hurling himself repeatedly against the doors of a glass cabinet, he is transported, astonished, but even more astonished in the end when he sees that in fact nothing is broken, nothing is even scratched or unhinged. There is not even a squeak. The shaman has journeyed between—and this betweenness must be stressed—between center and absence, where the between

---

18. Michaux, *Émergences-Résurgences*, in *OC* III, 552 (*Emergences/Resurgences*, 14).

marks no space or distance between a center that is always missing and an absence that is always ambiguously there, both named in the writing and disappearing back into the whiteness of the blank page. The vision passes; solitude leaves nothing behind but writing.[19]

Michaux's discovery of Paul Klee and Max Ernst was important for the way their images are not so much applied to the surface of the paper as seeming to emerge from it, whether through their use of watercolor or frottage. Struggling to find his way as an untrained artist, Michaux lets himself go, adopting a technique that emphasizes pure spontaneity rather than rules and planning. "I throw off my chains," he writes, "the chain of lies, of the falsity of my calm demeanor, or my various assertions of hope or confidence in the future, I who have lost all hope . . . everything has collapsed." These lines were written in the early days of 1948, during a time of profound personal crisis. His wife, Marie-Louise, gravely burned in an accident for which Michaux blamed himself, was dying in the hospital.[20] Spontaneous painting and drawing was a release from the anxiety. But it was not a time for writing. Michaux claims to have abandoned words and writing: too close to philosophies and the "sciences of man," never "rustic enough," always too much the machinery of preestablished rules and syntaxes that strangle creativity. Language, likened to an "immense, prefabricated house handed down from generation to generation, ever demanding faithful residence," becomes a weight. He now seeks a new, more direct, more immediate, more spontaneous movement that would upend such vast architectures. Using watercolors, in "jerky, disheveled gestures (*gestes saccadés*)" the heads emerge from the paper, mostly "irregular and unfinished."[21] But writing and images will conjoin once again in the form of invented calligrams that appear in works he shares with the Chinese painter Zao Wou-Ki.

Another text, *Turbulent Infinity* (originally published in 1957), continues this struggle between seeing and saying. This time the experience is of mescaline and the recurrent problem is how to record these experiences. The text posts a record of eight experiences with mescaline that Blanchot comments on at some length. From his childhood, Michaux had felt a

---

19. See Raymond Bellour, "Notices" on "Plume précédé de Lointain interieur," in *OC* I, 1241.

20. Jean-Pierre Martin, *Henri Michaux* (Paris: Gallimard, 2003), especially chap. XVII, 441ff.

21. Michaux, *Émergences-Résurgences*, in *OC* III, 550–51, 568, 571 (*Emergences/Resurgences*, 12–13, 28).

religious calling. Perhaps he even wanted to be a priest. Now, faithless in his fifties, he writes in the third mescaline experience of the second series, "I SAW THOUSANDS OF GODS. . . . They were *there*, present, more present that anything I've ever looked at in my life. And it was impossible. . . . Still, they were there, arrayed in their hundreds one beside the other. . . . They—those divine beings—and I: alone facing each other."[22] Although these lines were written by a lucid mind, "the most lucid," Blanchot writes, and we should have no reason to doubt that Michaux really did experience this vision and the reality of these "thousands of gods," do we have to upend everything, our occupations, our thoughts, in order to question ourselves on this important affirmation? Not at all. Even Michaux's admirers seem to pass by, unmoved.[23]

Under the title *Miserable miracle* (originally published in 1956),[24] describing several of his adventures with mescaline, Michaux says he wrote a "proud" book. He is in full possession of his powers; he is calm; in some of the accounts, masterful. He writes in a measured way about that which is without measure, describing an equality that is without equal. In the midst of these experiences brought on by a powerful drug, he is able to maintain a much more regulated and powerful sense of control than when he abandons himself to the "deregulated." But Blanchot notes a difference in tone between *Miserable miracle* and *Turbulent Infinity*. In the latter title, he is less approachable, more reserved; mescaline inspires his confidence where his readers do not. Has mescaline offered him the chance to cross the

---

22. Michaux, *OC* III, 852 (*Darkness Moves*, 209).

23. Blanchot, "L'infini et l'infini," 83. English versions of this text are mine.

24. Another, small book of mescaline inspired texts, *Paix dans le brisements* [*Peace in the Breaking*] (originally published in 1959), could also be mentioned in this context (in *OC* II, 980–1010). Here, Michaux writes of his visions of "ce tapis vibratile":

> This vibratile carpet, which had something in common with electrical discharges with ramified sparks, as well as with magnetic spectra, a certain something that trembled, that burned, that tingled, like spasms turned into nerves . . . that nervous projection screen, even more enigmatic than the visions that arose on it, I don't know, I will never know how to talk about it properly. . . . Fast, they come fast, fast in single file, passing, fleeing, disappearing, thoughts in a nascent state, thoughts in freedom, the only ones known to be free . . . about which neither you, nor your desires, nor your will can do anything, neither to sort them out nor to do anything else. (*OC* II, 996, 999; trans. Gillian Conoley in *Thousand Times Broken* [San Francisco: City Lights, 2014], 41, 47.)

threshold of human finitude? Has he passed to the other side, no longer just describing the infinite he experiences but having himself become infinite, through mescaline, "excessively finite?"[25]

Blanchot will not subscribe to this idea. Michaux has not delivered himself to any such thing. Michaux will not surrender to the mescaline, just as he will not surrender himself to the "enemy." Perhaps the mescaline imposed itself even more immoderately in order to make itself better understood, better "seized" by the forceps of writing. Whatever the case, the experience is described with clarity. Yet, where mescaline may generally be an amusing experience, a fourth experience recorded in *Miserable miracle* is much worse due to Michaux having made an error in the dosage. Now he is delivered over to an experience that is unforeseeable and insupportable. Yet deception is again in play here. Michaux writes how "terrible, beyond terrible" the experience is, yet the miserable miracle of mescaline is still nothing more than a frightful mirage of the mind (*l'esprit*). Its powerful upheaval is a power of the mind.

For Blanchot, the word "infinite" is essential—it appears in the title to his own writing, *The Infinite Conversation*—for the way it designates an open, infinite movement becoming something Other, a reality or an extreme region that cannot be approached or grasped through the power of concepts. Is thought infinite, thought as a power of the infinite, that even art does not seek it insofar as art does not seek power? There is another infinite in Michaux, a "turbulent infinite," one closer to an unutterable powerlessness, that is at stake in Michaux's art. Mescaline has a power, a cold, pure power in which the impurity of the mind can take refuge to increase its power. But this power, plus the turbulent infinite that it puts to work, do they not evoke, despite themselves, the cold and chaste tyranny of science? This is Blanchot's thesis: the madness of mescaline is the madness of science itself, the "dry horror of an implacable precision."[26] The madness of mescaline can be regulated to some extent, as the proper dosages are known and regulated by scientific experiments. Michaux is thus in a position both contrary to mescaline, fighting its terrible and terrifying power, not wanting to give in to his enemy, the poison, as he calls it, and at the same time in complicity with it, following and observing its power, in comparison to which even the

---

25. Blanchot, "L'infini et l'infini," 84. Blanchot writes: "Elle (la mescaline), dépasserait la façon humaine qui est incertaine et indécise; infinite, étant excessivement finie" ("It [mescaline], would go beyond the human way which is uncertain and indecisive; infinite, being excessively finite"; trans. mine).

26. Blanchot, "L'infini et l'infini," 86; trans. mine.

finest pages of literature seem flat, "uninteresting, stingy, and cramped."[27] But from the standpoint of scientific observation, mescaline also has its faults, as Michaux duly notes: its apparitions, its visions, come and go too quickly. In the preface to *Miserable Miracle*, Michaux writes, "The insurmountable difficulties come from the incredible rapidity of the apparition, transformation, and disappearance of the visions." To undertake a mescaline experience is to become subjected to "gusts" of movement, gusts of images, gusts of yes and no, and all of it stereotypical, Michaux notes. The pace is maddening. And they are too many; its multiplicity is a problem. It is also unemotional, cold, unforgiving.[28]

"Shaken, broken, but refusing to give in to it,"[29] Michaux considers mescaline as both enemy and friend, an indefatigable enemy up to the point of offering what Blanchot calls a secret friendship, a friendship for which it demands all secrecy.[30] Yet mescaline's revelations are something that becomes a written and figured thing in Michaux's books. The secret friendship it may have afforded is brought to light, exposed, described, resisted, subjected to typologies and experimentations, its infinite thereby becoming something finite. It is always there, the infinite speed of its movement having become something almost static, finished, seized in signs, descriptions, typologies. It has thereby lost the essential "imminence of a revelation" and has become instead "the imminence of a thought which is ever but the thought of an eternal imminence."[31] In his pursuit of a knowledge of mescaline's effects, in his recording of its infinite movement, in his creation of what might seem a new genre of literature, has Michaux abandoned literature through these mescaline books, not just through his scorn but precisely by abandoning what Blanchot calls literature's "eternal imminence?"

---

27. Michaux, quoted by Blanchot in "L'infini et l'infini," 87.

28. Michaux, quoted by Blanchot in "L'infini et l'infini." See *Misérable miracle*, in *OC* II, 620 (*Miserable Miracle*, 6–7).

29. Michaux, *Miserable Miracle*, 6–7. "Je 'n'etais pas neuter non plus, de quoi je ne me defends pas. La Mescaline et moi, nous étions souvent plus en lute qu'ensemble. J'etais secoué, cassé, mais je ne marchais pas." *Misérable miracle*, in *OC* II, 620.

30. Blanchot, "L'infini et l'infini," 87. "Comme si l'artificieuse mescaline ôtait lucidement ce qu'elle donne, ennemie de tous et d'elle-même, infatigable ennemie, jusqu'a cette secrete amité pour laquelle elle exige le secret" ("As if the artful mescaline lucidly took away what it gives, enemy of everyone and of itself, indefatigable enemy, even that secret friendship for which it demands secrecy"; trans. mine).

31. Blanchot, "L'infini et l'infini," 88.

Mescaline, Science, or Sorcerer?

> Les drogues nous ennuient avec leur paradis.
> Qu'elles nous donnent plutôt un peu savoir.
> Nous ne somme pas un siècle à paradis.[32]
>
> —Henri Michaux, *Connaissance par les gouffres*

Seeing and seizing were always linked and mingled in Michaux's work. There are two ways of seeing and seizing in Michaux: the written, discursive document and the figural drawing, the graphic sign. Whereas the first seizes by naming and conceptualizing and so often fails, the latter, insofar as it is seen as a representational image, both sees and seizes the moment of mescaline's effect. This is more successful, or so it would seem.[33]

Our thesis is that these ways of seizing are also ways of Michaux's being seized by the very "turbulent infinity" he denounces by naming. He is seized by what he cannot himself seize.

In the mescaline experiments, as recorded in *Miserable Miracle*, for example, or in such texts as the one quoted below, seeing (*le voir*) is also having (*l'avoir*). Michaux compares the experiments with mescaline to looking for hours through a microscope, a task that left him distraught and tired of being distraught.[34]

Seeing implies separation of the seer from the seen. Seeing can also be a seizing that attempts to cross that gap. The mental image experienced seems to be an outside brought to the inside (*dedans*). This is not the case.

---

32. Michaux, *Connaissance par les gouffres*, in *OC* III, 3. ("Drugs bore us with their paradise. / Let them rather give us a little knowledge. / We are not a century in paradise"; trans. mine.) Raymond Bellour notes the "celebrated" opposition active in *Connaissance par les gouffres* between "connaissance" and "paradis," the one implying self-possession and the "démon de la connaissance" and the other, the violent, destructive loss and fragmentation of self. The term "paradis" in this sense contains an implicit reference to Baudelaire's 1860 work on wine, opium, and hashish, *Les paradis artificiels*. See also Laurent Jenny, "Voir le paradis?" in *Passages et langages de Henri Michaux*, eds. Jean-Claude Mathieu and Michel Collot (Paris: Librairie José Corti, 1987), 271–81. Cited in *OC* III, 1468–1492.

33. See Margaret Rigaud-Drayton, *Henri Michaux: Poetry, Painting, and the Universal Sign* (Oxford: Clarendon Press, 2005), 119.

34. Michaux, *Misérable miracle*, in *OC* II, 621. Trans. Louise Varése and Anna Moschovakis as *Miserable Miracle* (New York: New York Review Books, 2002), 7.

The outside is already on the inside. The seen in this case is but a construct of the perceptual apparatus and the human imagination. The drawing is the direct recording of this thing seen qua inner, psychological experience. The mescaline experience and its visions are remembered, grasped as memories, then captured by being drawn by a hand that may be following its own courses, an enchanted hand. The images are then exhibited in galleries. As graphic signs on exhibition or published in books, they close the gap between Michaux's experience, mediated by the image, and the spectator, the gallery visitor, the one who contemplates Michaux's drawing. In this way, the terrifying original inner experience is transmogrified, becoming a communication but also a property or a possession circulating in a market. A communication broken on the pulverized shards of these images, all that remains of the original experience *dedans*, inside, a footprint in the sand.

Who has not wanted to see and to grasp in some way what is seen? To seize more and to seize beings and things in new ways, not just with words, phonemes, or other poetic means but with graphic signs, a new way, a new possibility for writing—a way of writing that is a way of being seized by the madness of visions? These are the question Michaux poses to his readers. Who has not wanted to "make an alphabet" or even a vocabulary from which the verbal component was excluded? "Not wanting to be receptive," rejecting passivity, Michaux's desire was to seize, to grasp so as see, where to seize is to know, not by words but by signs of his own invention, where, in his desire to grasp, he ends up being the one grasped, in and through the images he makes. A passivity emerges sponsored by his resistance to it.

> I refused to be receptive,
> I fought against taking it in
> Seizing
> Wanting to seize, seizing grabbed me (*m'accapara*)
> I was no longer anything but grabbed
> All my mind (*l'esprit*), seized, a being seized
> Gripped, invaded
> Seized and striking
> With the style itself of the seizing.[35]

How does this work out in the context of the mescaline experiences?

---

35. Michaux, "Saisir," in *OC* III, 936, 951. Trans. by Richard Sieburth as "Grasp," in *Stroke by Stroke* (Brooklyn, NY: Archipelago Books, 2006), unpaginated.

Again, Michaux is not looking for an "artificial paradise" when he consumes mescaline. "This is not a century for such a paradise," he writes. He wanted knowledge "une peu de savoir." Where Blanchot doubts Michaux's attempts to make a new literature from his mescaline experiments, a literature that would be discursive matter of words and phonemes, other commentators, most notably Franck Leibovici, have shown how Michaux pursued neither paradise nor literature, but "a little knowledge" in the experiments.[36] But Leibovici and Michaux himself also question the possibility of the mescaline visions ever being fully translated, transmogrified from their ephemeral, phantom-like states into lasting, stabilized discursive or figural forms that might be useful to knowledge. Without this, how is a *connaissance* (knowledge), as in *Connaissance par les gouffres*, possible?

The problem, as we have said, lies in seizing beings, images, movements that are inherently vanishing as they appear. As yet another commentator has said, there is a gulf between what the drug presents to the person who has actually ingested it, its interior images, and what the drug leaves behind for others to see, the leavings or scraps, a "déchiquètement d'écriture," a glacial moraine of broken drawings and notes that would supposedly constitute the objective record of the experience.[37] Even the emergence of the phenomena cannot be controlled or even anticipated. As Michaux recounts, "In my present interior movement certain animals arrived without having been solicited. Others obstinately refused to appear. I could not annex them with my drawings" (*OC* III, 938; trans. mine). Any attempt to seize or represent the mescaline experiences in the manner of a scientifically controlled experiment is doomed to failure. Mescaline's images and words are not susceptible to being represented or described as objects. They are unsolicited emergences, the imprint or signature of forces outside of the government of syntax, concepts, or a will, forces that cannot be seized insofar as they seize Michaux in all their sudden and vanishing appearances, seizing and passing, a thunderbolt, through his mind's eye and hand and onto the empty pages before him. Thousands of pages of scratchings and graspings are produced, the seismographic imprints of the turbulent infinity that is here the unseizable *fond* of text and image, a *fond* that rises and seizes Michaux's "interior movement."

The mescaline experiences occurred in a tightly controlled circum-

---

36. Leibovici, *Henri Michaux*, 186ff.

37. Henri-Alexis Baatsch, "Déserts peints," in *Henri Michaux* (Paris: Centre Georges Pompidou, 1978), 122.

stance. In 1954, Jean Paulhan invited Michaux to a study of mescaline's effects on the human brain, initiated by Doctor Julian de Ajuriguerra and Pierre Pichot at Sainte-Anne's hospital in Paris. Michaux himself had never been one to experiment with drugs. He was a drinker of water who had only had a few casual experiences with ether; never alcohol. "Fatigue is my drug," he claimed (*OC* II, 767). He was not the type to suffer addictions. Michaux took several precautions for the experiments: the curtains in the room were closed, silence reigned, there was some tea available and the music of Alan Berg. Michaux took notes, attempting to make an account truly in accord with what he was experiencing. The act of ingesting drugs has little or no benefit to knowledge. What counts is the faithful, accurate record of the experience. But the "écriture mescalinienne" was a disappointing mess. Words or phrases were written only to quickly fall apart on the page into illegible, melting scribbles.

Some years later, in 1963, Michaux and Éric Duvivier made a short film about the mescaline experiences, *Images d'un monde visionnaire*. It may have seemed somewhat of a failure in its attempt to re-create a mescaline experience, but what Michaux appreciated about film in this regard was its being a moving continuum, twenty-four frames per second, and not a discrete discontinuity of words and sentences or still images spread across a page. The drawings of mescaline visions lacked the temporality of film, its capacity to communicate the vertiginous, breakneck speed of the mescaline visions in a way that neither words nor drawings ever could. Time is seemingly a dominant dimension in Michaux's mescaline experiences, much more so than space.[38] Moreover, with the viewer sitting alone in the darkened cinema, the hallucinatory, dreamlike quality of the film was also conducive to communicating something of Michaux's original mescaline visions. These were crucial elements that writing and drawing could not equal. The shortcomings of writing and drawing in working up a scientific record of the mescaline experiences became an important stumbling block in the experiments Michaux underwent beginning in 1954.

---

38. Blanchot, for just one example, remarks on the priority of time over space in Henri Michaux's mescaline writings. "D'autres substances donnent l'immense espace. . . . La mescaline est presque sans espace, elle fait de la pensée la ligne cruellement droite, indéfiniment réduite à l'émiettement ponctuel: une éternité réduite à un point" ("Other substances give an immense space. . . . Mescaline is *almost* spaceless, it makes thought a cruelly straight line, indefinitely reduced to a punctual crumbling: an eternity reduced to a point"; trans. mine). Blanchot, "L'infini et l'infini," 87.

The first stage of the experiment consisted in Michaux taking notes in a state of "full perturbation." There were about 150 pages of such notes, but only thirty-two were reproduced in the book *Miserable Miracle*. They comprise the "proof" of the experience, the first attempt at a graphic translation of the mescaline-induced visions. A typed draft is then prepared. The experiences are thus filtered through a "typographic wall." The drawings, largely made from memory, are a third state of composition. A series emerges, beginning with the experience, passing through the note taking, together with whatever drawings were attempted, then a verbal and visual translation of the experience, which takes place in the days after the experience. But at best, these can only be a general equivalent. Actually, one is never quite certain of what one is experiencing in the interior visual experience of the drug. You really do not see, so you must guess, you must interpret what there is to see since the images are always in such a torrential flux that even memory is disabled. Seeing, seizing, reading the mescaline visions constitutes an arc that is always fragmented and unstable.

Compare this with a philosophical way of treating sensation and perceptual experience as described in Kant's transcendental deduction of the synthesis of perception. Kant's synthesis of perception is a synthesis of multiplicity that begins with the "apprehension," or intuition, of successive parts of sensation, follows through the "reproduction" of preceding experiential parts, and results in a "recognition" of the object of perception in and through the subsumption of perceptions, or intuitions, under concepts of the understanding. Thus, a general object (object = x) of experience emerges as the basis for objectivity in science. The subsumption of the sensible under a concept is an act of what Kant calls judgment. Kant and Michaux are at different levels or orders of experience: Kant is concerned with the visible, with sense experience, whereas Michaux is concerned with visions, inner visions. There is no judgment in Michaux; there is no standard of measure for the fury of the mescaline visions, no way of deciding what constitutes "a part" in the experience, no concepts that could grasp his visions, no "synthesis of the imagination" as between "center and absence"—there is only infinite movement. Mescaline leaves Michaux not with an object in general, the stabilized appearing of an object = x, something that could be seized and translated, but only with visions that appear and disappear before any such synthesis can be enacted. Thus, there can be no objectivity, which is essential for knowledge. Michaux's is always an inner experience, but one that challenges and contests any notion of a continuous, unified subjectivity and Cartesian-like inwardness. There is a *dedans*, as he calls it, but it is neither objective nor subjective. This is not to say that there is no *one* self; nor is to say that there are many selves, or that the self is a multiplicity. Rather, it is to affirm that there is *no* self. But who or what is the "I" of this experience? Who or what is the author of these pages we read in *Miserable Miracle*, for example? Mescaline's torrent shatters the very notion and possibility of there being a single unified, prelapsarian subject that might sustain this experience. For Michaux, the ego is at best an illusion, or a construct, reconstructed only later, piece by shattered piece. The idea of a single abiding and substantial, cognizing, judging self or subject, the philosopher's "thinking I," somehow standing behind these experiences as their witness and constituting source, has no place in the experiences recorded in *Miserable Miracle*. The "I" is transformed into a subject-less gaze. So too the "I" that paints. There is a generalized collapse, an erasure of the "will" whereby art lives only where the will and the subject that is its domain, pass away, are lost, abandoned, flowing out and away through the ink on paper.

Moreover, however intimate/ex-timate perception and representation may be, they can never completely overlap. To say that I am presently seeing something, a mescaline-induced vision, is but a report, not a vision, as Wittgenstein wrote in his *Philosophical Investigations*. "The language-game of reporting can be given such a turn that a report is not meant to inform the hearer about its subject matter but about the person making the report."[39] Can we ever get back behind the report to the raw, primary, initial vision by way of words or images? A text and image can only be but a rough framework for the experience, they cannot actually restore it or present it as something to be studied and reviewed. Michaux's notes and drawings are always at a distance from the original experience and constitute a report, a new order, a new level of experience. There always remains much of the experience that is incommunicable. How, for example, can one present in the form of drawings, images, or words a vision of infinite movement, a vision of a "turbulent infinity," which was indeed one of the most persistent and essential experiences brought on by mescaline? Wouldn't writing itself have to be infinite as it sought the impossible: to be the infinite?[40]

---

39. Ludwig Wittgenstein, *Philosophical Investigations*, 3rd ed., trans. G. E. M. Anscombe (New York: Macmillan, 1971), 190.

40. Writing *avec* Michaux, Alain Jouffroy writes, "l'homme qui écrit fait appel au 'Tout,' à la totalité. Ce qui l'empêche d'écrire, à la limite, n'exist pas: c'est pourquoi l'objet de l'écriture, son seul objet—est l'infini." *Avec Henri Michaux* (Paris: Rocher, 1992),

Michaux admits the impossibility of this in *Miserable Miracle*. He was an "infinity machine." But he could not actually touch the infinite since it is not an object of thought but the insane, unapproachable undercurrent that embraces every attempt to conceptualize or seize it. All he could do was to accept "infinite fragmentation, the teeming state composed of what is smallest, which divides and overruns everything." What does emerge is a provisional "model" of the infinite, narrated as the exhausting task of continuously extracting himself from one error only to fall into another, countless times, like a man running from one empty room to another in a palace that had numberless rooms. Counting, the reproduction of preceding parts, was impossible. And the whole rapid experience was such a fury of movement, an infinite speed of trial and error, that it probably only lasted about fifty seconds.[41]

Let us see another instance of this. Michaux tries to assure us that the mescaline vision lives in a "world of signs."[42] He experiences a long, infinitely long, trench or furrow (*le sillon*), a "furrow with little, hurried, transversal sweepings. In it a fluid, its brightness mercurial, its behavior torrential, its speed electric. . . . Where is this furrow exactly . . . crossing my skull . . . a furrow without beginning or end . . . a furrow that I'd say comes from one end of the earth, goes through me and on to the other end of the earth."[43] The furrow remains a constant in his visions, a constant "problem." He tried to reproduce it through the many sketches gathered in the pages of *Miserable Miracle*. Could it, too, have been a sign made by the "baboon mescaline through its silly images?"[44] Even the noises he experienced constitute signs. In mescaline's world of uncertainty, of transport and fleeting movements, signs become the only means of support. But this does not make that experience any more communicable, for these signs are not really signifiers, for they lack a signified or referent. The sign vanishes along with whatever it may have signified.

The binding together of the transfixing vision and the seizing or transfixing of that vision in writings or drawings, the translation of such

---

103. ("The man who writes appeals to the 'All,' to totality. What prevents him from writing, at the limit, does not exist: this is why the object of writing, its only object—is infinity"; trans. mine.)

41. Michaux, *Misérable miracle*, in *OC* II, 682 (*Miserable Miracle*, 70–79).

42. Michaux, *Connaissance par les gouffres*, in *OC* III, 115.

43. Michaux, *Misérable miracle*, in *OC* II, 626 (*Miserable Miracle*, 13).

44. Michaux, 695 (*Miserable Miracle*, 84).

a spellbinding intuition into significations, or into stable images or representations, is always a deceptive and vain process that both requires and ruins the symbolic orders of writing and drawing. Art, poetry, and prose are twisted into new, unexpected forms. The attempt to make art and poetry a means or conduit of knowledge, to empower them to communicate the unknowable, is to take language to the limit where it falls into silence, into a "dissemination into the flux," as Bellour wrote. It is to take *savoir* to the limit where it is *non-savoir*. It is to press and shred the symbolic order, perhaps in an attempt to touch what Jacques Lacan called "the Real" that dark, unnamable hole that disrupts discourse, causing it to stammer, bringing it to a stop. It is unlikely that there can ever be a true, faithful representation of the drug's visions in whatever form, whether discursive or figurative. Translating the vision annuls it. The vision shatters the chains of signifiers. The translation, the seizing, always defaces that initial, undeniable and powerful presence that marks the veracity of the vision. To seize what cannot be seized can only end in error and failure, signs without any transcendental signified or reference, lines that twist and fall off the page. The powerful presence encountered in the visions is overpowering and cannot be re-presented, destined only to disappear as though disappearance is the essence of appearance.

We have been dealing with the tension in Michaux's work—the "double pulsion"—whereby the pursuit of knowledge (*savoir*) is constantly both facilitated and upended in and by his poetics and painting. The pursuit of knowledge produces statements and concepts but always brushes up against the limits of language and conceptualization. The work of writing about or on the mescaline experience produces or results in not so much an oeuvre but a *desoeuvrement* of the discursive forms of knowledge.

Let us explore this further. Leibovici's remarkable book on Michaux says that the primordial question for Michaux is how to make the visions stand up, stick, hold on, stay (*tenir*) so that they can support the psychological sciences.[45] The term "presence," the undeniable, irrevocable presence of the vision, reinforced Michaux's faith that his visions were not just hallucinations but something that could be objectified, saved, or worked up into if not a conceptualization of the mescaline experience then an experience that unravels the methods and goals of knowledge in this case, that even unravels the more general possibility of there being a science of the visions at all but that still holds out hope for a science of the mescaline experience

---

45. Leibovici, *Voir*, 241.

that could possibly assuage the maladies of tormented souls. Michaux's "electrified writing," his "l'écriture mescalinienne," as Alain Jouffroy calls it, would also place him as though under a great dome in the great hall of a train station where voices and sounds are reflected, a zone located between consciousness and the unconscious where everything arrives and departs almost simultaneously, the great hall where he would find a new definition of consciousness, one that would put all consciousness into question.[46] Where writing would surely fail in this task, art, drawing, was to be the way in which the vision's presence could be made to stand up, stick, and hold on. To what extent then, Leibovici asks, can art be the producer of forms of knowledge? In Leibovici's reading, Michaux proposes a "redistribution of the frontiers" between poetry, painting, and science, a new alliance between them, as though at one level they are all doing somewhat the same thing. Like science, Leibovici argues, poetry "invents intellectual technologies," thus permitting a process of objectification. Descriptions allow one to leave the inner, private domain of the "I," the domain of inner certainties, in order to constitute images that could be made public, published as texts, and so help ensure the process of objectification. The nature of the image ties Michaux's enterprise to the production of knowledge. The mescaline drawings amount, in other words, to something like an "atlas" of maps of the experience.[47]

A Turbulent Infinity

But it is the infinite, the turbulent infinite, that is decisive here. How does one map the turbulence of the infinite? How can one give form to formlessness? This is the crucial problem for Michaux. If a map could index the infinite, if it could provide the formal points that would correspond to an actual topography, then the problem can be resolved. Could that work in this case? There are no points in the turbulent infinity that one could be seized and symbolized on a map. Constant flux would preclude such an operation. Are Michaux's drawings of the infinite "trench" (*sillon*), for example, an "intellectual technology" invented by drawing? Or is this infinite always something else, a madness, a terrible and terrifying power, a pulsation of movement that shreds writing and drawing, a chaos for which a map could only be provisionally worked on what Deleuze has called drawing's plane

---

46. Jouffroy, *Avec Henri Michaux*, 112.
47. Leibovici, *Voir*, 242–43.

of composition? Isn't the turbulent an infinite disaster—literature's infinite imminence, as Blanchot called it[48]—that the work of art and poetry might wish, thereby, to forestall, the writer writing so as to keep madness at bay? The turbulent infinity that must be seen as an enemy and as a danger yet that also flows into and through writing and drawing, a force from the outside, as it were, that flows through the inside of writing and drawing. Is this not what Michaux's mescaline drawings and writings attempt to say and to see but always fail in every attempt?

Gilles Deleuze has discussed the philosophical legacy of the infinite in his commentaries on two of his seventeenth-century intellectual heroes: Leibniz and Spinoza. For Spinoza, substance is infinite in its attributes. The attributes constitute an infinity. Thus, infinity "has a nature" for these philosophers, which they called a positive infinity, or what Daniel W. Smith's important book on Deleuze calls an "actual infinity."[49] This positive infinity, which Merleau-Ponty, quoted by Deleuze in his commentary, calls a most difficult notion of seventeenth-century thought, arises from Spinoza's theory of individuation, whereby an individual is thought to be composed of an infinity of parts. There are two approaches to this, entailing a distinction between an indefinite conception of the infinite and one that rests on a finite analysis. Following Daniel Smith's helpful commentary, we see that a finite analysis breaks down the individual into its component parts; eventually one obtains a part or a term that is ultimate: the atom, for example. By contrast, the indefinite analysis holds that one can never reach an ultimate or final term, the breakdown into parts would go on indefinitely.

Deleuze sees another alternative in the notion of a positive or actual infinity. The analysis of terms can go on to infinity, but the parts are not atoms but infinitely small, "vanishing terms," as Leibniz would say.[50] Thus, the terms of a positive infinity cannot be quantified, can never be treated individually, can never be counted one by one. But, as Smith writes, "infinitely small terms can only exist in infinite collections."[51] They are "multiplicities"

---

48. Blanchot, "L'infini et l'infini," 88.
49. Gilles Deleuze, *Expressionism in Philosophy: Spinoza*, trans. Martin Joughin (New York: Zone Books, 1992), 29. See Daniel W. Smith, *Essays on Deleuze* (Edinburgh: Edinburgh University Press, 2012), 249.
50. Smith, 249. Leibniz quoted by Smith.
51. Smith, 249.

that have no parts. They are intensities.⁵² Spinoza's modes are infinite in this way, not as quantified countables, not as mathematizable parts, but as multiplicities that are intensities. This becomes the crucial point for Michaux's notion of an intolerable infinite. It is not an infinite of form but of formless intensities. Since it cannot be counted or be treated as the referent for a mathematical proposition concerning the nature of the infinite, it can only be approached on a plane of composition as a drawing, as a poetry. These will constitute what Lacan might call the *matheme* for the turbulent infinite, an infinite that is as much outside as inside, an infinite that invades, that overwhelms the observing eye.

This formlessness of the turbulent infinite recalls Bataille's text "Formless," published in *Documents* no. 7, December 1929.⁵³ Bataille writes, the word "formless" does not have only a grammatical, adverbial function but can also serve to " 'bring things down in the world,' specifically, the philosophical claim that each thing has its form."⁵⁴ Formlessness has no "rights." It is no better or no different than a spider or an earthworm squashed on the street. But "academic men" are only content with a world in which everything has its form. "All of philosophy . . . is a matter of giving a . . . mathematical frock coat (*une reddingote mathématique*), to what is." To say that the universe is formless is to say that the "universe is something like a crushed spider or spit (*crachat*)."⁵⁵ And this is precisely what Michaux says, that nature is something like "une pâte d'on ne se quoi," an ill-defined blob, a wad of paste.⁵⁶ Hence art cannot represent this formlessness in artistic forms with any success, but it must rather perform it in blobs of paint, or in the gesture signs or the scribble drawings. Such drawings that accompany

---

52. Smith, 249.

53. Bataille, "Informe," in *Oeuvres complètes I* (Paris: Gallimard, 1970), 217. Trans. by Allan Stoekl as "Formless," in *Visions of Excess: Selected Writings, 1927–1939* (Minneapolis: University of Minnesota Press, 1985), 31.

54. Bataille, *Oeuvres complètes I* (Paris: Gallimard, 1970), 217. Trans. by Allan Stoekl as "Formless," in *Visions of Excess: Selected Writings, 1927–1939* (Minneapolis: University of Minnesota Press, 1985), 31.

55. Bataille, *OC* I, 217/31.

56. Michaux, *Ecuador*, in *OC* I, 151. Trans. by Robin Magowan as *Ecuador* (Seattle: University of Washington Press, 1970), 25. Quoted in Rigaud-Drayton, *Henri Michaux*, 117.

Miserable Miracle and the Mercure de France edition of *L'Infini turbulent* are not attempts at mimesis or representations. On their own plane of composition, they are performances. Not re-presentations, they are presentations, the points of emergence for turbulence and misery as "blocs of sensation" and as "affects" (Deleuze) of the infinite.

Perhaps the infinite becomes for Michaux very vaguely something like the regulative ideas of World, Soul, and God in Kant's first critique: it is a problem, an objective problem. Take the Idea of the World, or the Universe. For Kant, to speak of the totality of the Universe is an illusion generated from a false problem that arises from the category of causality. In this conception of causality, an event A would lead to B and to C and on and on until a causal network is established that would go infinitely in all directions. Grasping this network mathematically and in its entirety would mean that we could grasp the universe in its entirety, in its ideality, and we could then know it for what it is. The noumenal would thus be phenomenalized, made an object for science. But we cannot grasp this infinite series. The causal network shows not how the totality can be grasped, made into something formed and known, but how it is a problem. We should not begin by looking at the universe or at the world as though it is an object, something formed and defined by the causal series that constitute it, but rather as something to be questioned without suppositions. A similar situation arises when we try to conceive the eternity of the universe. We are again in the domain of a "transcendental illusion," looking for ideas or objects to be known rather than as a "problem to which there is no solution."[57]

These perspectives once again underscore the difficulty of trying to seize the visions of the turbulent infinity and make them available for psychological science. At every moment in its presentation or in its actuality in the visions, the infinite is objectively unassignable, its structure, if indeed we can speak of the Michaux's experience of the infinite as having a structure, is constituted by an infinite set of divergent and unceasing movements without having any centers of gravity. To seek to grasp this turbulent infinite as a thing to be known rather than as an objective problem, as something to be questioned, is to betray it, make it into a "transcendental illusion," when in fact its powerful presence—an insistent, despotic accentuation like that he experienced of the "thousands of gods"—is the hallmark of Michaux's "faith"

---

57. Immanuel Kant, *Critique of Pure Reason*, trans. Norman Kemp Smith (London: Macmillan, 1929), 319. See Smith, *Essays on Deleuze*, 251.

that his visions of the infinite are not in fact illusions or hallucinations. They are really there, as he writes.[58]

The encounter with the infinite leaves in its wake a new vision of the human body, one that might compare with Deleuze's "body without organs." Michaux's images of the human figure were played in the rhythms of the infinite. Images of bodies traversed, seized by mescaline, bodies that have crossed a threshold, leaving behind a world of steady forms and solid regularities. His body has become a force field invaded and possessed by the infinite. Such a body, such an experience, recalls in its intensity Deleuze's body without organs. We could suggest at this point that Michaux's mescaline books, perhaps alongside Spinoza's *Ethics*, is another book of the body without organs. Deleuze's concept of the body without organs connotes a body without the organic grammar or fleshy syntax of organs, without "organ-ization," so to speak, without the hierarchies of organs as one might find in classical images of the body with the head, the guiding, thinking, directing brain at the top; the heart, seat of courage and spiritedness, in the center; and the stomach, the alimentary canals, and the sexual functions at the bottom as the sources of nourishment and reproduction, a classical hierarchical body of human functions. By contrast, in its lack—it is not a "scene," nor a "place," nor even a "support upon which something comes to pass"[59]—Deleuze's body without organs is a body of intensities, a body where intensities pass and circulate, "producing them in a *spatium*," the space of an infinite turbulence that is itself "intensive, lacking extension."[60] Thus Deleuze envisions the "body without organs" as an "intense egg," lacking the strata of organs, and "defined by axes and vectors, gradients and thresholds" rather than organic functions.[61] Organs are thus not constants; they can change when they cross a threshold; they become "pure intensities, involving the transformations of energy." They become kinematic movements, gestures, dances, movements in play. We see this in Michaux's mescaline books, where his own body, tossed and transformed by the turbulent infinity of the mescaline visions, undergoes fabulous changes and migrations, losing

---

58. Michaux, *L'Infini turbulent*, in *OC* II, 812.

59. Gilles Deleuze and Felix Guattari, *A Thousand Plateaus: Capitalism & Schizophrenia*, trans. Brian Massumi (Minneapolis: University of Minnesota Press, 1987), 153.

60. Deleuze and Guattari, 153.

61. Deleuze and Guattari, 153.

all hierarchical functioning, or in his drawings of animal bodies and human bodies published in such books as *Mouvements* or *Emanations-Emergences*. We see bodies in motion, bodies and heads undergoing changes of color and consistency, subject to "split second adjustments," or in Deleuze's words, gesture-bodies, emanations without preexisting models or prototypes, emanations that seem to arise from and point toward a vide-substance. Like the mescaline drawings and visions, these are not bodies that can stand up and pose as regularities for the production of scientific discourses about the body and what it can do. They are pure intensities, a body of writing, a writing of the body braced at the limits of drawing and writing.

Perhaps, then, returning to Leibovici, we can see the drawn image and the written texts as preparing us for what is without image, the *VIDE-SUBSTANCE*, as Michaux calls it in capital letters, where the plane of composition collapses.[62] The image appears on a plane of composition that arises from chaos and sections off a bit of chaos, the diabolical movements that between center and absence arise and disappear into Night and Nothingness (*Vide*). In *Miserable Miracle*, the images and texts, drawings and writings, translate Michaux's vison of something like a ladder, a Jacob's ladder, having a seemingly infinite number of steps leading to "the abstract,"[63] the without-image, where images, in their *usage*—and not due to anything in their intrinsic nature—fail, are rendered "work-less," where writing and drawing fail, can no longer be made to "stand up."[64]

The Void, the emptiness masked by every screen, every image whether written or drawn, haunts every attempt to describe it, to reduce it to words, to concepts, to the sorts of things that can "stand up." To make language "stand up" would be to push language and signification violently into the "Real," driving the luminosity of words into the Night where they can no longer "stand up" or find shelter, where the house of language soon falls, fails, breaks. Poetry shall find its paradoxical "peace" in this breaking, a "vibratory hell" having become a "vibrating paradise" unfolding to infinity. What Lacan would call the Real, or Blanchot, Night, "the disaster," what Michaux called the *VIDE-SUBSTANCE*, are last words, words to end all

---

62. Michaux, "Les Rêves vigiles, in Façons d'endormi, façons d'éveillé," in *OC* III, 531. Quoted n Leibovici, *Voir*, 241. The vide-substance seems a contradictory phrase, vide meaning void or emptiness and substance meaning something substantial, full, perhaps, of being and existence—the opposite of the Void.

63. Michaux, *OC* II, 649 (*Miserable Miracle*, 37).

64. Leibovici, *Voir*, 241.

words. Without words to seize it, to lend it signification, poem and painting become but masks of the Void in its passage, revealing and concealing its inexpressible torrent. Disconnected from "the pleasures and controls of the finite," beyond all matters of the "question" of the nature or the essence of things, the poem is submitted to the turbulent infinite, carried on a wave infinitely unfolding. Is this also its "immortality"? Its "immutability?"

> He who has disconnected himself from the finite, from all the pleasures and controls of the finite, he who has submitted (to the infinite), has acted in a better way.
> While a vibratory hell has become a vibrating paradise and this new environment unfolds its folds to infinity, he experiences in his being astonishingly and rhythmically struck, quite simply, immortality, which is immutability. . . .
> Drunk, possessed, he no longer asks himself what to do with the infinite, whether to love it, adore it, merge into it, or whether it is an illusion or a fake, or only a step, or already promises his nirvana—he is both submerged and carried away by the wave whose nature he questioned. Having gone beyond the question, the food of the gods nourishes him. . . . Infinite badly deserved.[65]

Lignes-Signes: The Adventures of Lines and Signs

Let us now turn to a second pursuit in Michaux, one that also circulates around this nexus of visions, drawings, and writings—namely, his desire to create a universal language.[66] After all we have seen regarding the impossibility of communicating the mescaline visions, it is not surprising to see Michaux in a more generalized questioning of the possibilities and limits of communication through conventional language. He sought a more a

---

65. Michaux, *L'Infini turbulent*, in *OC* III, 933. Mercure de France ed., 20; trans. mine.

66. Rimbaud, in 1871, anticipated Michaux: "The poet, therefore, is truly a thief of fire. He is responsible for humanity, for animals even; he will have to make sure his visions can be smelled, fondled, listened to, if what he brings back from beyond has form, he gives it form; if it has none, he gives it none. A language must be found; besides all speech being idea, a time of universal language will come!" Arthur Rimbaud, "Letter to Paul Demeny," in *Arthur Rimbaud: Complete Works*, trans. Paul Schmidt (New York: Harper Colophon Books, 1976), 103.

universal, perhaps extra-linguistic mode of communication, but one he continued to call a *langue*. He sought "une langue commune," a way whereby beings of other worlds, human and animal, could communicate. It was his personal ambition, his dream, a language envisioned on the other side of "the curtain of dreams."[67] Such a universal language would not only be the result of dreams or voyages into a dream world, but there would also be physical and spiritual journeys that were part of this quest.

Let us begin by outlining these voyages in Michaux's almost Homeric quest for a universal language.

Consider first a 1939 text, *Peintures*, and a first chapter entitled "Qui il est" (*OC* I, 705). Several voyages, physical and spiritual, are recounted here, as we have seen discussed by Margaret Rigaud-Drayton: a first voyage when he was twenty-one years old from his birthplace in Belgium to Paris, from the North to the South, followed by voyages to the West, to the Amazon and the Equator, then to India and China, the Far East. He may have experimented extensively with drugs, but as his biographer Jean-Pierre Martin writes, "the first drug was always India."[68] After several voyages abroad, he may have journeyed through several lives and several bodies: born Belgian, reborn in Paris as French or southern European, then reborn again in India and China as Indian and then Chinese, though living in Paris. It is little wonder he sought a universal language that could communicate across so many borders.

But, as Michaux writes in *Qui il est*, one of the strangest voyages that one can undertake is "the displacement of creative activities" (*OC* II, 705). This voyage of creative displacement brings about a "strange decongestion," where the Western self that writes in linear lines, word after word—"mots-pensées, mots-images, mots-émotions"—is "decongested," broken up, or put to sleep and "is no longer" (705). The budding writer from the 1920s and 1930s is put to sleep. "Night." A "local death." Nothing more to want, no "appetite to speak" (705). A strange experience occurs, already noted in this 1939 text: as a painter, he finds himself looking at the world as though through another window. New difficulties ensue, new temptations arise (705). The experience described is a total transformation, like an emergence from a chrysalis. The voyages are always displacements, a drifting deterritorialization of identities and practices, of localities and languages.

---

67. Michaux, "The Curtain of Dreams," in *Darkness Moves*, 229.
68. Martin, *Henri Michaux*, chap. XXI, 569ff.

As Margaret Rigaud-Drayton has suggested,[69] Michaux's "passages," his voyages, were not only to the Orient (nor Ecuador and the exotic lands that entranced the Western imagination, voyages that had already been made by so many French authors and painters before him, including Klee's voyages to Tunisia), nor were they just spiritual, mystical voyages into the interior of a primitive and primordial self, voyages of liberation of that primordial self. They were voyages to an outside of reclusive, Western writing; voyages to an *autre*, an Other, far from the confines and stifling limitations of Western writing; voyages into drawing and painting.[70] No more words, he writes, "à bas les mots" ("Down with words!").[71] Two overall directions emerge. First, a passage, subject to questioning and interpretation, from Western cursive writing to painting, a passage that assumes an opposition between writing and painting. Second, the search for a universal basis of communication that would span Orient and Occident, human and animal. Could the line, in one of its adventures, be the basis for the alphabet of a universal language, a line as figure, gesture, and movement that would also communicate?

Michaux's writings and drawings may be seen as contesting the European logocentric conception of language, which privileges speech, not writing. The phonic substance of the living word, especially the hearing and understanding oneself in speech in which truth is primordially heard, is fundamental to the logocentric, European conception of language.[72] For this logocentric tradition, writing has a reduced, secondary role: it is but the

---

69. Rigaud-Drayton, *Henri Michaux*, 113–16.

70. Henri-Alexis Baatsch writes, Michaux was "l'un des artistes les plus profondément voyageurs de ce siècle, l'un des ces hommes qui ont besoin d'entendre de leurs yeux, de voix de leurs oreilles, avant de pretendre formuler une opinion sur quelque chose, Henri Michaux, jeunne homme, a fait quelques voyages classiques en pensée avec ceux qui étaint déja les grands maîtres d'une juenesse exaltée." Baatsch, *Henri Michaux: Peinture et poésie* (Paris: Hazan, 1993), 36–41ff. (Michaux was "one of the most profoundly journeying artists of this century, one of those men who need to hear with their eyes, with their voices, before claiming to formulate an opinion on something, Henri Michaux, as a young man, made some classic journeys in thought with those who were already the great masters of an exalted youth"; trans. mine.)

71. Michaux, *Émergences-Résurgences*, in *OC* III, 568 (*Emergences/Resurgences*, 26).

72. Jacques Derrida, "The End of the Book and the Beginning of Writing," in *Grammatology*, trans. Gayatri Chakravorty Spivak (Baltimore, MD: Johns Hopkins University Press, 1974–1976), 7ff.

silent, stillborn, and secondary script that signifies the spoken word, repeating it in its phonemic system, "all speech being idea," as Rimbaud wrote.[73]

Michaux also wishes to distance himself from this. The path leading away from this legacy of the European philosophy of language, away from its legacy of logocentrism that traditionally privileges the spoken word, the phoneme, over writing, is traced in the 1972 *Emergences/Resurgences*. From the opening pages, Michaux recalls a desire to escape "a culture and an environment uniquely given over to the verbal." The path he would open and follow leads to participating in the world in a new way: not principally via the voice, not through a writing that would merely signify the living voice (writing as the "signifier of the signifier"), but via lines. "I managed to liberate myself from words, these sticky hangers-on (*ces collants partenaires*)."[74] The voyage away from the culture and environment of the word, a voyage at once external (*dehors*) and internal (*dedans*), would take him away from the North (Belgium) and to the South (France), from the Occident to the Orient, toward the Chinese ideogram and toward his own experiments with gestures (*gestes*) and lines (*lignes*).

The route of the Western poet and artist through China is well traveled. The first book that launched European studies of China was Louis Lecomte's *Nouveau memoires sur l'état de la Chine*, published in 1696. European Jesuits, including Lecomte, in China became early and important conduits for information about the country and its language. But Europeans, especially merchants, had been fascinated with China and the Chinese language since the time of Marco Polo. In 1569, the Dominican Gaspar da Cruz published a first description of the Chinese language. He postulated that Chinese ideograms refer not to sounds but to ideas—as in Rimbaud's "all speech being idea." They were able to communicate ideas across Asia—not only China but also Japan, where Chinese characters were readily adapted. Thus, ideas could be understood by the huge variety of Asian cultures and communities, making Chinese something like a first universal language. Another historian of languages, Juan Gonzalez de Mendoza, said much the same thing in 1585. Another author, John Wilkins, observed in 1641 how the Chinese and Japanese differed in their languages, much like the Hebrew and the Dutch, yet both cultures could communicate and understand the books and letters of the other culture as if they were their own. Francis

---

73. Arthur Rimbaud, "Letter to Paul Demeny (May, 1871)," in *Arthur Rimbaud*, 103.
74. Michaux, postface to *Movements*, in *OC* II, 198–99. Trans. by Richard Sieburth, quoted in *Ideograms in China*, trans. Gustaf Sobin (New York: New Directions, 2002), 46.

Bacon, the first European to suggest the possibility of a "universal character," cited the case of Chinese writing as convincing evidence supporting that possibility. The Chinese character had both attributes of universality and direct contact between ideogram and idea. Chinese ideograms from then on enjoyed a powerful influence on the European search for a universal philosophical language.[75]

But none of this is precisely what Michaux finds in his encounters with Chinese ideograms. He does not seek a "universal *philosophical* language" dedicated to being the representation and communication of ideas, a system of signifiers representing concepts or ideas, transcendental signifieds, which in philosophical terms would be the presence of thought to itself. For Michaux, there is no direct contact between written sign, the drawn figure, the ideogram or the epigram, and an Idea it re-presents. His "strokes" (*traits*) are captured by turbulence, not the calm, momentary stability of philosophical concepts. If this were the case, it would suggest that Michaux's voyages into the Other by way of his immersion into exotic languages—Annamite, Chinese—are but routes leading right back into the same conceptual framework he thought he was escaping; his conception of language would be fundamentally "logocentric."

Is Michaux's conception of a universal language essentially logocentric? If so, we are arguing, despite his travels and experiments with the limits of his language and culture, his thought would remain rooted in a classically European metaphysics of language and the immediate presence of thought to itself. Where he had longed to escape Europe and the West, to escape its languages, its books and its ways of writing and thinking, to escape a world in which he no longer felt at home, his journeys beyond would have been but journeys homeward, back to the very European languages and cultures he had wished to escape. Are the intimations of a universal language Michaux thinks he sees in the Oriental ideogram but the intimations of a universal *philosophical* language? All of this Michaux would reject. It seems in the end he sought a language neither of speech nor writing, nor a relation of signifiers and signifieds, but a gestural writing leaping across a void, as in the spontaneous writing of a calligram. It is this gestural language he discovered in the writing of Chinese calligrams.

The universal language that Michaux sought has a gestural base. Lines are more than the shadowy representations of universal ideas. They are rooted,

---

75. Umberto Eco, *Serendipities: Language and Lunacy*, trans. William Weaver (London: Orion Books, 1999), 82–84.

202 | Apparitions, Daemons, and Emanations

a rhizome, not in speech or words or even conventional writing but in the human body. Again, with its physical gestural base, it is the Chinese calligram that is the most appropriate prototype for Michaux's universal language.

But it is not just the calligram that inspires him; it is also the human body. We have seen how the mescaline visions were related to a new experience of the human body. So too we must insist on the importance of the body for Michaux's universal language. The lines, the alphabet-like figures we see in such works as the 1946 *Peintures et dessins*, emerge from living bodies, the body of gestures and the bodies seen in visions. His is always a voyage through the body, through his own sometimes drugged, sometimes hallucinating body; a body often fatigued, often ill, often irritated, a trembling-beholder-of-death-and-visions body; a body that breaks and is laid low and at other times is incensed by the rhythms it makes on a tam-tam; a body that, when it is free from the "swaddles of health," wanders in worlds, with worlds wandering in it.[76] Michaux travels, he observes bodies and faces, their movements, their infinite variety of poses and postures. His impressions and descriptions of the Asiatic people he encounters—*Barbarian in Asia*—are often unflattering, while in other passages they are humorous and touching, yet always schematic, as though viewed and written from afar. What happens to these bodies he observes in India, China, and Japan? They sink into his memories and reveries, only to be revived later, taking form as his "double," as he writes in the postface to *Mouvements*, for example. They appear newly reborn as black, dancing and leaping lines, carried along on a wave of movement and rhythm, and Michaux declares himself to be their *moteur* although he himself was immobilized in bed, "the despair or the god of active people." "On paper, in India ink," he continues, "I could only repeat some of the innumerable minutes of my useless life."[77] They return in *Épreuves, exorcisme* (1945), for another example, where he writes of confronting death, one of many *épreuves*, tests, trials, or ordeals he withstands by putting them into writing, which Blanchot calls "this life that endures death and maintains itself in it."[78] In *Épreuves, exorcisme* we read how, in the dreamy, half-hallucinating state he was in, embraced by the cold grip of death, he was visited by "beings" (*êtres*). He observed them

---

76. Jérôme Roger, "Henri Michaux: malaise dans la pensée," in *Henri Michaux: Le corps de la pensée* (Tours: Farrago, 2001), 55–61.
77. Michaux, postface to *Mouvements* (Paris: Gallimard, 1982), unpaginated.
78. Blanchot, "Literature and the Right to Death," in *The Work of Fire*, trans. Charlotte Mandell (Stanford: Stanford University Press, 1995), 300–44, 322, 327, 336.

profoundly, until everything but the essential had disappeared. These beings then became quite diminished, thin (*ils s'amenuisèrent*), stick-like, until finally they were reduced to "a sort of 'alphabet.'" Thus, the path leading toward a new universal language of lines begins with bodies that evolve into a sort of alphabet. Although derived from the reduction of the bodies of his visions, it shall be one that could serve "in the other world, in any world."[79] The universality of this alphabet thus begins with embodiment, but this is a paradoxical embodiment because it reduces the body to writing, to what "endures death and maintains itself in it." Even this new writing must murder, in some sense, the bodies it renders visible by making them elements of an alphabet, reducing them to the sort of stick figures one sees in *Peintures et dessins*, which are remarkably similar in some cases to the stick figures depicting the human form at the Lascaux cave paintings. Michaux's becomes a voyage of embodied gestures, lines, and imaginary ideograms, a voyage abandoning the culture and environment of the voice in favor of the silent lines of writing and drawing, an "alphabet," conceived in a new, non-phonemic way. Slender and joyous, they emerge only because such lines and forms "pleased" him. "Their movements were so easy for me to execute." Turning his back on the verbal, he sees his new alphabet figures (*signes*) as "liberators," an "unhoped for writing, a new language, whereby, far from words, far from the words of others, he will finally be able to express himself."[80]

Again, expression is not re-presentation. Michaux's lines express but do not have a referential structure. Rather, more like seismographic indicators, they trace the pulse of movement, the pulse of life on the page.[81] He "turns his back" on the culture of references and the environment that privileges the speech over the silent rapidity of gestures. Not by actively adopting a new conceptual framework, not through a willful, thought-directed action, but—his will abandoned—by *passively* allowing himself to be led "by a single line, giving it free rein without so much as lifting pencil from paper."[82] As the passage quoted indicates, this was not only a movement away from the privileging of words and willful action. It was also a way for him to clear the page of clichés, to clear it of "other people's words." The new universal

---

79. Michaux, "Alphabet," *Épreuves, exorcismes*, in *OC* II, 785.
80. Michaux, *Mouvements*.
81. Richard Sieburth, afterword to *Ideograms in China*, 47.
82. Michaux, *Emergences/Resurgences*, 9–10.

language that emerges along the way of this path would thus be a language that no one has spoken so far, a language that has never existed.

Michaux's universal language is thus first a language not of words but of lines, strokes (*lignes*, *traits*) that leap from the gestures of the body. Writing and drawing both begin with such lines, a complex network of lines that appears little by little. Lines that walk around, the first the West had ever seen; lines that travel, that make trajectories and pathways rather than objects; lines that leave and go away; lines that penetrate but do not enclose or possess; elusive lines, presenting a new, "base" materialism (Bataille), sign-lines, poetry tracing, making what is heaviest light.[83] Michaux published these passages in his 1954 preface to W. Grohmann's *Paul Klee*.[84] The line is the common ground, the common origin of drawing and writing. Recall Merleau-Ponty's "Eye and Mind," which tells us something "already familiar to the painters," namely the idea that "there are no lines visible in themselves," that contours defining an apple, for example, or the border of a field are never in "this place or that . . . they are always on the near or the far side of the point we look at . . . are always between or behind whatever we fix our eyes upon."[85] Undefinable lines, trembling lines that mark thresholds, lines neither inside nor outside, always between. For Michaux, as for Klee and Merleau-Ponty, it was a matter of freeing the line, letting it "muse," as Klee had said. Lines that do not imitate but "render visible," in Klee's words, the paths of lines not enclosing but rather tracing a rhythm, a certain level or mode of the linear, but one that disobeys the rectilinear, lines that curve, swerve, break for the margins of the page.

Michaux's encounters with the art of Paul Klee and the Chinese calligraphers were decisive for his adventures in lines. He did not seek a hidden meaning in their work but only the way these artists played with lines in their different ways, creating something that is always new and fresh. He

---

83. Michaux, "Aventures de lignes," *Passages*, in *OC* II, 362–63. Trans. as "Adventures in Signs," in *Darkness Moves*, 316–17.

84. In his notes to "Aventures de lignes," Bellour recounts that Michaux's preface to Grohmann's monograph was republished as "Aventures de lignes," in *Passages*, an anthology of Michaux's writings from 1937 to 1963 (Gallimard, 1963), and now in *OC* II, 280–403. Grohmann's book was first published by Librairie Flinker in 1954. Flinker, who was also a "galeriste," was rather close to Michaux. Michaux's saw Klee's art in 1948 at the grand exposition consecrated to Klee at the Musée National d'Art Moderne." Bellour, *OC* II, 1191.

85. Merleau-Ponty, "Eye and Mind," trans. Carleton Dalleryn, in *The Primacy of Perception*, ed. James Edie (Evanston, IL: Northwestern University Press, 1964), 183.

even wrote a slender book on the subject, *Idéogrammes en Chine*, published in the mid-1970s.[86] In the calligram, in the Chinese line, there is no straight linear unfolding as in Western script. "Lines going off in all directions," as Michaux writes, "a bewildering thicket of accents."[87] It may not be the case that a Chinese calligram "goes off in all directions." This is only the way it seems to Michaux. Rather, as Yolaine Escalande tells us, each calligram is in fact constructed around a center, on a space with two dimensions.[88] Yet the important point remains that Klee and the Chinese calligrapher both distinguish their work from the classical, Western hyle-morphic conception of things and images. A line does not distinguish one thing from another, it is not a form enclosing a matter but a plenitude already constituting in itself a dynamic body.[89] But, unlike Klee, the Chinese line is not invested in making visible because it is already a living body. Its visibility is not in its making something else appear but in its own dynamic life, a life that comes from the rhythm of gestures by which it came to appearance on the white page. Written and qualified by resonance, a calligraphic line is not an aggregate of points but the trembling of vibrations. Like the Chinese calligraphic line, Michaux's lines are organic movements, lines of force moving in thrusts, spontaneously, across a page, transformed by ink and watercolor. Such calligraphic lines, emerging as lines of force, cannot emerge at the command of a will. "The will is the death of art," Michaux writes (*OC* II, 320). Lines not printed onto a page or a support but rather emerging from it, emerging from and incarnating the *Vide*, the Void, lines that bear the Void within and between themselves. Lines almost without any materiality, almost something unformed or formless. Traced by a gesture, awaiting imminently at the tip of a brush, a calligraphic line evokes the whole body, summons it forth in the gesture of brush or pen.

Michaux's universal language would arise from the prelinguistic materials of gesture and lines, strokes (*traits*) as seen in the Chinese calligram

---

86. Henri Michaux, *Idéogrammes en Chine* (Paris: Fata Morgana, 1975); *OC* III (1986), 817–49; *Ideograms in China*, unpaginated.
87. Michaux, *Ideograms in China*, unpaginated; *OC* III, 817.
88. Yolaine Escalande, "Le jeux du trait et de l'encre," in *Henri Michaux & Zao Wou-Ki dans l'empire des signes* (Paris: Flammarion, 2015), 67. Escalande quotes Zao Wou-Ki's, *Autoportrait* (Paris: Libraurue Arthème Fayare, 1988), 137–138. ("It is therefore because it makes a direct link with the origin of writing that in 1949, Zao Wou-Ki's painting catches Michaux's eye"; trans. mine.)
89. Escalande, "Le jeux du trait et de l'encre," 70–71.

but worked otherwise. Pages of lines, comprising an "alphabet." Lines like "young fish," Michaux writes. Lines that arise from a feeling, a "sentiment"; lines that talk (*parle*), laugh, ravish, or sometimes stab (*poignard*); indefinite lines; lines that skip school. Lines that plunge downward, lines that plunge dreamily, lines for absent-mindedness, lines passing into desires, that stretch away and deliver. Lines without any language or writing—without any belonging, without filiations. Lines, only lines.[90] We see pages and pages of such lines in another of his texts from 1974, *Par la voie des rythmes* and the 1975 *Idéogrammes en Chine*.[91] Finally, the 1979 *Saisir*, a book of "graphic signs," signs that arise spontaneously, resembling animals and insects, a sign-bestiary of "savage species," by which he could create an "alphabet" from which the verbal element would be completely excluded. They are signs without words, without phonemes or onomatopoeia. Ostensibly, his signs resemble a very ancient Chinese "oracle script," which has signs strongly resembling natural forms as in the character for "horse." But Michaux is not attempting to recreate very ancient Chinese script. He says his signs are not mimetic but involve a force at once spiritual and physical. Lines and signs by which he could seize (*saisir*) and be seized by beings and things, lines, strokes that are something other than a mimesis by which he could seize visions, put them in hand as though with a rapid force. They arise from the page, not from ideas or from intellectual self-possession but from an "interior turmoil" (*OC* III, 935ff). Pierre Vilar sees them as arising from states or modes of the body situated in space and time, arising from states of illness and joy.[92] Jérôme Roger describes Michaux's writing by lines ("*par des traits*") as an "écriture du trouble."[93] These lines and sign-figures might be elements of a "figural" dimension, a term from Deleuze and Lyotard related not to the representation of objects but to the effect of sensation, the violence of sensation as it acts directly on the nervous system. In any case, they do not allow the question of any identity to remain fixed, even the identity of the painter himself. They arise from a primordial material. Michaux seems to project himself onto them, a movement in which every response is but a new question. They arise from an activity of hand and

---

90. Michaux, "Lignes," *Moments traverses du temps*, in *OC* III, 730–31.

91. These texts are all collected in *OC* III.

92. Pierre Vilar, "Henri Michaux, mode et posture," in *Henri Michaux: Le corps de la pensée*, 29.

93. Jérôme Roger, "Henri Michaux: *Malaise dans la pensée*," *Henri Michaux: Le corps de la pensée*, 59.

eye, a movement inhabited by sensation. A total life of the body is involved. Lines that arise from an inner turmoil, Michaux says, as from an "inner sea," our inner sea, a space in which we are all immersed, forming a tissue at once material and sensible, and populated by incessant movements and contingencies, a theater without dramatic narrative, a sea of language, of figures, at once interior and exterior, an organic tissue where the world seizes us through sensations.[94]

A new language, a universal language, thus arises from the joy and malaise that every human being experiences, arises from the turbulence somehow hidden yet embracing everyone. A language of images, lines, and signs, emerging from an interior voyage, from a spiritual ascent. Signs not invented but seized, seized and offered to our regard, signs like the faces of monsters dissimulated in the folds of souls, monsters that spring from within. A language of exorcism, not representation.[95]

Is the gesture the eye of language, its blind spot so to speak, through which one could pass from the dominion of Western logocentric language to the great silence, to the flow of life and time, the source, the stillness on the other side of the blah-blah of language? Here, on this other side of words and images, at this source, as he calls it of all writing, a "tree of life" emerges from the flurry of Michaux's gestural lines "dotted with words and images."[96]

With all the emphasis on lines, is there an abstract opposition between writing and painting in Michaux's work? Commentators like Virginia La Charité have adopted this point of view, greatly supported by Michaux's own texts.[97] But the important point to see is how the voyages are not ruptures or breaks with writing and painting, not death and rebirths, but, like a voyage, they were transitions, a coherent deformation that results in new forms of signs that combine elements of both writing and painting.

Michaux the painter, as it turns out, was not a new birth or discovery. Even when the writer was budding in the 1930s, he was already a painter, as he writes in a letter to Paulhan in 1936, "I have found my way of

---

94. Jean Starobinski, "Le monde physionomique," in *Henri Michaux* (Paris: Centre Georges Pompidou, 1978), 65–67.
95. Octavio Paz, "Le prince; le clown," in *Henri Michaux* (Paris: Centre Georges Pompidou, 1978), 16.
96. Michaux, *Paix dans les brisements*, in *OC* II, 1000 ("Peace in the Breaking," in *Thousand Times Broken*, 48).
97. Rigaud-Drayton, *Henri Michaux*, 111. *Charité* is cited on page 111.

painting."⁹⁸ But he had no formal training ever. Always a dabbler, always finding his own way and his own rhythms. So the writer was never really "put to sleep," dead, once and for all, for he was as awake, alive, as ever, a fellow traveler, a fellow voyager right through the later years of his life.

What about the destiny of this poet-painter? What becomes of his own self or ego in these voyages? His quest for a universal language that takes him on a voyage away from the West to the East is also a voyage away from the Western idea of a unified self, ego, or "I" communicated in and through language toward a more mystical vision of the Void and a loss of self. Escaping the tyranny of the ego and the self enables an escape from the imprisoning will. Writing is also always too bound up with the will that binds into forms, the will that when wedded with an eye measures and reaches from afar, that combines and subordinates, the will that works and does not know how to play. Addressing this, Michaux unleashes the *gestural* possibilities of writing and painting, which shall always remain a treasure for Michaux. The freedom and spontaneity of the calligraphic gestures enables the painter (one could mention Francis Bacon in this regard) to forget themselves, forget their will that dictates every thought and every move, and so clear their canvas of the conventions and stereotypes, products of the ego and the will, that stifle their creativity. Unwilled, unforeseen gestures will help clear the page of all the clichés, all the infernal babble, all the preconceived, readymade ideas, all the stifling readymade images that already populate and fill the empty page, images and words imported from the massive symbolic order that comprises the human situation. How to clear the page of all this so that one can start something new, something that is drawn only out of one's own visions and experience? Whether it is writing or painting, Michaux's problem was to be rid of this massive legacy that cripples and confines creativity. He would start from nothing. He would teach himself. He wanted to have his own rhythms, his own way of doing things. He would have his own language. Other books, other paintings, other people's work would only prove to be a massive impediment to his progress. Reject them all, "Clear the slate!" He felt he had to begin as a child begins, in a kind of innocence, peering as though through a porthole at a new world. Yet he always begins again with writing and drawing, pushing them ever onward toward an impossible goal, to reach a "figure," a Void, a silence that dwells within words and images.

---

98. Michaux, *OC* I, *civ.*, cited by Rigaud-Drayton, 111.

Does this contestation of the Western notions of subjectivity and self (ego) find its parallel in the shift from writing toward painting? Uprooting this ego would entail uprooting the Western grammar that sustains it with its subject-object oppositions. Where one self, the writing self, Michaux as author, collapses, another, Michaux as famous painter, arises. Is there perhaps a double identity persisting throughout Michaux's career? Is there a "split self," the "articulation of a double identity," as Margaret Rigaud-Drayton suggests?[99] She writes about verbal and visual representations—and this is what they are for her, "representations"—"articulate dichotomous identities." But should we see in Michaux's work such a divided self, a schizophrenic practice, two sides, two "identities" vying against one another? Alternatively, a Lacanian reading would show how from the very beginning, the self, its identity, already has more than one foot in the symbolic order: it is formed by language, it comes to be in and through language, it is formed by writing rather than existing apart from it, a language self, in short, not a deep prelinguistic self, not a primordiality that writing or painting would only explore, kill, or put to sleep. The self is already multiple, already a discursive and figurative functioning, not something, whether monad or "dichotomous identities," deep and interior, that would be represented, expressed, or "articulated" by either writing or painting; nor a mythic pure spirituality, however sullied and divided against itself, that would then be externalized or materialized in and by the materiality of writing and painting. The Other that Rigaud-Drayton refers to is not outside of language, an impossible beyond of language. The Other is what Lacan called the Big Other, the Symbolic Order. To be a "subject" is to be subjected to language, to be named, placed, and colonized by a massive symbolic order that the subject inherited and did not create for itself. Through language, the subject is the folding of outside and inside. Michaux's work abounds in references to folds and foldings. Did we not just quote such a passage? "A vibrating paradise unfolds its folds to infinity."[100] Or, as he writes in *Paix dans les brisements*, "I fold myself in a thousand folds that fold me, unfold me."[101]

Even where he may have wished to escape from what he calls the murderous tyranny of either his own ego or Western languages, he could not. Drawings may offer a way to envision universality if not to communicate it

---

99. Rigaud-Drayton, *Henri Michaux*, 116.
100. Michaux, *L'Infini turbulent*, in *OC* III, 933. Mercure de France ed., 201.
101. Michaux, *Paix dans les brisements*, in *OC* II, 1005 ("Peace in the Breaking," 61).

in a manner that betters the stumbling discontinuity of words. Like words, drawings too are positioned at this threshold between inside and outside. In a text from 1957, "Drawing the Flow of Time," Michaux writes about his desire to draw "the moments that little by little make up life, to let people see the phrase within (*la phrase intérieure*), the phrase without words, a rope indefinitely unrolling, winding, accompanying in its intimacy all that comes in from the outside, and the inside, too."[102] *La phrase intérieure* is here described as "without words," yet it exists only in words, in the words of this text, words that come from the outside and the inside, too. He had wanted to make a film of this. His drawing was to be "cinematic." But this is yet another language, the language of film, that unfolds like a rope but that has its own syntax, its own grammar, its own semiotic system.

Whether through the art of Paul Klee or the Chinese calligram, Michaux's quest for a universal language, his adventures in lines, as with his mescaline sessions, all seek a way to undo his subjection to conventional language, escaping its way of killing off things and visions with words and syntax, its way of alienating the speaker from life, from the "flow of time," and from "the ineffable Void." This is Michaux's complaint. "Languages all so strong, so possessing."[103] Would his universal language not also be so possessing? Or would it be an escape from language? Why the need to escape? Can what is inside (*dedans*) ever be communicated objectively and universally?

As Michaux himself knew, it is only through the conventions of language that one can break out of language. But can art, can drawing, escape the limitations of discursive language? A passage from Lyotard makes this point: art, for its connection not only with figuration but also with the figure or figural may be a "refutation of the position of discourse." Michaux would have agreed. But what Lyotard is here calling "the figure," which he also calls "that manifestation," like Michaux's "vision," is still a linguistic space and a linguistic construct but one that language cannot incorporate without being shaken. The figure, the vision as the other side of language, is an "exteriority language cannot interiorize as signification." But must one keep silent, Lyotard asks, in order to bring this absolutely-other of language to light?

---

102. Henri Michaux, "Dessiner l'écoulement du temps," *Passages*, in *OC* II, 371 ("Drawing the Flow of Time," in *Darkness Moves*, 320).

103. Michaux, *Paix dans les brisements*, in *OC* II, 998 ("Peace in the Breaking," 45).

But the silence of the beautiful, of perception—a silence that precedes speech, an innermost silence—is impossible: there is simply no way to go to the other side of discourse. Only within language can one get to and enter the figure . . . the figure (a function which is not signified) is embedded in (language). One only has to allow oneself to slip into the well of discourse to find the eye lodged at its core, the eye of discourse in the sense that at the center of the cyclone lies an eye of calm. The figure [Deleuze's "figural"] is "both without and within."[104]

The vision and the "eye," the gaze embedded in language, ride the crest of a double folding of outside and inside. Thus Michaux's opposition to writing and to words, his voyages from words to drawings, his visceral rejection of books and words, does not register a rejection of writing and a rejection of language in favor of drawing, putting them into a false opposition, so much as it does a struggle at the limits of language, a limit where writing and drawing fold into one another, where the outside and the inside of language fold into one another, putting language in a perpetually unstable tension.

But in escaping the conventional use of language, does Michaux risk developing just another "private language" that could never be universal? This situation is nicely summarized by Octavio Paz where he points out the extraordinary tensions at the heart of Michaux's language: language is an "effective tool," but the use of language "bare(s) something that is completely ineffective by its very nature, the state of nonknowledge that is beyond knowledge."[105] It is beyond by being inside, the unknown that is *dedans*. Language is effective only so long as it stays within the limits of what can be communicated to others. Language is effective because it is first exterior, outside, public, the inherited basis for community. Yet, the "non-knowledge" impossible to communicate is always there, the beyond, the other that is inside, the seemingly private, dark counterweight to the "guérison" and the "savoir" Michaux was seeking. Michaux approached such non-knowledge,

---

104. Jean-François Lyotard, *Discours, Figure* (Paris: Klincksieck, 1985), 13. Trans. by Antony Hudek and Mary Lydon as *Discourse, Figure* (Minneapolis: University of Minnesota Press, 2011), 7.

105. Octavio Paz, "Henri Michaux," in *Alternating Currents*, trans. Helen R. Lane (New York: Viking Press, 1973), 79–80.

as did Bataille, in his own *expérience intérieure*, yet too Michaux wanted somehow to translate it into a form or a model that would be useful to knowledge, that would communicate it rather than leave it in its incontestable silence. For this, Michaux no doubt struggled. The effectiveness of language quickly stumbles up against its own ineffectiveness. The unity of thought with itself, its total interior self-transparency, is impossible for Michaux, for such unity and transparency of mind as we have seen is always violated by the unstoppable visions of heads and forms springing forth from the Night. Moreover, interior experience can only be sustained, as Paz writes, in "the whirlwind" of language. It is always folded into an exteriority that dissolves and displaces interior unity across the exterior space-time of writing where it is always and already irreparably broken, divided against itself, its intimacy fragmented across the exteriority of language. The possibility of a private interior world, a private language that would be both the silence of a perfect interior unity and its exteriorization in the loquacity of writings or drawings, is foreclosed. Michaux is caught in this tension between a desire to create an effective universal language that would both be private in the sense of springing from his own *dedans*, from his own visions and memories, and be exteriorized with claims to universality. Universality would require conventions, yet at the same time Michaux envisions a new universal language that would be an escape or release from the possessing and limiting conventions of existing natural languages. Such insuperable tensions always tear and open Michaux's work, the torsions of language, its effectiveness always doubled by ineffectiveness, a cohesion always inseparable from breaking, unity and consolidation always doubled by fragmentation, the center identified with absence. Such tensions remain at the heart of Michaux's writing and drawing and his search for a universal language.

Michaux's alphabets of lines, his bestiary, is not so much a private language, nor is it the restoration of a pure natural language, an Adamic language. Rather, he bequeaths a language at once visual, tactile, and physiological, a melding of writing and drawing. Where Plato's *Cratylus* discusses whether language arises from nature, from the direct representation of natural things, or from culture, from cultural convention, Michaux's lines and signs suggest a third alternative, a language that arises from gestures, from sensations and affects, escaping thereby the nets of concepts and the will, as well as the domination of habits, clichés, and conventions, a language both interior and exterior, from the folding of exterior and interior.

Born of gestures, sensations, and memories, born from his many voyages, Michaux's lines and drawings, his voyages, his search for a universal language ultimately becomes a route of "masks"; lines having drifted away from working as signifiers or calligrams emerge as masks, *Masques du vide*, as he entitles one of his paintings collected in his *Peintures et dessins*.[106] Here, in connection with Michaux's search for a universal language and for what he might have called a utopia of the sign, in connection with his contestation of the grammars of language and the self or ego it sustains, we encounter a "tendency" Bellour distinguishes in Michaux's work, not only toward the body and its gestural powers but toward a spiritualized mysticism, an ultimate voyage toward an "ineffable Void," as in Michaux's poem "Peace in the Breaking."[107] This is coupled with yet another tendency, one toward a "utopia of signs," the tree of life, the true cross, and the Haut of the Vide.[108]

The mystic approaches carefully. A modern Perseus, Michaux approaches the Medusa of the Void with masks. The mask that springs from his hand is the threshold between signs, between writing and drawing, and the ineffable Void. As he writes in a brief text, both prose and poem, that accompanies one of his paintings of a multiheaded mask-like apparition, "In a state of a withdrawal from myself apparitions appeared before me, the masks of a void."[109] Not a mask he wears, but a mask of the Void, a way for absence to appear and disappear in its appearing. We brushed up against this earlier when, in connection with the mescaline experiments, we cited Michaux's *VIDE-SUBSTANCE*.

The Vide also has a crucial role to play in Chinese painting, where it is active and dynamic, not something vague and nonexistent. For Michaux, writing in *Miserable Miracle*, in an "Addenda" composed between 1969 and 1971, the Void is the withdrawal of the existent, of the profane, of the density of material life, a loss of the longing to seize, to possess. "Abandoning acquisitions, reserves, desire, now that a shrewd lysis has liquefied everything, what is left? The Void, Emptiness," a Void that is as much "excess as loss . . . violent, active, living . . . incessantly augmented . . . ever

---

106. Henri Michaux, *Masques du vide: Peintures et dessins* (Paris: Point du Jour, 1946).

107. See Raymond Bellour's notes to the text of *Idéogrammes en Chine* (*OC* III, 1655); and Rigaud-Drayton, *Henri Michaux*, 112–13. The postface returns to "Peace in the Breaking."

108. Raymond Bellour's notes to the text of *Idéogrammes en Chine* (*OC* III, 1655). The reference to the *Haut* is found in "Peace in the Breaking," to which we shall return in the postface.

109. Michaux, *Peintures et dessins*, in *OC* I, 918. See also François Cheng, *Vide et plein: Le langage pictural chinois* (Paris: Seuil, 1991), 45.

surpassed and renewed . . . a shower of Emptiness that returns without end . . . (that) has no reason to stop itself, that dispenses with everything other than Emptiness itself and makes a sovereign rule to aid in nothing but the Emptiness, to have its fill of Emptiness." An "intense force field expands to form this almost infinite Void," Michaux continues. This "force field" consists of pulsions, driving a longing "for more, for better, for what is beyond the known, the expressible, the representable, the thinkable, the admirable, beyond everything imaginable."[110]

Let us expand on this by relating it to what Blanchot has said in "Literature and the Right to Death." Michaux's writing/drawing is a mask of the ineffable Void, not the sign for a transcendental signified. Rather than signifying anything, Michaux's drawing/writing is the mask-like inscription or "affect" of a dynamic void. Not the writing that is a dead sign, whose stillborn life is only obtained second hand in its reference to the living word, but, after Blanchot, writing that is the dissimulation of being qua nothingness in language. The function of writing and drawing in Michaux would then be the function of death in the existent. Death, then, would be the death that is also the incessant longing for the ineffable. Language, desire, longing, the desire to seize and to possess, are the "death drive." Writing, drawing, the watercolor emanations, would be but masks of the Void, profane masks that must be torn away so that "the sacred," what cannot be spoken or possessed, be there in its nothingness. The mask is an image, an image that is the presence of an absence of being, an emanation of the Void, the presence of nothingness. The mask, writing/drawing: a similitude grounded in nothingness, the nothingness that is similitude itself, and language, the bearer of death for the things signified. As Blanchot writes,

> Of course my language does not kill anyone. And yet, when I say, "This woman," real death has been announced and is already present in my language; my language means that this person, who is here right now, can be detached from herself, removed from her existence and her presence, and suddenly plunged into a nothingness in which there is no existence or presence; my language essentially signifies the possibility of this destruction; it is a constant, bold allusion to such an event. My language does not kill anyone. But if this woman were not really capable

---

110. Michaux, "Ineffable Vide (L'aventure de la perte de l'avoir)," in *OC* II, 775–79. Trans. as "Ineffable Emptiness," in *Miserable Miracle*, 172.

of dying, if she were not threatened by death at every moment of her life, bound and joined to death by an essential bond, I would not be able to carry out that ideal negation, that deferred assassination which is what my language is.[111]

What Michaux seeks is the murdered sign, the writing of disaster, not the sign that murders. Blanchot: "Writing is . . . already (it is still, *encore*) violence: the rupture there is in each fragment, the break, the splitting (*morcellement*), the tearing of the shred (*le déchirement du déchiré*)."[112] Writing that masks, that dissimulates and communicates the Void and in doing so is itself torn, shredded. Yet being—the Void—still speaks to him: Michaux: "L'être qui inspire m'a dit: Je sui celui qui tremble. Je suis celui qui rompt, qui glisse, qui rampe. Je suis celui qui rend."[113] And what is this "gift" being gives back? The gift of new visions, new masks, new ways of creation. Michaux's writing and his art are thus situated between the desire of existent beings, their desire to seize and possess, and the infinity of being without end where meaning is lost. It is this encounter with the Void, the ineffable emptiness, that shapes and twists Michaux's writing and drawings into ever new forms and shapes, always struggling to shred and cast off the profane, to cast off the dominance of words and the longing they embody, to hasten its withdrawal so as to open the space for the sacred, for the time of the immaterial, ineffable sacred, the gulf of the Void, to be strangely manifest. Michaux's search for a universal language is a search for a new way, a new Tao of writing, one no longer reduced to being but the secondary, material signifier of a spoken word. Illness itself becomes a voyage that carries him away from the European culture of the voice and the dominance of the word. "While I was out of the restful swaddles of health, I saw how men wandered and the worlds wandered in men."[114]

It is a writing "before" writing, an "arche-writing,"[115] a writing of gestures and movements, writing the rhythm life, the source of artistic creation;

---

111. Blanchot, "Literature and the Right to Death," in Mandell, *The Work of Fire*, 323–24.
112. Blanchot, *L'Écriture du déastre* (Paris: Gallimard, 1983), 78. Trans. by Ann Smock as *The Writing of the Disaster* (Lincoln: University of Nebraska Press, 1986), 46.
113. Michaux, "Épervier de la faiblesse, domine," *Épreuves, exorcismes*, in *OC* II, 779. ("The being who inspires me said to me: I am the one who trembles. I am the one who breaks, who slips and crawls. I am the one who gives back"; trans. mine.)
114. Michaux, "Les équilibres singuliers," in *OC* I, 780.
115. Derrida, "End of the Book," 60.

writing that opens time and space, that is a relation with otherness and the outside, a writing that opens from within language, from the gaze of the eye at the bottom of "the well of language"; writing that blinds the eye of thought and the will—an eye opened and blinded by the rapid, excessive pace of the brush across the page, blind to conventions of the visible and so able to see what he fears seeing, the stirrings of night (*la nuit remue*) (*OC* I, 944), the apparitions of floating forms, faces, foundlings. We have mentioned his confrontation with death; in other special moments when fatigue, illness, weariness, or *malheur* set in, in such lost moments, pencil in hand, he sees what cannot be seen: "Those who have come to me" (*ceux qui sont venus à moi*), visions of figures with two faces, or a figure with an enormous eye detached from its head as though floating by my window (910, 940–41). Faces of criminals, faces that have become masks, faces of that which hides. "Is it me, all these faces?" Or are they the faces of others? From what fathomless background (*fond*) have they emerged?[116] Faces of the other; faces seen now in profundity and reduced to their essentials. Faces of an alphabet.

The imaginary ideograms, the stick-men, the black, dancing figures traced by India ink across a death-white page constitute Michaux's language before language, an *avant-langue*, language as the inscription of a living rhythm, a resonance on the surface.[117] In the 1979 text *Saisir*, Michaux writes, "Who did not want to grasp (*saisir*) more, to seize better, to seize otherwise beings and things, but not with words, not with phonemes, nor with onomatopoeia, but with graphic signs? Who has not wanted one day to make an alphabet, a bestiary, even a whole vocabulary, from which the verbal element would be excluded?" (*OC* III, 936). Michaux's path out from the prison of the European conception of speech and phenomena found its way to the pages of insect drawings and the dribbled, dripping graphemes one sees on the pages of *Saisir*. Both his writing and drawing are graphic practices that leave nothing behind, certainly not a constellation of concepts and ideas, not a philosophy, not a meaning, not even the space or the place where a commentary might gain purchase, but only these silent traces, black star trails that turn and return incessantly across an empty white page, in the grips of an uncanny rhythm. The *traits*, the black insects that incessantly return and crawl across Michaux's pages, are certainly not an access to the

---

116. Michaux, "En pansant au phénomène de la peinture," in *Peintures et dessins*, in *OC* I, 857.
117. Escande, "Le jeux du trait et de l'encre," 64.

unconscious, nor a "return of the repressed," as Rigaud-Drayton suggests. Rhythm and return have another role in Michaux: they are the forces in which the materiality of ink and color becomes expressive. Rhythm does not bear anything to return, not a meaning or a "repressed," but only return itself, the turning and returning of writing in the form of the stroke, the *trait*, always moving toward an encounter with Otherness, bearing within it a silence greater than the opposition of speaking and silence, the silence of death. They approach a perilous threshold against which poetic writing hurls itself, and where it must abruptly turn back, only to return again to the limits of writing, the threshold between life and death. Not a "return of the repressed," but return as the ceaseless turning and returning of writing to and from this threshold, its limits, marking thus a rhythm in which, as Prometheus said, "I am caught" and in which I am lost. "Know what rhythm holds men," the ancient poet Archilochus wrote. Indeed, rhythm is a key word for Michaux, as it is for Deleuze and Blanchot, but it never resolves itself or congeals into a concept. It remains, as Blanchot's wrote, "the enigma of rhythm."[118] Not the fractured articulations of a dichotomous, divided "self," the rhythm of Michaux's *traits* are a contact, perhaps, with the infinite, with the Void, not as Ideas but as the rhythms of movement, as the formless chaos of nature. Arche-writing and arche-drawing's figures—the faces, the dancing stick figures, the black bestiary, the furrow (*sillon*)—emerge from and return toward a "fond," the "other Night," embodied in the terrifying open background terrain of the page. This is a background that never closes or congeals but always opens onto a Void (*Vide*). The page forms a "plane of composition" (Deleuze), the tenuous surface where the seismic needle of pen and ink traces, performs, or facilitates in these figures not the emergence of the repressed or the unconscious, but the emergence of the formless chaos of nature.

In summary, Michaux's gestural language always fights against the glare of visibility and the spoken word and yet, somewhat ironically, is distantly linked to the tradition of a Descartes for whom analytic geometry renounces the construction of figures, renounces making the figure visible as the solution to a problem.[119] However, it is the "tree of life" that Michaux's universal language will communicate, the tree of life that, like rhythm, is "the source traversing man from the first to the last of life" (*OC* II, 1000). Is life not what vulgar writing, the writing of concepts, betrays? Does writing

---

118. Archilochus quoted in Blanchot, *L'Écriture du déastre*, 14 (*Writing of the Disaster*, 5).
119. Blanchot, *L'Entretien infini*, 359 (*Infinite Conversation*, 257).

not menace the breath, spirit, and rhythm of life as the latter is immobilized in the dark repetition of letters? Yes, it does insofar as writing places one word after another in a segmented, syntactical chain that is measured, extensive, and composed of hierarchical orders. Writing spaces and defers. The written sign is also a "stop sign," punctuated and ordered grammatically, full of spaces and spacings; it breaks up the continuum Michaux seeks, the "murmur without end," the sinuous, smooth "phrasing of life." No writing is "rustic" enough, impoverished enough to embody the continuum of life.[120] To "show" (*montrer*) life, the tree of life, to render visible (*montrer*) that rope of time that links all "men," to show this requires a different practice of writing, a writing unrecognizable as an object of science, a writing as voyage, as *trait*, as stroke, as dance and gesture opening a temporalization and a relation with the other night Michaux shows in his painting *The Prince of the Night*.

Perhaps such a different practice could be glimpsed, anticipated, in the work of such Chinese masters as Shih-T'ao, the seventeenth-century master who spoke of "the Holistic Brushstroke" as the root of all images. Such a brushstroke, he says, is not exhausted by materiality but is perceptible spiritually and works mysteriously in the human mind: "My contemporaries are unaware of it." All journeys begin, he continues, by traversing the shortest of distances. "A single brushstroke can define that which lies beyond the borders of the universe. An infinity of brushstrokes all begin with it (the Holistic Brushstroke), and are completed by it."[121] Perhaps here we might find adumbrations of Michaux's universal language: not a language of concepts and meanings but the brushstroke that goes to the borders of the universe, that thus shows the tree of life that traverses all human beings "from the first to the last of life."

Writing as Emanation

Thus, Michaux's quest for a universal language entails an ethical dimension: it is the affirmation of life's infinite movement against all that would wish to contain it or control it. An uncompromising affirmation, it is not just

---

120. Michaux, *Émergences-Résurgences*, in *OC* III, 546 (*Emergences/Resurgences*, 11–12).
121. Shih-T'ao, *Enlightening Remarks on Painting*, trans. Richard E. Strassberg (Pasadena, CA: Pacific Asia Museum Monographs 1, 1989), 61.

lonely howl of protest but a creative force writing against the machinery of words that would seize and grasp through concepts the visibility of vulgar things; writing against the sheer deadening weight of Belgium; writing against all that would seek to limit, to reduce, to enclose or to in-form life, as Bataille said, in the straitjacket of figures, numbers, and concepts. This is the writing that Michaux explores in his strokes and emanations, a writing invested with the power of insubordination with regard to order, to institutions and conventions; a writing that breaks writing's prison-house of mirrors. Such a writing would begin by turning back upon itself, seizing itself in seizing its visions—the vision and the rhythm of visions—twisting and tormenting language, ceaseless becoming. "Formation," not "form," is the key, life's ceaseless metamorphosis into new forms of life. Writing wakes up one morning and finds itself in "par des traits" transformed into a beetle or a centipede, enduring all sorts of becomings, crawling across a page, an insect or a jet of black ink, the non-signifying elements of a new alphabet. Or cartoon strips in *Peintures et dessins*, a simple line drawing, the powerful leaping profile of a bison (*OC* I, 931) whose precedent is at Lascaux. Or the caricature stick figures of creatures half-human, half-fantasy, a cyclops, lines suggesting animal beings. Writings equal new becomings. Thus Michaux's "contra-writing," in the words of Bernard Noël, is a writing that is a "decalage," a shifting, gap, or dislocation standing apart from ordinary writing, a contra-writing unlike any other in that it "does not say anything because it is not separated from what it says."[122] This is perhaps the ultimate sense of the emanations that so fascinated Michaux, not only the ideograms from India ink but also the heads and mask-like faces that emerge from the drops of watercolor on an empty page. Color, figure, hand, vision, and trembling horror are all linked into a single intensity, a tree of life, the zigzags of a thunderbolt, a "single brushstroke that can define that which lies beyond the borders of the universe" and what lies beyond the universe within, *dedans*, an interiority as tumult folded with the outside: "thousands upon thousands of rustlings were my own thousand shatterings."[123]

Writing is emanation, emerging like a Lazarus from behind the page, like heads rising from the tomb of the night into the light as though from the dead, emanations rising into the labyrinth of the between of life and death but escaping the fate of Orpheus, locked in the silent dark world of

---

122. Noël Bernard, *Vers Henri Michaux* (L'Hay-les-Roses, France: Unes, 1998), 41–45.
123. Michaux, *Miserable Miracle*, 12.

death he had hoped to open with his song. Michaux's universal language, his experience with visions, his paintings, his other writings, the strokes and alphabets, the journals and travel writings, however they may begin in the night, are all voyages into the light. After all, how could those heads and faces emerge from the obscurity of darkness, how could they arise from the night if they did not already belong to the light? Klossowski quotes the Apostle in this regard: "All things that are condemned are made manifest by the light, for whatever makes manifest is light."[124] Michaux's praise of the night celebrates the light and what comes into the light. His song is not like that of Orpheus. It does not look back and so return to darkness. His is a song of life and light. "On the edge of a tropical ocean, in a thousand reflections of the silver light of an invisible moon, among undulations of restless waters, ceaselessly changing."[125]

The Tree of Life and the Legend of the True Cross

The mescaline visions, the search for a universal language, and the mystical journeys constitute a triad of interrelated adventures for Michaux. Let us now turn to his mystical visons of not only the Void but the tree of life and the Cross. Is it ultimately a spiritual salvation Michaux is seeking, whether through the mescaline visions or through his gestural lines and his various voyages physical and spiritual?

There may have been two trees in the Garden of Eden: a tree of knowledge of good and evil, bearing apples, and a tree of life, in the image of Christ, holding the secret to immortality. The tree of life grows in light, not in death and darkness. That is what he wanted "to show" (*montrer*), where "to show"—Klee's "to render visible"—is often translated as "to indicate." Translating *montrer* as "indicating," "pointing out," would suggest a mediation or an interval between a subject that points and an object that is indicated. Would such "indication" not endanger the very continuum, the supple phrasing of life that Michaux seeks? Whereas translating *montrer* as Klee's "to render visible," on the other hand, might better communicate

---

124. John 1:5, quoted in Pierre Klossowski, "Nietzsche, Polytheism and Parody," in *Such a Deathly Desire*, trans. Russell Ford (Albany: State University of New York Press, 2007), 109.
125. Michaux, *Miserable Miracle*, 12.

the essential nature of emanation, emergence, and resurgence that are the keys to Michaux's paintings, "showing" as the *élan* (*trait*) in which subject and object are dissolved and where life itself becomes expressive. It is not enough that the artist merely indicates the tree of life. He must find himself in it, he must first be the tree of life in his very artistic practice, like putting an apple on the table in front of him and then putting himself inside the apple. "What peace!"[126]

> Thus I believe I am indicating (*montrer*), having spent hours in its then-prodigious presence several times, I believe I am rendering visible (*montrer*) the endless tree (*l'arbre sans fin*), the tree of life, the tree of life that is a source, that is dotted with images and words and proposing enigmas, the flow that, without interruption, even for a single second, passes through man from the first moment of his life to the very last one, a stream or a hourglass that stops only when life stops (*ruisseau ou sablier qui ne s'arrête qu'avec elle*).[127]

The tree of life has its correspondent in another image, another sign, another symbol: the cross of the crucifixion, the image of death that is also the hope for salvation. As Nietzsche wrote in 1885–1886, "Christ crucified is the most sublime of all symbols—even in the present."[128] For Bataille, the crucified Christ was a figure of the "summit," the summit of evil, the "most equivocal expression of evil." The "criminals" who crucified and wounded Christ were not only the Roman actors who actually did the terrible deed. Each and every "man" is also implicated in this crime. This culpability is, moreover, the terrible wound rending the integrity of every culpable being. The image of the crucified Christ became so essential to Christian dogma, Bataille continues, it is as if Christ's wounds, his sacrifice, were the primary way human beings could communicate with their God, a communication in fact opened and assured by the evil, by the suffering and wounds of the Christ on the Cross. This means that the summit of communication obtains not between beings full and intact but only between beings put into play

---

126. Henri Michaux, *Lointain intérieur*, in *OC* I, 559 (*Darkness Moves*, 45).

127. Michaux, *Paix dans les brisements*, in *OC* II, 1000 ("Peace in the Breaking," 49; trans. altered).

128. Quoted by Bataille, *Discussion sur le péche* (Paris: Lignes, 2010), 54.

(*mis en jeu*), placed at the limit of death and nothingness.[129] Ultimately, the suffering, the wounds, the breaking of the integrity of beings itself becomes a source of life: at the summit of evil, the Cross becomes then a source of life. At the summit, then, one does not suffer evil but actually wants it, desires it, as one would want the source of life itself.[130]

Michaux himself may have experienced such limits. His drawings for his *Four Hundred Men on the Cross* shares Bataille's meditations on the communication of the sacrifice and suffering of Christ on the Cross, a meditation reenacted across the four hundred beings he depicts on the Cross. The Cross is thus a major, sovereign sign for Michaux, one that becomes a dominant almost obsessive figure in this text dating from the mid-1950s and that anticipates his vision of the tree of life, as recounted, for example, in his 1959 text *Paix dans les brisements* (*OC* II).[131]

According to the Legend of the True Cross, as shown, for example, in Piero della Francesco's mural cycle, the wood of the True Cross came from the Garden of Eden, where Adam and Eve first tasted the fruit of the knowledge of desire and death. From the Garden of Eden to the agony in the garden of Gethsemane, the wood of the True Cross traces the course of human destiny from paradise lost to transfiguration and salvation. Michaux's image-text, *Four Hundred Men on the Cross*, recounts Michaux's own journey with Christ, beginning from the spiritual paradise of his youth, the "serious years of my life," when he was embraced by Christ, "united with Him, surrounded by images of Him on the cross, finding all meaningful life in Him," until his final rejection of Christ: "How far I wandered from Him," he writes, wandered all the way to Asia and the Buddha. He had wanted at times to "hold on to the Man to whom I was once bound by passion and faith, in drawing. That was the plan. Shabby resurrection! How far I had wandered . . . so far that I could no longer represent him."[132]

Michaux's text returns to this task of failed representation, but by showing rather than describing. *Four Hundred Men on the Cross* combines

---

129. Bataille, 55–57.

130. Bataille, 65.

131. *Quatre cents hommes en croix*, *OC* II, appeared in 1956, but "its genesis is difficult to date with precision," according to Raymond Bellour (*OC* II, 1320). The drawings date from 1953, as Michaux himself notes in an early section of the text's subtitle "Diary of a Draftsman." Bellour further suggests that it may be something of a transitional text preceding the mescaline diaries, *Miserable Miracle*, for example, which also dates from 1956.

132. Michaux, *Four Hundred Men on the Cross*, in *Thousand Times Broken*, 157.

writing and drawing, words organized not into sentences and paragraphs but into forms, images, the shape of a cross; words and images here find their reconciliation. One such word-image shows the title of the text, its words composing an image of a cross written in capital letters, "FOUR HUNDRED MEN ON THE CROSS." At the top of the cross, instead of the name Jesus of Nazareth, as on the original cross, is the name HENRI MICHAUX, and at the foot of the image is the date, also written in words, "NINETEEN FIFTY-SIX."

While the diary's title might suggest that one will see four hundred men on the cross, only two hundred and sixty are actually named or in some way defined. Why "four hundred men," and not just one or a thousand men? Would the crosses not be the counter-image to his vision of "thousands of gods," one cross for each of the gods encountered and fallen in his life? Are these four hundred men other than the one man, Henri Michaux? Do the four hundred suggest the potentially infinite number of selves, both human and animal, that compose the persona Henri Michaux, as in Nietzsche's "at bottom I am every name in history"? Thus, God-Christ would not be the absolute guarantor and judge of the identity of the singular, unique, and responsible self but would itself be multiple. There are thousands of gods to see, he writes in *Turbulent Infinity*, there are "four hundred men on the cross," each portraying one of the different possibilities of life that, taken together in these scenes from the Cross, would comprise being itself, the totality of existence.

Let's look at some of these figures. Number 42, for example, is said to be a lout; number 51 is a duck, "a real quack-quacking on the cross"; 54 bears the expression "DEATH FOR NOTHING"; 60 is an intense figure, "so intense he bursts into flames. He's sure to consume the cross"; "eighty-three" is a "deserter, secret, bowed, sunk, twisted"; 84 is a quarrel-seeker; "NINETY-ONE" is a little Shiva; and 93 is "a ghost in the air, wretched ghost who conjures up a cross." The enumerations continue erratically until 104 is named as a "MAN-CROSS" and TWO-HUNDRED-AND-FIFTY-SEVEN is described as a "thinker, a recluse, a contemplative" who does not even notice that he's nailed to a cross. Number 212 is named "Christ as a cable. More than a rope, a rope fixed to a cross," thus recalling the rope of time of the tree of life. The numbering stops at 260, a little black angel.

It is always a man on the cross. There are no female figures in this strange diary. Is the image of a crucified woman too ghastly to contemplate? Another failure of representation? Multiplicity, difference, and the potentially infinite series are the principles of construction for this text-macabre. Only the cross itself is singular, always silent. Identified with "MAN," it sometimes "floats," ghostly like the ghost of Christ, "wretched ghost who conjures up a cross." Man and cross are united in their suffering. The Man-Cross: both in their baleful unity have "at last begun to suffer." Tragedy descends upon it. It is distraught. MAN-CROSS: at once the support and the supported, the sufferer and the instrument of suffering. The MAN-CROSS embraces the suffering of the "prophet," parts of whose body have been seized by the "impossible wood" of the cross, seized without respite. Michaux writes apropos figure "EIGHTY-SEVEN": "With what infinite withdrawal (*infini repliement*), he retreats into himself, into the depths of his body," as the figurative English translation has it. There's an almost Heideggerian resonance to the word "withdrawal," for the way it evokes the withdrawal of Being. But *repliement* can also be translated more literally as an "infinite folding," Christ's infinite folding into the depths of his body (*au fond de se corps*), a figure of infinite suffering, seized by the impossible wood of the impossible cross. Why impossible? Because of its fabled provenance from the tree of knowledge of good and evil in the Garden of Eden? Because of its unnamable links with death? Or is its impossibility due to its "not recognizing the prophets, even now as these joists hold one in its arm?" The impossibility of the cross arises from the impossible silence of its being, ever-bearing witness to the suffering that unfolds in its arms. Impossible being of the cross as support and supported, sufferer and instrument of suffering. The cross itself has begun to suffer, which is impossible. It becomes the stage, support, and instrument for the struggle against suffering. Michaux evokes the infinite forbearance required by the *épreuve* of suffering, Christ's infinite withdrawal into the fonds of his being. Alternately, there is also fury, the opposite of withdrawal, kicking against the pricks of suffering: Figure 53 has Christ "furious at being on the cross, making huge efforts to free his arms. . . . Christ or parachutist?"[133]

In the infinite folding into itself, in the infinite withdrawal from suffering, "infinite desiring suddenly recedes," as René Char writes. Is there a fiendish, unheard rhythm at work in these pages from Michaux, the infinitude of a desire that both demands suffering and is repelled by it, desire's "measureless retreat through measureless attraction" to suffering?[134]

---

133. The many above-quoted passages are from Michaux, *Four Hundred Men*, in *Thousand Times Broken*, 123–47.
134. Char quoted in Blanchot, *Writing of the Disaster*, 113.

The cross is thus not only an evocation of infinite life, the infinite tree of life that flows through each and every human being, it also and especially embodies the infinite suffering of life that stretches to infinity. Suffering, infinite suffering, is the theme of this text. The cross is thus the sign of a suffering that "stretches," like the man on the cross, "stretched out" on the cross "in the middle of the sky (*étendre in plein ciel*), the way human suffering stretches." In this way, the cross is perhaps a sign that appeals in some way to all of humanity. It is a key sign in the alphabet with which Michaux had hoped to create a universal language. The cross may be the universal sign of the triumph of life over death, but for Michaux, it is also the sign of the triumph of life over suffering, the kind of suffering that Michaux depicted humorously in his Chaplin-esque character Plume, or in his many other texts of "Ordeals and Exorcisms." Infinite suffering accompanies the life of infinite desire, hence his wandering toward the Buddha and Buddhism, for which the irreducible fact of human suffering constitutes the First Noble Truth of Buddhist doctrine. This is why Nietzsche says he preferred Buddhism to Christianity. Buddhism is not a religion of "pity." Moreover, "Buddhism no longer says, 'struggle against sin.' Duly respectful of reality, Buddhism 'struggles against suffering.' "[135]

In this connection between life and suffering, life and time, life and desire, the True Cross is the link and the continuation of the tree of life, with its infinite rope of time, the rope of desire and suffering, passing through each and every being. This is what Michaux wanted to render visible: what always withdraws from visibility, withdraws from enunciation into silence. In some way, the suffering of life that Michaux evokes in his *Four Hundred Men on the Cross* is the suffering of writing and drawing, the suffering of words seeking to pronounce what they cannot say, what they cannot show or render visible even when they are bent and twisted into new forms and shapes, images of the impossible silence of the cross.

The infinitude of suffering and desire is the infinitude of writing, its miserable miracle, its turbulent infinity, an ineffable and unspeakable infinite inscribed but not circumscribed in a writing raised to infinity. This is its rhythm and its disaster, writing and drawing always turned toward that which turns aside from it, a writing and drawing that turns itself aside. A silence and an invisibility that always withdraws or folds itself away from

---

135. Friedrich Nietzsche, *The Anti-Christ*, in *The Portable Nietzsche*, trans. Walter Kaufmann (New York: Viking Press, 1954; repr. Penguin Books, 1959), 587.

writing and drawing as from all speaking and seeing. Writing and drawing inscribe the detour of an infinite attraction that is also a turning away, a turning and returning to infinity, a turning of language and images toward that from which they must turn away in an original torsion concentrated in the rhythm of being. Blanchot names this rhythm in a quotation attributed to Hölderlin, the rhythm that is everything: "Everything is rhythm. The entire destiny of man is a single celestial rhythm, just as the work of art is a unique rhythm."[136] Michaux speaks of his drawings and texts in *Four Hundred Men on the Cross* as the pathways of exorcism, a way of purging, clearing away the babbling clutter of words and images that had been blocking a return to the pure silence of "the cherished face." But the success of this is highly doubtful, he concludes. More likely it is the opposite that will prevail. There can be no return, no rebirth for a life gone by.[137]

There is no release from this for Michaux, just as Christ shall not be released from the embrace of the impossible wood of the cross. Even though He may flail against it, as Michaux flails against the limits of language, there is no release, for either Christ or Michaux. Furious at being there, both are nailed, as it were, to the cross of language, suffering, and desire. Does the realization not occur to him that the limits of language are somehow without limits, the limit of the infinite? The infinite limit? Is this why Michaux writes of a "last letter that remains to be written, but that shall never be written?"[138] He may try to render visible what must remain outside the reach of language: hallucinations visual, auditory, tactile, emotional; visions of floating heads, Death, the impossible Real as Lacan might have once called it. But he always falls before it, a pure silence imagined in and by the impurity of speech, an impossible silence, the impossible wood of the Real, rendered visible, rendered into writing and speech but never seized by impure speech and noisy silence. Written or drawn, only to vanish again in the very act of inscription, the frenzy ever renewed. To render visible is not only to betray; it is also to conceal. Michaux's poems and drawings do not reveal anything hidden behind or within words; they do not name or signify pain but communicate it, not as a meaning or a significance but as a force, an intensity that is incommunicable, approachable only through its signs and symptoms, through the traces, marks, and masks it leaves on the human body and memory. But it is only through the masks of such words

---

136. Quoted in Blanchot, *Infinite Conversation*, 30.
137. Michaux, *Four Hundred Men*, 159.
138. Michaux, "Façons d'endormi, façons d'eveillé," in *OC* III, 525; trans. mine.

and images, through their disaster, their miserable miracle, their turbulent infinity, that this silence beyond words can receive Michaux, in the silence of his being, what he is as a painter-poet-musician, these "four hundred men on the cross."

We conclude with a last emanation: here we see him, Henri Michaux, one more time, one more man on a figurative cross, from the pages of *La Nuit Remu*, in "Crier," a poem that communicates the intensity of pain in a rather memorable manner. An emanation that, like the others, marks the threshold where *savoir* becomes *non-savoir*, where the universal suffering of life is transformed into a joy that cries out from a "red-throated voice" (*crie d'une voix bordée de rouge*), a stupefying, mad joy.[139]

> An inflamed toenail makes for dreadful suffering. But a far greater one was not being able to cry out as I was in a hotel. Night had just darkened my room and I was stuck between two sleeping neighbors.
>
> So I began to unload my brain of all sorts of things: great footlockers, cooper plates, an instrument more sonorous than any organ. Thus taking advantage of a prodigious fever's full force, I assembled a deafening orchestra. Everything shook with its vibrations.
>
> Finally, sure that in all this tumult my voice would not be heard, I began to scream, to scream for hours on end, so that little by little, I managed to soothe myself.[140]

This is not the red-throated cry of the flesh but the "other cry," the silent, written cry unfolding its folds in the turbulent infinity of writing. As the True Cross is transubstantiated from an image of death and suffering into one of salvation, so the suffering, written body is transubstantiated into an

---

139. Michaux, *Connaissance par les gouffres*, "Derrière les mots," in *OC* III, 68. Michaux writes a short interpretation of a text fragment or sequence that suddenly comes to him: "Paolo! Paolo! Crie d'une voix bordée de rouge." Is the sequence a phrase half-recalled? A fragment from literature? A drug-induced dream? Michaux calls it an unforgettable "hyper-sensation," a "cri agressif, qui entre violemment en moi et paraît venir du fond d'une cour" ("an aggressive cry, which enters me violently and seems to come from the back of a courtyard"; trans. mine). Also quoted by Jouffroy in *Avec Henri Michaux*, 117.

140. Michaux, "Crying Out," *The Night Moves*, in *Someone Wants to Steal My Name*, ed. Nin Andrews, trans. Sydney Lea (Cleveland, OH: Cleveland State University Poetry Center, 2003), 15.

immutability, hell into paradise, a paradise of immutability withheld in his mescaline visions. Is this what Michaux sought in his mescaline visions and his quest for a universal language, the "savoir" and "guérison" that would be the transubstantiation of suffering into joy? Recall the lines from Michaux's hand, cited earlier:

> Tandis que l'enfer vibratoire est devenu paradis vibratoire et que le nouveau "milieu" déplie ses plis à l'infini, il éprouve en son être étonnamment et rythmiquement frappé, tout simplement l'immortalité, qui est immutabilité

> (While a vibratory hell has become a vibrating paradise and this new environment unfolds its folds to infinity, he experiences in his being astonishingly and rhythmically struck, quite simply, immortality, which is immutability).[141]

---

141. Michaux, *L'Infini turbulent*, in *OC* III, 933. Mercure de France ed., 201; trans. mine.

Postface

Poésie par le gouffre

> A l'instar de Pascal, la poésie française n'a pas cessé de côtoyer un gouffre.
>
> —Claude Esteban, *Critique de la raison poétique*

In these concluding pages, no final conclusions, no summary, no closure shall be offered. Closures or conclusions are not possible for an in-finite writing, the writing of Michaux, Bataille, and Klossowski, a writing *par le gouffre*. Rather, we shall take up a short series of meditations or reflections on what we might term the "in-finite"[1] writing of Michaux, Bataille, and Klossowski. Just a sketch to suggest the profile and trajectory of poetry and painting in these authors, one that is suggestive rather than definitive of much that could follow.

Critics may ask, How can Bataille or Klossowski be called a "poet?" Michaux, yes. But Klossowski wrote in prose, and Bataille was not much of a poet. Perhaps they are not poets at all, not the familiar poets and poetry we are used to. Are they not poets who resist poetry, who would like to smash poetry? Did Bataille not speak, in fact, of a hatred for poetry?

There was perhaps a time, at least in the books of a philosopher, when it seemed that, like man himself, the poet stood firmly on the earth and beneath the open blue sky. A time when the task and the destiny of the poet was recognizable as a mediator between gods and men. A time when poetry may have been sheltered in the "house of language," when Being's

---

1. The "in-fini" as it shall be invoked in this conclusion, I owe to Bernard Noël's "L'in-fini de Bataille," in *La Place de l'autre* (Paris: P.O.L., 2013), 646–48.

"four-fold" of earth and sky, gods and men, was still a recognizable albeit remote possibility, if only we would heed the call, if only we would listen to and hear the sacred word of the poet.

The poetry encountered in the work of Michaux, Bataille, and Klossowski cannot in all good faith be considered as contributions to an established literary form. Rather, the poet's words seem vaporized. No longer giving voice to the laughing creation of gods, these poems are what can best be described as vibratory emanations, apparitions, the stratagems of a "daemon" that stretches out and prolongs itself over a *gouffre*, a poetry suspended over the nothingness and night of an abyss that resists all signification, that marks the point where signification collapses.

Yet the poet continues to dramatize this life at the edge of a *"VIDE,"* as Michaux called it, marking this experience by naming it, naming this unnamable *gouffre* as the "night" and so returning it to the play of significations. But this night, this written night, is not the Night "delivered of stars," a *"des-astre"* of writing, a "multiple night"[2]—Night that is the death of God, the setting of all Suns, the collapse of all True Worlds, a horizon wiped clean, that is death itself, the death of the poet. Having crossed into signifiers and significations, translated into legible cultural forms, the Night then returns to its hollow, to the abyss that it is, leaving the word "night" floating over its absence. The poetic experiences of these authors leave behind in their passing a writing, a *côtoyer un gouffre*, that has its basis in this nameless absence. The poems, the paintings, are but apparitions suspended over it, as over a gulf. They speak not *about* it, but *from* it, through (*pars*) it, a *gouffre*, a Night that however marked and named cannot be distanced, set aside as a mere trifle, that cannot be escaped, that is always there, the ground collapsing beneath the feet of the poet.

Two hundred years after Hölderlin, poetry is unheeded today. If, as in Hölderlin, poetry once gave voice to the sacred, that may not be its role in today's secularized, industrialized world.[3] Yet, poetry's links with the sacred survive. In poetry by Michaux or Bataille, the "sacred" still resonates,

---

2. Marie-Claire Ropars-Wuilleumier, "On Unworking: The Image in Writing According to Blanchot," in *Maurice Blanchot: The Demand of Writing*, ed. Carolyn Bailey Gill (London: Routledge, 1996), 138. Quotes from Blanchot, *The Writing of the Disaster*, trans. Ann Smock (Lincoln: University of Nebraska Press, 1986), 5.

3. See Blanchot, "La Parole sacrée de Hölderlin," in *La part du feu* (Paris: Gallimard, 1949), 115–32. Trans. by Charlotte Mandell as "The Sacred Speech of Hölderlin," in *The Work of Fire* (Stanford: Stanford University Press, 1995), 111–31.

but as an apparitional sacred, not, in other words, as a religious notion or belief, nor as a fixed concept, or even a word, but as what emerges from experiences of great loss, or suffering, or even of laughter and joy. A new space and time opens from within the poem, a time after the gods and before their impossible return, and the space of a new journey, the space and time for a new destiny and direction for writing at the limits of the possible, a writing at the summit, the Très Haut. What, indeed, do we hear in the poetic words of Michaux, Bataille, or Klossowski? Is there a new and more ancient way of conceiving the sacred words of the poet?

What is important for our purposes is to recall the "double pulsion" Raymond Bellour delineated in Michaux's writings and drawings: a pulsion of concentration, a powerful gathering force that pulls toward a mystical unity, a pulsion doubled by that of a "dissemination into the flux" ("*Indéfinition par dissémination dans le flux du divers*"). This double pulsion is important for the following discussion Michaux's poetry.[4] But it shall also be in the background of the discussion of the poetics of Bataille and Klossowski, as well.

Today (or was it yesterday, all the way back to the yesterdays of a Pascal or even a Hölderlin?) the poet's experience is greatly altered by this chasm that has swept the ground from beneath poetry's feet. Whence the poet's place today? Not still standing within a four-fold of earth and sky, gods and men, the voice at the center, the modern poet, since Pascal and no doubt since Hölderlin and Mallarmé, is "without place." As Claude Esteban writes, "le poéte est par excellence l'homme sans lieu, l'errant, l'exilé."[5] The *gouffre* is not a place, neither a locale nor a location for the building of poetry's architectures. The poet's experience is described as without place (*sans lieu*), a wandering, exiled encounter at the edge of an abyss that opens from within (*dedans*, Michaux's word), the poet and poetry itself. Is this an experience of despair? As Mallarmé writes, by "digging into verse," not beyond verse but "into" it, behind or beneath or inside its words and rhythms, he has encountered not one but two abysses that caused him to despair: the death of God and his own death.[6] Do Bataille, Michaux, and

---

4. Raymond Bellour, "Notices to Plume," in *Henri Michaux, Oeuvres complètes* vol. III, 1468, ed. Raymond Bellour with Ysé Tran (Paris: Gallimard, Bibliothéque de la Pléiade, 2004). Bellour is speaking especially of Michaux's *Misérable miracle* and *Paix dans les brisements*, which will be discussed in the pages that follow.

5. Claude Esteban, *Critique de la raison poétique* (Paris: Flammarion, 1987), 219.

6. Mallarmé, quoted in Blanchot, "Mallarmé's Experience," in *The Space of Literature*, trans. Ann Smock (Lincoln: University of Nebraska Press, 1982), 38.

Klossowski share in this despair? To the contrary, do they not speak of a joy in the face of this death? What Blanchot, in his article on Hölderlin's sacred language, has called the poet's "poetic existence," in all its strength, now stretches out into that nothingness and emptiness, "without ceasing to accomplish itself."[7] Is such strength still manifest in the poet's joy in the face of death? Not a poetry of resignation and despair, but to the contrary, impossibly, unexpectedly, one of joy?

The *fond*, the "experience," even the strength from which these poets speak, is nothing substantial, nothing like a firm foundation from which poetry could be launched, assuring its continued possibility as a recognized cultural genre. Rather the poet here undergoes the impossible, writing as an experience where there is no possibility of an experience: Night, death, and the ruin of poetry, a great giving way to collapse. The poet and poetry are now without vocation, a wandering, difficult passage to ever new forms of writing and painting in a world without the shelter of Truth, Goals, Destinations.

Little wonder that Bataille's or Michaux's poetry from the start did not set out to be "poetry," not a beautifully worded poem *about* experience, but to be a poem or a writing that is the least inappropriate form an *expérience intérieure* could take, poetry must *be* that experience, not just a writing *about* it; it writes from the absent center of that experience. Poetry, is transformed, displaced from the regulated orders of syntax and semantics, a metamorphosis emerging from the protective cocoon of traditions and stereotypes of culture, emerging in strange shapes, cries, and screams from the center of an experience, the *gouffre*. An anti-tradition of poetry takes flight, *une poésie par le gouffre*, no longer satisfied with the dominion of names and the genre of verse and rhymes, no longer sheltered in the conventional forms and settings of thought. Poetry and painting become emanations, apparitions, even the daemon, dwelling at the edge of a *gouffre*; not representations or significations, in other words, but a scream from a strangled throat.

The books of Michaux, Bataille, and Klossowski once challenged all of literature to get beyond itself as "literature," opening it to the experience of new thrusts and pulsions, new modalities and levels of writing, challenging

---

7. Blanchot, "Sacred Speech of Hölderlin," 114. In *La part du feu* as "Interroger Hölderlin, c'est interroger une existence poétique si forte que, son essence une fois dévoillée, elle a pu faire elle-même la prevue qu'elle était impossibilité et se prolonger dans le néant et dans le vide, sans cesser d'accomplir" (118).

it not to ask as to meanings and totalities but to what sustains poetry, what makes it possible in its impossibility. Writing at the limits, writing *par le gouffre*, writing can prolong and find its strength there, in its prolongation into the Void, *into the gouffre*. It may have its roots in mud, but it reaches for the stars. It now stands, stately, in Éditions Gallimard. What do these writers, Michaux, Bataille, and Klossowski, have to give when it is the lightning they have received? "The poet," René Char writes, "does not retain what he discovers; having transcribed it. He soon loses it. In that resides his novelty, his infinity and his peril."[8]

Michaux

. . . des signes mais comme des ondes
aucun autre but que la vibration.[9]

Et c'est toujours vers plus d'insaisissable, qu'il lève sa limite. Lui que son nom n'arrête pas, ni ses livres, ni sa peinture, car tout cela n'est pas son acquis, mais l'espace justement d'un dessein qu'on ne saurait pas davantage fixer que l'aile ne se fixe sur l'air qui la porte. Depuis l'origine, l'écriture va du visible à l'invisible et nous laisse devant la page sombre où lire n'est voir; mais voice inventée, comme par un retournement originel, l'écriture visible de l'invisible.[10]

"Fragmented thoughts that will remain so, individual, ungovernable, unusable, intractable, impermanent, apparitional, lost as quickly as they appear, not remaining, not preparing anything, impossible to direct, to resume, to place otherwise, to find again, to dream over, impossible to note within their wild ejection, sometimes malicious, but always

---

8. Char, "The Library Is on Fire," in *Furor and Mystery & Other Writings*, trans. and eds. Mary Ann Caws and Nancy Kline (Boston: Black Widow Press, 2010), 385.
9. Bernard Noël, *Vers Henri Michaux* (Paris: Unes, 1998), 24. ("Signs but like waves/ no other purpose than vibration"; trans. mine.)
10. Noël, *Vers Henri Michaux*, 54. ("And it is always towards more elusiveness that He lifts his limit. He whom his name does not stop, neither his books, nor his painting, because all that is not what he has acquired, but precisely the space of an intention that one cannot fix any more than the wing can fix itself on the air that carries it. From the beginning, writing has gone from the visible to the invisible and leaves us in front of the dark page where reading is not seeing; but an invented voice, as if by an original reversal, the visible writing of the invisible"; trans. mine.)

> innocent, never strategists, impudent, but incredibly dazzling, clarifying, thoughts that pass into a syntactical nothingness, which one does very well without . . . as long as one does not attempt to write."[11]
>
> —Henri Michaux, "Meaning of the Drawings"

We are far from the horizons of the *nous* and *logos* of Parmenides's philosophical poem that declared, from the mouth of a goddess, that one must think and say that Being is; thinking Being in its unity; Being as Truth, as a compact One, lacking nothing, a solidity without spaces or spacings, gaps, or breaks in the skin of its consistency; excluding all plurality. Darkness, the nothingness of Untruth, is identified with the paths of the many, with directionless plurality. A third path, the chiaroscuro of opinion, meanwhile, shall be allowed as a path of wandering, the admixture of the One and the Many, as one finds in writing and painting.

But Michaux's work is not simply the poetic overturning of this philosophical poetry, this unity of *nous* and *logos*. He does not simply affirm a reversal of plurality over the One, an assertion of plurality that would make plurality into yet another One. We ask, Does Michaux think and say that "Pluralism ≡ Monism," as Deleuze's "magic" formula has it?[12] Michaux's path is the paradoxical belonging of unity and plurality, their chiasmatic interweaving, opening the poem to think and say what silence, what *nuit*, what daybreak opens beyond all such notional discourses, silence as the excess of dialectical oppositions and philosophical relations between the One and the Many, beyond the domain of both *logos* and *nous*. Michaux: not a philosophical assertion of this but a fragmented poetry, yet bearing his name and signature; a playful, not purposeful, not "strategic" transcendence of the philosophical poetry of the One and the Many but their displacement, putting

---

11. Michaux, "Meaning of the Drawings" ["Signification de dessins"], in *Peace in the Breaking*, in *Thousand Times Broken*, trans. Gillian Conoley (San Francisco: City Lights, 2014), 46–47.

12. *Oeuvres complètes*, vol. III, ed. Raymond Bellour (Paris: Gallimard, 2004), 1468–1469 (hereafter cited in notes as *OC*). Bellour quotes Deleuze and Guattari's formula, "PLURALISM ≡ MONISME," from *Mille Plateaux* (Paris: Minuit, 1980), 31. Trans by Brian Massumi as *A Thousand Plateaus* (Minneapolis: University of Minnesota Press, 1987), 20. English trans.: "Passing through dualisms, we arrive at a process that challenges all dualisms . . . each time mental correctives are necessary to undo the dualisms we no wish to construct but through which we pass. Arrive at the magic formula we all seek—PLURALISM ≡ MONISM."

this opposition out of play. Michaux's poem "Peace in the Breaking" has a telos, a summit it is reaching for—the poet, a suffering penitent, crawling on his knees toward this summit. Yet the poem is neither in thought or saying nor outside of them, but it is at a threshold, a "non-place" somehow beyond or at the limits of all thinking and saying, a vision beyond oppositions that sees them in their embrace, with the corollary "transmutation of body and soul" in the silence of a mystical spiritualization of experience (*OC* III, 1468–1469).

Such, at least, is the thesis of Michaux's great editor and commentor Raymond Bellour, who, in the third volume of Michaux's *Oeuvres complètes* (*OC* III, 1468), writes, apropos to the whole of Michaux's work, that from the earliest works there is an "unbridled plurality of doubles," a proliferation of bodies, names, personae, masks, stolen non-identities,[13] and animals that populate his books. "There is no single self," Michaux writes. "There are *not ten selves. There is no self. SELF is but a point of equilibrium.* . . . In the name of many, I sign this book." The necessity is always undertaken to free himself from the idea of a single, sustaining Self, the Self of identity and unity. Under that or within its equilibrium lies the domain of fragmentation, of cries and shouts, the murmuring of the many, the multiple. All the dualisms and tormenting schizophrenic experiments are engulfed (*s'engouffre*) in the void left behind by the collapse of the poet's "too simple monisms"—essentially Christian-inspired—of his youth. Plurality does not sink into the nothingness of *la nuit*, the night of the poem with which the author feels identified, "at one with the night," and the other night, the night of the cross, as in all the four hundred figures left pinned to their crosses in *Four Hundred Men on the Cross*. The nothingness of *la nuit*, the *gouffre*, rises to it, into a body and soul transformed into a "pure state of multiplicity."

We can see this equivalence of unity and multiplicity in Michaux's 1959 book *Peace in the Breaking*.[14] Published between the more well-known mescaline books *Miserable Miracle* and *Turbulent Infinity* on one side and the more scientifically inclined *Connaisance par le gouffre* on the other, it

---

13. Michaux, postface to *A Certain Plume*, trans. Richard Sieburth (New York: New York Review of Books, 2018), 189.

14. Originally published as *Paix dans le brisements* (Paris: Éditions Flinker, 1959). Nine of those published were luxury editions printed on Japanese Imperial paper with original drawings and signed by the author. In the first collectible editions, the drawings were spread across multiple pages somewhat like a Chinese scroll painting.

is a "unique book," Bellour writes, not only for its position in Michaux's oeuvre but for its construction of multiple levels of textual performance: prose essay, the wildcat drawings, and the long poem. Image, essay, and poem: three experiments, three ways of unfolding a spiritual, sacred journey; three ways Michaux heeded, reconstructed, and distanced the embrace of the *gouffre* that opens from within; three experiments communicating a desire for the impossible, for *la nuit*, for a union ("*oh ce désir d'union*") in which the imprisoning walls of dualities, subject-object, inside-outside, beginning and end, unity and multiplicity, would break.

It most singularly escapes the "abstract opposition between the multiple and the one." Multiplicity is no longer "treated as a numerical fragment of a lost unity or totality, or as the organic element of a totality yet to come, but, whether discreet or continuous,"[15] as a multiplicity freed from the numerical, no longer defined by it, without return or reserve. Multiplicity is in the infinity of Michaux's "vibrating carpets" (*tapis vibratile*) or the furrow (*sillon*); multiplicity is named in the magnetic spectra that spring to life from the opening pages of *Peace in the Breaking*. It appears in the strange drawings of a torrent, which are not just drawings but a frenzy of pencil strokes ("*une poussière de signes*"),[16] a sometimes spiny, skeletal figuration that extends over several pages, a horror that opens the book *Peace in the Breaking*.[17] But through the horror, the poem closes with a vision of a shattered attainment. At the end of this poem, in images that reconstruct a spiritual and physical struggle with its almost Sisyphean ascensions and falls, the poet can be seen rising, in a final hard-won ascension, to the *haut* ("heights"). Is there "peace" for the poet? The summit brings not a tranquil unity of Self, but its fall and dispersion, its dissemination. There is perhaps an emptying of Self at the summit. Unity realized, it breaks into a "pure

---

15. Deleuze and Guattari, *A Thousand Plateaus*, 32.

16. Bellour, "Notice" to "Paix dans le brisements," in *OC* II, 1363.

17. In Michaux's short prose essay in *Peace in the Breaking*, "Meaning of the Drawings," he says that his images, their sudden uncontrollable streaming into presence, recalls his earlier "Tree of Life." Quoting Michaux, "Je crois montrer l'arbre sans fin, l'arbre de vie . . . l'ecoulement, qui, sans interruption, même d'une seule second, traverse l'homme du premier instant de sa vie au tout dernier, ruisseau ou sablier qui n s'arrête qu'avec elle" ("I believe I am indicating the endless tree, the tree of life that is a source . . . the flow that, without interruption, even for a second, passes through man from the first moment of his life to the very last one, a stream or an hourglass that stops only when life stops"). *OC* II, 1000; and Michaux, "Meaning of the Drawings," in *Peace in the Breaking*, in *Thousand Times Broken*, 48–49.

multiplicity." "Fragmented thoughts that will remain so, individual, ungovernable, unusable, intractable, impermanent, apparitional, lost as quickly as they appear, not remaining, not preparing anything."[18]

The long poem that composes the third, concluding part of *Peace in the Breaking* communicates the poet's spiritual journey toward a summit, seeking a physical and spiritual transfiguration. His journey is in the poem he has written. It cascades down the page, a torrent broken into stanzas, forming a visual image recalling the drawings of spiny furrows that open this fragmentary book. Michaux seems to have believed that his experiences of images and words were inherently and unconquerably multiple, initially pouring out too fast to do anything about them; too fast to sort them, name them, piece them together; too fast to glimpse their possible logic; such experiences were touching upon a "primitive and exceptional state" of consciousness or preconsciousness, an experience that leapt from the turbulent infinity that underlies even the most placid man, the most directed and willful intelligence.[19]

Peace in the Breaking thus has its own rhythms of unity and multiplicity. The essays, drawings, and the poem each have their own particular rhythms, but beneath these there is a great, silent wave-like rhythm of being, an infinite wave-like rising and falling, a pulse of offerings and disguises that surfaces in the discontinuities of words and images. It flows from images, through essays setting forth "the meaning of the drawings," and culminates in poetry's halting dance. The rhythm of the poem engenders the poet, marked by discontinuity, marked by finitude. What is this primitive, rhythmic pulsion that infuses the poem, that underlies the illusory continuity of daily words and beings with their rat-a-tat, marching rhythms? Is it a greater rhythm of silence, of darkness and light? A rhythm of gathering and dispersion, the rhythmic opening and closing of being, the rough, organic rhythms of the poet's shouts and cries, his lurching steps toward the summit, toward the chasm (*gouffre*)?[20]

---

18. Michaux, 47.

19. Michaux, 49.

20. This question of different rhythms in Michaux's poetry has been studied in the collection of essays "L'ecriture: Entre 'la colle' des mots et le dégagement des rythmes," in *Passages et langages de Henri Michaux*, eds. Jean-Claude Mathieu and Michel Collot (Paris: Librairie José Corti, 1987), 131–208. Bellour also speaks of a "pression rythmique sans égale, une insistance presque respiratoire ou s'inscrit, comme sur un sismogramme, le vie même d'un corps . . . abstrait par le caractère de la quête dont il devient l'enjeu."

In attaining the summit, the equivalent perhaps of the *gouffre*, Michaux's "peace," his "peace *in* the breaking," is found where he disconnects from the pleasures and controls of the finite and submits himself to the infinite. *Peace in the Breaking* is the poem that breaks poetry into "a thousand crushings crushed extended to infinity . . . the witness to infinity." The poem is an experience of the summit, the *haut* (the *VIDE*?), and of the fall, the *chute*, that comes with it. We can see why Raymond Bellour would write, "Never before has Michaux been able to express so closely, and so physically, what he wants to communicate."[21] Communicate what? Not ideas, and certainly not a dialectical ascension to truth and freedom. The poem gives us only "pegs" strewn "across the bone column that forms the furrow," the infinite furrow of a spiritual experience, the struggle against crippling dualisms, in all their forms and models, the double pulsions of unification and fragmentation, the doubling, the enfolding of the many and the one.[22]

It would be difficult in these slender pages to recreate or reproduce in some way the enormity Michaux had in mind for his *Peace in the Breaking*. Michaux envisioned it to be written and drawn like a Chinese scroll painting, a rolling fabric that would bear his images and texts, an endless poem read vertically, its words becoming images, like Chinese characters, having only a loose syntax.[23] Michaux's mystical and mescaline visions, untraceable no doubt, fragmentary and fleeting, are the basis for the experience appearing in this poem; the words and images of the poem are not the representations of that experience but its apparitional occurring. Hence the striking rhythms of *Peace in the Breaking*, the points of momentary and provisional unity and gathering broken by fragmentation and dispersal. The poem is to be both seen and read as though written on a scroll or a screen that unfolds to infinity; a "nervous projection screen," as he calls it; a "tapis vibratile," a white sheet he sees from his window; a torn, vibrating sheet, noiselessly snapping, on which "a world unfolded," on which the images and blocks of words appear and disappear—apparitions, emanations—without a substantial Self to witness their movement, without the sovereignty of a will to command their rising

---

OC II, 1365. (English: "Unequaled rhythmic pressure, where an almost respiratory insistence is inscribed, as on a seismogram, the very life of a body . . . abstracted by the character of the quest of which it becomes the stake"; trans. mine.)

21. *OC* II, 1362. The first editions did attempt to recreate the visual and poetic qualities of a Chinese scroll painting.

22. Bellour in *OC* II, 1362–1363.

23. Bellour in *OC* II, 1363.

and falling.²⁴ The poem is the record, the reconstruction of the emergence of thought, a visionary thought rising through exceptional states of mind and body.²⁵ A double movement that is a "breaking" and a "peace in that breaking" of Self. Let us now follow, like stepping stones across a turbulent stream, a few prismatic shards from this vibrating carpet of writing, Michaux's poetic trajectory toward the summit, the *haut* (*Trés-Haut?*).

> de mille écrasements écrasé
> allongé à l'infini
> témoin d'infini
> infini tout de même
> mis à l'infini
>
> (from a thousand crushings crushed
> Extended to infinity
> Witness to infinity
> Infinite all the same
> Set to infinity)²⁶

The "infinite" is an important signifier for Michaux. The writer appeals to the "All," to totality, Alain Jouffroy writes. "That which prevents or stops him/her from writing, a limit, does not exist: This is why the object of writing, its sole object—is the infinite."²⁷ Is this the infinite also named in Baudelaire's poem "Le Gouffre" ("The Abyss"), the Abyss that is "All—action and dream, language, desire?" "My windows open on an infinity," Baudelaire writes, like the noiselessly snapping white sheet Michaux sees from his window. The vertigo of the infinite haunts the poet, making him envy the indifference of the void, the Abyss.²⁸ Michaux shares much of

---

24. Michaux, *Peace in the Breaking*, 43.
25. This recalls the Surrealist project, as stated in the *First Manifesto* (1929), which André Breton defined as "psychic automatism . . . in which one proposes to express—verbally, by means of the written word, or in any other manner—the actually functioning of thought." Breton, *Manifestos of Surrealism*, trans. Richard Seaver and Helen R. Lane (Ann Arbor: University of Michigan Press, 1972), 26. Yet, Michaux did not travel with the Surrealists.
26. Michaux, *Peace in the Breaking*, 53.
27. Alain Jouffroy, *Avec Henri Michaux* (Paris: Rocher, 1992), 103.
28. Charles Baudelaire, *Les Fleurs du Mal*, trans. Richard Howard (Boston: David R.

this. The infinite in Michaux's poem is the infinite cascade, the infinite fall (*chute*), the infinite other side of the ascension described in the poem. Not a metaphysical abstraction distinct from and opposed to the temporality of the finite, Michaux's infinite is enfolded into the finite, folded into the rhythms of being, the infinite depth of the blue sky touching the finite curvature of the earth, marking the edge of all seeing and saying.[29] Finite and the infinite belong to one another, a rhythm of dissemination and gathering, breaking and collecting. It invades, it torments him, laughing at the finitude of his body, like a god. As he writes,

> infini
> infini qui au corps me travaille
> et rit de mon fini . . .
> infini qui m'étend
> et sans effort, sans spectacle
> de mes prises me dessaisit.
>
> (infinity
> infinity that torments my body
> and that laughs at my finish . . .
> infinity that extends me
> and without effort, without spectacle from my holds relinquishes
>   me.)[30]

Godine, 1983), 174.

29. See Jacques Colette's article "Chute et sentiment d'infini," in *Passages et langages de Henri Michaux* (Paris: Librairie José Corti, 1987), 63. Colette writes that Michaux has escaped the philosophical-metaphysical alternatives of idealization or materialist radicalization. Michaux writes in a register that is not of philosophical thought. Thus, the infinite is neither a philosophical term nor a concept. It is, in Michaux's words, a "transport éprouvé." The feeling of the infinite, Collette writes, "Servient lorsque, cessant de fixer le ciel comme un objet solide, on est précipité dans un abîme, (now quoting Michaux) 'donc rien ne vous sépare plus,' alors même que par la chute, descente ou ascension, le moi se trouve dans un definitive distance à l'égard de soi" (The feeling of the infinite "Arises when, ceasing to fix the sky as a solid object, one is thrown into an abyss [now quoting Michaux], 'therefore nothing separates you any more,' even though by the fall, descent or ascent, the Self finds itself in a definitive distance with regard to oneself"; trans. mine). Collette quotes Michaux, *Les grandes épreuves* (Paris: Gallimard, 1966), 126, 117.

30. Michaux, *Peace in the Breaking*, 61.

Michaux is possessed of the idea that he is the place, the site but not the source of an infinite unfolding, not the source of the infinite flux. Effortlessly, the infinite relinquishes him "from his holds," from the seeds of the Self that bind him by "extending" him to infinity, to the "swarm," in a "dissemination into the flux."

> à l'essaim je retourne
> des milliers d'ailes d'hirondelles tremblent sur ma vie.
>
> (to the swarm I return
> Thousands of swallows' wings tremble across my life.)[31]

Images of the broken seeds of the Self, a Self relinquished, wings beating across his life. The illusory, unifying Self relinquished; multiplicity becomes a sonorous, horrifying vibration that, like waves, can also be brilliant. Images both seen and heard that write the passages of relinquishment.

> sillon
> La forme fendue d'un être immense
> m'accompagne et m'est soeur
> J'écoute les milliers de feuilles.
>
> (furrow
> The split form of an immense being
> Accompanies me and is my sister
> I listen to the thousands of leaves.)[32]

The furrow is also drawn in the suite of images that opens *Peace in the Breaking*. Drawings that resemble fossils—the spiny, powdery signatures of passing life. A vertical torrent, he calls it, an image of time: "My time? Or the presence of that time?"[33] Recall the lines from *Miserable Miracle* quoted earlier: "Furrow with little, hurried transversal sweepings. In it a fluid, its brightness mercurial, its behavior torrential, its speed electric. . . . Where is this furrow exactly . . . crossing my skull . . . a furrow without beginning or end . . . a furrow that I'd say comes from one end of the earth, goes

---

31. Michaux, 53.
32. Michaux, 55.
33. Michaux, 39.

through me and on to the other end of the earth."³⁴ The furrow trembles, tingled with spasms that turn into nerves, a tree with fine branches, the tree of life evoked earlier. All revealed, all experienced on the "unexpected small screen," the mental panorama, "which was incredibly luminous, within a complete silence, within a bewildering silence."³⁵

> un désir d'union
> oh ce désir d'union
>
> (a desire for union
> oh that desire for union)³⁶
>
> Paix
> Paix par graine broyée
> Je fais la paix
>
> (Peace
> Peace through crushed seeds
> I make peace)³⁷
>
> Le mal est immolé au bien
> l'impur au pur
> l'à-côté au droit
> le nombre à l'unique
> et le nom est immolé au sans nom
>
> (evil is sacrificed to the good
> the impure to the pure
> the nearby to the straight ahead
> the number to the unique
> and the name is sacrificed to the nameless)³⁸

---

34. Michaux, *Misérable miracle*, in *OC* II, 626. Trans. by Louise Varése and Anna Moschovakis as *Miserable Miracle* (New York: New York Review Books, 2002), 13.
35. Michaux, *Peace in the Breaking*, 41.
36. Michaux, 55.
37. Michaux, 69.
38. Michaux, 71.

After the tumult of rapid-fire movements, through the dispersal of electrified images and words, there is a counter-movement of condensation, three images of collection, gathering, and union, three apparitional foreshadows on the *pente* (slope) toward the *haut* where the ultimate peace in the breaking awaits, always in retreat, the poet drawn by its very withdrawal. In the first image, a union is evoked. Not the ultimate form of metaphysical synthesis found in Hegel, a logical outcome or result, the union of a "tetanized soul," but a union that does not set aside the atrocious suffering and the separations sustained by this desire for unity. This is a "peace *through* crushed seeds," a "peace *in* (*dans*) the breaking," not in the aftermath. But a union with what? Death? "I love, I marry my death," he writes.[39] A union with totality, the "all" of the infinite? Or a union identified with loss and relinquishment? A mystical union with the "open petals" of a flower perfumed with the "unsayable," "the flower of the perpetual"?[40] While the image of a flower may suggest a sexual union, Bellour writes that Michaux's poem stands in the grand central train station between consciousness and the unconscious. Perhaps the union he speaks of is nothing sexual, nothing Freudian. There is no repression to conquer, no desire to set free. A mystical union, rather, that comes with the casting off of the Ego, of Self, of Me, casting off all the names and nomenclatures that seal the fate of suffering. In an almost Socratic turn of phrase, he writes, "I have broken my shell . . . I leave the prison of my body."[41]

Finally, the poem closes with the moment of ascension that could also be a plunge (*chute*) to the depths, making this an almost Heraclitean vision in which the way up and the way down are one and the same.[42] Peace,

---

39. Michaux, 65.

40. Michaux, 55.

41. Michaux, 69.

42. Is this "ascension" that is also a "fall" spatial or temporal in character? As stated in chap. 3, "Emanations," Michaux's drawings and writings in *Miserable Miracle* evoke a Jacob's ladder, having an infinite number of steps that lead to something formless, "abstract," without image or face, where writing and drawing fail. The image or metaphor seems spatial, yet to many commentators, there is a prioritization of time over space in Michaux's texts. See Colette, "Chute et sentiment d'infini," 60, which speaks of infinity in temporal terms. Commenting on *Peace in the Breaking*, he writes, "Que le temps de la chute puisse être aussi celui de l'ascension indique peut-être la secondarité de l'espace par rapport au temps qui seul nous prend au dépourvu. Descente dans les profondeurs au montée en altitude peuvent l'une et l'autre suggrérer l'accès à ce qui fonde, à condition que cet accès ne soit ni conquête du commencement, ni disparition

unity, is found in the "breaking," in the sacrifice of names to the nameless (*sans nom*). But insofar as this "peace" still floats over a flow of signifiers, it too remains illusory, a mask over the void.

> mon âme déchargée de la charge de moi
> suit dans un infini qui l'anime et ne se precise pas
> la pente vers le haut
> vers le haut
> vers toujours plus haut
> la pente
> comment ne l'avais-je pas encore rencontrée
> la pente aui aspire
> la merveilleusement simple inarrêtable ascension
>
> (my soul unburdened of the burden of myself
> follows in an infinity that animates it and does not take shape
> the slope towards the heights
> towards the high/top
> always farther upward
> the slope
> how had I not encountered it before?
> The slope that aspires
> The marvelously simple unstoppable ascent)[43]

A trajectory is here affirmed, a double, rhythmic pulse of existence, of life itself, the force of breaking, the shapeless, ever aspiring upward slope of a force effecting an "unburdening" of "myself," the force of breaking that is

---

fantasmatique dans un espace iréel" ("That the time of the fall can also be that of the ascent perhaps indicates the secondary place of space in relation to time, which alone takes us unawares. Descent into the depths or ascent to a [higher] altitude can both suggest access to what grounds, provided that this access is neither the conquest of the beginning, nor the phantasmic disappearance into an unreal space"; trans. mine). The questions, however, remain: Is this a temporal infinity, "an infinity that animates it and does not take shape"? Is this "ascent" a mystical vision, a mystical journey, and so beyond space and time? Yet the drawings, like the poems, are temporal and spatial on the page. The infinity of the vision must be both inside and outside of writing and drawing where there is both space and time.

43. Michaux, *Peace in the Breaking*, 73 (trans. altered), writes, "the upward slope // towards the high/top." For Bataille, the summit is a "summit of death," "à hauteur de mort," he writes. "La joie devant la mort," in *OC* II, 244.

the force that saves, that brings peace,[44] the rhythm of a mystical union of unity and disintegration, concentration and fragmented dispersal.

Bataille

Bataille's differences with Michaux turn up quite clearly and strongly in a phrase that had three successive versions: in *L'Orestie*, the first poems of which date from 1943, contemporary with *L'Expérience intérieure*; a few years later in *La Haine de la poésie* (Éditions de Minuit, 1947); and in *L'Impossible* (Éditions de Minuit, 1947) also published under the title *La Haine de la poésie* and then republished in 1962 with an augmented preface. As Bernard Noël quotes the phrase: "l'éclat de la poésie se révèle hors des beaux moments qu'elle atteint; comparée à l'échec de la poésie, la poésie rampe."[45]

This phrase announced Bataille's opposition to poetry, not to poetry as such but to a beautiful poetry of words, a poetry that justifies nature or relations between human beings in a world dominated by the rubrics of commerce and utility, a poetry launched from a world of words and discourses always evasive of the human in situ in the "in-fini," as Bernard Noël calls it in his essay on Bataille.[46] In-fini not only in the sense of surpassing finitude, an impossibility, but of entering more deeply into finitude and without looking away, in-fini in the sense of being unbound from any goal or finality, God, Truth, the Good, even that of the infinite itself, all are signs, metaphors for a desire for salvation in a world where no salvation is possible. In-fini as without the finitude of salvation, freed from all transcendence. But the in-fini in the sense of a world without end, the re-birth of the world within each new poem. Thus, where Michaux was seeking, at least in the thesis of Raymond Bellour, a "salvation" or a transfiguration of body and soul, a salvation that might echo the mysticism of the Upanishads and the Indian yogi who seek a union or a return from "Self" to the origins, the nameless, selfless Atman Brahman, the non-self;[47] where for Michaux

---

44. See Bellour's notes to *Paix dans les brisements*, in *OC* II, 1365.

45. Quoted by Bernard Noël in *Vers Georges Bataille*, in *L'Espace de l'autre*, 617. ("Poetry's radiance is revealed apart from the beautiful moments it attains; compared to the failure of poetry, poetry crawls"; trans. mine.)

46. Noël, "L'in-fini de Bataille," 646–48.

47. See Bataille, *L'Expérience intérieure: Quatrième partie*, which announces a *Nouvelle théologie mystique*, in *OC* V, 127–30. Trans. Leslie Anne Boldt as *Inner Experience* (Albany: State University of New York Press, 1988), 108–12.

the poem was the tormenting experience of that ascension to a summit, to a namelessness beyond or beneath all names, Bataille's *poésie* stems from a new configuration of *poésie* and *expérience*. Poetry and experience are of the same cloth, but poetry must always be a revolt against poetry, a poetry that holds out no possibility for salvation.[48]

Bataille's poetics in-fini takes these directions: first, a philosophical direction, with and against Hegel's dialectic of absolute knowledge; second, a more general combat against poetry delimited by utility; and third, the evocation, by way of a discussion of metaphor in Bataille's poetics, of a sacrifice of poetry, the poetry of the mystical experience at the limits of language. All this to shred any ties that poetry might have with transcendence, whether religious, philosophical, or scientific. Is Bataille's poetics merely a metaphorical play or is there another dimension, the labyrinth of another relation between poetry and experience in Bataille's work?

First, a more general revolt against the discourses of knowledge that might try to tame and trammel upon the darker and more unspeakable dimensions of experience, namely death and eroticism, by wrapping them under a "frock coat" of moral and scientific concepts by which their passion, their horror and terror, are neutralized, put to sleep under a blanket of finely turned phrases. Where the poets, Rimbaud most pointedly, seek a poetry in flames, a poetry that can illuminate the night, a poetry of vigilance and wakefulness in a somnambulistic world, Bataille finds only "bien-parler," as in the idealism of the surrealists, which to Bataille seemed desperate for sleep. Passing by the sleeping poet's bedroom, the surrealist notes the sign on the door: *pass by quietly, poet at work*. For Bataille, it is not a question of telling a bedtime story—composing a *récit*, a narrative—but of awakening. A writing that awakens shall be a poetry that sacrifices poetry, that sacrifices words, perverting them by opening them to a level beyond utilitarian concerns and communications to what Bataille still refers to as the sacred, identified with the collapse of transcendence and objectifications, finding the holes

---

48. See Leslie Hill, *Blanchot: Extreme Contemporary* (London: Routledge, 1997), 127, which follows other commentators in marking the difference between Heidegger and Blanchot on this theme of "salvation." To Heidegger's "only a God can save us now," Blanchot offers not a new divine, not a new sacred, but only "the absence of the presence of the absence of the gods, the only situation that allows the question of art" (and poetry?) "to be raised at all." Or, in the words of Bernard Noël, "We are the time of the silence of the gods. This is why poetry is possible: it is the vibration of this silence." From Noël's *Château de Cène*, quoted in Hervé Carn, "Gravir le silence: Parole et silence dans les récits de Bernard Noël," in *Noël: Le corps du verbe* (Paris: ENS, 2008), 162.

and displacements within language that allow the sudden lightning strikes that before no words could say and see. Writing comes to be the experience of experience, Noël writes, the experience, in Bataille's case, of the limits of the possible of experience, an experience of abyssal loss that the poetic word approaches only to fall back away from. Rimbaud sets the tone and the pace for Bataille's "hatred" of poetry. His rejection of poetry is unsurpassed. But where Rimbaud's is a more sweeping and generalized rejection of poetry, Bataille's is a more incendiary, eloquent revolt against any and all that might be celebrated in poetry as an aesthetic artifact, revolt against a poetry of goals, ideals; projects of truth, love, or beauty; or whatever else one might seize to hurl down the throat of the void that opens wide and darkly with the death of God and the consequent loss of any guarantee for the personal Self. And he continued to write poems. A poetry purified of working like a shovel becomes a torch that brings the *gouffre*, this chasm, into view, and the leap that before had been hidden under the parades of quotidian footsteps. Yet poetry—not despite the profile of rebellion it occasionally strikes—is the sealing wax whose fine phrases close it off from any encounter with radical finitude, thus protecting both the poet and the reader from the irresistible temptation to hurl oneself into that yawning gulf of darkness.

Such was Bataille's complaint against Hegel's monumental system: it built a grand conceptual architecture on the claim of having stood up against the *gouffre* of death. This gave it the strength to take up the whole of truth and being—to take death up—into its logic and so bring history to its end, its realization, its freedom. If it was to be, the system had to make itself the annulation of abyssal loss, the absolute triumph of life over death. Hegel's *Phenomenology*, that great book of Truth, succeeded only by cheating death, taking away its rending power by giving formless death a form and a place in the dialectic of Truth, bringing death's terrifying absence to appearance in and as a Gestalt, as a shape within consciousness and its journey to absolute self-consciousness. Thus death is driven inwardly, deep into the heart of Hegel's system of absolute knowledge. Death's *gouffre*, death's abyss, the most disquieting form negativity can take, is transformed, put to work in the task of realizing absolute knowledge. Hegel's achievement was to build a monument to the triumph of life over death. As a figure in the dialectic of absolute knowledge, death is thus mummified, put to work—the "labor of the negative"—building the pyramid of Truth. Death thus became something like a domesticated horse. This was Hegel's success and his failure. Hegel, in Bataille's view, was nothing but a "modern man," a "shovel handle."

Bataille knew what Hegel's absolute knowledge did not: that the death taken up and put to work producing the discourse of science is not Death itself, but that "other death," the one that takes shape in the discontinuity of a discourse, the one transmogrified by becoming a signification, a word taking on the heavy burden of signification. Far from being that horror before which consciousness shrinks, death is now put to work as a "negativity," playing a role in the system of absolute self-consciousness, working toward its own self-annulment as a figure in Hegel's science of absolute truth. As a Gestalt, a form, rather than a formless abyss, death annuls the very violence from which it was born: the violence of death. Whereas Hegel's philosophical discourse made death into an experience of consciousness, into a possibility of being, for Bataille's poetics—and here we can include many sections of *L'Expérience intérieure*, as we shall see—death is an impossibility, never brought to appearing, an abyss opening beneath our feet, an abyss having absence as its center, impossible to return to signification and expression. It is abyssal loss, the flight of being.

This refusal of any annulation of loss and the flight of being is at the core of Bataille's *expérience intérieure* and his *poésie*. This is why those commentators who say that Bataille's "sovereignty" is freighted with a metaphysical notion of a subject are mistaken, because sovereignty is the loss of subjectivity.[49] And this is why Pierre Klossowski is right when he links Bataille's a-theology with the "vacance du moi," with the abeyance or emptying of the ego, a holiday from the Me.[50] A scorn for notional discourses, a scorn for a poetry of words that would make even Death into a conversation piece of beautiful words.

Bataille: "Un poète ne justifie pas—il n'accepte pas—tout à fait la nature. Le vraie poésie est en dehors des lois. Mais la poésie, finalement, accept la poésie. Quand accepter la poésie la change en son contraire (elle deviant médiatrice d'une acceptation)! je retines le saut dans lequel j'excéderai l'univers."[51]

---

49. See Hill, *Blanchot*, 199. Jean-Luc Nancy's *Inoperative Community* is cited.

50. Pierre Klossowski, "Du simulacre dans la communication de Georges Bataille," in *Ressemblance* (Provence, Alpes, Côte d'Azur: Office Régional de la Culture, Éditions Ryoan-ji, 1994), 23.

51. Bataille, *Être Oreste, L'Impossible*, in *OC* III, 217–23. ("A poet does not justify—he does not accept—nature altogether. True poetry is outside the law. But poetry, finally, accepts poetry. Accepting poetry changes it into its opposite [it becomes the mediator of an acceptance]! I retain the leap in which I will exceed the universe"; trans. mine.)

The laws named are the laws of language. Poetry is the violation of those laws, *dehors des lois*, but never clearly either inside the laws of language, reinforcing them in beautiful phrases, or outside, strengthening those laws by contesting them. Poetry runs in the between, the indeterminate, open zones at the edge of the laws of language. Such poetry cannot be a function or a workhorse for the system of absolute knowledge. Distanced equally from day and night, poetry belongs to neither. Its place is a non-place, as Claude Esteban has said. A mixture of shadows and equivocations, but shadows and equivocations that are never overcome or set aside, sustained in a higher shape of knowledge. Sometimes they are dramatized but never in a way consistent enough to form a Gestalt having a place in the logic of Truth. From the perspective of the Parmenidean goddess, poetry is the shadow language of mortals, the way of "seeming," of "much-experience . . . to ply an aimless eye and ringing ear."[52] Poetry can be the labyrinth, Bataille is telling us, not the straight path to Truth. Ironic that poetry was the medium of the Parmenidean goddess. Was it not poetry in this case that pointed out the noble way to Truth? That's not the vocation for the poet today, not since Pascal, Mallarmé, Baudelaire, or Rimbaud.

> C'est la pénombre et l'équivoque. La poésie éloigne en même temps de la nuit et du jour. Elle ne peut mettre en question ni mettre en action ce monde qui me lie.
> Je m'approche de la poésie: mais pour lui manquer.[53]

Poetry cannot do anything against the ties that bind the poet to the world. But this powerlessness is not poetry's weakness. This utter lack of utility is poetry's strength. Its secret power is in its powerlessness to provide anything, any answers, solutions, promises, hopes, or ideals. A *poésie in-fini*. Bataille, the poet, approaches poetry but fails it, as he must, since poetry is still bound with language; bound with the discreet, linear economy of words that can liberate as much as enslave; bound to language, beautiful language, poetry fails the poet, fails to cut the ties that bind him to the

---

52. See "Fragment 73," in *Parmenides of Elea: Fragments*, trans. David Gallop (Toronto: University of Toronto Press, 1991), 63.

53. Bataille, *Être Oreste, L'Impossible*, in *OC* III, 218. ("It is penumbra and equivocation. Poetry moves away from night and day at the same time. She cannot call into question or put into action this world that binds me. I approach poetry: but in order to miss/fail it"; trans. mine.)

world. In a comment on authors who exhausted the meaning of poetry in a "hatred of poetry" (*un sentiment de haine de la poésie*), Bataille makes the following proclamation: "Poetry which does not rise to the nonsense of poetry is only emptiness (nullity?), just beautiful poetry."[54]

And, contrary to the system of philosophy on its way to absolute knowledge in which a merciless and implacable logic leads from the unknown, from death for example, to the known, to Absolute Knowledge, poetry (even knowledge itself) leads from the known to the unknown; poetry is not a self-knowledge, or "even less the experience of a distant possibility (of what previously was not), but the simple evocation by words of inaccessible possibilities" (trans. mine).[55]

Bataille's is a *poésie in-fini* in all of these senses. It writes an in-finite, immense experience, one that is interior, but an experience that is always the contestation of experience, language writing an experience impossible to experience.

And this is why his is essentially a poetry of simulacra, an apparitional *poésie* extended out into the absence, the void, the *gouffre*. Only a language of simulacra, apparitions, will be the least inappropriate for the extremes of inner experience Bataille evokes in novels, narrations, and poems; a writing and a life extended over the immensity of the absence of being. His originality in relation to this poetry is to enact a new "experience–poetry" configuration, which Bernard Noël's preface to Bataille's book of poetry *L'Archangélique* (1967 edition), entitled "Poésie et expérience," brings to prominence. Language betrays silence, Noël writes, the meditative silence of the poet and the priest, by making that silence speak, attempting to understand silence, dramatizing it. Thus poetry and experience were separated insofar as experience—mystical experience—was but the object or the meaning of the poem. For Noël, a new configuration between poetry and experience arises with the *Grand Jeu*[56] and Georges Bataille. For the poets of Romanticism who preceded them, the

---

54. Bataille, *OC* III, 220. "La poésie qui n'élève pas au non-sens de la poésie n'est que le vide la poésie, qui la belle poésie," (French original).

55. *OC* III, 221. "La poésie n'est pas une connaissance de soi-même, encore moins l'expérience d'un lointain possible (de ce qui auparavant n'etait pas), mais la simple évocation par les mots de possibilities inaccessibles," (French original).

56. *The Grand Jeu* was an incandescent set of fellows, poets, seekers, and mystics for whom death was the "great game." René Daumal and Roger Gilbert-Lecomte were prominent among them. Some of their writings, which originally appeared in a magazine, *Le Grand jeu*, the first issue of which appeared in the summer of 1928, have been translated into English: *Theory of the Great Game* ed. Dennis Duncan (London: Atlas Press, 2015).

poet was one who has "ceased to speak in order *to be* spoken." The one who is spoken becomes the subject of poetry, the one who speaks the poem, but not its author, not its ultimate source, which was always somehow transcendent, in Nature or in God. For Bataille, it is the silence of the absence and flight of being that speaks through him, like the phantom mouth of a seer or a shaman; immensity, the in-fini, speaks through his poems and is erased in and by them. Indeed, as Bataille's biographer Michel Surya suggests, the poems of *L'Archangélique*, for example, were composed during the early 1940s, when France was under Nazi occupation and Bataille himself had retreated to smaller towns outside of Paris where he lived a quiet, withdrawn life, the life of a monk, of a mystic.[57]

But with the death of God, with the collapse of belief in an eternal salvation for the human soul, both the priest and poet were unemployed, so to speak, without vocation. What, henceforth, could be the authority, the basis for poetry and experience? For Bataille, through Blanchot, that authority was to be experience itself, inner experience, and poetry became identified with that experience, an "ecstasy" outside of "faith." But his was not an experience that had shed all outside necessities or belonging to the world. Insofar as the experience necessitated communication—community, the "other," the reader, the community of researchers as in Bataille's group Acéphale (active from 1933 to 1939) or the Collège de Sociologie more than ten years later—it necessitated writing, an almost confessional writing, words uttered into the aghast ears and eyes of a reader. As Noël writes, "In order to transmit (communicate), his experience, he was constrained to write it, and it was by consecrating himself to this writing, which definitely laicized experience, that he encountered poetry."[58] Mallarmé made poetry more of an interior experience, the poem as the screen where impressions play. In his *Un coup de dés*, he brought a previously unfathomed spatiality of the poem to the fore, emphasizing the background blankness of the page. It is a poetry with gaps, openings, gulfs, spatialized across the page, the abyssal white void below the writing shining through. Bataille prolongs this sense of space in his *L'Expérience intérieure* where experience becomes more identified with an immensity, a bursting, shattering immensity, the immensity of a tomb.

---

57. Michel Surya, "Sickening poetic sentimentality," in *Georges Bataille: An Intellectual Biography*, trans. Krzysztof Fijalkowski and Michael Richardson (London: Verso, 2002), 322–28. Surya devotes an entire chapter to a discussion of Bataille's poetry. His articulate discussion closely follows Bataille's essay "De la âge de pierre à Jacques Prevert."

58. Noël, "Poésie et experience," in *Vers Georges Bataille*, 617.

From *L'Archangélique:*

Le tombeau
Immensité criminelle
vase fêlé de l'immensité
ruine sans limites

. . . .

la folie ailée ma folie
déchire l'immensité
et l'immensité me déchire

. . . .

je tombe dans l'immensité
qui tombe en elle-même
elle est plus noire que ma mort[59]

Noël writes that Bataille encountered poetry as Nietzsche had before him, as a "necessary poetry." Not despite its almost built-in need to fail, not despite its being hopelessly caught in the aporia of attempting to express what cannot be expressed, Bataille was still "driven" to write poetry, even though poetic compositions are a relative rarity in his oeuvre. Most of the writings collected in his *Oeuvres complètes* are devoted to his criticisms of poetry and other poets rather than to his own original poetry. Aware of poetry's insufficiency, especially evident in the poetry of surrealism, Bataille sought to outline an poetry in-fini in the sense that it would do without the finitude of aesthetic theory; there is nothing poetic about this poetry, nothing beautiful.[60] And unlike the poetry of the surrealists, for whom the poem sprang from the dreams of a good night's sleep, Bataille's poetry in-fini would be acutely awake, the poetic word ignited by the moment standing at the edge of the abyss of death, as experienced in sacrifice. Bataille sought a poetry without utilitarian dimensions; a poetry of expenditure, squandering, and gaspillage; a poetry that would look into the abyss of human existence without turning away. He equally condemned the vain gratuitousness, the sheer idleness, of art for art's sake. But not "la poésie," the poetry that is the

---

59. Bataille, *L'Archangélique*, in *OC* III, 75. "The Tomb" "Criminal vastness // cracked vase of immensity // limitless ruin //. . . the winged madness my madness // tears apart the immensity // and the immensity tears me apart //. . . I fall into the immensity // which falls into itself // it is darker than my death"; trans. mine.

60. Noël, "Poésie et experience," 617.

sacrifice of poetry, a poetry as a sacrifice of all poetic and aesthetic ideals. Poems dictated by experience ("*son expérience les dicte*"), poems that were, thus, "la plus juste de sa vision."[61]

To sharpen these points now raised against poetry's throat, let us consider the cultural and economic metamorphosis of the horse in its appearance through several of Bataille's texts.

Bataille's poetic vision of the horses drawn on the walls of Lascaux evoked and brought into sight an animality that did not know bondage and the harness of work and ideals. There was a vibrant, burning force that becomes expressive, apparitional, in these images. For Bataille, they posed a stark contrast to the yawning modern world of work and purposeful things that spread out far beyond the ancient caves at Lascaux. In later writings, the horse, considered as a plastic image, is shown ensnared in the cultural opposition between the barbarian beast and the classical Greco-Roman horse, the "academic horse." How did the horse, common or extravagant as the case may be, ever come to be "academic?" When it joined the Academy, Plato's Academy. "*Le cheval académique*" (*Documents* 8, 1930)[62] shows us this path of becoming, the animal-becoming-academic, stretching from the Gallic horse—extravagant, fantastic, and barbarous—to the "academic horse," especially the Greco-Roman exemplar, the Ideal, or Idealized horse, a real, finite horse but seen as the reflection of an eternal Ideal: "Horseness," a noble, humanized animality, animality now standing tall, sometimes on its back legs, but still a broken animal (as in, to break a horse) willing to accept the harness. An academic horse pulls a carriage for the heavy weight of Ideals. Bataille writes: "The absurdities of barbarous peoples are out of step with scientific arrogance, nightmares with geometrical traces, and the horse-monsters imagined in Gaul with the academic horse."[63] The horse that was once free, as witnessed at Lascaux, is now domesticated, a "good horse," which usually means that it is a supremely useful animal, either for work or sport or for making war and money. But when that horse is taken from the "known" of the pasture and the barn to the "unknown," to the abattoir, there is a change. At the flash of the butcher's knife, the horse is no longer academic nor bonded to any harness. It stands, a finite being,

---

61. Noël, 618.
62. Bataille, *OC* I, 159–63. English: "The Academic Horse," trans. Krzysztof Fijalkowski and Michael Richardson, in *Undercover Surrealism: Georges Bataille and Documents*, eds. Dawn Ades and Simon Baker (Cambridge, MA: MIT Press, 2006), 237–39.
63. Bataille, *OC* I, 161 (*Undercover Surrealism*, 238).

before the abyss of death. As Bataille writes, for the butcher, the horse, even though still living, is only meat with a price on it. No doubt this dulls his sensibility and enables him to kill the animal without feeling sorrow for it. But the animal that humans have raised, nourished, and put to work in some fashion is now "a presence on the edge of an abyss (whose pit is absence)."[64] This is not to adopt a sentimentality for the animal's fate at the slaughter house but to see in the cry of death the animal's change in status from domesticated to "sacred" (Bataille's word, as we shall see). Let us recall that one of the first possible instances of animal sacrifice depicted in European painting was in the scene from the pit, the most inaccessible pit in the labyrinth of Lascaux's cave (c. 15,000 BCE), which showed a shaman beside a large bison, its entrails spilling out. Whether in the Lascaux paintings or in the photographs of the Parisian abattoir, the image of animals, of horses in Bataille's books, shows a sovereign animality, an existence or death that puts a barrier between animals and humans in question. Bataille writes, "To kill the horse is to suppress it as a distinct object . . . the horse is no longer . . . something distinct from me. The suppression of this object (the horse) by its death is the suppression of a barrier between 'the animal' and myself: it becomes the same thing as I am, a presence on the edge of absence."[65] This suppression of the barrier is the sovereign moment when the horse and I are indistinct beings, animal beings. The sovereign moment, as was already shown, is a moment somehow inside and outside of expression.

Must Bataille's poetry not fall back here onto the use of metaphors to communicate in poetry or prose such a sovereign moment? Does Bataille's poetry—or his prose writings too, for that matter—fall back on a conventional use of metaphor to communicate its *expérience intérieure*? The question here is whether or not Bataille's poetics is the metaphorical representation of the sovereign moment, of the *expérience intérieure*. Or is it the apparition, the verbal body of that experience, its moving flesh, so to speak, and not just a signifier representing or portraying it? How can metaphor be apparitional rather than representational?

Metaphor may in its most basic form be but a transposition, a transference or transmutation, a carrying over from sensation, from *expérience* to

---

64. Bataille, "De l'âge de pierre à Jacques Prevert," in *OC* XI, 103. English trans.: "From the Stone Age to Jacques Prévert," in *The Absence of Myth: Writings on Surrealism*, trans. Michael Richardson (London: Verso, 1994).

65. Bataille, "De l'âge de pierre à Jacques Prevert," 103. French original: "le voici la même chose que moi: comme moi presence au bord de l'absence."

signification.[66] In this way, metaphor and analogy are essential to poetry, as Michel Deguy has shown, and may have a deeper underlying ontological dimension.[67] There is no word for the limits of expression, for what Bataille might call the "impossible," or the "sacred," or *expérience intérieure*. Are these but metaphors? If the "sacred" is but a metaphor for a sacrificial squandering (*gaspillage*), then, according to the definition just evoked, metaphor would have to be the transposition or carrying across of the force, the sensation or experience of sacrifice and not its representation. In this way, Bataille's metaphors would have to be a sacrifice of conventional metaphor. Metaphor would transmute not significations or meanings but some of the raw force of such a squandering, carrying it from the level of sensation and experience into language. The sacred, a wordless communication would thus be said or written in this way in metaphors. What is quite beyond language in some way could only be said to be "like this": it is "impossible," or "sovereign," or "ecstasy." But these terms, these "metaphors" communicate the force of that experience, not its signification. Phrased ontologically, while we can speak of "beings," or entities, a "horse" for example, we cannot say what Being itself is, except that it is not an entity. "Being is said in many ways," said Aristotle. In metaphor we can say Being is "like" this. Being "likes to hide"; Being cannot be contained or exhausted by words. Even the word, Being, must be crossed out, written and erased. It may be present in words, but equally withdraws behind them.

What Bataille calls the "impossible" or a "sovereign moment" would be like this. It is *like* "laughter," "joy," or *like* the grip of erotic desire and the flows of sacrifice, and so on. But we cannot say "what" it is. It is impossible to say. Words become useless. Likewise, all that is senseless and excessive in death and what Lacan calls the Real can be carried over

---

66. As Michel Deguy writes in his *Poèmes en pensée* (Bordeaux: Le bleu du ciel, 2002), 11, "Ainsi faire dire aux choses le contraire de ce que leur mutism, leur indifférence, leur clameur ou leur aversion paisible manifestent, c'etait la condition pour le sens" ("Thus, to make things say the opposite of what their silence, their indifference, their clamor or their peaceful aversion manifest, was the condition for meaning"; trans. mine).

67. See Michel Deguy, *La poésie n'est pas seule* (Paris: Seuil, 1987), especially chap. II, "*Les faits*," 39–60, chap. III, "*De la figure aux figures*," 61–88, and chap. IV, "*Être-comme*," 95–141; also "*Feuillure 4*," the essay "*La poésie n'est pas seul; ou: privation et comparaison*," 142–53. But this theme is pervasive throughout Deguy's writings. Metaphor, the *comme*, is essential to *poésie*. See also Martin Rueff's lengthy commentary *Différence et identité, Michel Deguy, situation d'un poète lyrique à l'apogée du capitalism culturel* (Paris: Hermann Éditeurs, 2009).

in metaphors. A nameless signified would then be transposed into words, given a signifier that might in some way communicate such an impossible experience of death and the Real.[68] But is "the night," is this word, in any way the equivalent of the "Night," that vast, abyssal unknown, that *gouffre*?

Does metaphor seek to establish a signification for what lacks signification? This is what Lacan's treatment of metaphor suggests. Lacan shows that metaphor has a vertical structure while metonymy has a horizontal structure. There is a barrier, or "bar," between the signifier above and the signified written below this bar. The bar serves to separate a signifier from entering the Real, or the unconscious, to separate it from what resists or disrupts signification. This bar is the bar of signification, the threshold so to speak, the fold between a signified and a signifier. The bar both forecloses and opens signification. Crossing it occurs in the play of metaphor, which is essentially the substitution of one signifier for another. Thus, in crossing the bar of signification, the signifier, the metaphor, is substituted (or carried across) for the signified, the unknown, the senseless, with the effect of allowing the emergence of new signification. Of course, this crossing can be otherwise, when the nameless Real crosses and disrupts signification, disrupts the play of signifiers, which accounts, in Lacan's view, for the "effects of the unconscious."[69]

Is the horse evoked in Bataille's text such a metaphor? Does it extend signification to what lacks it? We could ask, in these Lacanian terms, is Batailleann poetics just a play of metaphors, whereby the bar (*la barre*) separating the signifier from the signified, or the bar separating language from the Real, is crossed, as language "eats its way into the Real" hollowing it out, making "a hole in the Real,"[70] with words, signs, "furrows," and, in

---

68. "Real" is here capitalized to indicate it is being used as a specialized term from Lacan's seminars.

69. See Jacques Lacan, *Le Seminar, Livre XX, Encore* (Paris: Seuil, 1975), 35. Trans. by Bruce Fink as *The Seminar of Jacques Lacan, Book XX, Encore (1972–1973)* (New York: W. W. Norton, 1998), 33–34. Lacan says that the "bar" (*la barre*) of signification is a bit superfluous and even futile, insofar as it only brings out what is already active in the spacing of signifier and signified (the signifier S over a bar separating it from the signified, s), "indicated in the distance of what is written. . . . The bar is precisely the point at which in every use of language, writing (*l'écrit*) may be produced. . . . The effects of the unconscious have no basis without this bar." See also, "The Metaphor of the Subject (which could also be 'The Subject That Is a Metaphor')," in *Écrits*, trans. Bruce Fink (New: Norton, 2002), 755–56.

70. See Jacques Lacan, *Le Séminaire, Livre XXIII, Le Sinthome* (Paris: Seuil, 2005), 31. Trans. A. R. Price as *The Sinthome: The Seminar of Jacques Lacan; Book XXIII* (Cambridge: Polity Press, 2016), 21.

this case, poetry? The Night, the Void, Ecstasy, the Impossible, are they but potentially new metaphors for this crossing of the bar of signification, this attempt to extend signification into the Real? Metaphor, in the Lacanian definition, adapted from the Jakobson prototype, is the substitution of one signifier for another. According to this, the Bataillean "sovereignty," "the impossible," are just sliding signifiers, ways of attempting to cross the bar separating language from the unknown, always pushing sign and signification, always seeking to "inject," as he says, signifiers deeper into the signified, always attempting to cross that bar and dig deeper into the Real, making way for the emergence of signification, new meanings. Except in the case of Bataille's poetics, the signifiers—"animal," "night," "sovereignty," "the impossible"—have lost their singular, substantial referents. These signifiers do not cross into the unknown, into the *gouffre*, so much as the latter rises to it. They are thus more emanations of this than they are pure metaphors. The signified is the unknown, about which nothing can be written, but which, as void, "*gouffre*," drives writing from its unseen, unwritten force. There is a fine example of this sliding signifier in the curious itinerary of the word, the signifier, "horse," in Bataille's texts on poetics.

Bataille describes the cultural and economic metamorphosis of the horse—its metaphoric itinerary—in both its plastic and verbal forms. This directly relates to his poetics. How does the horse, whether as word or image, eat its way into what Bataille calls "the Impossible," the impossible Real? Is the intent here to bring forth new significations, new metaphors, as one might find in poetry, or is there something else afoot here? What is the link between the sacrifice, the slaughter of horses described above, and poetry?

Bataille sees the sovereign horse, the images of horses that adorned the darkness at Lascaux, not as representations but as apparitional signs, masks, having, doubtless, a sacred value. They are apparitional metaphors for the kind of sovereignty Bataille was seeking in the mystery of Lascaux. Bataille shows how this sovereign horse, effortlessly leaping and running across Lascaux's walls, has today become a common word, a "workhorse," a horse with no sacred associations whatsoever, just another horse. The animal itself, not despite its animal appeal, is largely reduced in representational language to purely utilitarian roles. This domination of utilitarian values is challenged by Bataille's poetics. Poetry is the sacrifice of words. Its play of sliding signifiers may attempt to cross Lacan's bar of signification into death, into the Real, but what it carries across, what it brings to the surface, is not signification but the loss or squandering of signification. Poetry attempts to write in this way what cannot be written, to write the erasure or the absence of writing, a visible writing that writes the invisible, as Bernard Noël has said.[71] The "impossible" experienced in some way in Bataille's every venture, failure, and loss is thus communicated, carried across, appearing and disappearing in these ragged, shattered bodies of language.

This is the link in Bataille's poetics between the killing of horses and the poet's sacrifice of words. Not just a play of metaphors, not just the facilitation of new signification, but the writing at the limitless limits of language, a writing that is also a sacrifice of writing. In *L'Expérience intérieure*, Bataille writes, "Of poetry, I will now say that it is, I believe, the sacrifice in which words are victims. Words—we use them, we make of them the instruments of useful acts."[72]

He expands on this with the examples of two words, "horse" and "butter." In a typical, everyday scene, it would be known by speakers of a language, namely a keeper of horses and a farm girl, who are Bataille's characters in this story, to know what object distinct from them, distinct from the words in their mouths, is being named in and by the word "horse." They would know the referent (the signified) of the term, the signifier so to speak. The speakers, the horse keeper and the farm girl, know what to do with the horse in the field, the butter in the churn or on the shelf, because each and all, word and thing, are all in their place and deployment in an economy and a world of signification and utility. But the poet can take these two words and put them into new configurations, far from the dominion of utility. Poetry can make way for the unknown to rise up and enter upon the known, or for the void to rise up into language. Poetry can say, "butter horse." Bataille: "It places one, in this way, before the unknowable"[73] When the words "horse" or "butter" are enunciated, when they accompany familiar images of horses and butter, their poetic combination seems impossible. What can one do with a "butter horse"? Horse and butter combined in new ways by the poet are names that "solicit" the words horse and butter "in order to die," not really to die but to die in their signification, to die the death of all the old familiar links and associations between words and things whereby words were just another workhorse in the production of meaning. Poetry is the "sacrifice of words," Bataille continues, the "most accessible sacrifice

---

71. Noël, *Vers Henri Michaux*, 54.

72. Bataille, *L'Expérience intérieure*, in *OC* V, 156–57 (trans. by Leslie Anne Boldt, *Inner Experience*, 135–36).

73. Bataille, *OC* V, 157 (trans., 136).

available."[74] Is this the "holocaust of words" Sartre disparaged?[75] The poet is to words in their everyday employment what the knife is to the throat of the tired horse, a moment when weariness and utility are set aside. Sacrifice of poetry is a sacrifice of conventional signification. Pushing the "bar of signification" into the Real to the point where signification itself is sacrificed. But in poetry nothing dies, not even the poet, as much as they might like to promise their own death. This is the aporia, the paradox of poetry and the poet, which the previous chapters stressed, that poetry's sovereignty may not lie in *attainment* but in its in-finite *movement toward* that supreme moment, that sovereign moment of laughter, anguish and tears, toward the night, toward the abyss. A movement that never attains its goal so long as it moves in poetic forms because it writes without any predetermined goal; it writes in the age of the end, the generalized collapse or devaluation of transcendental finalities and destinations.

As a "sacrifice of words," poetry is the sacrifice of definitions. Without direction as what is True, Good, or Beautiful, the poet wanders in the labyrinth. A poetry of simulacra, from the horse to the labyrinth to the halo of flames that awaits.

Poetry, a "pure" poetry, a poetry purified of utility, is not a word that means something. It is a "cry which bestows sight—which reveals what we could not otherwise see." But the word that "bestows sight is also what later prevents it."[76]

Poetry, at its limits, is a sacrifice of poetry, a cry that bestows sight. A strangled cry that bestows the sight of what cannot be seen. Such a cry carries language to its limits where words fail or fall apart from an overload of meanings and sufferings, carries it into the labyrinths where Orpheus once walked. The propositional forms of language break down into rhythms and songs in Bataille's poetry, even as in his writings on prehistoric art. His writings are prolongations of the rhythms of a vibrant animality that one sees there, a chant, a visual song—a gift?—addressed to a future humanity the hunter-painter at Lascaux could not know, left in the silence of a labyrinthine darkness deep in the earth. Voices from the labyrinth. Bataille's

---

74. Bataille, *OC* V, 157 (trans., 136).

75. Jean-Paul Sartre, "Departure and Return," in *Literary and Philosophical Essays* (New York: Collier Books, 1955), 150.

76. Bataille, "De l'âge de pierre à Jacques Prevert," in *OC* XI, 99 (*The Absence of Myth*, 147).

260 | Apparitions, Daemons, and Emanations

poetry is the apparition of this labyrinth. The labyrinth leaps from language and words, leaps from the darkness of Lascaux and becomes an image, as in the Masson's mascot figure for the journal *Acéphale*,[77] which also has its labyrinthine dimensions, an image, a simulacre that portrays and writes the impetus of the journal. The song of the labyrinth that humanity is to itself. Bataille speaks of the "labyrinthine structure of the human being," yet, despite this use of the term "structure," it seems the structure is not just a word or a place but the wandering lack of a structure, a lack of transcendence, a *débordement* that constitutes the leap (*sauter*) out from "*les prisons lexicales*."[78]

This mascot, this visual metaphor, literally embodies the labyrinth, the labyrinthine structure of the human being, humanity's "base materialism," as Bataille called it. As such, it "puts to the test the pertinence of the diacritical couple, *homme*/animal," which it strikes (*frappe*) at once "l'immanence du moi et la transcendence de l'autre."[79] The *Acéphale* image of the headless man inspires Bataille's comment "Man has escaped from his head as the condemned from prison."[80] The animal/human doubling at Lascaux is one instance of this, with its bird-man inscribed on the walls of the pit in the heart of the labyrinth, or the minotaur and the *Minotauromachie* in Bataille's *Les larmes d'Éros*, or in the cover-image of *Acéphale*,[81] a writing at the limits, a "cry" that takes on these many simulacral forms. *Acéphale*'s images are not symbols, signs, or signifieds; nor are they conventional metaphors. Such images are apparitional metaphors, metaphors *as* apparitions, *as* emanations, *as* the work of a daemon. Not the conventional metaphors

---

77. This image is published in *OC* I, 444. See "*La conjuration sacrée*," in OC I, 442–45.

78. Denis Hollier, "La labyrinth et la pyramid," in *La prise de la Concorde* (Paris: Gallimard, 1974), 114–15. Hollier also quotes Bataille's 1935–1936 essay "Le labyrinthe" in *OC* I, 436, 109.

79. Hollier, "La labyrinth," 115.

80. Bataille, Klossowski, and Masson, "La Conjuration Sacrée," in *Acéphale* (Paris: Jean Michel Place, 1980) viiff.; and *OC* I, 442–45.

81. Masson's famous black ink line drawing was published on the cover of the first edition of *Acéphale*, June 24, 1936. Bataille and Klossowski, together with Masson, are listed as coauthors, editors, contributors, and participants in what the journal announces as La Conjuration Sacrée. Masson's image shows a muscled man, decapitated, a fleshless skull stuck in his groin, his stomach open, and the labyrinth of his intestines revealed. The figure's outstretched hands hold a torch in its right hand and a dagger or small sword in its left hand. The posture of the figure suggests Leonardo's image of the Vitruvian Man. Is this the new Vitruvian Man, his head in his groin, his essence a labyrinth? ("La Conjuration," vii).

that exchange signifiers and signifieds, they are apparitions in which what resists or withdraws from appearance—the abyss of death, bottomless night, or the laughter of gods—here marks its ambiguous appearance in simulacra. Whether in Lascaux's labyrinthine shadow play of animal images or Michaux's inkblot heads emerging as though summoned by a shaman from within the white void of a blank page; whether in the rhythms of a poem or in the mysterious, floating reflection of a goddess at her bath or in the ambiguous gestures of a woman, this woman, Roberte, as she is, *ce soir*, what could not be seen or said here rises to appearance and withdraws behind that appearance. The poem-image, the emanation, is metaphor as a mask for the void, both the employment and sacrifice of metaphor. Lascaux's horses, like Bataille's new Vitruvian Man or Michaux's "Prince of the Night," are all of these. They are a "sacred conjuration," communicating not the triumph of a signification that will endure but a condensed and shattering intensity.

Without sense or direction, the labyrinth's riddle is left unanswered: Where is the way out? Bataille's labyrinth is the other side of Michaux's *haut*. Labyrinth and void are the apparitions of an ultimate loss of signification, where even the play of metaphor is suspended, a solecism in the dance of death and desire, images left suspended over an unfathomable absence.

Is the labyrinth also *le vide*?

"Le Vide" is the title to the final suite of poems in *L'Archangélique*.

des flammes nous entourèrent
sous nos pas l'abîme s'ouvrit
un silence de lait de gel d'ossements
nous enveloppait d'un halo[82]

(flames surrounded us
under our feet the abyss opened
a silence of bone gel milk
enveloped us in a halo)

"Us"—the writer and the reader of these words—"surrounded by flames?" Does a new community appear in these lines, a community between the writer and the reader of poetry, a community of flames? Is this immolation the destiny of writing and poetry? An a-theological immolation that restores the true sacred now identified with a true poetry as the sacrifice of words and gods? What

---

82. Bataille, "Le Vide," in *L'Archangélique*, 95. English version is mine.

abyss opens beneath us? Why can we not even ask the question, "What?" Do we fall into it or does it rise to us? The silence is there: the "bone gel milk" of silence, where milk, like silence, is a liquid that can change states of being. It becomes a halo that envelops us, a halo of silent milk where the flames used to be. Is this a transformation of words and language into a holy silence? Is this, too, a sacrifice of words, a *conjuration sacrée*, a transfiguration? Are we not enveloped by the poem in a halo, in the sacred?[83]

Klossowski: "The Persistence of a Name"

> Je réfère au nom de Roberte ce que je vois et que je ne verrais point à défaut de ce nom.[84]
>
> —Pierre Klossowski, *Les lois de l'hospitalité*

The poetic thrust of writing in Bataille and Michaux is clear. But it is not so clear in the *récits*, the narratives, of Pierre Klossowski. Singular, unique works though they be, they are not recognizably "poetic." While Klossowski has recourse to several "idioms," as we might call them—narratives, stories, lectures, newspapers, paintings, film, photographs, drama, debates, discussions, and picture shows—he makes little or no use of poetry. There is the distant memory of his tutelage under Rilke, yet he is first and always a prose writer. Even in the midst of a narrative, however, poetry does have its place, in Klossowski's novel *Diana at Her Bath*, for example, where his translations of Ovid are quoted. But are there other forms or layers of Klossowski's narrative that, although they may not be read as evincing the standard genre-specific characteristics of poetry (having rhymes and rhythms), can be read nonetheless as exercising a poetic function? Look not for the lines and stanzas that characterize the visibility of a poem on the page, but look for the work of a single word, a powerful, poetic word, a sign, a unique sign, that is the contestation of received, everyday language, as much as it is the contestation of the narrative form. It is, in its own way, a sacrifice of words.

---

83. For a more probing look at Bataille's poetics, see Jacques Cels, *L'Exigence poétique de Georges Bataille* (Brussels: Universitaires De Boeck, 1989). Also cited in Surya, "Sickening poetic sentimentality," 350.

84. Pierre Klossowski, postface to *Les lois de l'hospitalité* (Paris: Gallimard, 1965), 335. "The name Roberte refers to what I see and what I could never have seen without this name"; trans. mine.)

Whence this "power" of a single word, the power of a name—the name Roberte—a nomination that annuls? A poetic function that here transforms the impious body of language into the purity of the silence of a sacred moment. A power that Klossowski describes as an intensity, which, designating itself with a sign, a unique sign, introduces a dimension of silence and death into language, a dimension where the power of conventional signification fails and where little else seems satisfactory to fill that gap, certainly not the great theory-systems of theology, psychoanalysis, and philosophy.[85] Rising from and within narrative forms, the unique sign is a hole in writing, a blind and workless grave of memory and words, a circle, its place marked by a name—the name Roberte—a name linked to a body, to a sexuality, to a game of desire, and from which cohesive singularity the necessity of a writing, a narrative, unfolds, toward the limit of narrative forms, a poésie par le gouffre.[86]

Klossowski, like Bataille, stands in the vortex of the texts and authors that swept through twentieth-century French culture: Nietzsche, Sade, Marx, Hegel, and Freud. For Klossowski, there is also the theology of Church Fathers and Roman polytheism. Writing took on new forms as it confronted the void left by the death of God, the loss of any ultimate grounding for identity or meaning in the natural or cultural worlds. The consequent swirl of multiplicities and of the experience of the Eternal Return made the very possibility of any creativity a wager and a risk in the face of futility. Klossowski's "novels" are an important example of the new modes of literary work that appeared mid-century. But are they in any way "poetic"?

However unique this work, to speak of its poetic function arising in the midst of its narrative and pictorial forms would require reading these texts in new ways, looking for an undercurrent or the glimmer of possibilities that so far have gone unnoticed. One could argue, for example, that the condensed intensity of the writing of *Diana at Her Bath* makes that narrative close to poetry, suggesting a prose-poem, perhaps. One could even go out on a limb and argue that Klossowski's drawings, with their rhythms of movement and "freeze-action," with their vision of a present moment to

---

85. Maurice Blanchot, "Le rire des dieux," in *L'Amitié* (Paris: Gallimard, 1971), 195. Trans. by Elizabeth Rottenberg as "The Laughter of the Gods," in *Friendship* (Stanford: Stanford University Press, 1997), 171.

86. Daniel Wilhem, *Pierre Klossowski: Le corps impie* (Paris: Union Générale d'Éditions 10/18, 1979). Wilhem's book argues that Klossowski, Bataille, and Blanchot contest the limits of traditional narrative forms. See "Et Clandestin," 175–214, for a long study of the body and its relations to narrative in Klossowski.

communicate, are poems, in the tradition, perhaps, of Horace's *Ut pictura poesis*, painting as "silent poetry," as the classical Greek poet Simonides of Keos called it. Klossowski, the Latinist, might have felt at home in this classical tradition. Daniel Wilhem asks how to define or characterize Klossowski's genre: Is it a novel, a romance (*romanesque*), a psychological narrative? Is it pictorial? Wilhem points out that Klossowski's text is indeed more pictorial and sculptural than literary. So, the paintings could also be trans-genre, literary as well as pictorial, making Klossowski's drawings poems that are both textual and figurative, not just between them but in each case a crossing of painting and writing, thus making Klossowski's books, in Wilhem's phrase, "le récit du bord," "le récit limite."[87]

Henri Michaux also blurs the distinctions between painting and writing. The idea of the painting as poem could be argued in the case of Klossowski's color drawings on the grounds that paintings replaced all writing and that drawings were the way Klossowski ultimately allowed for the many layers and dimensions of his work to be seen with immediacy—and this is just one of the advantages of drawing over writing for Klossowski—with the viewer immersed in this immediacy of seeing. The subject–object relation fades. Of course, there is still a space between the viewer and the drawing, just as there is between the reader/writer and the page. But seeing is still an experience of immediacy and of immersion, not one of subject over and against an object. The eye crosses that space immediately as though it were all a part of vision and not something between seeing and the seen. Such immediacy would be attractive to the poet were he to paint rather than write. Claude Esteban writes that poetry may not accept the mediated relation with the world that language necessitates, and due to this it sinks into representational discourse. Poetry may thus seek "un statut different, privilégié ou non, par rapport a l'économie du sensible . . . à refus la dichotomie rassurante des mots et des choses, pour faire retour, mythiquement, à l'origine de l'acte où le dire and l'être sont inséparables."[88] Is the painting-as-poem a way toward this mythic return to the original unity of word and being, of language and existence, but now in the language of line, shape, and color? Such a silent poetry of painting is ultimately rejected by Esteban. Language is the

---

87. Wilhem, *Pierre Klossowski*, 230, 244.

88. Esteban, "Un lieu hors de tout lieu," in *Critique de la raison poétique*, 218–19. (Poetry may seek "a different status, privileged or not, in relation to the economy of the sensible . . . rejecting the reassuring dichotomy of words and things, to return, mythically, to the origin of the act where saying and being are inseparable"; trans. mine.)

medium, mediated, "mediatized," or not, for poetry.[89] It is language that is the crucial site for Klossowski's contestation of language.

Yet this desire for an immediacy between words and things, Saying and Being, language and experience can help us approach Klossowski's situation, for it is both inside and outside of this opposition. Seeing is all-important for Klossowski's novels and drawings. Yet there remains in his work a moment where both seeing and saying are suspended: the capital moment when Roberte's dress catches fire (described in chapter 2). Can one say what has happened? Can one say what they have seen, what do they see or do not see? Does it relate to what has happened, an event seen and yet not seen? There is also the capital moment Klossowski calls "the unique sign," which here, in Klossowski's painting and poetry, is always, Roberte, *ce soir*, caught, named and denounced as she is, *tonight*. In other words, where the picture-poem would be the unity of seeing and saying, for Klossowski the immediacy of that relationship between seeing and saying is always disrupted at the height of the capital moment, at the moment something of Roberte's secret is about to be disclosed. As the poetic words of the goddess tell the lusty youth, turning into a stag, hiding in the bushes, hoping for a glimpse of her naked body,

> nunc tibi me posito visam velamine nares
> si poteris narre, licet?[90]

The male gaze disrupted, blinded at the moment it sees what it desires. Let us consider the poem in relation to not only Klossowski's drawings but also the unique sign that is so crucial to his novels. Is this a poetic thrust

---

89. Esteban, "Un lieu hors de tout lieu," in *Critique de la raison poétique*, 218–19: "Je le crois volontiers de l'art des images qui prend en charge et subsume du même coup un élément de l'immédiate en lui donnant forme visible, lisible pour nos yeux physiques et mentaux, Mais la poésie . . . pour sa part, ouvre, non pas sur du concrete—matière, couleur, sonorité—mais déja au sein de ce milieu médiatisé que constitute le langage" ("I readily believe this in the art of images, which at the same time takes charge of and subsumes an element of the immediate by giving it visible form, readable for our physical and mental eyes. But poetry . . . for its part, opens, not on the concrete—matter, color, sonority—but already within this mediatized medium that constitutes language"; trans. mine.)

90. Pierre Klossowski, *Diana at Her Bath*, trans. Stephen Sartarelli and Sophie Hawkes (Boston: Eridanos Press, 1990), 63. Klossowski: the goddess Diana is speaking to Acteon, "Now you may tell you saw me here unclothed / If you can tell at all!"

that bursts from within the form and discourse of the novel? A thrust associated not with visibility or the making visible of painted images but with silence and blindness?

As we have seen, the axis of his work is the name, Roberte, his unique sign. Klossowski lived—at least in the 1950s—under the obsessive name Roberte. An "obscure law," he writes, prevents him from seeing and describing Roberte or her "situations." In order to describe her, it is not necessary to actually see her. The name Roberte designates not just a physical person but an obsession that forms from within Klossowski's life, the crest of an intensity that blinds and causes an obsessive arrangement to take hold as thought. A "poetry," therefore, that wishes to see, that is governed by a will to see but that reaches that limit-point where seeing and blindness coincide. Between this unique sign, between the simulacre that goes by the name Roberte, between this and ordinary language, there is a ceaseless contestation, a combat against culture, a radical opposition.[91] It is in this contestation that puts the silence of a unique sign, the silence that coils and seduces in Roberte's gestures, over and against the loquacity of the everyday codes of signs that usually facilitate communication, just as poetry contests and prolongs conventional expression.

Is there a silent poetry that may be evoked in Klossowski's images and *récits*? One that begins in the imposing silence of a unique sign, by which an intensity of thought designates itself in a moment or an instant that could be described as poetic in the way it seeks not for metaphors but for its equivalents in the words and sentences of that code, that seeks its equivalents in a certain physiognomy, in the silent poetry of gestures and provocative situations, a silence from within or behind the images of a woman, whether discursive or drawn, that drives the writer, Klossowski, mad. Our writer finds himself enclosed, as it were, within the intensity of a thought that folds back upon itself so as to designate itself in and by a sign, a folding that becomes a constraining circle, a unique sign, the writer's life and memory nearly destroyed by such a thought defined only by its extreme, Parmenidean self-coherence for which there is no before and after, no beginning and end, nothing to remember. For it is a circle, a constraining circle, the circle of the eternal return, a unique sign that is not a sign, where a sign is defined by its relations and not its isolated self-coherence. A thought and a sign that are incommunicable and yet requiring a communication; its exorcism, its "denouncement" in a name and in an act of

---

91. Hervé Castanet, *Pierre Klossowski: La Pantomine des esprits* (Nantes, France: Cécile Defaut, 2007), 154. Castanet quotes Klossowski's "Avertissement" to *Les lois de l'hospitalité*, 7.

naming, a naming that returns silence to the discontinuity and incoherence of a signifying code, the "code of everyday signs," everyday language, in short. Not, obviously, a silence or an intensity that can be represented by the everyday code of stereotypes and mediatized language. Under the hubbub of the daily prattle, the intensity of this silence always remains, a threat, a stain, a spreading darkness. Klossowski's narratives testify to that. The "equivalents," the simulacra that designate this obsessive circle of the unique sign, are both the imprint of and the escape hatch from its crushing silence.

Paradoxically, Klossowski also links this unbearable silence of the unique sign with purity, a purity imposed with an iron rule that must be escaped. Pure because, as a circle in complete coherence and continuity with itself, it lacks all content; it is just the turning of thought upon itself as it reaches a moment of highest intensity. Pure because it is purified of all names that only disrupt and distance purity, the purity of silence. As such, it shall always be in combat against the "impure" signifying codes, impure because of their intrinsic discontinuity, because the coherence of identities assumed in and by the tyranny of names amounts to nothing more than "grammatical pleasantries."[92] Yet such pleasantries are taken by those who bear them and repeat them as communicating a "real world." "My" world, where mine also designates a highest intensity, one of both being and having ("I am," "I have an identity, a dignity, a human right"). Truth is in the correct and right use of such names.

But, strange as it may seem, it is also the purity of this intensity that itself selects the impurity of terms by which it shall designate itself. Such an impure discourse that delimits silence by naming it, wrapping it up in and by the word "silence," a word that can never be what it names, is such a discourse not by definition false in the sense of *pseudos*? But intensity is not a "True World." The "laws of hospitality" unfold in a time and place when the True World has become a fable. The telling of this fable is not just a holiday but a necessity, imposed by the intensity of thought. Is there not an exigence here that must be answered to? The exigence of a pure silence, the exigence of the *gouffre* of silence, is an exigence that can only be answered in the exigence of writing, of poetry. A silence that can only be silenced when it is named, Roberte, or evinced by her austere, gloved palm. Klossowski himself is not the source of these visions and experiences he names, the "glove," the "darkness," the white "glow of the skin" beneath the glove that contrasts so sharply with the *pénombre* of the glove. It is thought, the intensity of thought, that selects these designations. Klossowski himself seems

---

92. Klossowski, postface to *Les lois de l'hospitalité*, 337.

utterly passive in this face of a thought, of an intensity, that reaches out to him. The exigence of poetry is to write this intensity, to receive it, taking up the terms intensity has offered in order to survive its deadly silence.[93] In this way, Klossowski seems a modern counterpart to the ancient poet who listened, who waited and was filled with the gods (as in the Greek *enthousiasmos, entheos*) when they spoke through him. Klossowski's poetry is a classical "pantomime of the spirits" strategically brought into play in an age when the gods, the spirits, have withdrawn.

Pure silence, the pious silence behind or within the physiognomy of *le corps impie*, like the purity and whiteness of her palm wrapped and hidden in the darkness of the glove, is always set apart, wrapped in the language of limits and prohibitions, set apart from the noisy loquaciousness of impure discourse, and so calling forth the very words, the very gaze that seeks to violate it. A special apparatus, a special new code of phantasms and pantomimes, shall be required in order that silence can be seen by being named or enacted, disclosing itself, its purity, on the stage and screen where the impurity of names—those of Roberte, Antoine, and Octave—shall perform their necessary roles in the laws of hospitality. A special new set of laws (poetic laws?), the laws of hospitality, shall be enacted so that the gloves can be taken off, so to speak, in a parodic transgression outside the laws of marriage—as all poetry is, in its way, outside the laws of discourse—outside everyday proprieties, exposing them for what they are: ways of exchanging the unexchangeable.

Introducing his laws of hospitality, Klossowski names the place and role of animality that necessitates these laws. Animality is also outside the laws of discourse. Animality's place in relation to the laws of language, which

---

93. "La penombe, la lueur de l'épiderme, le gant, autant de désignations non pas de chose existants ici à ma portée, mais formant un ensemble au gré de l'irréelle pénombre . . . Dirai-je que ce n'est pas moi qui me désigne ce que j'entends par 'pénombre,' mais la pensée, hors de moi, qui se regarderait dans les termes 'pénombre,' 'épiderme,' 'gant,' etc. . . . Mais alos n'est-ce pas je traduis de façon tout à fait arbitraire pas les terms 'pénombre,' 'lueur d'épiderme,' 'gant' . . . quand je ne serais moi-même qu'intensité pure qu'attendait la pensée de personne pour se désigner par ces termes." Klossowski, postface to *Les lois de l'hospitalité*, 335–36. My trans.: "The penumbra, the gleam of the epidermis, the glove, so many designations not of things existing here within my reach, but forming a whole according to the unreal penumbra. . . . Shall I say that it is not me who myself designates what I mean by 'darkness,' but the thought, outside of me, which looked at itself in the terms 'darkness,' 'epidermis,' 'glove,' etc. . . . But then, am I quite arbitrarily translating the terms 'penumbra,' 'skin glow,' 'glove' . . . when I would be myself only a pure intensity that waited for no one's thought in order to designate itself by these terms?"

we have touched on in connection with Bataille and Michaux, returns in Klossowski's *Laws of Hospitality*, where, in a striking passage, Klossowski describes how Octave and Roberte's situation is one in which traditional matrimonial laws and customs defy and distort their animality, their animal desires. The laws of hospitality are thus a challenge to the laws of procreation, or, on the other hand, a *revanche* ("revenge" or "retaliation") of the couple against their animal necessities. But, as Klossowski writes, animality "plays its part in this challenge. And such is the force of this part that, detached from its very function, animality in its turn seeks its own sign and lends, like an idiom, an elasticity to thought, a flexibility, a monstrous viscosity."[94] Is this an animal thought, an animal poetry with its own sign and idiom, flexible and monstrously viscous (shape-shifting?) as we have already seen in his *Diana at Her Bath*?

It is not, in any case, a silent thought fallen into the linearity of time and discourses that pass from a beginning to an end. It is not a thought fallen into a discourse of transcendence; not a poetry of the divine. Is it, as Castanet's reading claims, is this "unique sign," the *matheme* (the poetic word?) for an obsessive object? Does it function in Klossowski's récit as something like "object *a*" in Lacan's formula of the phantasy, standing for or marking the place in the structure of desire for a lost jouissance?[95] Does the unique sign, in the Lacanian vocabulary, mark the place and structure of an unconscious phantasm of desire? Does it mark a hole in language, the hole of the unconscious, around which it is organized and against which its defenses are always erected? Klossowski always rejected the Freudian unconscious, so this may be problematic for Castanet's reading. The question, however, is still viable: Is Roberte's allure phantasmic, an "object *a*" as Lacan might have called it, a lure and trap, concealing nothing behind it,

---

94. Klossowski, "Avertisssement," in *Les lois de l'hospitalité*, 8. "Peut-être s'agit là d'un defi de la pensée aux lois de la procréation, d'une revanche du couple sur sa nécessité animale, encore que l'animalité ait sa part dans ce défi. Et telle est la force de cette part que, détachée de sa fonction même, l'animalité à son tour cherche son propre signe et prête tel un idiome une élasticité à la pensée, une souplesse, une viscosité monstreuses." On animality and the law, see also Jacques Derrida, *The Beast and the Sovereign*, "First Session, December 12, 2001."

95. Castanet, *Pantomine des esprits*, 157: "La spécificité de (Klossowski) est de fétichiser ce unique signe, de l'enluminer comme cetttte lettre dessine le bord du trou dans le savoir inconscient par laquel qui s'invoque la jouissance perdu à laquelle il ne résout pas." (The specificity of [Klossowski] is to fetishize this unique sign, to illuminate it like this letter which draws the edge of the hole in the unconscious knowledge by which a lost jouissance is invoked without being resolved"; trans. mine.)

no higher Truth, no greater Beauty, no radiant One, no Secret but only the daemonic play of death and desire? Being not just a thought, a God-like thought, Klossowski's narratives begin from a desire, a mania or an intensity impossible to represent, define, or communicate in the norms established by the worldly discontinuity of language.

But whether psychological, theological, or metaphysical, there is first the exigency to write in Klossowski, as we have also seen in Bataille and Michaux. An exigency that takes on the formless forms of poetry, that pushes poetry toward the abandonment of all writing, always wanting something more immediate than words, more powerful in its horror and its humor. Paintings replace words. A silent poetry commences. A poetry, neither of words, exactly, nor images but of apparitions, emanations, and simulacra, emanations marking the flight of images, the flight of being.

Is this exigency to write or to draw not the other side of the exigency to leave nothing behind, not even a sign? An exigency both fulfilled and frustrated in Éditions Gallimard?

These apparitions, emanations, and simulacra, these "thousand crushings crushed," have indeed become something left behind, an artistic legacy, almost a legend. Did the authors of the volumes in which their simulacra are now published ever imagine these "fragmented thoughts, ungovernable, unusable, intractable, impermanent, apparitional,"[96] congealing into books destined for museums and libraries, their rage now quiet, having become important cultural statements? Books that once offered a "holocaust of words" between their regal covers, what has become of the lightning that used to strike their pages? Has its brilliance been the cause of its having been diminished, extinguished, almost forgotten? Published in beautiful volumes, lined up on a shelf, can they be what Blanchot calls, an "absence of the book?" In the midst of changing times, from within the libraries of the world, they bequeath not a monument but a hole in the utilitarian prattle of everyday language, a poet's infinitesimal point of solitude opening onto the infinite, worlds ever dying and renewed in their dying, written and erased as they are written, "rising from (their) well of mud and stars . . . bearing witness, almost silently, that (they) contained nothing which did not truly exist elsewhere, in this rebellious and solitary world of contradictions."[97]

---

96. Michaux, "Meaning of the Drawings," in *Peace in the Breaking*, 47.

97. René Char, "Le poème pulverisé," in *Furor and Mystery & Other Writings*, 244–45 (trans. altered).

Bibliography

Ades, Dawn, and Simon Baker. *Undercover Surrealism: Georges Bataille and DOCUMENTS*. Cambridge, MA: MIT Press, 2006.
Arnaud, Alain. *Pierre Klossowski*. Paris: Seuil, 1990.
Baatsch, Henri-Alexis. "Déserts peints." In *Henri Michaux*, 119–23. Paris: Centre Georges Pompidou, 1978.
———. *Henri Michaux: Peinture et poésie*. Paris: Hazan, 1993.
Backès-Clément, Catherine. "Incarnation fantastique." In *l'Arc* 43. Paris: Librairie Duponchelle, 1970.
Badiou, Alain. *Handbook of Inaesthetics*. Translated by Alberto Toscano. Stanford: Stanford University Press, 2005.
Bataille, Georges. "Abattoir." In *Documents 6*, 167–68. Paris: Mercure de France, 1968.
———. *l'Abbé C*. In *Oeuvres complètes*. Vol. III, 233–66. Translated by Philip A. Facey as *l'Abbé C* (London: Marion Boyars, 1983).
———. *Acéphale*. Paris: Jean Michel Place, 1980.
———. *L'Archangélique*. In *Oeuvres complètes*. Vol. III, 71–96. Paris: Gallimard, 1978.
———. "L'amitié de l'homme et de la bête." In *Oeuvres complètes*. Vol. XII, 167–71. Paris: Gallimard, 1988.
———. "Le bas matérialisme et la gnose." In *Documents 6*, 93–104. Paris: Mercure de France, 1968. Translated by Allan Stoekl as "Base Materialism and Gnosticism." In *Visions of Excess: Selected Writings, 1927–1939*, 45–52 (Minneapolis: University of Minnesota Press, 1985).
———. *Être Oreste, L'Impossible*. In *Oeuvres completes*. Vol. III, 217–23. Paris: Gallimard, 1978.
———. *The Blue of Noon*. Translated by Harry Mathews. New York: Urizen Books, 1978.
———. *Discussion sur le péche*. Paris: Lignes, 2010.
———. *L'Érotisme*. Paris: Les Éditions de Minuit, 1957.
———. "Formless." In *Visions of Excess*, 31.
———. "La guerre et la philosophie du sacré." In *Oeuvres complètes*. Vol. XII. 47–57. Paris: Gallimard, 1988.

———. *The Impossible*. Translated by Robert Hurley. San Francisco: City Lights, 1991.
———. "Informe." In *Documents 6*, 177. Paris: Mercure de France, 1968.
———. *Inner Experience*. Translated by Leslie Anne Boldt. Albany: State University of New York Press, 1988.
———. "Le labyrinth." In *Oeuvres complètes*. Vol. I, 433–41. Paris: Gallimard, 1970.
———. *Les larmes d'Éros: Nouvelle édition augmentée*. Paris: Société nouvelle des éditions Pauvert, 1981.
———. "Lascaux ou la naissance de l'art." In *Oeuvres complètes*. Vol. IX, 7–102. Paris: Gallimard, 1979.
———. *Lascaux or the Birth of Art*. Translated by Austryn Wainhouse. Geneva: Éditions d'Art Albert Skira, 1980.
———. "Madame Edwarda." In *Oeuvres complètes*. Vol. III. Paris: Gallimard, 1978.
———. *Madame Edwarda*. In *My Mother, Madame Edwarda, The Dead Man*. Translated by Austryn Wainhouse. London: Marion Boyars, 1989.
———. *Manet*. Translated by Austryn Wainhouse and James Emmons. New York: Skira, Rizzoli International, 1983.
———. "La Mére-Tragédie." In *Oeuvres complètes*. Vol. I, 493–94. Paris: Gallimard, 1970.
———. *La passage de l'animal à l'homme et la naissance de l'art*. In *Oeuvres complètes*. Vol. XII, 259–76. Paris: Gallimard, 1988.
———. *Oeuvres complètes*. Paris: Gallimard, 1970–1988.
———. "Slaughterhouse." Translated by Annette Michelson. *October* 36, no. 11 (Spring). Cambridge, MA: MIT Press, 1986.
———. "Terre inviable." In *Oeuvres complètes*. Vol. XII, 514–17. Paris: Gallimard, 1988. Translated by Michelle Kendall and Stuart Kendall as "Unlivable Earth?," in *The Cradle of Humanity: Prehistoric Art and Culture*, 175–78 (New York: Zone Books, 2005).
Baudelaire, Charles. *Artificial Paradises*. Translated by Stacy Diamond. New York: Citadel Press, 1996.
———. *Les Fleurs du Mal*. Translated by Richard Howard. Boston: David R. Godine, 1983.
Baudrillard, Jean. "La précession des simulacres." In *Le simulacre, TRAVERSES/10* 39, 3–37. Paris: Minuit, Centre National d'Art et de Culture Georges Pompidou, 1978.
Beaumelle, Agnès de la. ". . . l'ombre pour la proie." In *Pierre Klossowski: Tableaux vivants*. Directed by Sarah Wilson. Whitechapel Gallery, London, and Museum Ludwig, Cologne. Paris: Gallimard, Centre Pompidou, 2007. Exhibition catalog.
Bellour, Raymond. "Notices to Plume." In *Henri Michaux, Oeuvres complètes*. Vol. III, 1468. Paris: Gallimard, Pléiade, 2004.
Bernard, Noël. "L'in-fini de Bataille." In "Vers Georges Bataille." In *La Place de l'autre. Oeuvres* III, 646–48. Paris: P.O.L., 2013.
———. *La Place de l'autre. Oeuvres* III. Paris: P.O.L., 2013.

———. "Vers Georges Bataille." In *La Place de l'autre. Oeuvres* III, 611–76. Paris: P.O.L., 2013.

———. *Vers Henri Michaux*. L'Hay-les-Roses, France: Unes, 1998.

Berressem, Hanjo. "The 'Evil Eye' of Painting: Jacques Lacan and Witold Gombrowicz." In *Reading Seminar XI*, 175–82. Edited by Richard Feldstein, Bruce Fink, and Maire Jaanus. Albany: State University of New York Press, 1995.

Blanchot, Maurice. *l'Amitié*. Paris: Gallimard, 1971. Translated by Elizabeth Rottenberg as *Friendship* (Stanford: Stanford University Press, 1997).

———. "The Birth of Art." In *Friendship*, 1–11.

———. *La bête de Lascaux*. Paris: Fata Morgana, 1982.

———. *L'Écriture du désastre*. Paris: Gallimard, 1980. Translated by Ann Smock as *The Writing of Disaster* (Lincoln: University of Nebraska Press, 1986).

———. *L'Entretien infini*. Paris: Gallimard, 1969. Translated by Susan Hanson as *The Infinite Conversation* (Minneapolis: University of Minnesota Press, 1993).

———. *L'Espace littéraire*. Paris: Gallimard, 1955. Reprinted in 2018. Translated by Ann Smock as *The Space of Literature* (Lincoln: University of Nebraska Press, 1982).

———. "L'infini et l'infini." In *L'Herne: Henri Michaux*, 80–88. Paris: l'Herne, 1966.

———. "Literature and the Right to Death." In Mandell, *The Work of Fire*, 300–44.

———. "Mallarmé's Experience." In Smock, *The Space of Literature*, 38–48.

———. "Naissance de l'art." In *l'Amitié*, 9–20.

———. *La part du feu*. Paris: Gallimard, 1949. Translated by Charlotte Mandell as *The Work of Fire* (Stanford: Stanford University Press, 1995).

———. "Le Rire des Dieux." In *l'Amitié*, 192–207.

———. "The Laughter of the Gods." In Rottenberg, *Friendship*, 169–82.

———. "The 'Sacred' Speech of Hölderlin." In Mandell, *The Work of Fire*, 111–31.

Breton, André. *Manifestos of Surrealism*. Translated by Richard Seaver and Helen R. Lane. Ann Arbor: University of Michigan Press, 1972.

Butor, Michel. *Improvisations sur Henri Michaux*. Paris: Fata Morgana, 1985.

Carn, Hervé. "Gravir le silence: Parole et silence dans les récits de Bernard Noël." In *Noël: Le corps du verbe*, 143–64. Paris: ENS, 2008.

Castanet, Hervé. *Pierre Klossowski: La pantomime des esprits*. Nantes, France: Cécile Defaut, 2007.

Cels, Jacques. *L'Exigence poétique de Georges Bataille*. Brussels: Universitaires De Boeck, 1989.

Char, René. "Homme-oiseau mort et bison mourant" [Dead Bird-Man and Dying Bison]. Translated by Nancy Kline. In *Furor and Mystery & Other Writings*, translated and edited by Mary Ann Caws and Nancy Kline, 357. Boston, MA: Black Widow Press, 2010.

———. "La Béte innommable" [The Unspeakable Beast]. In *Lascaux*. Translated by Nancy Kline. In *Furor and Mystery & Other Writings*, 359.

———. "The Library Is on Fire." In *Furor and Mystery & Other Writings*, 385.

———. "Le poème pulverisé" [The Pulverised Poem]. In *Furor and Mystery & Other Writings*, 245.
Cheng, François. *Vide et plein: Le langage pictural chinois*. Paris: Seuil, 1991.
Clément, Catherine. *La syncope: Philosophie du ravissement*. Paris: Bernard Grasset, 1990.
Clottes, Jean, and David Lewis-Williams. *Chamanes de la préhistoire*. Paris: Seuil, 1996. Translated by Sophie Hawkes as *The Shamans of Prehistory: Trance and Magic in the Painted Caves* (New York: Harry N. Abrams, 1998).
———. *Pourquoi l'art préhistorique?* Paris: Gallimard, 2011. Translated by Oliver Y. Martin and Robert D. Martin as *What Is Paleolithic Art? Cave Paintings and the Dawn of Human Creativity* (Chicago: University of Chicago Press, 2016).
Colette, Jacques. "Chute et sentiment d'infini." In *Passages et langages de Henri Michaux*, 57–64.
Daumal, René, and Roger Gilbert-Lacomte. *Theory of the Great Game*. Edited by Dennis Duncan. London: Atlas Press, 2015.
Deguy, Michel. *La poésie n'est pas seule*. Paris: Seuil, 1987.
———. *Poèmes en pensée*. Bordeaux: Le bleu du ciel, 2002.
Deleuze, Gilles. *Expressionism in Philosophy: Spinoza*. Translated by Martin Joughin. New York: Zone Books, 1992.
———. *Francis Bacon: Logique de la sensation*. Paris: la Vue le Texte, Harry Jancovici, 1984. Translated by Daniel Smith as *The Logic of Sensation* (Minneapolis: University of Minnesota Press, 2002).
———. *Logique du sens*. Paris: Les Éditions de Minuit, 1060. Translated by Mark Lester, with Charles Stivale, as *The Logic of Sense* (New York: Columbia University Press, 1990).
Deleuze, Gilles, and Félix Guattari. *Mille Plateaux*. Paris: Minuit, 1980. Translated by Brian Massumi as *A Thousand Plateaus: Capitalism & Schizophrenia* (Minneapolis: University of Minnesota Press, 1987).
Derrida, Jacques. *The Beast and the Sovereign, Volume I*. Translated by Geoffrey Bennington. Chicago: Chicago University Press, 2009.
———. "The End of the Book and the Beginning of Writing." In *Grammatolgy*, translated by Gayatri Chakravorty Spivak. Baltimore, MD: Johns Hopkins University Press, 1976.
Eco, Umberto. *Serendipities, Language and Lunacy*. Translated by William Weaver. London: Orion Books, 1999.
Escalande, Yolaine. "Le jeux du trait et de l'encre." In *Henri Michaux & Zao Wou-Ki dans l'empire des signes*, 60–71. Paris: Flammarion. 2015.
Esteban, Claude. *Critique de la raison poétique*. Paris: Flammarion, 1987.
Evans, Dylan. *Dictionary of Lacanian Psychoanalysis*. London: Routledge, 1996.
Foss, Paul, Paul Taylor, and Allen S. Weiss, eds. *Phantasm and Simulacra: The Drawings of Pierre Klossowski*. Special issue, *Art & Text* 18 (July 1985), Melbourne, Australia.

Foucault, Michel. "The Prose of Acteon." In *The Baphomet*, translated by Sophie Hawkes and Stephen Sartarelli, with a foreword by Michel Foucault, xxi–xxxviii. Hygiene, CO: Eridanos Press, 1988.
Freud, Sigmund. *The Standard Edition (SE) of the Complete Psychological Works of Sigmund Freud*, vol. XIV. Translated by James Strachey. London: Random House/Vintage, 2001.
Gasché, Rodolphe. "The Felicities of Paradox: Blanchot on the Null-Space of Literature." In *Maurice Blanchot: The Demand of Writing*, 34–69. London: Routledge, 1996.
Hegel, G. W. F. *Phänomenologie des Geistes*. Hamburg: Felix Meiner Verlag, 1952. Translated by A. V. Miller as *The Phenomenology of Spirit* (Oxford: Clarendon Press, 1977).
Hill, Leslie. *Blanchot: Extreme Contemporary*. London: Routledge, 1997.
Hollier, Denis. *La prise de la Concorde: Essais sur Georges Bataille*. Paris: Gallimard, 1974.
Jouffroy, Alain. *Avec Henri Michaux*. Paris: Rocher, 1992.
Jenny, Laurent. *Voir le paradis*? In *Passages et langages de Henri Michaux*, 271–81.
Kant, Immanuel. *Critique of Pure Reason*. Translated by Norman Kemp Smith. London: Macmillan, 1929.
Klossowski, Pierre. *The Baphomet*. Translated by Sophie Hawkes and Stephen Sartarelli. Boston: Eridanos Press, 1988. Originally published as *Le Baphomet* (Paris: Mecure de France, 1965).
———. *Diana at Her Bath*. Translated by Sophie Hawkes and Stephen Sartarelli. Boston: Eridanos Press, 1990. Originally published as *Le bain de Diane* (Paris: Gallimard, 1980).
———. *Du signe unique: Feuillets inédits*. Paris: Les Petits Matins, 2018.
———."Du simulacre dans la communication de Georges Bataille." In *Ressemblance*, 21–34.
Provence, Alpes, Côte d'Azur: Office Régional de la Culture, Éditions Ryoan-ji, 1994.
———. *La Différence*. Paris: Centre National des Arts Plastiques, 1990.
———. *Les lois de l'hospitalité*. Paris: Gallimard, 1965.
———. *Nietzsche and the Vicious Circle*. Translated by Daniel W. Smith. Chicago: University of Chicago Press, 1997. Originally published as *Nietzsche et le cercle vicieux* (Paris: Mercure de France, 1969).
———. *Origines culturelles et mythiques d'un certain comportement des dames romaines*. Paris: Fata Morgana, 2010.
———. *Pierre Klossowski*. Repères. Cahiers d'art contemporain no. 14. Paris: Galerie Maeght Lelong, 1984. Exhibition catalog.
———. *Pierre Klossowski: Tableaux vivants*. Directed by Sarah Wilson. Whitechapel Gallery, London, and Museum Ludwig, Cologne. Paris: Gallimard, Centre Pompidou, 2007. Exhibition catalog.
———. "Protase et apodoses." In *l'Arc* 43, 8–20. Paris: Librairie Duponchelle, 1990.

———. *Ressemblance*. Alpes, Côte d'Azur: Office Régional de la Culture, Éditions Ryoan-ji, 1984.

———. *Roberte Ce Soir & The Revocation of the Edict of Nantes*. Translated by Austryn Wainhouse. New York: Grove Press, 1969.

———. *Le Souffleur, ou le theatre de sociéte*. Paris: Jean-Jacques Pauvert, 1960.

———. *Such a Deathly Desire*. Translated by Russell Ford. Albany: State University of New York Press, 2007. Originally published as *Une si funeste désir* (Paris: Gallimard, 1963).

———. *Tableaux vivants: Essais critiques 1936–1983*. Paris: Gallimard, 2001.

Klossowski, Pierre, and Alain Jouffroy. *Le Secret pouvoir du sens*. Paris: Écriture, 1994.

Klossowski, Pierre, with Rémy Zaugg. "Simulacra." In *Phantasm and Simulacra*, 48–71.

Krell, David Farrell, and Donald L. Bates. *The Good European: Nietzsche's Work Sites in Word and Image*. Chicago: University of Chicago Press, 1997.

Lacan, Jacques. *Écrits I* and *II*. Paris: Seuil, 1999. Originally published in 1966. Translated as *Écrits*, by Bruce Fink, in collaboration with Héloïse Fink and Russell Grigg (New York: W. W. Norton, 2002).

———. *The Four Fundamental Concepts of Psychoanalysis*. Translated by Alan Sheridan. New York: W. W. Norton, 1978.

———. "Presentation on Psychic Causality." In *Écrits*, 123–57. Originally published as "Propos sur la causalité psychique," in *Écrits I*. Paris: Seuil, 1999, 150–94.

———. *Le Seminaire. Livre XX. Encore*. Paris: Seuil, 1975. Translated by Bruce Fink as *On Feminine Sexuality: The Limits of Love and Knowledge* (1972–1973), *Encore: The Seminar of Jacques Lacan; Book XX*. New York: W. W. Norton, 1998.

———. *Le Séminaire, Livre XXIII, Le Sinthome*. Paris: Seuil, 2005. Translated by A. R. Price as *The Sinthome: The Seminar of Jacques Lacan; Book XXIII* (Cambridge: Polity Press, 2016).

Lamarche-Vadel, Bernard. *Klossowski l'énoncé dénoncé*. Paris: Marval/Galerie Beaubourg, 1985.

Laporte, Roger. "Une passion." In *Deux lectures de Maurice Blanchot*, 53–156. Paris: Fata Morgana, 1973.

———. "Maurice Blanchot: 'Une passion, nouvelle version.'" In *A l'extrême pointe: Proust, Bataille, Blanchot*, 65–95. Paris: P.O.L., 1998.

Leibovici, Franck. *Henri Michaux: Voir (une enquête)*. Paris: Presses de l'université Paris-Sorbonne, 2014.

Leroi-Gourhan, André. *Le Geste et la Parole*. 2 vols: *La mémoire et les rythmes* and *Technique et langage*. Paris: Albin Michel, 2022. Originally published 1964–1965.

———. *The Dawn of European Art: An Introduction to Paleolithic Cave Painting*. Cambridge: Cambridge University Press, 1982.

———. *Préhistoire de l'art occidental*. Paris: Éditions d'Art Lucien Mazenod, 1965.

Lugan-Dardigna, A.-M. *Klossowski: L'homme aux simulacres*. Paris: Navarin Éditeur, La collection du Studiolo, 1986.

Lyotard, Jean-François. *Discours, Figure*. Paris: Klingksibeck, 1971. Translated by Antony Hudek and Mary Lydon as *Discourse, Figure* (Minneapolis: University of Minnesota Press, 2011).

———. *Économie libidinale*. Paris: Les Èditions de Minuit, 1974. Translated by Iain Hamilton Grant as *Libidinal Economy* (London: Bloomsbury Academic, 2021).

Maldiney, Henri. *Regard, Parole, Espace*. Paris: Cerf, 2012.

Martin, Jean-Pierre. *Henri Michaux*. Paris: Gallimard, 2003.

Merleau-Ponty, Maurice. "Eye and Mind." Translated by Carleton Dalleryn. In *The Primacy of Perception*, edited by James Edie. Evanston, IL: Northwestern University Press, 1964.

———. *The Visible and the Invisible*. Translated by Alphonso Lingus. Evanston, IL: Northwestern University Press, 1968.

Michaux, Henri. *A Barbarian in Asia*. Translated by Sylvia Beach. New York: New Directions, 1945.

———. "A Dog's Life." Translated by Anne McGarrell. In *Someone Wants to Steal My Name*, edited by Nin Andrews. Cleveland, OH: Cleveland State University Poetry Center, 2003.

———. "A Head Comes Out of the Wall." Translated by Richard Ellmann. In *Henri Michaux: Selected Writings*, 195–96. New York: New Directions, 1968.

———. "Aventures de lignes." In *Passages. Oeuvres complètes*. Vol. II, 2001, 360–62.

———. "Adventures in Signs." Translated by David Ball. In *Darkness Moves: Henri Michaux Anthology 1927–1984*, 316–17. Berkeley: University of California Press, 1994.

———. *A Certain Plume*. Translated by Richard Sieburth. New York: New York Review Books, 2018.

———. *Connaissance par les gouffres*. In *Oeuvres complètes*. Vol. III, 3–161.

———. "Crying Out." In *The Night Moves*. In *Someone Wants to Steal My Name*, 15. Edited by Nin Andrews. Translated by Sydney Lea. Cleveland, OH: Cleveland State University Poetry Center, 2003.

———. *Darkness Moves: Henri Michaux Anthology 1927–1984*. Translated and selected by David Ball. Berkeley: University of California Press, 1994.

———. "Dessiner l'écoulement du temps." In *Passages. Oeuvres complètes*. Vol. II, 371–74.

———. "Drawing the Flow of Time." Translated by David Ball. In *Darkness Moves*, 320.

———. *Ecuador*. Translated by Robin Magowan. Seattle: University of Washington Press, 1970.

———. *Emergences/Resurgences*. Translated by Richard Sieburth. New York: Skira Editions and The Drawing Center, 2000.

———. *L'Espace du dedans*. Paris: Gallimard, 1966.

———. "Four Hundred Men on the Cross." In *Thousand Times Broken*, translated by Gillian Conoley. San Francisco: City Lights, 2014.

———. *Henri Michaux: Oeuvres récents*. Paris: Le Point Cardinal, 1985. Exhibition catalog.

———. *Henri Michaux: Peindre, composer, écrire*. Organized by the Bibliothèque nationale de France. Under the direction of Jean-Michel Maulpoix, and Florence de Lussy. Paris: Gallimard, 1999. Exhibition catalog.

———. *Henri Michaux & Zao Wou-ki: Dans l'empire des signes*. La Fondation Martin Bodmer, Cologny, Suisse. Texts and notices by Bernard Vouilloux, Yolaine Escande, Madeline Laurence, and Michel Butor. Paris: Flammarion, 2015. Exhibition catalog.

———. *Idéogrammes en Chine*. Paris: Fata Morgana, 1975. Translated by Gustaf Sobin as *Ideograms in China* (New York: New Directions, 2002).

———. *L'Infini turbulent*. In *Oeuvres complètes*. Vol. II, 807–952.

———. *Life in the Folds*. Translated by Darren Jackson. Cambridge, MA: Wakefield Press, 2016.

———. *Misérable miracle*. Paris: NRF, Le Point du Jour, 1972. Translated by Louise Varése and Anna Moschovakis as *Miserable Miracle* (New York: New York Review Books, 2002).

———. *Mouvements*. Paris: Gallimard, 1982.

———. *Oeuvres complètes*. Edited by Raymond Bellour with Ysé Tran. Paris: Gallimard, Bibliotheque de la Pléiade, 1998–2004.

———. *Par des traits*. In *Oeuvres complètes*. Vol. III, 2004, 1233–1285.

———. *Passages (1937–1963). Nouvelle edition revue et augmentée*. Paris: Gallimard, 1963. Also in *Oeuvres complètes*. Vol. II, 1998, 80–403.

———. *Passages et langages de Henri Michaux*. Edited by Jean-Claude Mathieu and Michel Collot. Paris: Librairie José Corti, 1987.

———. "Peace in the Breaking." In *Thousand Times Broken*. Translated by Gillian Conoley. San Francisco: City Lights, 2014.

———. *Plume, Précédé de lointain intérieur*. In *Oeuvres complètes*. Vol. I, 1998, 557–665.

———. "Le Prince de la nuit." In *Oeuvres complètes*. Vol. I, 1998, 712.

———. "Les Rêves vigils." In *Oeuvres complètes*. Vol. III, 2004, 519–37.

———. *Saisir*. In *Oeuvres completes*. Vol. III, 2004, 933–83.

———. "Signes." In *Oeuvres complètes*. Vol. II, 2001, 429–31.

———. *Stroke by Stroke*. Translated by Richard Sieburth. Brooklyn, NY: Archipelago Books, 2006.

———. *Tent Posts*. Translated by Lynn Hoggard. Copenhagen: Green Integer, 1997.

———. "Une vie de chien." In *Oeuvres complètes*. Vol. I, 1998, 469–70.

———. *La vie dans les plis*. In *Oeuvres complètes*. Vol. II, 1998, 159–70.

Montrelay, Michèle. " 'Les Lois de l'Hospitalité' en tant que lois du narcissisme." In *l'Arc* 43. Paris: Librairie Duponchelle, 1970.

Nietzsche, Friedrich. *The Anti-Christ*. In *The Portable Nietzsche*, translated by Walter Kaufmann. New York: Viking Press, 1954 (Penguin Books, 1959).

Parmenides. *Parmenides of Elea, Fragments*. Translated by David Gallop. Toronto: University of Toronto Press, 1991.

Paz, Octavio. "Henri Michaux." In *Alternating Currents*, translated by Helen R. Lane, 78–84. New York: Viking Press, 1973.

———. "Le prince; le clown." In *Henri Michaux*, 16–22. Paris: Centre Georges Pompidou, 1978.

Perros, Georges. "Le Moins qu'on puisse dire." In *L'Arc* 43, 45–47. Paris: Librairie Duponchelle, 1970.

Reuff, Martin. *Différence et identité, Michel Deguy, situation d'un poète lyrique à l'apogée du capitalism culturel*. Paris: Hermann Éditeurs, 2009.

Rigaud-Drayton, Margaret. *Henri Michaux: Poetry, Painting, and the Universal Sign*. Oxford: Clarendon Press, 2005.

Rimbaud, Arthur. *Arthur Rimbaud: Complete Works*. Translated by Paul Schmidt. New York: Harper Colophon Books, 1976.

Roger, Jérôme. "Henri Michaux, malaise dans la pensée." In *Henri Michaux: Le corps de la pensée*, 55–70. Tours, France: Farrago, 2001.

Ropars-Wuilleumier, Marie-Claire. "On Unworking: The Image in Writing According to Blanchot." In *Maurice Blanchot: The Demand of Writing*, edited by Carolyn Bailey Gill, 138–52. London: Routledge, 1996.

Rouaud, Jean. *La splendeur escamotée de frère Cheval*. Paris: Grasset, 2017.

Sartre, Jean-Paul. *Being and Nothingness*. Translated by Hazel E. Barnes. New York: Philosophical Library, 1956.

Shih-T'ao. *Enlightening Remarks on Painting*. Translated by Richard E. Strassberg. Pasadena, CA: Pacific Asia Museum Monographs no. 1, 1989.

Smith, Daniel W. *Essays on Deleuze*. Edinburgh: Edinburgh University Press, 2012.

Starobinski, Jean. "Le monde physionomique." In *Henri Michaux*, 65–67. Paris: Centre Georges Pompidou, 1978.

Surya, Michel. *Georges Bataille: La mort a l'oeuvre*. Paris: Garamont, Librairie Séguier, 1987.

Translated by Krzysztof Fijalkowski and Michael Richardson as *Georges Bataille: An Intellectual Biography*. London: Verso, 2002.

Thomas, Chantal. "The Indiscreet Gaze." In *Phantasm and Simulacra*, 100–7.

Vernant, Jean-Pierre. "The Birth of Images." In *Mortals and Immortals*, edited by Froma I. Zeitlin, 164–85. Princeton, NJ: Princeton University Press, 1991.

———. "Death in the Eyes: Gorgo, Figure of the Other." In *Mortals and Immortals*, 111–40.

Vilar, Pierre. "Henri Michaux, mode et posture." In *Henri Michaux, le corps de la pensée*, 27–40.

Wilhem, Daniel. *Pierre Klossowski: Le corps impie*. Paris: Union Générale d'Éditions 10/18, 1979.

Wilson, Sarah. "Épiphanies et secrets." In *Pierre Klossowski: Tableaux vivants*. Directed by Sarah Wilson. Whitechapel Gallery, London, and Museum Ludwig, Cologne. Paris: Gallimard, Centre Pompidou, 2007. Exhibition catalog.

Wittgenstein, Ludwig. *Philosophical Investigations*. 3rd ed. Translated by G. E. M. Anscombe. New York: Macmillan, 1971.

Index

Acéphale (journal), 6, 7, 260–261
Altamira (prehistoric site), 16, 17, 23–24
Aristotle
   on art as catharsis, 141
Arnaud, Alain, 87n16, 127, 142
   biographical notes on Klossowski, 7
   on the gaze in Klossowski's novels, 152n83, 154
Art
   see also Aristotle
   as affect, 102
   animality and art, 21–22, 36, 53, 59, 60, 66, 69, 72, 73, 73n85, 174, 253
   see also Bataille, Georges
   betweenness of art, 101, 117–118, 215
   cosmological dimensions of, *see* Rouaud, Jean
   historical origins, 16, 17–19, 24, 36, 37, 42, 43, 52, 62, 70n82
   homo ludens, 72
   see also Klossowski, Pierre
   see also Michaux, Henri
   modern art, 20, 71–72, 103
   and the nude, 80
   optical vs. haptic, 32–35
   as phantasm, or simulacre, 115, 117
   see also Plato
   prehistoric (Altamira, Lascaux), 21, 22, 24, 25, 31, 39, 60, 65, 67, 74, 259
   and shamanism (Bataille, Clottes), 48, 66
   representational vs. non-representational, 13
   see also Rouaud, Jean
   silence of art, 76
   and slave culture, 103
   and sovereignty, 118
Bacon, Francis (painter), 34, 84, 208
Bacon, Francis (16th century philosopher), 200–201
Backès-Clement, Catherine, 162, 163
Badiou, Alain
   on art, 139–140
Baatsch, Henri-Alexis, 199n70
Bataille, Georges
   art, 252, 259
      as apparitional, 15
      and passage between human and animal, 68–69
      and rhythms, 259
      and ritual sacrifice, 4–5, 67–68, 71
   base materialism, 55–58, 75
      base materialism and animality, 59, 70
   double birth art and man, 75

282 | Index

Bataille, Georges *(continued)*
  expérience intérieure, 212, 232, 248, 254, 255
  formless, 193
  on Gnosticism, 56
  hatred of poetry, 247, 250
  human figure as shaman, 61–62
  on Gnosticism, 55–57
  on masks, effacements in prehistoric art, 58–60, 62
  on modernity, 53–54
  on prohibitions-transgressions, 62–65, 69
    transgression defined, 65
  on the scene in the pit at Lascaux, 65–68
  shamanism, 62, 64, 178, 251, 254
  sovereignty, 59, 69
    animality and sovereignty, 62, 70, 76, 253, 254
    Klossowski on, 137
    void, 64, 70n82, 250n54
    in *L'Archangélique*, "Le Vide" (poem), 261
  writings/interpretations of prehistoric art, 4–5
Baudelaire, Charles, 239, 249
Bellour, Raymond
  on Michaux, Henri, 12, 204, 213, 222, 231n4, 234n12, 238
    double pulsion in Michaux's work, 175, 183n32, 190
  on "Peace in the Breaking," 235–236, 243
Bernini, Gion Lorenzo (sculptor), "Ecstasy of St. Theresa," 81
Berressem, Hanjo, 89
Blanchot, Maurice, 1, 2n2, 8, 17, 19, 82, 95, 202, 246n48
  the "hilarity of the serious" in Klossowski, 133n61

Infinite Conversation (*L'Entretien infini*), 18, 181
  the Night, 196
Body (human)
  body without organs, *see* Deleuze
  defined by impulses, 97, 102
  in Klossowski's work, 86, 92, 104, 113, 116, 122
    daemonic body, 148
    Diana's, 150, 151, 153, 157, 158, 161, 166
    Roberte's, 113, 122, 124, 125, 263
    and signs, writing, 127–128, 129, 132, 134, 150
  in Merleau-Ponty's work, 20
  in Michaux's work, 12, 178, 195, 196, 202, 203, 206, 235, 243
    gestures, lines 204, 205, 207, 213
  in Nietzsche's work, 93, 97, 98, 102, 104, 105, 106
  suffering body, 224, 227, 240
Breton, André, 24
Breuil (abbé), 58–60, 62
Buddhism, 225

Caillois, Roger, 7
  L'Homme et le sacré, 5
Castanet, Hervé, 144n76
  on Octave (Klossowski's character) and the gaze, 121, 121n43
  on the phantasm and the unconscious in Lacan, 266n91, 269, 269n95
Cézanne, Paul (painter), 20, 34
Char, René, 13, 224, 89
  Homme-oiseau mort et bison mourant, 32
  La Bête innommable, 15
  La poem pulverisé, 1, 13, 270
  The Library Is on Fire, 233

Chauvet (prehistoric site), 16, 17, 21, 23–26, 31
China, Chinese, European studies of, 200–201
   calligrams, 201–202, 205
Clottes, Jean, 16, 73
   shamanism, becoming-animal, 47–48
   criticism of anthropology as a science, 28–29
   criticism of Leroi-Gourhan, 44–45
   discussion of cave walls, 46–47
   on shamanism, 22, 43–49, *passim*
   stages of entopic figures, 44
   images of human hands, 47
Code of everyday signs, 105–107, *passim*, 130, 267
Collège de Sociologie, 5
Combat against culture, 13, 97
   as combat against herd morality, 106
   Klossowski on, 104, 139
   Nietzsche on, 90–93, 103–104
Courbet, Gustave (painter), 143

Deleuze, Gilles
   on becoming-animal, 48–49
   on body without organs, 195
   gesture-bodies, 196
   on haptic art, 34
   figure (figural), 74, 76, 206
   on the infinite, 192, 194
   on Klossowski, 8, 127
   magic formula, 234, 236n15
   plane of composition, 191, 217
   rhizomes, 86
   zone of indeterminacy, 149
Derrida, Jacques, 48n43, 199n72, 269n94
Descartes, René, 53, 98
   Klossowski's reversal of, 93–95, 96

Eco, Umberto, 201n75

Ernst, Max (painter)
   influence on Michaux, 10, 179
Escalande, Yolaine, on the calligram, 205, 205n88
Esteban, Claude, 229, 231, 249, 264, 265n89
Eternal Return, 52, 84, 85, 90, 93, 94, 263, 265
   Klossowski and, 94–97, *passim*, 266
   Diana (Klossowski's character) and, 151, 167
   Nietzsche's vision of, *see also under* Nietzsche
   see also Rouaud, Jean

Foucault, Michel, 145n79
Freud, Sigmund, 7, 114, 143, 263
   death drive, 165
   on narcissism, 163–164
   pleasure principle, 105
   unconscious, Klossowski's rejection of, 108, 113

Gaze (le regard), 88–90, 152, 139, 166
   differs from perception (seeing), 89
   Lacanian formulations of the gaze, 89, 157
   and narcissism, 161
Gaspar da Cruz (16th century Dominican), 200
Gide, André, 10, 84
Gonzales de Mendoza, Juan (16th century historian), 200

Hegel, G. W. F., 57, 94, 95, 98, 103, 110, 118, 125, 243, 246, 263
   Bataille, Kojève's Hegel seminar, 3
   death, *The Phenomenology of Spirit*, 247–248
   master-slave dialectic, 101–102, 157

Heraclitus, 42
Hölderlin, Friedrich, 5–7, 230–232, *passim*
Hollier, Denis
  on the labyrinth, 17, 23n10, 66
Horace, 264
Hurst, Damien, 72

Jouffroy, Alain, 81, 152, 188n40, 191, 199, 220, 227n39, 239
Kafka, Franz, 178
Klee, Paul, 10, 35, 179, 199, 210, 220
  and Chinese art, 205
  Michaux on, 77, 179, 204, 204n86
Klossowski, Denise, 8, 86, 89, 151, 152
  as double of Roberte, 151
Klossowski, Pierre
  animality, 167, 268–269
  art, drawings of, 81, 82, 101, 102, 107, 139, 141, 145, 150
    and daemon, daemonic, 144, 145, 147
    drawing of Roberte and Acteon, 158–160
    effect on the viewer, 141–142, 146
    as ludic suspension of reality principle, 117
    painting as silent poetry, 264
    style of, 143
  on Bataille's *L'Abbé C*, 133–135, 135
  on Blanchot, 100
  conscious-unconscious distinction, 92, 95, 96, 108–109, 113–114, 142, 156, 161, 191
  on the daemon/daemonology, 138
    in *Diana at Her Bath*, 145–148, 150
    compared with psychoanalysis, 142
  hypostatic union, 108
  metaphysical oppositions, rejection of, 108
  on Nietzsche, 107

  pantomime, 149, 150
  the phantasm, 115–118, 150, 116
  ressemblance, metaphor, 110
  semiology of intensities, 108
    doublings, 109
    intensities becoming signs, 109, 114–115
    reflexivity of intensity, 109–110
    philosophy as semiology of intensities, 105
  on signs, 112
  simulacre, 135–138, *passim*, 147
  theatrical character of works, 82–84, 101
  theological studies, 7, 8
  void, 106, 119n41, 166

Lacan, Jacques, 7, 8
  on Diana and Acteon, 143
  divided subject, 113
    as product of symbolic order, 112
  the gaze, 89
  narcissism, theory of, 165
  phantasy, 163n98
  the Real, 196
  signs vs. signifiers, 112
  on sexual difference, 41
  unconsciousness, structured like a language, 112, 113, 156, 256, 256n68, 269
Laporte, Roger, 172, 172n6
  criticism of Bataille, 3–4, 63, 107
Lascaux
  compared to Sistine Chapel paintings, 60
  double economy of, 62, 75–76
  as shamanistic, 77
  types of images, 29
Lecomte, Louis (17th century Jesuit), 200
Leiris, Michel
  on *Documents*, 4

Leroi-Gourhan, André, *passim*, 35–43, 73
  animality in prehistoric art, 36
  on form, 36, 39–41
  influence on Bernard Noël, 37n21
  on the meaning of prehistoric art, 42
  on rhythmic gestures, 37
  on superimposition of images, 39
  on sexual difference in prehistoric art, 41
  types of prehistoric figures, 38
Leibovici, Franck (*Voir*), 185, 190–191, 196
Lotar, Eli (photographer), 54
Lyotard, Jean-François
  figural space, 74, 76
  phantasm as nihilism, 116, 116n39

Marc, Franz (painter), "The Fate of the Animals," 60
Martin, Jean-Pierre, 10n23, 198
Maldiney, Henri, 35n19
Manet, Édouard (painter), "Olympia," 81
Merleau-Ponty, Maurice
  "Eye and Mind," 20, 204
  The Visible and the Invisible, 27
Metaphor, 70n83, 73n85, 246, 254–255
  Bataille and metaphor, 67, 70, 246, 255–257, 258, 260–261
  Deguy, Michel on, 255n67
  in Klossowski, 110, 111, 137, 138
  Lacan, Jacques on, 256–257
  in Michaux, 243n42, 245
Michaux, Henri
  alphabet, 174, 184, 199, 202, 203, 206, 212, 216, 219, 225
  animals, animality, 176, 206, 219, 223
  art, 10, 169, 174, 177, 181, 188, 190–191, 193, 204, 210
  contacts with Bataille, 10–11, 10n23

  Blanchot on Michaux, 172, 174–175, 182n30, 185, 186n38
  "book" vs. "work" in Michaux, 175–176
  writing of disaster, 175, 177, 215
  Christ, importance of for Michaux, 221–222, 226
  Christian Cross, 221–226
  Duvivier, Éric, mescaline film, 186
  formless, 169
  Heraclitean dimensions of Michaux's poetry, 243
  infinity (turbulent), 181, 182, 183, 185, 187, 188, 189, 191–197
  Kant, Immanuel on infinity, 187
  Marie-Louise (Michaux's wife), 179
  mescaline, 173, 181, 185
  descriptions of experiments with, 183–187
  furrow (*le sillon*), 189
  Miserable Miracle, 180, 182, 183, 188, 194, 196
  Turbulent Infinity, 180
  Paulhan, Jean and Michaux, 186
  see also Night, the
  rhythms in his work, 217, 237n20, 226
  self-descriptions, 11
  seeing, visions and writing, 184, 190
  tree of life, 220–221, 236n17
  unconscious-consciousness, 243
  universal language, 172
  between humans and animals, 174
  void (*vide*), 196, 197, 205, 208, 210, 213–215, 217, 220, 230, 232n7, 233, 238, 239, 244–263 *passim*
  in Chinese painting, 213
  voyages of, 9, 198, 199, 201, 207, 208, 211, 220
  voyages away from logocentrism, 200–201, 207–208

Michaux, Henri *(continued)*
　will, no will, in Michaux's work
　　188, 208, 212, 216
Mirrors, 101, 127
　in *Diana at her Bath*, 150, 152,
　　154, 158, 161, 167
　"Diana's mirror" (Lake Nemi, Italy),
　　139
　mirror stage, Freud and Lacan, 165
　Narcissis myth (Blanchot), 166
　in *Roberte ce soir*, 133
Montrelay, Michèle, 161, 164

Narcissism, 160–161, 162, 163
　divine narcissism, 148
　see also Freud
　see also Lacan
　Blanchot on, 165–166
　Merleau-Ponty on, 160
　primary and secondary in
　　Klossowski, 164–165
　psychoanalytic theory of, 163
　Roberte's (Klossowski's character),
　　151
Nietzsche, Friedrich
　on art and culture, 103
　on the role of the philosopher, 92,
　　93, 98, 104
　on Self (Selbst), agent (sûppot), 108
　identified with the body, 96–97
　thinking as fluctuation of intensities,
　　105
　vision of Eternal Return, 93,
　　96–100, 103
　Lou Salomé's account of, 98
Night, 1, 2, 12, 50
　in Bataille, 22, 23, 52, 77
　in Klossowski, 125, 126, 159, 167
　in Michaux, 171, 176, 196, 198,
　　212, 217, 218, 220, 230, 232,
　　235, 246, 256, 257, 259, 261
　in Nietzsche, 99

Noël, Bernard
　on Bataille, 219, 246n48, 247, 250,
　　251–258 *in passim*
　influenced by Leroi-Gourhan, 37n21
　in-fini, 229, 245
　on Michaux, 10n20, 233n10, 245

Ovid, *Metamorphosis*, 153, 165

Paulhan, Jean, 9, 11, 186, 207
Plato, 149
　Symposium, 145
　Republic, theory of art, 139–141
Psychoanalysis, *see also* Freud,
　　Klossowski, and Lacan
　Conscious-unconscious distinction,
　　156
　Klossowski's work compared to, 142
　Klossowski's criticisms of, 113

Rigaud-Drayton, Margaret, 209, 217
Rimbaud, Arthur, 197n66, 200, 246
Roberte (Klossowski's character)
　see also Body
　as double of Diana, 151–152
　as divided, 113
　physiognomy of, 128, 143–144
　as unique sign, 111–112, 119–133,
　　143, 265, 266
Roger, Jérôme, 206
Rouaud, Jean, 21, 22 49–53, *passim*
　cosmic, cyclic dimensions of
　　prehistoric art, 50–52
　comparison with Clottes, 51
　definition of poetic thinking, 49
　prehistoric art and nature, 52–53
　shamanism, 22

Sacred, 5, 16, 230, 231
　in Bataille, 8, 18, 23, 54, 63, 64,
　　65, 68, 69, 71, 75, 230, 246,
　　255, 261, 262

Blanchot on, 246
in Hölderlin, 230, 232
in Klossowski, 153, 263
in Michaux, 170, 209, 214, 215, 230, 261
Sartre, Jean-Paul
criticism of Bataille, Blanchot, 96, 259n75
Saussure, Ferdinand
concept of the sign, 112
Science of prehistory
criticisms of, 28–29
Self (agent or sûppot), see also Nietzsche
conscious-unconsciousness distinction, 108
as doubled, 109
as thinking, 111
Shaman, shamanism, 22, 29, 33, 49, 64, 178
see also Bataille, George
see also Clottes, Jean
and Gnostic archontes, 55
Michaux and, 261
and poetic-thinkers, 50
see also Rouaud, Jean
Shih-T'ao (Chinese poet-painter), 218
Simonides of Keos, 264
Simulacre, 105, 111, 133, 140
Klossowski on simulacra in Bataille's work, 134–138
simulacral return to animality, 68–69
Siva, 16
Smith, Daniel W., 192, 192n49
Spinoza, Baruch, 192
Ethics, 195

Surya, Michel
criticism of Bataille, 4
on poetry, 251n57
Sympathetic hunting magic, 22, 30–31

Tertullian, 95, 115, 146
Titian (painter), 80–81
"Rape of Europa," 80, 162
Trismégiste, Hèrmes, 144, 144n77, 145, 146

Unique sign, see also Roberte
Castanet on, 269
as constraining force, 131, 266
and Eternal Return, 99, 114
and everyday language, 262
intensity, semiology of impulses and, 104, 110, 115, 263, 266
Je, I (pronoun), as unique sign, 136, 167
and Lacan, 130, 269
silence of, 266, 267

Vernant, Jean-Pierre
on Greek art, 139
Vilar, Pierre, 205

Wilhem, Daniel, 119n41, 125n50, 129n55, 133, 144n77, 263n86, 264
Wilkins, John (17th century Anglican clergyman), 200
Wittgenstein, Ludwig, 188

Xenophon, 139

www.ingramcontent.com/pod-product-compliance
Ingram Content Group UK Ltd.
Pitfield, Milton Keynes, MK11 3LW, UK
UKHW041916140426
5217IPUK00013B/180